BORROWED LIGHT

BORROWED LIGHT

VOLUME I

Vico, Hegel, and the Colonies

Timothy Brennan

STANFORD UNIVERSITY PRESS
STANFORD, CALIFORNIA

Stanford University Press
Stanford, California

©2014 by the Board of Trustees of the Leland Stanford Junior University. All rights reserved.

No part of this book may be reproduced or transmitted in any form or by any means, electronic or mechanical, including photocopying and recording, or in any information storage or retrieval system without the prior written permission of Stanford University Press.

Printed in the United States of America on acid-free, archival-quality paper

Library of Congress Cataloging-in-Publication Data

Brennan, Timothy, 1953- author.
  Borrowed light : Vico, Hegel, and the colonies / Timothy Brennan.
     pages cm
  Includes bibliographical references and index.
  ISBN 978-0-8047-8832-8 (cloth : alk. paper) —
  ISBN 978-0-8047-9054-3 (pbk. : alk. paper)
  1. Colonies—Philosophy. 2. Imperialism—Philosophy. 3. Philosophy, Modern. 4. Vico, Giambattista, 1668-1744—Influence. 5. Hegel, Georg Wilhelm Friedrich, 1770-1831—Influence. I. Title.
  JV51.B74 2014
  325'.301—dc23
                              2013047796

ISBN 978-0-8047-9058-1 (electronic)

Typeset by Bruce Lundquist in 10/14 Minion

For Keya

In those days, the communists were, I tell you this in all truth, the only human ones.

Patrick Chamoiseau

CONTENTS

Acknowledgments   xi
List of Abbreviations   xv

INTRODUCTION   1
   The Interwar Moment 1   *Arguments and Lineages 4*
   Why Philology 7   *Rupture/Continuity 11*   *Overview of Chapters 14*

1   VICO, SPINOZA, AND THE IMPERIAL PAST   17
   Vico's Untimeliness 17   *Anticolonial Imagination 21*
   Vico as a Contemporary 36   *Spinoza and the Purity of Mind 45*
   "Spinoza" for the Moment 52   *Vico's Cadre 63*

2   HEGEL AND THE CRITIQUE OF COLONIALISM   73
   Vico's Hegel 73   *At the Court of Liberal Thought 80*   *An Other State 89*   *The Tale of Hegel, Africa, and Slavery 98*   *Dialectical Oblivion 108*   *Polemical Intelligence 119*   *Marx, Hegel, and Backwardness 124*

3   NIETZSCHE AND THE COLONIES   133
   Classics and Class War: Vico and Nietzsche 133   *Nietzsche in Colonial Discourse 139*   *The War on Philology 147*   *Odyssean Imperialism 154*   *Untimeliness in Real Time 159*   *The Interwar Fear Genre 175*   *What Nietzsche Means by Genealogy 184*

4   BORROWED LIGHT   197
   Bataille and the Party of de Sade 197   *Signifying on Hegel 207*
   Prophetic Suicide: Reading 218   *Posthumanism as Imperialism 224*

Appendix: Preview of *Borrowed Light*, Volume II   235
Notes   237
Index   271

ACKNOWLEDGMENTS

For the many days and nights spent trying out ideas, I would like to thank those friends whose opinions I sought, and from whom I learned so much. They aided me in ways material and intellectual—to the late Neil Smith, whose rumpled confidence and empathy were only matched by his demotic style; to Michal Kobialka, a constant intellectual resource and sensitive spirit with a different reading list; to Silvia Lopez, for her insights into Latin American sources and good taste; to Tim Heitman, for a nonacademic perspective and musical accompaniment; to Chris Chiappari, for his humanist pessimism of the intellect; to Marco Katz, for his extravagant generosity, his bucking up, and his view from the street; to Deb Cowan, for pushing back on the Foucault question and for showing me the possibilities of the politics of the demimonde; to Neil Larsen, for his implicit demand to up the ante; to Crystal Bartolovich, for her moral support in Ithaca and for teaching me the virtues of immersing oneself in the early modern period; to Ken Calhoon, for his style and aesthetic exactness; to Bob Hullot-Kentor, for the encounters in New York, and for his lamenting polemics in the Brooklyn Rail; and to Susan Buck-Morss for her restless integrity and inventiveness, and her unfailing personal warmth. My greatest debt is to Keya Ganguly, the most penetrating and principled mind I know. She is behind every line, and I dedicate every one to her hoping some of them measure up.

A special thanks to Neil Lazarus, for his friendship, and for being involved with the arguments of this book at every stage as we swam upstream; to Priya Gopal, for her unwavering vernacular spirit; to Rashmi Varma and Subir Sinha, for their solidarity and kindness from afar; and to Benita Parry, for being a daily confidant, and for the million conversations in Marton, where my thinking finds a home. I learned from two younger scholars whom I first met as students and with whom I corresponded. Their work on philology and Marxism complemented my thinking, so let me thank Eric Owens and Stefano Selenu for their insights. To irregular correspondents who sought me out because they shared some of the same passions and are themselves pursuing projects along similar lines: Matthew Abraham, Asher Ghaffar, Marcus Green, Jamil Kader, Aaron Kamugisha, Francesco Rocchetti, Francescomaria Tedesco, and Daniel Vukovic.

I would like to thank those who were kind enough to invite me to their institutions to present some of the arguments of these chapters: Silvia Albertazzi, Antonis Balasopoulos, Akeel Bilgrami, Rowan Boyson, He Chengzhou, Simon During, Ben Etherington and Jarad Zimbler, Walter Goebbel, Jens Gurr, Benjamin Hagen and Michael Becker, Ulla Haselstein, Chen Jing, Michal Kobialka, Rüdiger Kunow, Jairo Moreno, Wang Ning, Mariam Said, Tapati Thakurta and Rosinka Chaudhuri, Terri Tomsky and Eddy Kent, Antonio Vazquez-Arroyo, and Ban Wang.

It would be difficult for me to express how thankful I am to Amanda Anderson, who invited me to lead a seminar at the Cornell School for Criticism and Theory in 2010. Much of my thinking about the book over the last decade took final shape in that setting. My students in that seminar worked through its earlier forms with me: thanks, then, to Raquel Anido, Maureen Curtin, Rachel Feder, Anna Fisher, Roxana Galusca, Andrés Guzman, Saffron Hall, Colin Loughran, Ani Maitra, Seth Perlow, Nanna Thylstrup, Heather Treseler, Daniel Walker, and Laura Fan Xie; but let me particularly express my thanks to certain members of that cohort: Sayan Bhattacharyya, Eric Brandom, Robert Day, Christian Gerzso, Antonio Gomez, Stephan Hammel, Marco Katz, Salvador Mercado, Geordie Miller, Eric Owens, and Terri Tomsky. Thanks also to those from the seminar who later took part in panels at the American Comparative Literature Association conference on Hegel's relevance to anticolonial thought, above all to Jerilyn Sambrooke, who co-organized the panels with me, and to Nicholas Brown for participating. And to my students in Germany, where I spent a half year navigating officialdom and the archives; they taught me to see the challenges and contradictions of living in today's Europe: Jan an Haack, Milo Kanefaty, Philipp Kneiss, Frederike Offizier, Yami Quiroga, and Steffi Siewert.

Thanks to my colleagues in the Dialectics and Society Workshop at the University of Minnesota, above all its main organizer, Bali Sahota. Over a four-year period a group of us explored dialectical traditions with outside help from Gopal Balakrishnan, Susan Buck-Morss, Chris Connery, Raymond Geuss, Robert Hullot-Kentor, Neil Larsen, Max Pensky, Moishe Postone, and Shierry Weber Nicholson. And to my graduate students with whom I have worked through so many of these ideas in seminars, office encounters, and e-mail exchanges: Sunyoung Ang, Koel Bannerjee, Matthew Boynton, Madhurima Chakraborty, Anil Chandiramani, Dan Dooghan, Esther Edelman, Nick Hengen, Hyeryung Hwang, Jayashree Kamble, Jennifer Kang, Na-Rae Kim, Dennis Mischke, Barbara Pierre-Louis, Djordje Popovic, Nick Robinette, Gabe Shapiro, Lindsey Simms, Saloua ben Zahra, and Marla Zubel.

My work has been supported by grants from the Deutsche Forschungsgemeinschaft, the National Endowment of the Humanities summer stipends program, and the University of Minnesota Grant-in-Aid and Single Semester Leave programs. These allowed me to hire research assistants who are already well on their way in their own careers; I am very grateful for their labors and precision. These include Cecily Marcus, Gauti Sigthorsson, Thomas Haakenson, Jan an Haack, and, more recently and especially, Anil Chandiramani. A part of Chapter 3 appeared in *German Colonialism: Race, the Holocaust, and Postwar Germany*, ed. Volker Langbehn and Mohammad Salama (Columbia University Press, 2011), and a part of Chapter 2 appeared in *The Oxford Handbook to Postcolonial Studies*, ed. Graham G. Huggan (Oxford University Press, 2013). Thanks to Saranindranath Tagore for his help in obtaining permission to use the cover image.

ABBREVIATIONS

Giambattista Vico

AGV *The Autobiography of Giambattista Vico*, ed. and trans. Max Harold Fisch and Thomas Goddard Bergin (Ithaca, NY: Cornell UP, 1944).

ARh *The Art of Rhetoric* (*Institutiones Oratoriae, 1711–41*), ed. and trans. Giorgio A. Pinton and Arthur W. Shippee (Amsterdam: Rodopi, 1996).

FNS *The First New Science*, ed. and trans. Leon Pompa (Cambridge: Cambridge UP, 2002).

NS *The New Science of Giambattista Vico* (Unabridged Translation of the Third Edition [1744] with the addition of "Practic of the New Science"), trans. Thomas Goddard Bergin and Max Harold Fisch (1948; Ithaca, NY: Cornell UP, 1968).

OHE *On Humanistic Education: (Six Inaugural Orations, 1699–1707)*, intro. and notes Gian Galeazzo Visconti, trans. Giorgio A. Pinton and Arthur W. Shippee (Ithaca, NY: Cornell UP, 1993).

PSN *Principj di scienza nuova* (vols. 1–3), under the direction of Fausto Nicolini (1744; Turin: Giulio Einaudi editore, 1976).

SAC *Statecraft: The Deeds of Antonio Carafa*, ed. and trans. Giorgio A. Pinton (1716; New York: Peter Lang, 2004); a translation from the Latin of *De rebus gestis Antonj Caraphaei*.

UR *Universal Right*, trans. and ed. Giorgio A. Pinton and Margaret Diehl (Amsterdam: Rodopi, 2000).

Benedict de Spinoza

CBS   *Correspondence*, in *The Chief Works of Benedict de Spinoza*, trans. and intro. R. H. M. Elwes (New York: Dover, 1951), 2:275–420.

E   *Ethics*, ed. and trans. Edwin Curley (1677; New York: Penguin, 1996).

EGD   *Ethica: ordine geometrico demonstrata*, ed. J. Van Vloten and J. P. N. Land (The Hague: Martinum Nijhoff, 1905).

OIU   *On the Improvement of the Understanding*, in *The Chief Works of Benedict de Spinoza*, trans. R. H. M. Elwes (New York: Dover, 1951), 2:1–42.

PT   *A Political Treatise*, in *The Chief Works of Benedict de Spinoza*, trans. and intro. R. H. M. Elwes (1675–76; New York: Dover, 1951), 1:270–387.

TPT   *Theologico-Political Treatise*, in *The Chief Works of Benedict de Spinoza*, trans. and intro. R. H. M. Elwes (1670; New York: Dover, 1951), 1:3–278.

G. W. F. Hegel

ETW   *Early Theological Writings*, trans. T. M. Knox (Chicago: U of Chicago P, 1948).

FPS   *System of Ethical Life* (1802/3) and *First Philosophy of Spirit*, ed. and trans. H. S. Harris and T. M. Knox (Albany, NY: SUNY Press, 1979).

HA   *Hegel's Aesthetics: Lectures on Fine Art*, trans. T. M. Knox, vol. 1 (Oxford: Clarendon Press, 1975).

HGW   *Gesammelte Werke*, Hrsg. im Auftrag der Deutsche Forschungsgemeinschaft (Hamburg: Felix Meiner Verlag, 1968).

HL   *Hegel's Logic: Being Part One of the Encyclopedia of the Philosophical Sciences*, trans. John N. Findlay (Oxford: Oxford UP, 1975).

HPW   *Political Writings*, ed. Laurence Dickey and H. B. Nisbet, trans. H. B. Nisbet (Cambridge: Cambridge UP, 1999).

LPH   *Lectures on the Philosophy of World History*, trans. H. B. Nisbet (Cambridge: Cambridge UP, 1975).

PH   *The Philosophy of History*, trans. J. Sibree (New York: Prometheus Books, 1991).

PhS   *Hegel's Phenomenology of Spirit*, trans. A. V. Miller (Oxford: Oxford UP, 1977).

PR   *Elements of the Philosophy of Right*, ed. Allen W. Wood, trans. H. B. Nisbet (1820; Cambridge: Cambridge UP, 1991).

SL   *The Science of Logic*, trans., George di Giovanni (Cambridge: Cambridge UP, 2010).

Friedrich Nietzsche

BW   *Basic Writings of Nietzsche*, trans. and ed. Walter Kaufmann (New York: Modern Library, 1992).

KGW   *Nietzsche Werke: Kritische Gesamtausgabe*, ed. Giorgio Colli and Mazzino Montinari (Berlin: Walter de Gruyter, 1982).

KSA   *Kritische Studienausgabe*, ed. Giorgio Colli and Mazzino Montinari, vols. 1–4 (Berlin: Verlag de Gruyter, 1967).

NGW   *Gesammelte Werke*, vols. 1–3 (Munich: Musarion Verlag, 1920–29).

NPW   *Political Writings of Friedrich Nietzsche*, ed. Frank Cameron and Don Dombowsky (New York: Palgrave Macmillan, 2008).

NUP   *Unpublished Writings from the Period of Unfashionable Observations*, trans. Richard T. Gray with afterword (Stanford, CA: Stanford UP, 1999).

SLN   *Selected Letters of Friedrich Nietzsche*, ed. and trans. Christopher Middleton (Chicago: U of Chicago P, 1969).

WEN   *Writings from the Early Notebooks*, ed. Raymond Geuss and Alexander Nehamas, trans. Ladislaus Löb (Cambridge: Cambridge UP, 2009).

WFN   *The Complete Works of Friedrich Nietzsche: The First Complete and Authorized English Translation*, ed. Oscar Levy (London: T. N. Foulis, 1909–13 [vols. 2, 4, 17]; New York: Macmillan, 1924 [vols. 1, 5, 6]; New York: Gordon Press, 1974 [vols. 3, 7–16]).

BORROWED LIGHT

INTRODUCTION

> [Not] intuitions, pulled out of one's head, supported by statistical laws
> ... but "active and aware participation," "compassion," the experience of
> immediate particulars, and a system that might be called "living philology."
> Antonio Gramsci[1]

THE INTERWAR MOMENT

This is a book about historical continuities rather than sudden eruptions or revolutionary breaks. Although it may seem disconnected at first, my interest is to trace the direct and indirect influences of Giambattista Vico and (as an heir to Vico) G. W. F. Hegel on the historically new anticolonial spirit that arose in the early decades of the twentieth century. Within the intellectual lineage they created, this movement from the eighteenth to the twentieth century saw the development of ideas that, quite unlike the present, expressed their apostasy as humanism rather than anti-humanism, and saw the ability of the humanities to check the claims of the natural sciences as being not just an intellectual matter but a vital political goal. In a second volume, I look at the political and aesthetic forms that this influence took in the interwar era itself (see the Appendix for the contents of that study).

There are a number of rifts in the humanities today, and no lack of books and essays debating incompatible positions, with great energy and emotion, on the nature of the human, the politics of literature, the prospects for historical change, and the character of language. Even at the level of theme, it is striking what one group of critics finds compelling and another banal. The choices of topics—inspiring many, leaving others cold—are made for the most part without any attention to the past of thought. We have a great deal of "theory," in other words, but very little intellectual history. One of my purposes in writing this book was to speculate on whether understanding is fruitfully disrupted when theory knows the prehistory of its own formulations. Does it matter when one comes to understand the situation of the time when the ideas were first given form—to see ourselves suddenly in the guise of a person or cause that may now seem alien to our interests or intentions? Or, how does the debate alter when we realize that what we thought was new was really a repetition?

The interwar moment, I am going to argue, is one whose debates we are largely echoing today. It was the time when challenges to European control first reached global dimensions and when resistance to the old order had for the first time the strategic and military means to threaten European hegemony rather than simply shame it. The anticolonial common sense that most of us hold today was, in other words, a hallmark of the early twentieth century—especially the interwar period (not, as is often maintained, a result of the postcolonial turn of the 1980s and 1990s). The sense of a global common cause backed by sophisticated organizational networks and, as I try to show here, an already developed conceptual framework, was fully realized only between 1905 and 1940, when a new culture arose in the aftershock of revolution on Europe's semideveloped eastern periphery, with immediate reverberations throughout Asia. These events profoundly affected intellectuals on both the Right and Left.

To see why the thinking that emerged particularly within interwar Marxism is at the heart of anticolonial struggle and inseparable from it, one must return to a communism before communism. Indeed, its golden age between the European wars did not begin with Marx nor even with his principal inspiration, Hegel. If this is a surprising linkage, it may be more heterodox to propose that what is privileged in current forms of theory—especially its postcolonial avatars—owes its debts to motifs first developed within Marxism. Nonetheless, my hope is precisely to make such a case in order to recover an anticolonial philosophy and practice worthy of the name.

Between World Wars I and II, European consciousness of the colonies changed sharply and, to some, threateningly—and this was no less the case in the colonies themselves, as well as among intellectuals from the periphery who had participated in the revolutions on European soil and among Europeans and North Americans who joined forces with insurgents in Mexico, China, and elsewhere. From 1880 to 1939, artists and social theorists in the European metropole, many of them foreigners, brought a new attention to the non-Western world. These regions were no longer simply artistic raw material or an ethical site for expressing sympathy with the victims of various invasive business enterprises, but an array of emergent polities populated by colonial subjects rising in arms and pressing their demands. This convergence of forces was historically unique. An entirely new outlook was the result, and to a degree that has gone almost completely unmentioned, it lay behind the era's creativity and originality in philosophy, social theory, and the arts.

"Borrowed light," then, is a motif in the anticolonial imagination. My purpose is to perturb the expectation that accompanies this image: the colonialist cliché of the light of Europe brought to the world's benighted peoples. To turn the tables on this cliché and reverse its implicit value hierarchy, I draw attention to a position and a politics developed in peripheral zones whose inspiration is as much European as non-European. The light that casts its glow on the twentieth century as a whole derived from earlier sources: specifically, from ideas and attitudes I trace back to Vico. In time—and this is my key point—these ideas were taken up by anticolonial thinkers outside Europe and returned to Europe once more, via that influential detour. The light borrowed thus shines in two directions, without contradiction, depending on the flow of history and one's place in time. Indeed, this is why a historical logic predicated on continuity rather than rupture is essential; without a sense of how ideas have come down to us but also why they have traveled particular routes, the discourse of history may be rendered fashionably synchronic, but at the same time risks being orphaned or, at least, consigned to presentism.

One is likely to meet the objection at this point that, since it is about anticolonial thought, an argument like the present one relies too heavily on European forerunners. But this seems to me to express a disagreement that is less about national fealties or ethnic identifications than theoretical or political affiliations. Within postcolonial studies, certainly (but not only there), many of those invested in depicting their opponents as Eurocentric, or in attacking the covert Western epistemologies lurking in anticolonial declarations, tend to draw on thinkers such as Martin Heidegger, Immanuel Kant, Emmanuel Lévinas, Jacques Derrida, or Jacques Lacan, although these choices do not seem to produce an allergic reaction as do the writings of Karl Marx, Pierre Bourdieu, or Johann Gottfried Herder. Often, this is a matter of disagreement over what is important, but at times it is also a matter of misrecognition based on faulty logic (on the order of "I am anti-Eurocentric, I like X, ergo X is anti-Eurocentric"). In either case, what is at stake is a war of positions—not an exposure of ethnocentric assumptions or Western triumphalism. Given its unequal distribution of power and resources, the history of colonialism and imperialism dictates that the ideas at hand will include (inevitably, though not exclusively) those from Europe.

Vico's *The New Science* and Hegel's *Philosophy of Right* contain original propositions about vernacular modes of expression and civic values that speak to our contemporary focus on aesthetic forms of dependency, uneven development, and cultural incommensurability. Likewise, Vico's speculative theses on poetic speech and the origins of language, together with the role of collective authorship in epic, as well as his elevation of secular reading over biblical textual models, provide the basis not only for a nonparochial conception of world literature but also for a dissident model of international citizenship. This view, in turn, is enriched by Hegel, who in terms of intellectual history must be seen as a Vichian thinker. He, like his predecessor, shows at some length that Western conceptual forms relied on those from the East and would have been unthinkable without them. Across both volumes, *Borrowed Light*, then, addresses what amounts to a civic hermeneutics—an aesthetic and a style that conform more closely to the actual modes of non-Western or postcolonial literatures and the arts than do prevailing forms of European and American modernism. The emphases of this hermeneutic may be said to be on the vulgate rather than the classical; on secular and corporeal solidarities rather than sacred textual encounters; and on the circulation of demotic and experimental forms rather than their containment within notions of aesthetic autonomy.

A different version of the emergence of anticolonial thought like this one may provide a new point of access and a potentially new set of projects and directions for comparative literature and postcolonial studies. A closer reading of Vico and the tradition he launched not only shifts our focus to different sources and inspirations but questions how we currently argue and read. If, in fact, the content of form is historical, we can only discern the nature of our arguments by learning more about how they took their present form. In this book I adopt the long view in order to learn from history as Vico narrates it— that is, as punctuated, spiral, cyclical, accretive, filled with philological details, curious facts, learned accounts of dubious parentage, and so on. If, as Vico argues, history spirals as it continues, we can say that at the vortex of twentieth-century modernity is the interwar era. And since this is the period that saw the consolidation of international Marxist thought as well, we can begin to appreciate that Marxism happened long before Marxism—that Marxism as we think we know it in the figures of Karl Marx, Antonio Labriola, Alexandra Kollontai, V. I. Lenin, Walter Benjamin, and others is the rediscovery of what had taken shape much earlier, although not in that exact form. The radical new directions in early twentieth-century literary theory and language came from Left populist and revolutionary sources from eastern Europe, just as postwar redirections, when they were not recyclings of interwar ideas, came directly from or were inspired by the global peripheries (or in answer to them). In a general sense, then, "theory" is Marxism's borrowed light.

ARGUMENTS AND LINEAGES

This book is organized primarily around four thinkers. Let me clarify why these four serve as the basis of my revision. In philosophy, Vico and Hegel are the two thinkers, first of all, who did most to establish the methods and terms that would give later anticolonial thought its foundation, above all within the movements of international Marxism. More brashly polemical figures can certainly be found in European anticolonialist literature: Walter Raleigh, Bartolomé de Las Casas, and above all, the Abbé Raynal, all of whom made statements that would cause even modern readers to wither in the face of their invective—as when Raynal in 1770, for example, speaks of the Portuguese adventurers who "ravaged coasts . . . insulted rulers and . . . soon became the terror and the scourge of peoples . . . [and did] not scruple to pillage, to deceive, to enslave idolaters."[2] But Vico and Hegel, who at times speak just as bluntly, formulated a manner of thinking that other dissidents would assume as their own point of departure. They created an architecture of interconnected ideas that systematically attack on a number of fronts the religious authority of the Holy Book, the quietism of intellectualist abstractions, the damaging effects on thought caused by the system of labor and the market, the specious integrity of those whose wealth came from earlier banditry, the fake radicalism of self-styled philosophical eccentrics, and the emptiness of natural law (as opposed to civil law). Despite the elaborate structure of their systems, Vico and Hegel foreground life on the street and the bitter quarrels of parliament chambers; their ideas dwell on the everyday world of work, economy, colonial conquest, and the police, giving explanatory heft to the idea that politics is always about states, and that states themselves have to do with a much earlier and difficult process of discovery, compromise, and self-limitation. Each sheds a different kind of light on the other, enabling us in turn to see them in distinctive ways.

The other two figures are Spinoza and Nietzsche. For their part, the latter builds an important philosophical counterposition to Hegel by openly identifying with Spinoza's leads and simultaneously using many of Vico's techniques. Without adducing Vico as such, Nietzsche explores many of the same philological resources and indeed crafts his career out of similar elements. To put it another way, Nietzsche is the towering antipodal presence who sets out to displace both Vico and Hegel, setting up a confrontation that still influences us today between a mode of reading that acknowledges the authority of the past and a mode of reading that privileges the inventions of memory. Despite differing with Spinoza on this last point, Nietzsche names him as his model and true predecessor. The enthusiastic return to Spinoza's philosophy over the last half century—particularly among those seeking a revitalization of Marxism—must be seen through such a Nietzschean lens. Vico also names Spinoza, of course, but to entirely different ends, not least because he is at the head of the tradition, writing before Minerva's owl has flown. The battles today over the relative claims of science and the humanities derive in part from Vico's critique of Spinoza (later developed by Hegel), of the exclusionary scientism of the seventeenth century: that is, not science as such, obviously, but the kind of discourse that had sprung up then that considered the study of history defunct and the study of letters an arcane indulgence.

To move to a different consideration of the relationship between arguments and their lineages, let me say that, in contrast to the belle-lettrism of earlier decades, a very different tone is perceptible today in the response of humanistic critics to problems such as the global ecological crisis, the neoliberal ascendancy, and the almost unquestioned imperial actions of the United States and its allies abroad. In these crisis surroundings, we find a combative theoretical mode in which scholars feel they are involved in a new form of insurgency, or that their work bears directly on the revolutionary overthrow of capitalism.[3] Inquiries into subjectivity and affect that defined the field of postcolonial studies two decades ago have given way to criticism that directly invokes Abu Ghraib, steeps itself in economic terminology, and prophesies a coming insurrection, as though mediation were now a thoroughly outdated consideration. Along the same lines, conference postings bristle with references to Marx, Lenin, and Rosa Luxemburg, marking their affiliations to critical traditions both green and red. At the same time, and from the other side, there is a countertendency that wants to do away with any sort of critique at all and seeks a no less revolutionary solution in the *dis*solution of the human as such. Its strategic position is to abandon all positions and emphatically to take its stand with indecisionism.

With this latter move, we confront something of a historical pun: the humanities have come to stand against humans. There are at least three pronounced trends today that bear this out. The first is toward a posthumanism based on the figure of the animal or on the biotechnologically compromised uniqueness of the human body; its emphasis is on the nonpriority of a human species that has betrayed other animals through ecological devastation and its undeserved mastery—what might be called green misanthropy. A second trend posits the cybernetic triumph of thinking machines, arguing that the human mind has been overtaken by the possibilities of artificial intelligence, seen as decoupled entirely from human intervention; or that the machine, in this sense like the animal, is more moral than the human because it cannot be guilty of acting upon what it naturally intends. Third is the move in historical circles to replace the writing of history with the history of objects: a new kind of history writing, in other words, which only incidentally includes the human, and then only as one object among many—a natural history to replace the history of human beings. In this trend we also find a romance with death, a purification of inquiry by way of a desired oblivion of the social world and the contemplation of the end of the species; it obviates in this way any commitment or affiliation with the idea of political will or force.

No philosopher, though, exceeds Vico's and Hegel's fascination with the human being as actor, and so there is no other tradition today that so directly speaks to this aspect of the present of theory. This relevance has less to do with their being the by-product of what is cavalierly called "humanism" today than with their elaboration of a striking anthropological/political economy of the species. In this emphasis both Vico and Hegel remain in contact, albeit inversely, with the topos of the posthuman. For both, the human is the being beyond which we cannot think. We are the animal, the creature who, along with everything else, invents the posthuman—as though by doing so we had demonstrated our lack of will.

WHY PHILOLOGY

In an early essay written over twenty years ago, I argued that philology—or, at least, a philological sensibility—was positively involved in, and helped enable, the emerging interest in non-Western cultures and the legacies of imperialism.[4] Although the proposition was unusual at the time, there has since then been a great deal written about some of these connections; and certainly the link between Erich Auerbach's and Leo Spitzer's work in Romance philology and that of Edward Said in world literature and the study, throughout the 1980s and 1990s, of non-Western intellectuals and writers is by now familiar. But another aspect of my argument remained unexplored—the connection between Said's active anticolonial criticism and his early apprenticeship under interwar

Marxist intellectuals. Some of these intellectuals figured prominently in his essays and books, and they were the frequent topics of the seminars he taught throughout the 1980s. In this, he mirrored (and, of course, also helped create) an influential nexus that remains more or less unexamined today.

In the epigraph that heads this Introduction, Gramsci suggests that Marxism is not just a political tendency or economic program but a philosophy of active encounter. He declares that in the early twentieth century, Marxism stood against the stream and on behalf of ideas with which philology earlier had been associated and for which it was then (just as now) largely ridiculed. This move allows him to position himself within Marxist debates of the time by distinguishing himself from the neopositivists (or "Lorians," as he calls them), on the one hand, and Crocean idealists, on the other. For Gramsci, the calculative spirit of the bourgeois money economy had swept through the human sciences, stamping them with pseudoscientific instincts that movements within Marxism were busily combating throughout the period from 1880 to 1950. There is, I would argue, a mostly unnoticed philological dimension of Marxism embedded in this example—a dimension of which almost all the Marxist intellectuals of the era whom we read and admire today partake. This particular emphasis, moreover, played an important role in the development of anticolonial thought.

In public discussion, of course, philology—if anyone pays attention to the word at all—is usually written off as a tedious scholarly machinery and a spent method. While it enjoys some residual prestige in parts of the academy—mostly in humanistic area studies, classics departments, and the early modern wings of English studies—it is typically mocked by authors and journalists as being of a piece with the great speculative system philosophies of the eighteenth and nineteenth centuries. We do not have to look far to find parodies of philology's academic type today: take the recent example of Palipana, the "epigraphist" of Michael Ondaatje's *Anil's Ghost*, whose philologist character earnestly marches off to reclaim what any half-intelligent modernist knows is ridiculous: the truth of the past. Part archaeologist and part textualist, Palipana lives like a hermit prophet in the "Grove of Ascetics," "draw[ing] parallels and links between the techniques of stonemasons he met with in Matara and the work he had done during the years of translating texts and in the field. And he began to see as truth things that could only be guessed at. In no way did this feel to him like forgery or falsification."[5] Later in the novel, Ondaatje drives home this spurious fact-finding and invented certainty. The confident, well-armed hunter for the truth—careful, studious, exacting—discovers in the end that the truth has to be made up: "In the last few years he had found the hidden histories, intentionally lost, that altered the perspective and knowledge of earlier times. It was how one hid or wrote the truth when it was necessary to lie."[6]

For all that, philology keeps making an entry these days. It has again been taken up in high-profile journal articles and artfully written, often highly experimental, "avant" books as though its historical backwash were lapping against postmodern shores. A number of classicists, Sanskritists, and polyglots have been raising an entirely different complaint from the mainstream one about philology's outmoded status.[7] To them, the field's meanings are being diluted by the noncognoscenti. So, for example, Said's attempts to enlarge on the role of philology in colonial administration is seen by these critics as the efforts of a dilettante who tossed the word around too loosely. They also consider his inclusion of critics like Auerbach and Spitzer in the philological fold misplaced, since the latter, despite their many gifts and obvious erudition, had little to do with the philological trenches, that is, the labors of comparative linguistics, textual recension, and other aspects of the formidable scientific machinery of philology proper.

My use of the term is less technical. In fact, I argue that a broader definition of the philological is inherently Vichian—that is, interdisciplinary and based on a logic of intellectual generalism that was developed in Left Hegelian thought as the only approach possible for the study of the social totality. Vico's take on the term was to describe his method as "a new critical art that has hitherto been lacking." In his work, he pointed out, unlike in that of such predecessors as Tacitus and Sir Francis Bacon, "philosophy undertakes to examine philology," defining the latter as "the doctrine of all the institutions that depend on *human choice*; for example, all histories of the languages, customs, and deeds of peoples in war and peace."[8] Within philology, in this sense, there is a protest against the divisions of academic labor. It is a version of Vico's recognition that the principles underlying any claim on the real rely on attention to the modes of language, to the sorting of documents, internal consistency, and systematic comprehension.[9] At any rate, it seems pointless to attempt to police its meanings today as some critics have tried to do. Even Nietzsche points out that in his own time, when the field was at its academic zenith, it had a loose and shifting definition and referred to a wide range of inquiries, not all of them strictly verbal.

In his German translation of *The New Science* in 1924, Auerbach too welcomes this expansive sense of philology, arguing that Vico meant by it "anything that we now call the humanities: the whole story in the strict sense, sociology, national economy, the history of religion, language, law and art."[10] But he goes beyond this as well, arguing in the spirit of the interwar era that "classical philology has always been (and it almost still is) the only science that will include a *general social theory*, for in it are all branches of human activity contained in the lyrics and subject matter of its study."[11] Herder, the greatest of Vico's successors, is still more radical. In 1768, he formulates, in a strikingly modern way, the need to "de-center" European values and to learn modesty from studying the civilizations of others: "He is the greatest philologist of the Orient who understands the nature of the Eastern sciences, the character of the native language, like an Easterner"—an impossible demand, but a strategically welcome one in the face of the arrogance of his contemporaries.[12] The philological, as I mean it in this book, then, is a deliberately generalist understanding of language and literature—a theory of the social that is reliant on a theory of reading based on evidence, correspondence, and evaluation, situating authors in their motives and times. The attitude is one laid out by Gramsci when he writes of the need for "scrupulous accuracy and scientific honesty" in dealing with an author's writing: "It is necessary, first of all, to trace the process of the thinker's intellectual development in order to reconstruct it in accordance with those elements that become stable and permanent—that is, those elements really adopted by the author as his own thought, distinct and superior to the 'material' that he had studied earlier and that, at a certain time, he may have found attractive." He then goes on to sketch the possible method of such a project:

> 1. biography in great detail, and 2. Exposition of all the works, even the most negligible, in chronological order, sorted according to the different phases: intellectual formation, maturity, the grasp of a new way of thinking and its confident application. The search for the leitmotif, the rhythm of the thought, more important than single, isolated quotations.[13]

Both Marxism and philology adhere to historical forms of knowing, to the sedimentary traces of a past that happened, to the ultimate creativity of the unnamed, unheralded, popular elements of society. Both, it turns out, are skeptical about romanticism and literary modernism, and for the same reasons (the attractions to supermen, the evacuation of the subject, the calligraphic fetishization of writing, the addiction to secrets and enigmas, and so on). For his part, Gramsci puts the matter very plainly, again emphasizing the deliberate generalism that gives the humanities a certain political advantage over other methods of knowing: "The experience upon which the philosophy of praxis is based cannot be schematized; it is history in its infinite variety and multiplicity, the study of which can give birth to 'philology' as a method of scholarship for ascertaining particular facts and to the birth of philosophy understood as a general methodology of history."[14] From the rather different tradition of the Frankfurt School, Benjamin makes this connection even more strongly in *The Arcades Project*, when he expresses his intention "to prove by example that only Marxism can practice great philology, where the literature of the previous century is concerned."[15]

RUPTURE/CONTINUITY

One of the most provocative, if forgotten, figures in the arena of philological materialism, Sebastiano Timpanaro, made an observation of significant importance to the Vichian tradition. He focused on the closed nature of the Saussurean conception of language and remarked that it had resulted in early Prague and Copenhagen linguistics circles (1928–1939) in a "systematic mysticism."[16] As he put it, they exalted Cuvier over Darwin, which left them with no way to account for the movement from one state to another except by "sudden and miraculistic leaps, just like Cuvier's 'catastrophes.'" Our theoretical preferences over the last three decades seem equally drawn to sudden and miraculous departures. In Marxist sociology journals, almost every essay, it seems, is built around the notion of "crisis," as though a crisis could simply go on unchanged for decades; in other fields, such as history, literature, and cultural studies, we read of "epistemic breaks," "Copernican revolutions," and "historical ruptures." A whole industry of essays and books in one form or another avow theory's radical severing from Western metaphysics, the end of grand narratives, the linguistic turn as a sudden shift from reality to signification, and, of course, the end of history. The proposed revaluation, in a revolutionary shudder, simply leaps over whatever it has left behind.

A more careful account of the figure of rupture would have to contend with its philosophical and methodological other. The career of Neoplatonism, for example—which played such a prominent role in Martin Bernal's *Black Athena: The Afroasiatic Roots of Classical Civilization* (1987)—points us to the realization that a political break can be effected as much by historical continuities as by ruptures. As with any tradition, Vico's contemporary influence did not begin with Vico, an idea to which Benjamin also alludes, drawing on Karl Kraus, when he remarks that "origin is the goal"—that is to say, all concepts have a prehistory, and uniqueness is a form of repetition which it is our goal to retrace. So Vico's precursors can be glimpsed in Neoplatonism, which had as its purpose, among other things, to speak of submerged Afroasiatic inheritances hiding in the light borrowed from Egyptian and Phoenician civilization. Christian orthodoxy violently set out to *rupture* lines of connection between thought on the peninsular continent of Europe and Egyptian and Levantine learning. By contrast, at the core of Neoplatonism was the idea that Christianity was an oriental philosophy, that African secrets lay buried in the heart of European knowledge as its borrowed light, and that the life of the mind, of letters, and the first books were the work of the East. Vico himself, as Bernal rightly observes, inherited Neoplatonism's secularization and paganization of Christian wisdom and its de-centering of a Europe held to be the unique child of Greece.

As late moderns, our relationship to the (largely Marxist) heresies and organizational achievements of the interwar era is analogous to this earlier severing; for political and aesthetic reasons, we too have been cut off from its ways of seeing, or its sensibilities have been safely wrapped in repellent garments with garish colors. Paradoxically, then, the idea of tradition acquires a revolutionary sense in regard to the still viable but suppressed past set against the peremptory metaphor of modernist rupture and theoretical breaks. But I also contend that the conceptual dispute between continuity and rupture, captured often in aesthetic or literary-critical terms (and especially elaborated in that sphere), is precisely at issue in the attempt to see Marxism as a punctuated articulation of a civic spirit operating according to a logic that thinkers such as Vico and Hegel attempted to express and define.

The desire to be done with Eurocentric thought, after all, leads to very different itineraries. It is certainly possible to search for—and even perhaps find—non-Western forms of philosophy that offer radically incommensurable modes of thinking and value untouched by modernity, heroically resistant to it, and therefore invisible to it, with no place or sense in the current hegemony. Similarly, it is possible to argue not for a singular modernity but for alternative or peripheral modernities (in this way following the common gesture of pluralizing terms already meant to be comprehensive, as one speaks today in neologisms about "communisms" or "sexualities"). The political act of deliverance, then, becomes above all an act of articulation. The point becomes a simple way of conveying the reality of the other realm in a milieu of oppressive universality while employing alien terms and strategies of verbal circumnavigation to evoke what lies outside the vision of the dominant.

In practice, this imperative prioritizes the rediscovery of what can only be the indigenous, the original, the native. Given the offensive overtones of the term "native," critics hesitate to use it, for its ethnographic frame implies an ontological stability that is dangerous for those who seek to break out of its imposed limitations. And so what we are left with is a philosophy that cannot name what it enacts, and seeks so much to alienate itself from its referents that it must develop a conceptual vocabulary where language no longer means at all, or in any case means only arbitrarily, thereby universalizing its own gestures at the very point of condemning any claims to the universal as such. This is a prominent version of anti-Eurocentrism today—an othering of Europe that articulates itself, ironically, by paying homage to a particular and partial group of European philosophers and their various late twentieth-century disciples.

But what if we saw the matter differently, refusing to grant this polarization of the globe? What if it was argued that to insist on the absolute incommensurability of certain values and knowledges among modern peoples in the colonial aftermath surrendered too much? Modernity, if it is singular, is so not because of any theoretical declaration, or because theorists of a different persuasion find totality attractive or find comfort in a simple-minded formula about the universal. Rather, modernity is singular because of the overdeveloped and interlocking global systems of capital, always the prime motives of colonialism and imperialism. So, if in the present stage of colonialism we are all left with this single governing logic, what place then is left for the non-Eurocentric? A partial response has to lie in recognizing that the demarcation of Europe is itself a combinative creation, and that a singular modernity, as the willing or unwilling outcome of capitalism, bears the stamp of its own diversity and resistance.

What I hope to explore in this book is some of that sense of mutuality in the global articulations of modern life. On the one hand, I am interested in the immense implications for anticolonial thought in specific European intellectual traditions; on the other hand, I am also interested in what European intellectuals learned from those outside its orbit in the colonial encounter, as well as the original contributions, corrections, and adaptations of metropolitan ideas by intellectuals in the periphery. Crucially, this is a conjuncture of joint creations, encounters and dialogues, at least in those cases where the positions taken (and I am talking mainly of positions rather than ethnic or racial inheritances) were not already steeled in the confidence of their own superiority. I would like also to question the narrow ways we have of conceiving Europe today as constituting *the* center when the continent is filled with pockets of underdevelopment and residual backwardness, and experiences some foreign domination and military occupation. The mutuality that catches my interest here is present, even if in a negative form, in the recognition by some of Europe's earliest anticolonial thinkers that colonialism brought to the domestic setting itself some of the inequality and irrationality visited by Europe on others.

My intention is not to propose an exclusive tradition that displaces others, since it is the logic of exclusion that I want to contest. Nor am I trying to idealize a lineage by positing a trans-historical Vichian spirit that magically revisits thinkers sullied by misuse or disregard, or who have fallen out of favor because of their political stands. As I hope becomes evident, many of the principal figures I explore, including Vico, come in for extensive criticism. Still, the question that remains worth asking is, which traditions open up possibilities for a transformed future? In the chapters that follow, I explore how Vico and Hegel's thinking does this, paradoxically, by directing us back to the human past, which is the only one we have that we can make again.

OVERVIEW OF CHAPTERS

Chapter 1 explores Vico's anticolonial ideas in the doctrines of the nonpriority of peoples, the de-centering of Greece, and the account of inland colonies as forms of class warfare. I make a case for his incipient historical materialism, his formulation of a qualitative sociology, and his attacks on scientism and the greed of the first "heroic" age of civilization. Vico's contemporaneity is traced in three of his principles—the human as a being beyond race and territory, language as material exchange, and the need for philosophy to have a system character and a polemical foundation. A contrast is then set up with his near contemporary Spinoza, whose theory of reading in the *Theologico-Political Treatise* harmonizes with Vico's in ways that have been overlooked. The achievements, but also limitations, of Spinoza's thought are then considered in relation to his doubtful materialism, the monotheistic subtext of his philosophy, the problematic notion of a "perfect" nature (finished, impermeable, incomprehensible), his skepticism toward democracy, and the close affinity of his thought with Dutch mercantile impulses. I explore Spinoza's prominence today by way of the neo-Spinozist concept of "productive reading" (the obverse of Spinoza's own more philological mode of reading). The chapter concludes with a history of Vico's influence and how it became an actual lineage that influenced Marxism and anticolonial thought.

Chapter 2 begins by establishing the systematic parallels between Hegel and Vico: their exploration of their own peripheral status within Europe, their insistence on the methodological superiority of the humanities to the sciences, and their revolt against slavery, unchecked accumulation, and class. I make the case that anticolonial intellectuals understood Hegel's inventive defense of the state form in the *Philosophy of Right* as their own—the state as embodying the principle that freedom must defend itself. I argue that Hegel's radicalism rather than his conservatism is what scandalizes liberal thought, and show where Hegel draws on non-Western sources and where he identifies Eastern philosophy and African civilization as forerunners of European Mind. The chapter then takes up Fredric Jameson's claim that even dialectics must be dialectical (that is, self-overcoming) in order to suggest, by contrast, the importance of system and polemic in philosophy. The chapter ends with a reading of the history of Hegel's influence on anticolonial thought, above all in a positive sense in Marx's famous treatment of the *Philosophy of Right* and, in a negative one, in Alexandre Kojève's treatment of Hegel after World War II, which disparages peripheral independence movements.

Chapter 3 focuses on Nietzsche as a philologist to show the centrality of his training in classics to his views on European colonialism. The chapter examines the politics of form in the two genres that most define Nietzsche's style—the epigram and genealogy—and shows how they emerge from his philological repertoire. I account for the reasons why Nietzsche occupies a privileged position in postcolonial theory, particularly in light of the ways that earlier anticolonial intellectuals reviled him. He is placed in his time—one marked by both the apex of German colonialism and the dramatic rise of socialist parties and movements with which his work is in intimate dialogue. Nietzsche's influence on the interwar period is traced in the popular genre of the 1920s on European colonial encirclement. And finally, an argument is presented that genealogy in Nietzsche is not a new way of doing history but a new way of reading and arguing based on inheritance.

Chapter 4 recounts how Georges Bataille re-invented Nietzsche for postwar theory against the setting of third-world emergence and Soviet triumph. It relates how he ingeniously builds his masterwork, *The Accursed Share* (1949), around those very issues while declaring that humans now have a fatal choice—Nietzsche or communism. In this chapter I return to the image of borrowed light to describe in more detail what is meant by the trope and specifically how and why it alludes to the strategy of mocking while mimicking the texts and ideas of Marxism. The idea of genealogy is further developed as well, seen here as a principle of counterphilological reading. Finally, the Vichian dispute with Spinoza over the humanities and natural sciences is revisited in the form of current debates over posthumanism.

Frontispiece of Vico's *Scienza nuova* (1744)

1

VICO, SPINOZA, AND THE IMPERIAL PAST

> [Vico,] the true precursor of all German thought.
> Marcel Grilli[1]

VICO'S UNTIMELINESS

Like the *corsi* and *ricorsi* of his cyclical history, Giambattista Vico, it appears, had to be discovered twice. No longer can one pretend to introduce him for the first time, since from the age of the philosophes onward, he has been a thinker whose ideas were debated throughout his native Italy and avidly read, paraphrased, and plagiarized by many of the most famous intellectuals of France and Germany. Circles dedicated to his work could be found in nineteenth-century Buenos Aires. Montesquieu repeated him and Rousseau found in him the central ideas of his "Essay on the Origin of Languages" (1871). Among German thinkers, Goethe read him on his travels to Naples; the great German Enlightenment independent, Johann Georg Hamann, passed his secrets along to Herder, with lasting effects on Romance philology. And on the other side of the continent, Coleridge did his best to acknowledge, formally, the momentous impact of Vico in an England already familiar with his theories in their borrowings by Scottish empiricists. All across Europe and parts of the Americas, the history of ideas attests to Vico's distant presence—admired, contested, engaged, a source of ideas found to be expressing what later readers somehow knew but did not know why.

It is only the twentieth century, strangely, that discovers a different Vico. Despite the labors of Benedetto Croce in *La filosofia de Giambattista Vico* (1911) and in his *Bibliografia vichiana* (with Fausto Nicolini, 1947–48) in standardizing editions of Vico's works, popularizing his system, and explaining his significance internationally, Vico subsided into an obscurity he had not known since the 1720s.[2] Always an enthusiasm among specialists, antiquarians, and Italianists, he was no longer considered a serious source of philosophical learning as he had been for the ground-clearers of the French Revolution. There were exceptions. Georges Sorel's idiosyncratic study of Vico in 1896 based on Jules Michelet's equally selective translations from earlier in the century provided a weapon in Sorel's assault on the economic determinism of early interpretations of Marx.[3] A long chapter on Vico in *The Economic Determinism of Karl Marx* (1909) by Marx's son-in-law, Paul Lafargue, played a similar role.[4]

But neither they nor their contemporaries fully grasped the fact that entire fields of inquiry became imaginable only in his wake. For it is really in Vico that we see the first hints of what would later become qualitative sociology, cultural anthropology, social history, comparative linguistics, hermeneutics, world literature, and even, I would argue, Marxist cultural criticism. If the originality of Vico's revolt had faded from view, especially after World War II, it took with it the ability to see at a glance that thinkers such as Friedrich August Wolf, Ernst Cassirer, Arnold Toynbee, and R. G. Collingwood were following in his footsteps. It also made invisible the earlier fact that some of the most important eighteenth-century ideas—for example, aspects of Kant's ethics—are equally indebted to Vico.

Much of what mid-nineteenth-century French intellectuals after Michelet, Vico's tireless promoter, took for granted about the latter's project had to be relearned. This active rediscovery was, for example, Erich Auerbach's major postwar undertaking. In laying out his translation of *The New Science* in 1924 (not the first in German), Auerbach declared Vico his model and master, going so far as to argue that no one before him had penetrated Vico's ideas to the same degree. Indeed, part of the twentieth-century retreat from Vico can be attributed to Auerbach's incorrect comment in his introduction that "Herder, the Romantics, and Hegel knew nothing of him." He does, however, hedge on this claim by conceding that Vico was read in wider circles after the eighteenth century but then goes on to say that he was subject to "a long series of misunderstandings," making it important for Auerbach to be the one who "grasped the true content of Vico."[5] Vico remains as much an open secret as a puzzle today. Even though his name is immediately recognizable, his work has not been engaged in anything like the depth enjoyed by many lesser thinkers.

As a result of wars on Europe's periphery in the early twentieth century, as well as the waves of anticolonial insurrection that followed, Vico's ideas took on a particular shape in new surroundings. My contention at the outset is that this "particular shape" prompted a philosophical reaction that for complicated reasons sought not only to consign Vico to obscurity but also to disarticulate his philosophy's premises and methods. In turn, this reaction has led to an evacuation of the generalist mode of inquiry Vico called "philology," a term that in his hands had none of the quasi-technical and -scientific associations it acquired in its high–nineteenth-century form. The implications of Vico's challenge—polymathic, humane, vernacular, and irreverent—have consequently been rendered largely unintelligible to those seeking to understand the twentieth century as, above all, the anticolonial century.

Influential but heterodox thinkers such as Auerbach and Edward Said tested the waters by bringing Vico back into the conversation—the first devoted to the literary comity of Europe after the devastations of war, the second to a literary reckoning with colonialism itself. But their efforts to make Vico relevant remained tentative and somewhat cryptic. To be sure, scholarship on Vico, including theirs, has never stopped being brilliant and broad. But it says very little, finally, about what Vico offers for an understanding of the European colonial past or resistance to the imperial order.

His contribution, it turns out, runs deep. He invented a body of terms and concepts that set the stage later for others to deride chauvinism and undermine the authority of foreign conquest. For in Vico we find the human being exuberantly extolled without triumphalizing "reason" as it was passed down from the scientific Enlightenment. He importantly sees the disregard of the aristocracy toward the peasantry in terms of a rejection of foreigners and so links class prejudices with colonialist mentalities. His confidence in the epistemology of the archive is offset by his excitement for "metaphorical" knowledge—a literary knowledge that for him takes precedence over the physical sciences, and in that way he can be said to offer an entirely original and compelling theory of the politics of literature itself. In many ways, in his current reception, he is speaking directly to and against what we today call "posthumanism," particularly its reliance on the tropes of technoscience.

Vico, then, is helpful for letting us appreciate a different way of arguing than is common today. Consider the affective differences between reading Spinoza, whose star has been in the ascendant ever since Louis Althusser brought him back into vogue, and Vico, who now signifies only as a name. Spinoza wrote in a prose carefully shorn of all personality, a medieval scholastic Latin crafted precisely to remove all sense of personal character, opinion, or taste.

His findings are consciously made to appear to arrive from no particular conjuncture or setting, immanently—an important stylistic feature that captures the tone of his portrait of an impervious and eternal nature. In Vico, by contrast, there is color, anger, and mockery. He is not shy about foregrounding his debates with various antagonists, and *The New Science* is the first of his books he did not write in Latin, choosing instead (and also appropriately) the Italian vernacular. If Vico insists that his study does for philology what Bacon's did for scientific method and Newton's for the laws of motion, he is no mere iconoclast. He loves, in fact, to dwell on precursors, drawing on a number of obscure masters from antiquity to whom he readily pays homage—Diodorus Siculus, Eusebius, Marcus Terentius Varro, and others. Vico's sources are amazingly cosmopolitan, especially when one considers the breadth of ancient learning he derives from Damascus, Tyre, Alexandria, and Antioch.

Is Vico current? The linguistic implications of his work, for one thing, dramatically reorient the story of the turn to language in twentieth-century philosophy. But even more, despite the fact that Spinoza has been the philosophical source for an influential school of contemporary neo-Marxism, Vico is by far the more likely precursor to Marx. This is so not only because he defends history and historiography against their detractors (a move popularized by Althusser's rejection of historicism) or because he so elaborately portrays class struggle and the centrality of labor, but because Vico invents the idea that specific ideas, linguistic innovations, and forms of art correspond to a period's conditions of social organization. He inaugurates, in other words, a nonpresentist form of historicism that is the genesis of Marx's historical materialism. Vico's importance for Marxism may lie even more clearly, though, in his *ricorsi*. Against the backdrop of the fall of the Berlin wall, the emergence again, after great effort, of that which had been roundly defeated earlier is not simply possible but wholly logical in his particular mapping of human time. Because history as he imagines it is never exactly repeated, we can be sure that it will reappear in forms we cannot yet imagine.

The troubled sense of the term "philology" today (in the aftermath of *Orientalism*) is clarified in Vico along the lines of a generalist intellectual program that, in later centuries, would be vital to the Left Hegelian tradition. In Vico, finally, we find the early instruments for a de-centering of European culture and a respect for foreign peoples that is the basis of what would come to be known, further down the line, as world literature. My purpose here is to explore the reasons for the disjunction between Vico's appearance and reality.

How, in other words, can he today appear so out-dated and yet be at the head of a lineage from which many of our most contemporary ideas and frameworks are derived? My aim is to show the links between Marxism and philology in the ways in which they take shape in Vico's reception and in the form in which Vico's early eighteenth-century text contains them, however implicitly.

If Vico's predecessor Spinoza is the talisman of some current and popular versions of theory in the humanities, we might wonder at the exactly counterposed Vichian exclusion. For if there are obvious disagreements between Vico and Spinoza, there is also a lot of common ground, found above all in their hermeneutic theories. But the larger question that I want to address via this counterposition is how the contemporary creation of "Spinoza" (to be distinguished from Spinoza himself or his writings) is primarily about finding a foil to Hegel. To put it differently, how did the *non*-Vico become the *anti*-Hegel? My interest, then, is less in denying Spinoza's relevance to antinomian thought than in making a specific case for Vico because he has been overlooked. In addition, there are consonances between Vico and Spinoza that deserve to be treated in an account of the historical precedents of anticolonial thinking in the West.

ANTICOLONIAL IMAGINATION

The New Science (1725–44) is a vivid, bulky, formally innovative compendium of linguistic archaeology, iconographic readings of antique prints, and imaginative recountings of prehistory before the development of writing and the tools of the historian. A long and asymmetrical work, it was written over an extended period of time, with additions and amendments along the way. The study reads as such: a confabulation of brilliant, often brief, précis, factoids, apothegms, documentary snippets, and heated marginal commentaries. The work resists genre, filled as it is with dramas of class conflict, insurrection, intertribal warfare, and conjectures about the rise of the first cities and the first books, as well as the first empires. Vico's guiding principle throughout is that no one people, race, or region has priority in the story of human beings. His history, as he puts it, is "gentile" in the sense that it traces human origins from the first *gentes* (tribes, extended families), leaving to the side the providential story of the chosen people already revealed in the Bible.[6]

Consequently, the book's thesis is prophetically nondenominational. He provides a unified theory of fragmentary events and peoples, showing what is common in human practices over many millennia. And, although unified, *The New Science* is unorthodox in method—découpaged from oral myths, tattered scraps of ancient poetry and prose, commentaries of philologists from antiquity, and the iconography of early etchings. Like pieces of broken pottery reconstituted from their scattered shards, the study is less history than metahistory, showcasing an approach to reading that Vico proudly refers to as "a new critical art that has hitherto been lacking" (*NS*, 6).

The radicalism of Vico's project involves the challenge his theories posed not simply to the established authority of the church, to classical pieties, or to aristocratic power structures but to countertheories widely perceived as defining radicalism in his time. This is very important, for here, too, there are resonances with the current moment. His critique is, in this sense, two-pronged, and he is involved as much in shrugging off his own earlier, mistaken enthusiasm for views deemed at the time dangerous and subversive as in shaking up the complacent status quo. The most uncompromising critic of Cartesianism of his day, he could afford his anger, since he had been a dedicated Cartesian up to the writing of *Universal Law* (1720–22) and the first *New Science* (1725). In time he would reject Cartesianism from the Left, as it were, for he takes the view that the refined ratiocination of philosophy was the by-product of "the disputations of the Athenian assembly and courts"—a collective product unfolding over generations rather than the work of extraordinary celebrities.[7]

Despite Vico's perceived irrelevance in many circles, the shock of what *The New Science* proposes bears stating baldly to get a full sense of its insult to prevailing norms.[8] He is saying, after all, that civilization was the invention of brutes; that instinct, feeling, intuition, and figurative language are forms of reason; and that the first philosophical thought was based on poetic characters. Moreover, in a devoutly Catholic milieu, he builds his case on mostly pagan and Protestant sources.[9] With respect to the word "radical," his postulates had the capacity to scandalize followers of Descartes just as much as they did emissaries of the pope or, more to the point, the monks and priests who were his friends and whose goodwill he counted on in Naples, with his growing alienation from Cartesian freethinkers.[10] Vico's riposte to Cartesianism was a methodological coup. Humanistic studies have as their goal *vero* (the true), the sciences *certo* (the certain). It is in the fancies and rough verbal utterances of the vulgate, in other words, that Vico finds relief from the fictions of math. The scientist's arbitrary postulates (let x be 1) offer up a merely deduced, and therefore sterile, certitude.

> Perception is stricken by algebra, for algebra sees only what is right under its eyes; memory is confounded, since when the second sign is found, algebra pays

no further attention to the first; imagination goes blind, because algebra has no need of images; understanding is destroyed, because algebra professes to divine. [This leaves the young] less apt in the affairs of civil life. (*AGV*, 125)

This is not to say that Vico disparaged all scientific inquiry—far from it. He revered the discoveries of Newton, saw himself as carrying on the spirit of Bacon, and considered Leibniz one of the great minds of the age. At one point he praises his own efforts in employing Descartes's theory of heat and cold ("cold being motion inward from without and heat the reverse motion outward from within") to "build thereon a system of medicine" (*AGV*, 150). Vico's projected complete system of philosophy, *De antiquissima*, had as its second book the now-lost *De aequilibrio corporis animantis* (On the equilibrium of living bodies), dedicated to the medical implications of physics and the philosophy of nature. His position, rather, was that physics had to be grounded in a suitable metaphysics and rarely was, or, put differently, that the drift of scientific inquiry in his age was toward an "arid and dry" reasoning that "reduced natural signs of magnitudes to certain ciphers at will" (*AGV*, 124). From this thinking flowed his claim that ultimately we can know fully only what we have made. This is the view underlying Vico's famous *verum-factum* distinction. The word he chooses in Italian for this product of human making is *cosa* (literally, "thing," "affair," "matter," or "institution"). The use of the Italian equivalent of the Latin *res* permits him an allusion to Lucretius's Epicurean poem *De rerum natura* (On the nature of things) while rendering it demotic. *The New Science*, he implies, explains the nature of things too, only not of atoms but of political affairs.

The consequences of Vico's relative neglect can be appreciated when we consider how few of the readers of Sorel's hugely influential *Reflections on Violence* (1908) understood its Vichian points of departure—a fact of some importance when reckoning with the hidden story of Vico's twentieth-century Marxist reception. Vico was for Sorel at the turn of the century nothing less than the banner under which Marxism had to be reconfigured. *The New Science* was a caution against "all those who, in the Marxist orbit," saw "historical determinism as a simple variant of natural determinism."[11] Sorel observed that Vico effectively blasted the mechanical economism of late-century positivism and paved the way for the more voluntarist elements he sought to bring to political strategizing. Vico had understood that myth provided an "ensemble[ ] of images capable of evoking *en bloc* and solely by intuition, before any analysis, the mass of feeling corresponding to diverse manifestations of the war of socialism against modern society."[12]

Even thinkers whose own habits and methods parallel Vico's have, unlike Sorel, downplayed his importance. Raymond Williams, for example, in *Marxism and Literature* (1977), while crediting Vico with being responsible for "the effective origin of the general social sense of 'culture,'" adds that "the specific interpretations which Vico then offered are now of little interest."[13] He continues in this vein with the same divided judgment on Vico's disciple, Herder, whose interpretations "in terms of 'organic' peoples and nations, and against the 'external universalism' of the Enlightenment, are elements of the Romantic movement and now of little active interest."[14] Although he was allied with them in other respects, Williams's dismissal clashed sharply with his 1970s contemporaries Hayden White and Edward Said, who borrowed from Vico but without fully appreciating the possibilities his work opens up for anticolonial thought.

The attractions of Vico for anticolonial theory are obvious from three defining features of his work. First, his story of civilization's origins gives no priority to any one people, thereby refuting the principle of European centrality by way of Greece. If certain cultures were responsible for specific inventions such as navigation, the quadrant, the first alphabet, laws of the first free commonwealth, and so on, for him the drama of civic institutions is the work of everyone equally and separately (*NS*, 36): "By uniformity of ideas the orientals, Egyptians, Greeks and Latins, each in ignorance of the others, raised the gods to the planets" (*NS*, 4). Along the same lines, he notes that the "law of nations" is not an invidious natural law based on race or lineage but on the making of institutions (*cose*). His understanding of civic or national belonging depends on uprooting pedigree and natality as its main emphasis and replacing them with sociality.[15]

Vico locates civilization (as opposed to barbarism) at the center of human activity, but not in the sense of a technological imperative. He refers, rather, to a civic breakthrough common to all humans in prehistory: the inventions of religion, marriage, and burial.[16] The very conceptions of barbarism and backwardness are in his portrayal displaced from their imperial deployment, and he reminds us that the organization of human faculties by means of which the propensity toward murder, rape, and ignorance was overcome only later turned into a device for distinguishing between the civilized and the barbaric. By the same token, Vico does not reject the idea of law or civilization (as is common today) because these have at times been oppressive; nor does disappointment with civilization provide the grounds for heroizing an earlier nomadism.[17] On the contrary, the past sets the terms for a different outcome in the future. Every *ricorso* is a new possibility.

Second, Vico's theory of independent cultural creation anticipates the antidiffusion thesis prominent only later in the mid-twentieth century—one that was instrumental in countering the prejudices of the discredited "European miracle" thesis.[18] Vico proleptically displaces this still-mainstream twentieth-century variant on nineteenth-century notions of European supremacy. Proponents of the "miracle" held that instead of genetic inheritance, it was accident and opportunity that allowed Europe to surpass its global rivals: its favorable climate, the traditions of scientific inquiry made possible by the Reformation, the individualist ethos that arose from Christianity and encouraged innovation. Vico contests the view that Europe is the font of government, technology, and culture in ways that leave little doubt about his views on the equality of cultures, saying, for instance, that "the American Indians would now be following this course of human institutions if they had not been discovered by the Europeans" (NS, 414).

The third and final feature of Vico's aptness for anticolonial understanding can be discerned in his condemnation of conquest. Equating robbery and foreign domination, he says: "As in the first barbarian times, the heroes considered it a title of honor to be called robbers, so in the returned barbarian times [of the Middle Ages] the powerful rejoiced to be called pirates" (NS, 19). Similarly, he chastises the celebration of colonies in the ancient world, and his text is replete with asides that rebuke imperial attitudes—pointing out, for example, that Telemachus in the *Odyssey* calls non-Achaians the "other people," "which is to say a subject people" (NS, 235). And above all, his seminal insight (as elaborated below) is to associate the inequality of classes with the invention of the culturally foreign. In an analysis later picked up by Hegel, Vico believed that colonial domination was originally the work of victims who had come to the city's protections too late, who were eventually driven from home, and who ended up plundering other lands. Colonies are formed "in order to avoid oppression and to find escape"; people risk "the hazards of the sea" . . . in search of occupied lands along the shores of the Mediterranean, toward the West" (NS, 13). One of the principal causes of the great migrations of peoples out of Africa was to establish "heroic overseas colonies" (NS, 14)—certainly a strange reversal of the patterns of colonization in the modern era. But even as he makes this statement, its purpose has less to do with the distant lessons of antiquity than with confronting the colonial realities of his own time:

> Only by extreme necessities of life are men led to abandon their own lands, which are naturally dear to those native to them. Nor do they leave them temporarily, except from *greed to get rich by trade*, or from anxiety to keep what they

have acquired. This axiom is the principle of the migrations of peoples. It is an induction from the heroic maritime colonies, the inundations of the barbarians ... the latest known Roman colonies and *the colonies of Europeans in the Indies*. (*NS*, 89; my emphasis)

But these three dimensions hardly exhaust the theoretical implications of Vico's science for anticolonial theory. He considers economic development to be the means of establishing political independence—a view that becomes central to postwar anticolonial liberation intellectuals. This ostensibly stagist view of history has often come under attack in the work of Marx and Hegel, so it is important to understand the inaptness of that charge here. If the Cain and Abel story of Genesis extols nomadic shepherds over farmers, then the *Odyssey* (in the Cyclops episode, above all) sees shepherds as murderous and brutal. Vico, it is true, sides with the latter, gentile account of the rise of the settled, class-ridden world of the agricultural estates on the grounds that individual realization is not possible outside the cities' protections, however ugly these first forms of government were.[19]

He is rejecting, in other words, the natural law theories of Thomas Hobbes and Hugo Grotius, as well as their revision by Samuel Pufendorf, building his contrast not between human and animal but between humans before and after civil law (*FNS*, 4). The bestial, in short, does not necessarily end for Vico with the making of laws. Even the first governments of the *famuli* (slaves under the rule of noblemen-priests), he writes, are signs of the vestigial savagery from which the truly civil state will only later emerge.[20] In order to engage with his contemporaries, he invokes the terrible times before the flood, characterized in his words by "wandering, bestiality, ugliness, violence, ferocity, depravity and blood" (*FNS*, 274).[21] He calls the first polities founded on blood ties and the domestication of captive labor "heroic" because this is how the ancients spoke of them and because he is thinking etymologically; in his ethical universe, however, he means to say that they are precisely *not* heroic in the usual sense of the term, representing instead "the deeds of scoundrels" (*NS*, 226).

His argument anticipates Marx's contrast between country and city—a pairing treated, with frustrating brevity, in *Capital*, *The German Ideology*, and *The Communist Manifesto*: "The bourgeoisie has subjected the country to the rule of the towns," satisfying "new wants" with "the products of distant lands and climes" in a system that has transcended "national seclusion and self-sufficiency" in favor of the "universal inter-dependence of nations."[22] The conquered countryside of the periphery becomes the hands to the global city's mind as capitalism consolidates its holdings, a process Marx painfully records but does not applaud. This image of the global interdependence of peoples has as its corollary the growing gulf in social status between intellectuals and workers resulting from foreign conquest. It is a theme that runs throughout the pages of *The New Science* and is developed by Marx when he explicitly connects the "division of material and mental labour" to capitalism's bifurcation of town and country in *The German Ideology*.[23] Vico, too, had worried that "some men must employ their minds in the tasks of civil wisdom, and others their bodies in the trades and crafts . . . that the mind should always command and the body should have perpetually to obey" (*NS*, 236). The problem of intellectuals, therefore, is linked by Marx to the problem of the center's hold over the periphery, of the cosmopolitan's over the farmer and the worker.

And Vico's writing is saturated with images of labor. This, too, has a colonial dynamic: "The barbaric wars of the heroic times meant the ruin of conquered cities, and the surrendered foes became herds of laborers scattered over the countryside to cultivate the fields of the victors (such were the heroic inland colonies)" (*NS*, 385). He dwells, as Marx would later, on the entwinement of intellectual and manual labor, specifically in the way in which their conflict led to invidious social distinctions. By means of "crude metaphysical associations" (a positive for Vico) vulgar labor finds its sublimated form as religion, and later, philosophy. As Marx would argue in *The German Ideology*, so argues Vico: that the first nobles appropriated this plebeian creation, acting as priests who kept the laws "in a secret language as a sacred thing," living off the social surplus created by a legion of artificially illiterate serfs (*NS*, 21).[24] Opting out of the depoliticized vagaries of classical interpretation, he explains that the Herculean knot, for instance, refers to the *nexi*—those who have been tied to the lands they cultivate for the nobles. Some had an abundance of goods, others were in need of them, but both were the basis of the first *socii*, the serfs—those literally "of society" (*NS*, 198). The first inland colonies arose when bands of refugees escaped this system, where "colony" in Vico's lexicon refers to "a crowd of workers who till the soil (*as they still do*) for their daily sustenance" (*NS*, 200; my emphasis). Greek mythology bears witness, then, to a metaphorical displacement: the figures of Tantalus, Sisyphus, Mars, and Vulcan are really there to symbolize the cruel exploitation that governed the massive forest-clearing and earth-moving of the first agricultural lands.

Vico's theory of civil theology, after all, rests, as we have said, on vivid portrayals of the conflict of estates in the explicit language of foreign conquest and racial othering. It is an anthropological excavation with particular attention to the power dynamics within the family as society's ur-form. Structurally, the concluding sections of *The New Science* are almost identical in focus to what Marx later attempts in the *Economic and Philosophical Manuscripts of 1844*. But there are decisive differences as well, and these must temper our judgment of the friendliness of aspects of Vico's vision to the Left Hegelian legacy, even if, in "Beginnings of the Bourgeois Philosophy of History," Max Horkheimer went so far as to identify as brilliant Vico's projection of human traits onto the nonhuman world and his treatment of mythology as a mirror of political relations.[25]

As I noted above, his account of those divisions is inconsistent: in some places, it has to do with the fate of primacy, that is, that some arrived in the better lands first and consigned the rest to untillable fields; at others, of the unchecked brutality of the seaborne invaders (the Phoenician traders, Odysseus's sacking of defenseless villages along the Trojan coast), which seems to suggest a quasi theory of primitive accumulation (*NS*, 421). But in brief interludes, his focus is quite different: the heroes dominated the *famuli* because the latter chose to wander longer in the wilderness, practicing their bestial acts in the absence of all law or piety. Nonetheless, the protopolitical economy of his argument is unmistakable. The entire history of cities is captured, he remarks, by one myth above all: the labors of Hercules. He considers all references to gold in ancient fables to be allusions to grain; what made early humans "like beasts" is that they lived alone "for private utility." The very concept of justice comes about only as a by-product of piety, which is to say nothing more than that for him the sacred is the politically just: *Ious* (Jove) leads to *ius* (right). His text is consistently sympathetic to revolt, as when he states that the Chaldean aristocrats were "overthrown by means of the popular liberty of the plebeians of that people" (*NS*, 35), or when he points out that the first *socii* were "plebeians of the heroic cities and finally the provincials of sovereign peoples" (*NS*, 81). And yet, like Spinoza and Hegel (although not Marx), Vico finds constitutional monarchy attractive, and on the same grounds that Spinoza did. For the problem with popular commonwealths is that they leave the door "wide open by law to the greedy multitude, which is in command" (*NS*, 87). As a result, we get civil war and (as he points out explicitly) unjust wars abroad—a connection that will become important in Hegel, and later, Marx.

He considers the first forms of civil government, though, to have been "born either of open violence or of fraud" (*NS*, 180). His comparative praise for monarchy is precisely to distinguish it (again like Spinoza in *A Political*

Treatise) from aristocracy, which he considers a brutal tyranny (*NS*, 212). As a "commonwealth of optimates," the nobles of the first aristocracies "swore eternal enmity against the plebs" (*NS*, 214), which he considers a travesty. The first plebs, he adds, were considered *foreigners* (*NS*, 225, 239), and it was because they were outside the ethnic family, so to speak, that they were thought fit only to be laborers. Socialism and anticolonial thought are in Vico proleptically joined.

His city-centered theory is not a mere metropolitan swagger but rather tends in his hands to link civil life with a specifically institutional literary politics. The historian Pietro Giannone, Vico's Neapolitan contemporary and a profound influence on Edward Gibbon, had pointed out that the great legal historians of the era were philologists, and that Naples in Vico's time was crazy for philology.[26] In that light, Vico saw the origins of textual interpretation as modeled less on clerical disputes over scripture than on the diligence of jurisconsults poring over "praetors' edicts" in the working out of Roman jurisprudence. On his way to writing the first *New Science* (1725), he discovered that the act of literary criticism itself is the shadow of an earlier practice of humanist interpreters of legal texts whom he calls "philosophers of natural equity" and that interpretation is inseparable from the urge for social equality found in investigations of "the principles of universal law" (*AGV*, 116).[27] If cities were necessary for the concept of law, the refined study of law (first expressed in poetic form) became an ur–literary criticism.[28]

The tropes of exile, diaspora, and wandering, so attractive in contemporary theory, are downgraded in Vico's universe. He crafts his arsenal of tropes instead from notions of orality, physical language, and objects of production and exchange. Religious terms are regrounded. "Divinity," for example, is traced to the act of "divining," that is, predicting the future by understanding popular consciousness. His famous and, to some, puzzling term "providence" fits a similar pattern. By calling his book "a rational civil theology of divine providence" (*NS*, 4), he is laying out a theory of independent development. If the isolated communities of the ancient world, separated by culture, geography, historical experience, and mode of production, all arrived at similar civil institutions, there must be a social logic, some inner meaning to the human itself, that would cause this outcome.[29] His is a humanist anthropology, in other words, couched in an acceptably Christian idiom. In that sense, "providence," if not exactly a jest, is intentionally ambiguated. Vico is cleverly undermining the view found, among others, in Jacques-Bénigne Bossuet in his *Discourse on Universal History* (1681). Bishop Bossuet, a fierce opponent of equality, defender of absolute monarchy, and professional sycophant, borrows lavishly from the Bible to illustrate God's plans for history.[30] Vico's is a polemical reversal of that very piety.

Although I have spent some time here demonstrating Vico's centrality for later anticolonial thinking, he cannot be claimed uncritically for this tradition. Some of his language is troubling—for example, when God is said to allow a "new order of humanity" to be born in the Middle Ages to defend the "true faith" (*NS*, 397). He does, however, in the same breath call the Middle Ages a "return to barbarism," leaving the tenor of the new order more than a little uncertain. But we might also have a deeper objection to aspects of his emphasis on gentile history: he tends to sever a heroic Christian genealogy from Judaism, which is then rendered irrelevant to the concerns of the book. How can Christian triumphalism ever lend support to a global secular politics?

Here too, however, there are telling adjacencies that offset certain passages which seem at first discordant with the flow of his argument regarding the equality of all peoples. Having spent many pages attacking the "conceit of the scholars" and demonstrating the emptiness of ethnocentric claims of nations that say they are the source of all innovation, he suddenly treats the foreign cultures of his own time dismissively.[31] At moments he seems even to celebrate the centrality of Europe as the highest manifestation of virtue in the passage from barbarism to civilization (*NS*, 41–43), and in language so extravagant that it verges on self-parody: "The Christian religion is the best in the world, because it unites a wisdom of [revealed] authority with that of reason." And again, "Christian Europe is everywhere radiant with such humanity that it abounds in all good things that make for the happiness of human life, ministering to the comforts of the body as well as to the pleasures of mind and spirit" (*NS*, 414). On the very same page, though, as if making the insincerity of the earlier statement clear, he attacks Europe for its treatment of the American Indian, whose indigenous culture (he points out) was disrupted, not improved, by the Europeans' arrival. He is emphatic that the return to barbarism in Europe coincided exactly with the monopolization of Christian doctrine. Christianity, he points out very clearly and unambiguously, stands in for the religious monism of the earlier, savage "age of the gods."

All the same, his orations in successive years at the opening of studies at the Royal University seem to tell a different story. In *On Humanistic Education* (1705), he equates the military glory of commonwealths with the flourishing of letters, as though literary learning and artistic accomplishment were essential to acts of foreign conquest (his examples are Alexander's overthrowing of the

Persian Empire and Rome's conquest of Carthage under Scipio, both of which occurred, he argues, when Greek and Roman literatures were at their height) (*OHE*, 111). The martial spirit of the passage is unmistakable, and the value of Homer's poems is reduced to the examples they provide of martial prowess on the model of Achilles. Although he matches his crude references to barbarous Turks with balancing comments about "perfidious Christians" when marking the rise and decay of empires, he clearly gives primacy to Christian Europe as it developed out of antiquity and the Gothic invasions, suggesting that the accomplishments of the Islamic Middle East relied on treacherous aid from European renegades (*AGV*, 142–144).

Reading the oration more skeptically, though, one can see that he also undercuts imperial belligerence. What he seems to argue, in fact, is that the liberal arts should tame warlike spirits—that those who conduct war are "wasteful of their souls." Following the lead of Giannone, Vico drew comparisons between the Spanish monarchy and the Roman Empire in order to show the former's ruthlessness. When choosing between civilized and barbarian, "there is no difference whether it is Attila or Xenophon who is waging war" (*OHE*, 111). All the same, he concludes that the cultivation of the fine arts contributes to "the glory and greatness of arms and empire"—a statement nevertheless at odds with his counsel that the "universal right of the people is superior to the civil right inasmuch as the whole of mankind is valued more than any single national unit" (*OHE*, 122, 117). The prose of the oration is everywhere witness to this push and pull of sentiments.

His intent may be buried, although not irrecuperably so, in the many textual variants found as one moves from the 1725 to the 1744 edition of *The New Science*. It is always the latter that introduces the most offensively ethnocentric language, as though bringing his vexed and, at the time, largely unread book more into line with orthodoxy (he expresses happiness, for example, that China had recently opened its doors to "the advantages of trade with us Europeans" [*NS*, 90]). That these are attempts to find favor with the Italian authorities after the dismal reception of earlier editions of his book is possible. More to the point, the imperialist sentiments are rare and give the impression of having been tacked on at the end in a short "Conclusion" not found in other editions, rather than woven into the mood of an argument that unfolds over more than four hundred pages. They form an impertinent coda in 1744, as if to sanitize the more explosive implications of the scholarship that he realizes his benefactors may not even have read.

The formula of statement/controversion above is a pattern found in other parts of the text and not likely to be accidental, given Vico's immersion in the art of rhetoric. So there are two reasons to be cautious in taking at face value the triumphalist outbursts that seem in other ways so out of place. He is, for one thing, not above tactful subterfuge when taking unconventional positions. He often issues statements that he backs up pedantically with reams of documentary evidence that theatrically contradict what he has said only a moment before.[32]

Is Vico capable of irony? It is a crucial question given the consistent hostility toward irony throughout the Vichian tradition (in Vico himself, but also in Hegel, Marx, Gramsci, and others). For his part, the young Auerbach, in keeping with *Mimesis*'s lack of interest in comic elements in deference to the existential seriousness of realism, parts company with Croce over the latter's suggestion that part of *The New Science* employs irony. Vico, Auerbach says, moves in the "spirit of medieval realism" platonically, so that his mode of discourse is usually objective, sincere, and striving for importance.[33] Vico's explicit statements in *The New Science* seem to support this: "Irony," he declares, "is fashioned of falsehood by dint of a reflection which wears the mask of truth" (*NS*, 131). He is quick to point out at the very opening of his *Autobiography* that he "take[s] no pleasure in verbal cleverness or falsehood," which he says lacks "depth," and would rather aspire to the "candor proper to a historian" (*AGV*, 111, 113). In his *Art of Rhetoric* (*Institutiones Oratoriae, 1711–41*), he is more dispassionate, by contrast, but not out of line with these convictions, writing simply that "irony in Latin was called *dissimulatio* or *illusio*. It is the trope by which we say that which is other than what we feel" (*ARh*, 145). We can get a grasp on Vico's way of thinking by dwelling for a minute on this compendious handbook that dedicates a chapter to "false tropes."

> Tropes are those figures of speech which turn a word from its proper and native meaning to an improper and strange one which Terence in Latin calls the inversion of words (*verba inversa*). There seem to be two causes of this mutation—necessity and ornamentation. (*ARh*, 145)

Here, Vico does not specify what a "necessity" might be, although the pejorative "false" when counterposed to "proper and native" is given teeth when we see how he applies examples from antiquity to illustrate the present. As Giuseppe Mazzotta rightly points out, Vico connects modern irony with the cannibalism of the Cyclops, or one-eyed Polyphemus: "As a form of reflective consciousness, irony is a one-eyed, illusory, and violent perspective on one's own presumed intellectual superiority."³⁴ But in the guise of satire, it is recuperated somewhat by his related discussion on the tropes *antilogy* and *antiphrasis*, which traditionally mean to signify a thing by its opposite.³⁵ In other words, a dissimulation is proper when it is necessary, but only if its saying the opposite can be understood clearly by readers as a calculated deviation from its native meaning.³⁶

There are good reasons, then, to detect politically motivated play in his text. By remarking at one point that only "men of limited ideas take for law what the words expressly say" (*NS*, 93), he seems in some passages to be coaxing his readers to look beneath the surface of his prose for meanings that, given their political sensitivity, had to be concealed. The book begins with a chronological table, for example, which addresses competing historical claims of the past, and above all, the priority (or not) of certain peoples. He states that his intention here is to show "how uncertain, unseemly, defective, or vain are the beginnings of the humanity of nations" (*NS*, 29). And yet the account does not seem uncertain at all. He cites a number of authorities from antiquity who contend that Egypt is the oldest civilization, and he mounts voluminous evidence to that effect. It is a position to which he seems to assent, since he relies on the Egyptian account of the three ages of man to frame his entire discussion. And yet, because church doctrine dictates otherwise, he purports to side with the Bible, abruptly refuting the claim by summarily dismissing all Egyptian achievement, saying their medical knowledge was "mere quackery" and their pyramids nothing—just big. The overstatement is so sudden and so excessive that it calls attention to itself (*NS*, 30).

But even as he ridicules Egypt's claim to greatest antiquity (a claim that he, again, bolsters through references to several seemingly clinching observations found in ancient historians such as Tacitus), he calls it arrogant boasting. What he intermittently asserts to the contrary is overwhelmed by the matter between. Accordingly, and only a few pages later, he reverses himself, saying that his own undertaking is aided immensely by the "antiquity of the Egyptians," who preserved two great fragments "not less marvelous than their pyramids" (the concepts of the three ages and the three languages [*NS*, 34]). Because he is not averse to establishing precedence of various sorts, he concedes that the first vulgar wisdom comes from the East and that Assyria was the first monarchy: "the beginning of the entire human race was in the East" (that is, to the east and south of the Levant; *NS*, 282).

Despite its wide-ranging sources, the narrative in this crucial opening section is also riddled with small though significant contradictions. Following convention, he asserts that the Greeks were older than the Egyptians, but relates that it is Cecrops the Egyptian who brought twelve colonies into Attica, one of which became Athens (*NS*, 40). Later he speaks of Danaos, an Egyptian, founding Argos, and yet his theory of the non-antiquity of the Egyptians is based on their "having no dealings with other nations" and therefore no "idea of time" (*NS*, 45). He writes that the Greeks themselves did not know their own antiquity and so did not write of it, though he then goes on to remark casually that it was through Psammeticus that the Greeks learned Egyptian institutions "by way of commerce."

We get a better sense of what he is up to in the "Principles" section that sums up the chronology. In it he pointedly tells his readers to take note of the consistency of the earlier section, saying that an inconsistency in any one element would mean one in all. This then sets up his condemnation of earlier accounts of the rise of humanity as "a tissue of confused memories, of the fancies of a disordered imagination" (*NS*, 96). What could this suggest except that he meant to violate received biblical wisdom as well as Greco-centric thought? Rather like the purloined letter, he conceals his meaning superficially, which is to say that he hides his meaning openly, enlisting a form of irony that joins the public in derision rather than playing behind its back.

Despite there being good reasons, then, to resist placing Vico in a conservative Christian or patriotic camp, a few other qualms can be registered about his version of universal culture and therefore his value for anticolonial thought. The view that all peoples go through a process of development in a similar way is, as I said above, a stagist conception. But this would overlook the fact that stagism in this case is not about the gift of modern technologies bestowed on backward peoples but the self-invention of human civil life. He tends even within the primordial development story to flip the script by postulating that democratic communes preceded monarchies—that is, that although people solve their problems on their own terms, they do so irregularly, unpredictably, and according to structural opportunities that never arrive twice in exactly the same form.

A complaint could be lodged, similarly, against Vico's list of the first civil institutions: religion, marriage, and burial. In many cultures, after all, people do not bury their dead. They set them afloat on rafts, cremate them, leave them to rest atop ritual platforms, or place them in sacred chambers open to the sky to be devoured by birds. Although he demonstrates that the term "human" in the Romance languages comes from *humus* (the earth)—and so to deserve to be called human you must bury your dead—his point is not literal burial but the ritual commemoration of mortal remains. On his terms, all of the practices above constitute burial, and he is not subordinating other peoples to a Latin norm.

Still, I am not interested in making the case that there are no problematic dimensions to Vico's argument or in suggesting—as some have with Spinoza—that he is the first Marxist before Marx. The prejudices of his place and training are at times embarrassingly obvious—for example, when he speaks of the "Turk" or Islam—an almost universal feature of the discourse of European intellectuals at the time that he wrote (*AGV*, 143–44). Their repertoire of images, their allusive vocabulary, the very structure of their concepts were demonstrably Christian, of course, and could not have been otherwise. And yet, as Michelet puts it, the message Vico left his readers was that "humanity is divine, but no one man is divine." So much for Jesus. But the point can only be what Vico did with this inherited schema, one that demanded of him a degree of conformity if he was to be heard at all.

Needing wealthy patrons in order to be published, he was not above fawning and euphemism.[37] This is nowhere more evident than in his history of Antonio Carafa (written in Latin and commissioned by Adriano Carafa, his nephew): *De rebus gestis Antonj Caraphaei* (1716). But even this had its compensations. For it explores in detail, using no longer extant original documents and letters, the political history of Europe between 1664 and 1689, especially between the Hapsburgs of the Holy Roman Empire and their Ottoman antagonists. The action is set in peripheral Europe, in what is now Hungary, the city of Vienna, Serbo-Croatia, Poland, and Turkey. Vico's purpose was to show through Carafa's life "the abuses committed in the past by the Austrians throughout their conquered territories," and his larger argument concerns how philosophers are important to statesmen (a theme he dwells on in his *Autobiography* as well).[38] Even more, though, the career of Vico's writing cannot be grasped without recognizing that he wrote under the shadow of the Inquisition, which was active in Naples throughout his lifetime. The Holy Office's suppression of "Epicureans and atheists" in 1688 swept up two of his closest friends and may have been on his mind as he found ways to express himself in the pages of *The New Science*. The historian John Robertson points to the "agitated" political scene in Naples between 1690 and 1730:

> The intellectual culture of the city was that of post-Galilean natural philosophy: while the vitality bequeathed by the Academy of the Investiganti was checked by trials of supposed "atheists" early in the 1690s, the philosophies of Gassendi and Descartes provided a focus for continued, vigorous debate.... History was central to the interests of the leading intellectual institution at the turn of the century.... Many of the "Lezioni" read to the Academy were devoted to the history of empires, the Greek and Persian empires as well as the Roman.[39]

Like others from earlier centuries, Vico employed an alien idiom—it would be presentist to think otherwise. As the intellectual historian J. G. A. Pocock rightly puts it, a historical actor is "not fully in command of the 'meaning' of his own utterance."[40] He must in every sense be translated. Vico's Christianity in Naples has its meaning, finally, in what it made possible rather than in what at times it literally says. And this is not to suggest, of course, that Christianity itself has never offered anything to anticolonial thought. While applauding mythology, he is far from the religious return in some wings of postcolonial thought, which repudiates secularity itself, identifying it with a crypto-Christian content, a Eurocentric directive, and a condescending liberal tolerance.[41] Vico's apparent rejection of the very atheism that seems to mark his followers stems from doubts about its theoretical effects. The atheism he knew was based on what he took to be an appeal to a purifying, disciplining reason (in Pierre Gassendi, for example), which he considered elitist. To deprive historical actors of an animating spirit by consigning them to the machinery of an aleatory matter is to rip the motivation out of social movements. The spirit world of religion as a social institution had the great merit of countering the narrow rationalism of the early Enlightenment—a form of rationalism that Hegel criticizes at length in the *Phenomenology of Mind*. Vico anticipated the dialectical compromise with religion developed by some of his descendants, above all, Ernst Bloch.

VICO AS A CONTEMPORARY
The Human

Theory in the humanities is often divided by intransigent pairings: totality/heterogeneity, universal/singular, politics/ethics, structure/construction. But the interwar roots of theory as Vico looked forward to them rely on a more fundamental question—whether human beings any longer exist. If studies of colonialism have been acutely sensitive to the idea of the nonhuman—given its ambiguous deployment in speaking of non-Western civilizations and subject races—the specificity of interwar conceptions of the post- or antihuman demands attention.[42] Indeed, this question represents one of several ways in which the conflict between Spinoza and Vico has played out in contemporary discussions, making the character of Vico's take on it especially resonant.

What is at stake in this pairing is made vivid by, among other things, Stephen Greenblatt's *The Swerve: How the World Became Modern* (2011), which configures a contemporary debate between scientific knowledge and religious belief played out in the guise of an older and now-forgotten philosophy. Like Umberto Eco and Dan Brown, Greenblatt writes a popular mystery story involving rare texts set in the libraries of Renaissance monasteries under the watchful eye of papal censors. His project is to suggest that materialist science and a nondivine cosmogony, with the eloquent ambassadorship of Lucretius's Epicurean poem *The Nature of Things* (first century BC)—discovered by chance in a Renaissance library—works its way centrally into the thinking of the likes of Max Planck, Albert Einstein, and many others. *The Swerve* wants to protect the rights of endangered academic learning in the United States by joining the camp of science, although a science literarily linked with the first classical glimmers of the uncertainty principle of quantum mechanics, based, he implies, on the "swerve" of atoms described by Epicurus.

The study reminds us of the mainstream tradition of canonical Epicureans that included Thomas Hobbes, John Locke, Thomas Jefferson, Walter Pater, and Jeremy Bentham, suggesting that the tradition is a kind of hidden center of Anglo-American learning, not far from the democratic intellectual heart of free inquiry itself. All the same, it is important to add what he leaves out: that the tradition has many more of the characteristics of the Pyrrhonism of David Hume than of what Marx would later call "materialism," and that this appeal to skepticism and the undecidable is one on which the enthusiastic reception of his study rests: the story of how the irreligious and materialist elements of science are predicated on the unpredictable swerve of atoms worked out in Epicurus and immortalized by Lucretius's poem.

Greenblatt's embrace of Epicurus, then, warmly welcomed by reviewers and the public, can be seen to be part of a larger dominant, as we will see later in Chapter 4 in a discussion of the forceful reappearance of the uncertainty principle as a hermeneutic category in the early twenty-first-century humanities: the enshrinement, we might say, of a kind of contemporary Pyrrhonism.[43] Few of the enthusiasts seem especially aware of the traditions that begin with Vico which, with a more marked obscurity, have spent a good deal of time challenging Epicurus after an initial dedication to his teachings. Vico particularly questions Epicureans for considering society "solely in the order of natural things, giving the name of natural theology to the metaphysics in which they contemplate this attribute," whereas "they ought to have studied it in the economy of civil institutions" (*NS*, 102).

Along these lines, we find that throughout his early years in Naples, Vico was an avid follower of the city's extramural intellectual societies of freethinkers—the salons of Nicola Caravita and Giuseppe Valletta, and the Accademia degli Investiganti (Academy of Investigators), whose motto, *Vestigia lustrat* (he follows the tracks, reviews the traces), was taken from Lucretius. To be a freethinker in this milieu was to deny a provident God, to see the universe as composed of matter ruled by natural laws, and to insist on the primacy of a sober, methodical inquiry into sensual facts absent any impertinent doctrinal intrusions. Not only for Vico but also for many of his contemporaries, the Epicurean thought of Lucretius was seen as being of a piece with the insurrectionary science of Descartes.

What is crucial, however, is that as Vico acquires his own voice, he submits his earlier seduction to a self-critique, rejecting it not because it leads to the nihilism of faithlessness (the position of anti-Spinozans such as Friedrich Heinrich Jacobi, for instance) but because it fails to capture human action in its transformative encounter with materialities. Epicurus comes to stand for a suspect fixation on the aleatory. As Vico recalls it, he "could not accept either seriously or playfully the mechanical physics of Epicurus or Descartes, for both start from a false position" (*AGV*, 122).[44] Epicurus lacked any concept of historical patterns, of cultural determinants, or of the creation of opportunities in favor of a naturalism that concealed, ultimately, a naïve phenomenological confidence in appearances.[45] He could "take little or no pleasure" in the Stoics and Epicureans, "for they are each a moral philosophy of solitaries: the Epicurean, of idlers inclosed in their own little gardens; the Stoic, of contemplatives who endeavour to feel no emotion" (*AGV*, 122). Epicurus, in fact, explicitly counseled that his followers remain apolitical. Pursue *ataraxia* (tranquillity), he advised, which alone will give you relief from the anxiety of a struggle with power.

It is worth remarking that this line of argument is entirely reminiscent of Marx's doctoral thesis on "The Difference between the Democritean and Epicurean Philosophy of Nature." Marx was fascinated by the fact that Democritus and Epicurus shared an identical materialist theory of atoms that ended up producing in each thinker a mutually antipathetic "theoretical consciousness." The incompatible outlooks took a variety of forms, as Marx explains while quoting Cicero:

> [Democritus] wandered through half the world. But he did not find what he was looking for. An opposite figure appears to us in Epicurus. Epicurus is satisfied and blissful in philosophy.... While Democritus seeks to learn from Egyptian priests, Persian Chaldeans and Indian gymnosophists, Epicurus prides himself on not having had a teacher, on being self-taught.... [Epicurus has] no interest

in investigating the real causes of objects. All that matters is the tranquility of the explaining subject. Since everything possible is admitted as possible, which corresponds to the character of abstract possibility, the chance of being is clearly transferred only into the chance of thought.... [Epicurus] is a dogmatist.[46]

This linking of dogmatic thought with the materialist a priori of a self-satisfied, blissful consciousness has great resonance today when measured against theories whose apparent rootedness in the material world takes the form of an internal search for the experience of being an inert component of that world. Modernist inventiveness itself is at times enabled by the solitary consciousness seeking its own oblivion, as in Baudelaire. Marx's position in his thesis has typically been characterized as finding in Epicurus a rebellious, materialist common cause in harmony, say, with that of Greenblatt (for instance, see John Bellamy Foster's *Marx's Ecology* [2000]), but this is not accurate.[47] He fundamentally shares Vico's critique of Epicurus, in fact, and as we saw, with many of the same barbs. The most we can say is that Marx occasionally sought in his dissertation to recuperate aspects of Epicurus's philosophy by translating them, unpersuasively, into a Hegelian idiom. For instance, the striking of atoms against one another is cast (somewhat clumsily) by Marx as a principle of self-realization ("repulsion is the first form of self-consciousness"; the "abstract individuality of the atom"; its "negation ... in the void"). But for our purposes, what is more interesting is the sensibility he shares with Vico, the same likes and dislikes, their mutual rejection of the a priori and the complacency that accompanies the certitude of a stipulated "materialism" with no need for evidence. Here as elsewhere, his intellectual personality, and not only his specific assessments of philosophers, is Vichian.

Linguistic Thingliness

Vico considered his discovery that the first gentile peoples spoke in poetic characters (*NS*, 341–42) to be the vital center of his system. His theory, I shall argue, is unique in the radical Enlightenment for the leads it provides in thinking about peripheral aesthetics today—for articulating a civic materialism based on the beauty of the tactile word that has the calm iconoclasm of socialist realism couched in the rhetorical forms of movement and discovery, as in travel narrative. The first words, he begins, were actually things placed in the role of signs, what he calls "real language": originally, a frog, a mouse, a bird, a ploughshare, and a bow for shooting arrows (*NS*, 50). Words, then, are originally bodies, not signs; even less are they signifieds groping for mere concepts as distinct from the real things the concepts are intended to capture. Verbs, similarly, which refer not to things but to acts, develop only later out of this thingly obsession; they "were the last part of speech to be invented" (*NS*, 154). As such, he maintains that speaking did not precede writing, nor was it superseded by it; having arisen at the same time, the two remain forever merged, each partaking of the other's features without priority. Right away we can see that the Vichian outlook unseats the contemporary emphasis on the archetypal primacy of writing as the paradigm of language. The philosophical force behind the relative space he provides for orality offers theoretical support for a number of aesthetic initiatives in postcolonial writing—most obviously, perhaps, in contemporary *créolité*. Patrick Chamoiseau, Jean Bernabé, and Raphaël Confiant write of the Martiniquan "purveyor of tales, proverbs, 'timtim,' nursery rhymes, songs," pointing out that in the Caribbean, orality is not a style or choice but "our intelligence . . . the still blind groping after our own complexity . . . a system of counter-value" and "ordinary genius."[48] It is this merging of the written and the oral—what Edward Kamau Brathwaite calls "orature"—that Vico's theories historically authorize; and they provide as well a solid basis for the insistence on the philosophical seriousness (in *créolité*, "intelligence," "genius"), rather than merely stylistic option, of orality itself.

Challenging prevailing theories at the time, Vico contended also that the first language was poetry, not prose. But unlike the populist sublime of Wordsworth's "Preface to the *Lyrical Ballads*," he has in mind not only the wealth and vibrancy of a verbal idiom derived from the language of commoners, but also epistemology. To say that verbal creativity and expressivity are inversely related to the modern powers of abstract thinking is to state a preference for a writing that resists the pretensions of professional elites. For Vico, vulgarity, precisely for being vulgar, is more metaphorically adept and vivid than the sophistications of clerical or academic prose—and indeed, the figurative richness of his own idiom is more difficult to find after the eighteenth century, as though supporting his idea that the process of verbal abstraction is historically ongoing. His epistemological poetics suggests that the more figurative language is, the truer to the thing (*NS*, 149). In writing fables, the ancients knew this too, untheoretically; and instead of approaching allegorical inventions as a genre of indirection or diversion, they considered them simply "trustworthy histories of customs" (*NS*, 6). In short, the first poetry is practical, plastic, metaphysically penetrating, and material (their "vulgar metaphysics" *is* physics, he writes). Linking laborers with everyday epic in a communal gathering of utterances where expression is by definition poetic and can not be other, and yet where poetry has lost its ethereal or interiorizing connotations, Vico returns language to a profane illumination of quotidian objects of exchange. His whole approach has large potential effects for contemporary realism, tending to reground and concretize along sociological lines the political aspirations of early twentieth-century avant-garde poetry. In other words, the urge for literature itself to be immediately political, so often marred by idealizing the act of inventing fictional worlds while splicing the concept "political" onto a literary escape from politics, is here given a more plausible narrative: fledgling civil institutions took shape in poetic thought, and economics was an exchange of word-things.

The social imperatives of a politically committed poetry are equally embedded in his account of the three ages of language. "A mute language of signs and physical objects," as we saw, formed the first; the second age involved communication "by means of heroic emblems, or similitudes, comparisons, images, metaphors, and natural descriptions" in the "age of the heroes"; and finally, there is the age of human language, of "using words agreed upon by the people, a language of which they were absolute lords ... proper to the popular commonwealths" (*NS*, 20). The stages of political hierarchy and counterhierarchy imprint their character on linguistic forms, and concealed political interests communicate themselves as modes of expression, quite apart from the content of the message. The whole edifice of philological study oriented toward literary languages or to conferring canonical status on ingenious individuals such as Sophocles, Vergil, or Catullus is subordinated here to the inventive exchanges of communities in the act of solving problems of development and organization, where active choice (language "agreed upon") determines outcomes. The manifestos of Vladimir Mayakovsky and Sergei Tretyakov will come to recognize this sensibility perfectly and, what is more, understand it themselves as Vichian.

As we can see, a politics of knowledge is being developed here, with literary study placed at the center of the disciplines. For Vico, the vulgar metaphysics of poetic wisdom gives way to logic, morals, economics, and politics in one branch and to physics, cosmography, and astronomy in the other. From this perspective, the rejection of Cartesianism's privileging of the sciences comes full circle, cast here as a later and subordinate modification of the great evolutionary leap of original poetic thought. From this perspective, the tropes anatomized in rhetorical handbooks are not distillations of authorial style so much as the concrete figures of the logic of the mind before modern abstraction. Tropes are supposed to be "ingenious inventions of writers," but they were really just "necessary modes of expression of all the first poetic nations" (*NS*, 131). He goes on to list the axioms that allowed him to make sense of the documents of antiquity where others had failed. Whereas the key discovery of Marx might be the anthropology of human production as social *re*production, Vico's key discovery is a methodological guide for how to read: "Wherever it is lost in ignorance man makes himself the measure of all things" (*NS*, 60); "When men are ignorant of natural causes, they resort to analogy" (*NS*, 70); "The unknown is always magnified" (*NS*, 60); "To define was equivalent to naming" (*NS*, 140); "Different languages comes from different climates and natures" (*NS*, 148). In effect, he gives us a materialist aesthetics.

Vico challenges a newly confident Enlightenment rationality in order to understand foreign cultures on their own terms. Herder would later transpose Vico's emphasis on the foreignness of time to a foreignness of peoples, demanding that European scholars respect what they do not understand, and learn from those they pretend to save. Pocock compares Vico in this respect to the great fourteenth-century Arab Muslim historian Ibn Khaldun: both "possessed ... a great inheritance of knowledge about the past, which had little obvious function or significance in his society and was not furnished with one by that society's dominant intellectual techniques.... To both men philosophy of history and historical sociology were one and the same."[49] Unlike later literary modernism's attractions to the primitive, whose peripheral form is enlisted as a redemptive anticivilizing gesture, Vico, stealing a march on Freud, is saying that we are the products of a primitiveness we no longer recognize in ourselves:

> The nature of our civilized minds is so detached from the senses, even in the vulgar, by abstractions corresponding to all the abstract terms our languages abound in, and so refined by the art of writing, and as it were spiritualized by the use of numbers, because even the vulgar know how to count and reckon, that it is naturally beyond our power to form the vast image of this mistress called "Sympathetic Nature." (*NS*, 118)

The feel of this sort of literary criticism, quite apart from its importance in the history of early modern thought, is fashioned in such a way that contemporary readers can escape the formalism and scientism of theory, even while bringing form itself centrally into play. For all Vico's emphasis on things, economies, and classes, realism is neither prescriptive nor narrowly demotic; it is rather a philosophy of history. He calls this philosophy his "unitive method" based on montage, encyclopedic listings, circling around, repetition, and cumulative force: "uniting particulars to obtain universals" in the spirit of Bacon's *Novum Organum*.

Behind Vico's theory of reading lay a personality that informed it and was at one with it. He argued that "the Hebrews thought God to be an infinite Mind beholding all times in one point of eternity," whereas the "gentiles fancied bodies to be gods, that by sensible signs they might give notice of what was in store for the peoples" through divination" (*NS*, 7). A sense of the embodied, sensual worldliness of gentile religion permeates the text, in other words; it represents what he later calls "philosophy as *autopsia*," the evidence of the senses, a world occupied by the operations of the body (*NS*, 166–67)—a view that will be so important later in Herder's theory of language as affective and sensual. Eventually it finds its way into Bakhtin's trope of the carnivalesque body.

System and Polemic

Given that his own text is asymmetrical and improvisational, like a miscellany of loosely assembled scraps of speculative syntheses of the archive, it is surprising how vigorously Vico defends systematicity in his science. And yet the often strident repudiation of system philosophies in twentieth-century theory is not necessarily antagonistic to Vico's practice. Like Herder after him, Vico both rejects and embraces system-based argumentative modes, and so today's highly normative antipathy to systemic thinking probably does not provide the right perspective in coming to terms with this aspect of his method. Herder, for instance, was antisystem in arguing that abstract thought weakens the sentiments expressed by it; and so he opted for a style that was emotional, grammatically inventive, and colloquial, filled with casual asides, precisely to make it unsystematic in presentation, though not in substance. Indeed, he was all for the systematic when it came to insisting on a self-consistency based on argument and evidence.

The comparison to the later Herder allows us to reckon more appropriately with Vico, whose presentation is composed of what he calls "logical proofs" derived from "Axioms, Definitions, and Postulates." There is nothing here of the syllogisms of Spinoza's *Ethics* (1677), which could not be a more extreme example of a system philosophy; moreover, Vico's method is inductive rather than deductive and comes off less like a proof than a highly intelligent grab bag of textual facts interrupted by startling précis presented in no observable order. Still, to the degree that he considers the elements of his science to be interdependent, it is systematic (*NS*, 96). In an era that celebrated Leibniz and Newton, the high ground to occupy was that of mathematical exactness. As a result, when Vico describes his method in *The Synopsis of Universal Right* (1720–22)—the book he would rework to become the first *New Science*—he achieves this by appealing to the systemic nature of truth:

> You need to have built the habit of reasoning geometrically; and thus, when you decide to read, do not open at random nor skip from one place to another throughout these books, but follow the lessons from beginning to end. Seek out whether the premises are true and well connected. . . . You must have a comprehensive mind, because everything reasoned by this science is connected with so many innumerable other things that are in consonance with it, each thing is in a particular consonance with others, and each one with all of them together shaping the wholeness, in which all the beauty of a perfect science uniquely consists.[50]

The description is quite far from the demotic and messy character of *The New Science*. In particular, the positive comparison of his work with geometry leaps out, for as we have seen, the Vico of 1744 would have nothing to do with this deference to mathematics.[51] Although the aesthetic of *The New Science* stands on spiraling returns and reiterations, its system character remains essential and is nothing without it. Without claiming any of the airtight veracity of the geometrical method of 1722, he still takes the position that reading, if meaningful, depends on the cumulative effects of a theory informed by evidence.

A growing consensus at the time had it that the historical and literary sciences were incapable of such verifiability, or that their evidence, to be called such, had to resemble physical laws. To these charges Vico responded with a startling and almost venomous anger. This was less a character flaw on his part than a substantive feature of his own philological theory. For if the history Vico narrates is one of brutal conflict, so at times is his tone, as though it needed to be caustic for the gravity of the theme to be conveyed. His writing is confrontational, sardonic, astonished, conversationally intimate, and at times simply furious. He writes like an injured genius ignored by inferior minds, and the pitch of his voice anticipates that of others in the Vichian tradition in its polemicism. At a distance from today's standards of professional decorum, he opts in his autobiography (written for young students) for a clarity that is often antagonistic:

> We shall not here feign what Réné Descartes craftily feigned as to the method of his studies simply in order to exalt his own philosophy and mathematics and degrade all the other studies included in divine and human erudition. . . . For Réné [was] over-ambitious for glory, as . . . he tried to make himself famous among professors of medicine with a physics contrived on a pattern like that of

Epicurus and presented for the first time from the chair of a European university so famous as that of Utrecht. (*AGV*, 113, 129)

His aggressive tone, no doubt a sign in his own mind of honesty, is scarcely less evident in many other passages of *The New Science*.

Vico's polemical energy is essential to his brand of intelligence and a deliberate aspect of his method. Leaving aside the habits of his place and time, which allowed for more frankness and emotion in scholarly writing than our own, he wants to summon here the interested character of knowledge. It is tempting to see his derision as the maneuver of a marginal intellectual fighting to be heard at a time when the philosophical centers of Europe were elsewhere and when the aura of Italian learning had already begun to fade. More faithful to the whole of his argument, I think, would be to see criticism in his hands as requiring an agon in form to match the conflict and contradiction of his narrative. At a time of hyperprofessionalization and antidebate, Vico reminds us that to be a scholar and a philosopher does not mean losing the sense of having something vital to fight over.

SPINOZA AND THE PURITY OF MIND

As the title of this section (and the book) suggests, my intention throughout is to pose a set of contrasts between the four continental figures at the heart of this study: Vico, Spinoza, and (in later chapters) Hegel and Nietzsche. In doing so, I am of course pursuing the idea of "borrowed light," that is to say, the illumination of the anticolonial problematic by the light of Vichianism in its interwar Marxist form. Here, the juxtaposition of Vico and Spinoza is particularly illustrative of two contrapuntal models of heterodox thought, though it is Spinoza—with his conception of an abstractly immanent divinity—who has seemed peculiarly suited to the antihumanist bent of contemporary theory. This, however, does not diminish the bravery of his heresy or the model of radicalism he rightly became.

As brilliant satirical deadpan, Spinoza's refutation of the Old Testament God in the very act of proving God's existence inspired successors from Pierre Bayle and Goethe to Herder and Marx. The outcast quality of Spinoza's endeavor—a man brilliant enough to be offered a professorship and wise enough to turn it down in favor of continuing his subversive writings anonymously as a lens grinder—is as dramatic as it is compelling. His early banishment from the synagogue of Amsterdam for being an atheist made him an obvious symbol of principled dissidence under conditions in which iconoclasts risked their lives.

Although he skirted persecution personally and wrote anonymously to survive, allies and friends perished for proclaiming versions of his ideas.

If not exactly a protocommunist, he certainly reviled those who thought themselves "more blessed" because they were "more fortunate" (*TPT*, 43).[52] As Isaac Deutscher points out in *The Non-Jewish Jew*, Spinoza's uncompromising intelligence was helped along by his being a reprobate to begin with:

> [Jewish intellectuals and artists] were *a priori* exceptional in that as Jews they dwelt on the borderlines of various civilizations, religions, and national cultures. They were born and brought up on the borderlines of various epochs. Their minds matured where the most diverse cultural influences crossed and fertilized each other. They lived on the margins or in the nooks and crannies of their respective nations. They were each in society and yet not in it, of it and yet not of it. It was this that enabled them to rise in thought above their societies, above their nations, above their times and generations, and to strike out mentally into wide new horizons and far into the future.[53]

Deutscher adds, though, that these "wide new horizons" were approached only at a price. They were made available only by attacking the premises of their own inherited faith and rejecting its institutional practices.[54]

In this respect, Spinoza's most remarkable work was certainly the *Theologico-Political Treatise* (1670), which in contrast to the *Ethics* is relatively neglected in discussions of Spinoza's dramatic break from church authority and scholastic philosophy.[55] Here we find him in the raw mode of controversy, less lofty and guarded than in the *Ethics*, mounting a sustained assault on the manipulation of the popular mind by clerical and rabbinical interpretations of the Bible. With relentless sarcasm and anger, Spinoza methodically unpacks the absurdities of both allegorical and overly literal readings of the Holy Book by self-interested clerical watchdogs who wish to create for the multitudes an image of religion as a series of magic tricks, ethnic particularisms, and supernatural personified forces.[56] The issue for him is popular naïveté in the face of rhetorical finesse: "people endeavouring to hawk about their own commentaries as the word of God and giving their best efforts under the guise of religion to compelling others to think as they do."[57] Spinoza's radicalism, like Vico's, involved also revealing to common readers that earlier peoples thought differently and used language in ways "strange and obscure" (as he puts it). The prophets "perceived nearly everything in parables and allegories, and clothed spiritual truths in bodily forms, for such is the method of the imagination"

(*TPT*, 125). This is Vico's playbook, of course, although what is not yet evident is that Spinoza is not at all friendly to allegory. He is undercutting the prophets, not praising the earthiness or poetic sharpness of their insights.

The fact is that Spinoza took his stand by saying that there are better and worse, truer and falser interpretations of texts—and that, perhaps, is a heresy of another sort in his contemporary reception. He flatly charged false readings with being politically interested. What he proudly calls his "method of Scriptural interpretation" is based, by contrast, on "a careful, impartial, and unfettered spirit" without prior doctrinal assumptions (*TPT*, 8).[58] He outlines this method doggedly. Nothing should be accepted as true that is not seen "in the light of its history"; for this reason, his task is to explore the "nature and properties of the language in which the Bible was written," organize the contents to find internal correspondences, mark textual variants, and check for inconsistencies. He goes to great lengths to eliminate ambiguity by examining "context" and finally—and crucially—to consider paramount the motives of the author: "what was the occasion, and the epoch of his writing, whom did he write for, and in what language" (*TPT*, 101–3). Even given the epistemological pose of the *Ethics*, Spinoza's approach is philological in that it delves deeply into parts of speech, stylistic peculiarities, diction, and figurative language in determining plausibility and sense. Famously indifferent to history in the *Ethics*, Spinoza builds his case in the *Theologico-Political Treatise* on the interdependence of textual meaning and authorial intention, dwelling on a text's multiple, incompatible authors, for instance; contrastingly, he appeals as well to the historical impossibility of the Bible's events, thus proffering its centrality on the grounds of its interpretation rather than its actuality. And yet very little of this theory of reading has been discussed or even noticed in his recent revival, which is unfortunate, since it would tend to place Vico interestingly as an heir to Spinoza in some respects.

A philological political philosophy is not all that Spinoza and Vico share. As qualified defenders of constitutional monarchy, both arrive at a similar rationale for that position, expressing sympathy with commoners for the harsh conditions of their existence and believing the multitude to be the basis of all legitimate political authority. But in the end both philosophers find the multitude to be unfit to rule for the same reasons: credulity, distraction because of overwork, fickleness (*TPT*, 4, 11). Thus Spinoza: "The mass of mankind remains at about the same pitch of misery[;] it never assents long to any one remedy, but is always best pleased by a novelty which has not yet proved illusive" (*TPT*, 5). And in Vico: the "haughty, avaricious, and cruel practices of the nobles" are face-to-face with the "greedy multitude" (*NS*, 83, 87). For both, high-minded appeals to moral right have little place in a science of politics, which is in the end based on pure relations of force. When Vico declares that "political science is nothing other than the science of commanding and obeying in states" (*NS*, 235), he might well be alluding to Spinoza's *Political Treatise*, which makes an identical point, hoping to free like-minded dissidents from the illusion that redress of grievances comes about by appeals to natural right.[59]

Despite Vico's harsh words about Spinoza, he does not wholly reject the findings of the *Ethics*. Taking a page from him, in fact, Vico comments that "moral virtue began, as it must, from *conatus*" (*NS*, 171)—arguably a concise synthesis of Spinoza's entire argument. Their epistemologies have significant parallels. For there is no question that Spinoza's presence can be felt in Vico's insistence that "the metaphysics of the philosophers" relies on "clarifying the human mind" with the aid of "clear and distinct ideas" (*NS*, 170)—a phrase that encapsulates Spinoza's major conceptual building block in the *Ethics* (*TPT*, 14).[60] For Vico, similarly, to explain something is to know its cause, just as for Spinoza, to demonstrate essence (what it is) depends on demonstrating its cause (what makes it what it is).

What separates them is metaphor. An analyst, like Vico, of the antipathy of "imaginative power" to "abstract reasoning," Spinoza sides actively with the latter, arguing that "those who excel in intellect" need to "keep their imagination more restrained and controlled, holding it in subjection, so to speak, lest it should usurp the place of reason" (*TPT*, 27).[61] Like Hobbes in *Leviathan*, Spinoza reviles figurative language. To be ignorant is to "take the imagination for the intellect" (*E*, 29). The entire *Theologico-Political Treatise* can be seen as an exposé of the creative misapplication of rhetorical figures for political ends. Religious faith is for Spinoza "a tissue of ridiculous mysteries" concocted by "men who flatly despise reason"; imagination is a "phantom" and dreams "childish absurdities" (*TPT*, 6–7, 4). The whole character of the Spinozist philosophy, then, is turned upside down by Vico's conviction that the first intellectuals philosophized in myth and wrote in hieroglyphics. The first *nomoi* were songs, the first laws civic poems. As the two traditions play themselves out, it is unfairly the Vichian (especially in Hegel) that comes to be associated with an impatient insistence on the backwardness of all official religious thought. That is the view one finds much more uncompromisingly in Spinoza.

Spinoza cannot really live up to his injunction against the figurative, however. The *Ethics* hinges on plastic wording, locating in the interstices of syntax a negotiation among discordant features of key transitional moments in his argument. For example, in one of his more famous statements, he significantly does not say that God is everything. He says that "everything is *in* God," which creates for us, linguistically, a separable space for things to be "godly" without being equivalent to, or self-identical with, God. Specifically, he writes: "Et quamvis hoc non esset, nescio, cur divinâ naturâ indigna esset: quandoquidem extra Deum nulla substantia dari potest, a qua ipsa pateretur. Omnia, inquam, in Deo sunt," which Edwin Curley renders as "Even if this [reply] were not [sufficient], I do not know why [matter] would be unworthy of the divine nature. For apart from God there can be no substance by which [the divine nature] would be acted on. All things, I say, are in God" (*EGD*, 11; *E*, 13). If this is what Spinoza means by "immanence," then according to his theory the universe is immanent in God rather than the other way round, as it is more often taken to be, in the writing of Antonio Negri and Pierre Macherey, for instance. What is most striking about his wording here is his reliance on the passive voice ("dari," "pateretur"), which creates an atmosphere of anonymous, unpersonifiable natural laws without providential force, underlining the absence of human agency. But there is more to this stylistic move than that; for the corollary of the passive voice in this case is a looping, delayed, back way into thought, such that (to render the Latin more actively than Curley) "there can be no material substance that divine nature itself would not open out or extend. All things, I say, are in God." The effect is to create a syntactical space of suspension where Being is given the aura of an action, and where a God who does nothing exists not as material substance but as its warrant, as its terrain of extension. Pocock reminds us of the historical precedents for this ambiguous materialism:

> Among the radical sects—one has only to mention *Man's Mortalitie*, usually ascribed to the Leveller Richard Overton—such a heresy as mortalism could go hand-in-hand with chiliasm and enthusiasm; the paradox of the doctrine is that it could flourish among mystics whose belief in the primacy of the spirit was so absolute that they saw spirit as immanent in matter to the point where it could by no means be separated from it. Man's spirit was his body and his body his spirit. The resurrection of the one was the resurrection of the other, and it was blasphemous to try to separate the two.[62]

We can see the irony of Spinoza's postwar reception by looking more closely at the *Ethics*, whose title is paradoxical, since it is a work primarily about epistemology, not morals or ethics as we usually understand these terms. For Spinoza, the supreme good consists in the enjoyment of a human nature which, because perfectly aware of its place in and unity with the natural order of things, accepts the inevitability and necessity of that order. Moral perfection consists in getting beyond the contingency of affections, which is to say that we go wrong, according to Spinoza, when we seek to impose a narrative of redemption upon powers we do not possess or to invent religious mythologies of deliverance that see an interventionary God willing this world to be what it is while being capable of willing it another way.

From the point of view of giving new life to radical politics, that part of his message sounds welcome, since it is about overcoming illusions in favor of a sober study of real relations. But he is also saying that nature is the expression of the perfection that is God. "Perfection," to put this another way, is not a normative state but literally the end of all unfolding. It can be taken, certainly, to be in this sense a deeply conservative idea, for in Latin (as Spinoza himself stresses) *perfectus* means fully made, finalized, unchangeable—as though he had more or less transposed the Old Testament God into a new political ontology.[63] And it is with this feature of his thinking in a post–Carl Schmitt era, rather than with his ostensible materialism or his promoting of the "third level" of thought called intuition, that any neo-Marxism must reckon. The moral perfection he seeks in the *Ethics* is reached when, by the act of intellection, we come to concede the necessity of our being as the illusion of doing. Our only freedom is freedom from error.

From the point of view of a democratic politics, this is troubling. For when he writes that the "finite spirit possess its truth—and thus is moral—just insofar as it directs its knowing and willing upon God, and just insofar as it has the authentic Idea, which is the unique experiential cognition of God," he arguably reintroduces some of the same escape hatches for authority that he had exposed in the *Theologico-Political Treatise*.[64] Which inadequate part of nature among us (that is, which person), Vico might ask, is capable of discerning these "laws" and this "authentic idea"? We cannot, because we are too much in it and of it. By contrast, doubt has no room in Spinoza's philosophy except as a vacillation of the mind; the entire purpose of the project is to prove the substantiality of knowledge outside the *cogito*, the links that bind the idea to the object of extension. But because he never describes this process of coming-to-understand, or of perceiving essence, his declarations double back. To say, as he does, that "reality" is just another name for "perfection" (the static real, alien to the notion of becoming) or that existence is just the "intellect of God" is also a way of saying that what today's theorists call his "materialism" is better seen as an idealism so extreme that even ideas are objects and thoughts are acts (*E*, 33, 12). His immanence, to put this another way, is what most philosophers call transcendence.[65] By the same token, his atheism is monotheistic. A mechanism called "God" clings to every element of our thought and action, right down to the illusory thought that we have a choice in how to act.

The rhetorical elisions beneath the apparent serenity of the Latin, then, is a significant dimension of his argument itself. His carefully evasive wording reflects the suturing of contrary elements. His challenge to the mind/body distinction of Descartes is expressed as "the mind is united to the body from the fact that the body is the object of the mind" (*E*, 48). By this he does not mean that the mind thinks about the body but that the body possesses and envelops ideas as physical processes. Since human beings are, like everything else, a part of God, they are not separate, individual, or wholly constituted in a world of objects but are elements in the total, seamless system of Nature. For Hegel, even objects are subjects; for Spinoza, subjects are only objects. God, says Spinoza, is "a thinking thing." And so in his schema for categorizing types of thought into three levels—confused ideas (or "imagination"), adequate ideas (or "understanding"), and intuition—it is inevitable that in his system the last of these will be considered the highest (*E*, 12, 57). For it is really a letting-go rather than an act of conceptualization; "reason" is a feeling rather than an action. In a very different context and with different intentions, these emphases on affect, natural passivity, and environmental anonymity arise again as the foundational ideas of interwar phenomenology's accession of Nietzschean motifs. They are significantly authorized by the growing dominance of the natural sciences in intellectual life, which, in their own way, also relegate imagination to confusion, apotheosize nature, see matter as indifferent to our concepts of it, and subordinate will and aspiration to processes that involve neither.

Even as a reprobate, Spinoza set out as a disappointed but once-ardent believer to challenge official religion theologically, for his philosophy retains a version of textual law. The divine law may no longer be scriptural, but it permeates his proofs as a taste for the infinite, the transcendable, and above all, the unanswerable. He strives for an intellectual space that one can never think beyond and so never completely understand. What we do understand is that we are subject to it and an inferior part of it—a mere attribute of the divine Substance. Unlike other central figures in the scientific Enlightenment, Spinoza is deeply embroiled in theological refutations and assertions, which lurk beneath the surface of the mathematical-scientific architecture. Despite his engagement with political affairs elsewhere, the *Ethics*, although subversively rationalist in the seventeenth century, is not liberatory in a late twentieth-century sense, for the human world is reduced to insignificance.

As I have been implying, certain trends of post- or neo-Marxism found themselves well disposed toward a Spinozist resurrection by way of essentially Nietzschean categories.[66] They could appreciate—as Nietzsche himself did—that like Spinoza, he toys with an everyday understanding of ethics in order to expose the futility of self-restraint and to insist that freedom lies in letting nature express itself. Let us leave aside for now that Spinoza's politics are not at all Nietzschean, or what is more, that they are even at odds with his own epistemology when he claims, for example, that "the will of the commonwealth must be taken to be the will of all; what the state decides to be just and good must be held to be so decided by every individual" (*PT*, 302). What matters more in the revival is that both Nietzsche and Spinoza rely on a form of synesthesia, translating emotional states into forms of intellection. In fact, *affectus* (originally *adfectus*) does not refer to emotions, passions, desire, or even feelings so much as a condition of mind. Our current sense of "affect," at any rate, with all of its post-Freudian baggage, prepares us very poorly for what the word means in Spinoza's Latin. On the one hand, its sense is that emotions are really admixtures of ideas and concepts—that even feeling is intellectual for Spinoza; on the other, that even intellect is a feeling that moves toward the mind of God.

"SPINOZA" FOR THE MOMENT

Enlisting Spinoza for neo-Marxism seemed unlikely from the start, given his apparent theological residues and the closed quality of his mathematical-propositional form. Quite apart from the epistemological clashes, the very feel of the thought of Spinoza seemed wrong for the projects at hand. It lacked the vibrant anecdotes, spirited reversals, and existential palette of Marx's historical account of productive relations, for example, expressing itself in an austere and in some ways prescriptive idiom. But neither consideration impeded what Perry Anderson, in *Considerations on Western Marxism* (1976), rightly describes as "the systematic induction of Spinoza into historical materialism by Althusser and his pupils" after the 1960s.[67] Anderson observes that this recuperation "was intellectually the most ambitious attempt to construct a prior philosophical descent for Marx and to develop abruptly new theoretical directions for contemporary Marxism from it."[68]

As I have been trying to show, however, even though Anderson's statement is partially supported (though it would depend on what one considers to be "ambitious"), what he overlooks are the active Vichian lineages of Western Marxism, beginning before Marx in early German philosophy but more actively still in the relative intensities of the enlistment of Vico by such figures as Ferdinand Lassalle, Paul Lafargue, Antonio Labriola, and Leon Trotsky; then very emphatically in Antonio Gramsci and José Carlos Mariátegui; and subsequently, via Valentin Volosinov, in Anderson's near contemporary Raymond Williams. I would say that despite Anderson's groundbreaking work in this arena, it is now time to reconsider those considerations concerning the Marxist tradition.

What Anderson calls "construct[ing] a prior philosophical descent" for Marxism is precisely what Sorel, Croce, and to a lesser extent, Lukács all exemplified. We might say that the Vichian traditions of Marxism are the reverse image of Althusserian Spinozism, not controverting it so much as preempting it with a philological studiousness that still stands in contrast to the thought experiments and productive readings made famous in the Althusserian moment.[69] For this Spinozist project appeared to its various participants to be primarily about finding a way around Hegelian dialectics. As such, the historical contact of Vico with Spinoza was ignored. As it took shape, that war of positions became in some ways very blunt. For Althusser, Spinoza is flatly the materialist, Hegel the idealist. Marxism is cut loose from its idealist underpinnings by Spinoza's "materialism of the imaginary"—Althusser's progressive spin on Spinoza's subordination of reality to the determinants of God as a "thinking thing." Althusser's stress on structural shifts over the "expressive causality" of social actors was substantially derived from the Spinozist motif of an "absent cause immanent in its affects."

Among the most influential purveyors of this vision of an absent cause is Pierre Macherey in *Hegel or Spinoza* (1979), in which he attempts to push this non-Hegelian dialectic toward a kind of computer mapping of forces and relations of production, bracketing off any hint of the producers involved in this production or the subjectivities experiencing these relations. All struggle and conflict are excised from the narrative. Spinoza had argued that thought is a property of Substance, not a subject. In order for Marxism to be considered a science again, implies Macherey, it would be necessary to rethink its emphasis on conflict, negotiation, strategy, and organization. Spinoza's immanent objectivism seemed to offer such an option. But with this move, earlier debates on the French left over precisely the same issues went unaddressed. Sorel's objectives, after all, had been nominally identical to Macherey's ("science"), although he sought to accomplish them not through Spinoza but through Vico, not through the evolution of the productive machine but through a supreme act of willfulness, the general strike.[70]

Even within neo-Spinozism, there are significant internal differences that suggest other layers of hermeneutic disagreement and contestation. In *The Savage Anomaly* (1981), for instance, Antonio Negri dwells very little on absent causalities, his focus directed instead toward a politics of possibility. While drawing a distinction between the earlier, pantheistic Spinoza (who does not interest him) and what he considers the later, materialist Spinoza of the *Ethics*, Negri elaborates on motifs found in Macherey—the replacement of conflict with "ensembles" of pure productive energy and a passion held "in common." In place of a social contract or political authority, he summons a force immanent in the group. This particular take on Spinoza, however, confronts a difficulty that exceeds that of interpretation alone. For it is not that these two re-imaginings of Spinoza wrestle with the philosopher's alien idiom in order to discover ideas or methods germinating there—ones that can be adapted with changes to new surroundings or that can be acknowledged for the first time as the grounds of what Marx would later call communism. Spinoza's politics are much more explicit than Vico's, and this fact confronts them with an incommensurability. For it is hard to escape the sense that for all its ingenuity in translating and analogizing, neo-Spinozism is forced by the logic of its recovery to heroize the emergent bourgeoisie of the seventeenth century in a sense quite antipathetic to Marx's. Spinoza's Latin for the "state" is "imperium." The problems being mooted in neo-Spinozist political circles do not, for the most part, directly deal with imperialism; rather, they are concerned with the nature of political rule as such. But given the overlapping senses of the state and imperiality, they are drawn into the larger problems of imperialism, chief among them the techniques necessary for coercion on a global scale. This bothers them philosophically, as Warren Montag, one of the Spinoza revival's most persuasive interpreters, makes clear:

> We know the rise of the trans-Atlantic slave trade coincided exactly with the flowering of political philosophy in the seventeenth century but that the great philosophers had nothing or almost nothing to say about it, perhaps because it came too close to suggesting that property rights and the system of accumulation they justified depended on violence, whether in the first or last instance; or perhaps because its violence was a too visible reminder of the more subtle forms

of coercion that made acceptable the granting of formal rights, the tyranny of everyday life, the constant discipline of the market and the state, that ensured that the multitude would live their servitude as freedom.[71]

If we take Montag's comment to cover a more general lack, one that persists beyond the seventeenth into later centuries (and the context suggests this), his statement slights the very philosopher whom neo-Spinozism set out to circumvent. The urgent observation should have led, one would think, to a concession to Hegel, who in fact addressed all of these problems: in his attacks on slavery, in his concession that colonial settlement strategies were purely self-interested *Machtpolitik*, and in his persistent exposure of the excesses of the market economy. The denial is too perfectly symmetrical not to be meaningful, as though modern philosophy's silence on the important question of slavery and violence depended to some degree on forgetting not just Hegel's philosophy but the expanded forms it took in the twentieth century itself.

To understand how and why this came about, one has to explore again those fissures within Marxism and anticolonial thought that centrally concern philology. The Spinozist intellectuals of the postwar period realized that the new relationship they wanted to establish to the past was in some ways dubious. Macherey, for example, asks, "What allows one to say of a body of philosophical thought that it is actual, whereas historically it belongs to the past?"[72] His answer is that it is actual—that is, contemporary—because a number of thinkers, himself included, had lately turned to Spinoza and were writing about him. The issue of contemporaneity is thus given a circular meaning. Such actuality occurs, he goes on to say, only when a philosophy "independently of the objective conditions authorizing an authentic and actual reading of its *oeuvre*" becomes a "source of inspiration for other forms of philosophical thought" that are precisely *not* based on an authentic reading of the work but are given "the greatest margin of interpretation."[73] Althusser, too, was clear that he had knowingly attributed "to the author of the *Tractatus Theologico-Politicus* and the *Ethics* a number of theses which [Spinoza himself] would never have acknowledged, though they did not actually contradict him."[74] This was warranted, he insisted, since every movement is based on philosophical detours, as well as on the need to establish its own difference by way of division—in this case the rupturing of Hegel by way of Spinoza. The nineteenth century had its pantheist Spinoza, so why should the twentieth century not have its communist one? Both versions were "productive" in his terms and justified as such.

Althusser's theory of symptomatic reading, as well as the related notion of working through precursors without regard to their texts or contexts—a view he defends from his first sallies into Spinoza in the *Écrits philosophiques et politiques*—has left a lasting mark on the discourses of contemporary theory, expressed today in terms of an apparently resistant "reading against the grain." And it is on this basis, perhaps, that we can speak of a "Spinoza" rather than Spinoza without falling into the trap of having made a "Vico" out of Vico. It is the revival of the former, after all, without regard to Spinoza's hermeneutic theories, that relies on a negative incarnation of the philological, whereas the interpretive methods devised by the latter were empirical, in the sense of being faithful to the words of the text, and based on a correspondence with the nonverbal world. Taking account of the variations within language across periods and cultures, establishing chronologies, and wrestling with connotations are crucial for Vichians but decidedly not for Althusser and Macherey, who actually identify them as impediments to political strategy.

For the Vichian Herder, thought itself depends on the bounded scope of language. Meanings are not separable ideas captured by verbiage but infused by and coincident with the tactile usage of words. Along the same lines, he proposed a psychology of reading, a projection into authorial language by feeling one's way into perceptual and affective sensations, gaining in the process a situated, corporeal sense of place and time. Meanings are often ambiguous, of course, and there is no guarantee of a single, authoritative meaning; but Herder points out that ambiguity can also too often be manufactured by obsessing over the text in isolation from its production. He admits that in reading there is an aspect of "divination" (Vico's term), but only because the semantic layerings resist schemata. One has to take account of an author's textual performance, above all by locating the debate he was entering at the point of writing. Who was he arguing with? What is it that he wanted to oppose? Before readers could dwell on the latent "symptom" of the text's *un*said (symptomatic reading), they had to know the positions the author was trying to displace, modify, learn from, or erase. If textual and extratextual evidence were beside the point, then interpretation was no longer secular but precisely sectarian.[75] In short, Herder, the Vichian, spells out an essentially Spinozist hermeneutic practice, although one that the neo-Spinozists themselves dismiss.

The untroubled positivity that informs these theories of creative misreading relieves itself of much more than a Hegelian aura. It gets caught in the same trap from which Sorel hoped to free Marxism almost a century earlier: a teleological narrative of absolute determinations. The thought/extension distinction in the *Ethics* (an active intelligence supposing itself to be capable of will while thinking as a passive intelligence that responds to physical stimuli) contains the pattern embedded in the political projections of neo-Spinozism itself. As such, it shares a number of features with Sorel's original target: the evolutionary Second International Marxism that saw politics in terms of a pure relationship of forces, an economic unfolding without will. Finding it impossible to escape the logic of Hegel's thought, neo-Spinozism finds a way around it by projecting itself back into the thought of a seventeenth-century philosopher who wrote before Vico or Hegel even existed. Temporal distance enables subversive adaptation.

Slavoj Žižek observes along these lines that "every postmodern 'French' figure is accompanied by an obscene disavowed double or precursor: Althusser's proto-Marxist Spinoza—'with Plekhanov'; Negri's anti-Empire Spinoza of the multitude—'with Leo Strauss'; Deleuze's Spinoza of affects—'with Damasio.'"[76] But while Žižek refers to guilty associations, I would place the stress more on the problem of historical return and the advantage of being able to judge outcomes of certain courses of action because we are seeing them again, this time with the luxury of a retrospective glance. Already in *The Arcades Project*, for instance, Walter Benjamin is quoting Karl Korsch's critique of the imputed Spinoza-Marx axis in the interwar period:

> The formulas of materialist history that were applied by Marx and Engels . . . have been detached by the Marxist epigones from this specific application, and in general from every historical connection; and out of so-called historical materialism they have made a universal . . . sociological theory. . . . They have thus reintroduced their own backward attitudes into a theory which Marx had consciously transformed from a philosophy into a science. . . . The leading representative of this school . . . Plekhanov, in his eager pursuit of that "philosophy" which might be the true foundation of Marxism, finally hit upon the idea of presenting Marxism as "a form of Spinoza's philosophy freed by Feuerbach of its theological addendum."[77]

Korsch does not add, of course, what only the future would show—that whereas Nietzsche at the time was seen as a romantic, writerly alternative to positivist Marxism, neo-Spinozism would come in some ways to represent a curious mingling of the two.

Productive reading assigns meaning to a text on the basis of what is judged to be productive of a desired political effect. The criterion for a good reading, then, shifts from asking "Is it what the author wrote?" to "Does it create an effect?" Macherey explains it this way:

> What at first glance appeared to be on the order of planned or involuntary falsification turns into forms of expression which, by virtue of being deviant, are no less authentic in their own way, and in any case are necessary: these are, if I may put it this way, "true errors," which reveal meanings that no one can claim to be radically foreign to the work itself.[78]

By these means, one can conclude that Spinoza, the thinker who promoted an enclosed system of inflexible laws, was a champion of an open-ended "positive potential" outside any social plan. What for Spinoza was the victory of the intellect over the affections becomes in Negri the passionate relations of society whose primary mode of production is love. Just as the original meaning of nature and law for Spinoza are inverted by neo-Spinozism, so too it merges historical and natural *telos*. That is to say, Spinoza's quarrel was with the religious thinkers who had recourse to the argument from design (the telos of nature). By contrast, he has nothing against the progressive betterment of humans in history (historical telos), implicitly enlisting the idea inasmuch as the *Ethics* is an urgent appeal to think differently or, to borrow a title from Spinoza's study of 1662, to "improve the understanding" (*OIU*, 1–42).

The philosopher who banished the imagination from the adequate idea becomes a proponent of the imaginary. Freedom from all law and restraint is attributed to the philosopher who vanquishes freedom in the name of a liberating recognition of our objective place in a world of other objects. Macherey and later Negri propose that we see society as a collection of human singularities, a multitude of subjects outside prescription. But that would seem to place Spinoza's *natura naturans* (self-making nature) within the purview of the subject, whereas for Spinoza it is reserved strictly for God.[79] Politically, his emphasis is not on sovereignty without government but on the absolute necessity of the state "led, as it were, by one mind" (*PT*, 330). The opening three chapters of *A Political Treatise* are entirely dedicated to this point: "Were the commonwealth bound by no laws or rules, which removed, the commonwealth were no commonwealth, we should have to regard it not as a natural thing, but as a chimera" (*PT*, 310). In short, neo-Spinozism is "radically foreign to the work itself."

Spinoza advocated a modified, more responsive monarchy in a Europe still characterized by absolutism, but also within a country that during his lifetime saw new social actors emerge in the trades and in merchant life. Spinoza's democratic model was extremely modest by contemporary standards, failing to include under its suffrage most of the population on grounds of their being foreigners, criminals, women, or the poor. The gender politics of both Spinoza and Vico are atrocious.[80] But if the question of rights, including gendered rights, depends upon institutional backing for their enforcement, the revival has been led by thinkers who find in Spinoza an ideal of "constituent" power—one immanent in the multitude that is then set off against the constituted power of governments on the basis of a legal edifice of rights and restrictions.[81] In this thinking, political legitimacy itself appears to rely on a multitude whose individuals never meet, discuss, or propose policies.

It is true that Spinoza believed that the sovereignty of states rests on the assent of the multitude: "the right of the commonwealth is determined by the common power of the multitude." But this conviction has nothing to do with immanence, which is a concept taken from the *Ethics* rather than from his political writings and in a very different context—referring (as we saw) to the suffusion of material things in God (*PT*, 305). Indeed, Spinoza could not be more alien to the constituent power thesis when he remarks that "no society can exist without government, and force, and laws to restrain and repress men's desires and immoderate impulses."[82]

The use of the term "multitude" from seventeenth-century political theory, similarly, is problematic. The word manages to avoid the tainted or belated terms "people," "proletariat," "throng," "mob," and "masses" but creates at the same time unforeseen theoretical blockages. Writing in the wake of a protracted civil war fueled by religious fanaticism, Hobbes had stressed the attractions of order in a strong state founded on laws, justifying such a government as being characterized by a "people" (his term) unified in supporting the state even at the cost of some of its liberties. Hence, Hobbes—who is a more subtle thinker than he is generally credited with being in these discussions—emerges as a foil: an apologist for the state and a purveyor of the fiction that the state's authority is founded on an undifferentiated people. Hobbes, then, stands for the state, which in the neo-Spinozist argument, regardless of the state's contingent forms, stands in every case for the reduction of the many into the one fiction of "the people," whereas the multitude is a congeries of little worlds, quiet modes of affiliation, diverse pockets of association, and the uncontainable richness of the sum total of peoples who never can be reduced to Hobbes's dubious "one."

Spinoza, though, shares a great deal of political territory with Hobbes. Both assent to the transfer of right to the sovereign in payment for protection, and both disparage the moral and intellectual capacities of the multitude. He is far closer to Hobbes than neo-Spinozism presents the matter, but there are three important differences. First, Hobbes fears the multitude and wishes to control it, whereas Spinoza wishes to base all sovereignty on a recognition of its interests.[83] Second, whereas Hobbes argues for constitutional monarchy, Spinoza explicitly does not prefer any form of government so long as that form, whatever it is, bases itself on the sovereignty of the multitude—although his most adulatory language in *A Political Treatise* is reserved for constitutional monarchy, even as his very brief, unfinished entry on democracy emphasizes the latter's weaknesses. Finally, Spinoza, in arguing that all right derives from might, represents the military, insurrectionary power of the multitude in a positive light as the essential corrective to the excesses of sovereigns. This could not be less like Hobbes.

It requires some effort, at any rate, to suppose that a seventeenth-century concept developed in a small, underpopulated European nation during the early phases of capitalism—a concept forged prior to the French Revolution, ignorant of the rise of socialism, and unprepared for future anticolonial liberation movements—could claim adequacy when applied to late modern societies. One is driven to ask what other demurs, unrelated to Hobbes's now-four-centuries-old reservations, are possible with a concept like "the multitude." The question is more urgent since Spinoza's use of the term has by now mutated. Precisely its lack of precision, its ability to circumvent any focus on distinct social sectors in a struggle with one another over resources, appears inviting to many today for its reprieve from a discredited language of conflict.

But how can one miss that this appeal, quite unlike Vico's providence, uncomfortably echoes some of the religious enthusiasms that Spinoza was at pains to arrest—evident, for example, in Negri's phrase "multitudio fidelium," for example, or his emulation of St. Francis? Or Althusser's own early investments in Catholicism and his openness to the mysteries of the church even late in life? As metaphors, these rhetorical postures at the same time are uncomfortably close to positions that neither Negri nor Althusser would seem to support; they echo, perhaps without wanting to, the contemporary language of a mysterious mass order out of chaos purportedly achieved by market choice, the revolution of upward mobility repeatedly advertised in official U.S. political jargons, and the supposed leveling of power, interest, and status offered by new media technologies. The strategy of creative misreading behind the fashioning of "Spinoza" is not just a hermeneutic (or better, counterhermeneutic) operation but a relationship to the past founded on a persistent presentism. The radicalism of the early bourgeois era embodied in Spinoza is transformed metaphorically into the sign of a present need: a communism to displace historical communism on behalf of a seventeenth-century freedom which was, after all, mercantile through and through.

The point is crucial, since the drift of neo-Spinozism contradicts itself by establishing its own bona fides in the undermining of the bourgeois subject. Spinoza obliterated—Althusser is eager to claim—"the imaginary illusion, the Subject," reaching "into the very heart of bourgeois philosophy, which since the fourteenth century had been built on the foundation of the legal ideology of the Subject."[84] Montag, on the strength of this observation, goes even further: "[Spinoza's] refusal to set the human apart from nature, mind from body, thought from action thus makes him perhaps the most thoroughgoing antihumanist in the history of philosophy."[85] But this is what is meant by hermeneutic presentism, in that Spinoza does set the human apart from nature, which is, after all, only God's realm of being, since the human is only partial and therefore imperfect nature. Accordingly, for Spinoza one can be a part of nature (and not "above" it or master of it, as perhaps is true in some versions of humanism) while being separable from nature as a whole, since nature as a whole is a characteristic of God alone. The particular being within nature that is the human subject is, in this light, *not at all denied*, since by way of adequate reason the human can free the mind of illusions and arrive at more accurate correspondences. Spinoza's project, which is realized by subjects, is to discipline confusion and fence out error by means of a vigorous, even pitiless, display of the mind's capacity to suppress and tame unruly thoughts.

Vico, then, not only departs from Spinoza at the level of ideas, but develops a mode of reading that re-situates Spinoza in his own time. Since for Vico the secularity of civil society was often expressed through metaphors of religion, he had no real interest in purging reason of myth or religious belief. On precisely this kind of point Vico disparages Spinoza, in fact. Whereas Spinoza sees the people as potentially manipulable and driven to passion by fear and unreason, Vico, while sharing elements of this distrust, stresses the movements from below that have throughout history forced a new order of sovereignty upon reluctant potentates. While alluding to the need to stem natural "avarice, envy, and ambition," Spinoza points out that "inasmuch as men are led ... more by passion than reason, it follows, that a multitude comes together, and wishes to be guided, as it were, by one mind, not at the suggestion of reason, but of some common passion." Italian autonomists tend to see this as a prescription, but it is actually a fear on Spinoza's part, and so the desires of autonomism (paradoxically) are closer to Vico's practice. Spinoza wants to stem this passion: "men are not born for citizenship but must be made so" (*PT*, 316, 313). There is more than one reversal of this sort in the adventures of productive reading. For Vico, who speaks incessantly about providence and the Christian religion, has had an almost exclusively secular influence, whereas Spinoza, considered in his own time to be scandalously atheistic, was overwhelmed by the contemplation of divinity and carried on many of the catechistic rigidities of institutional religion.[86] The liberatory dimensions of popular myth arise again in interwar figures such as Bloch, Tristan Tzara, Louis Aragon, and Benjamin—Marxist redeployments of a Vichian theme.

If Spinoza takes the momentous step of atheism, it is a move that for him involves no sense of active striving, incongruity, or planning—no exercise of what Hegel calls "Mind" or "Spirit." The attractive extremes of Spinoza's leap into the future are based, to that extent, on the relatively narrow human instinct for self-preservation and advancement. Negri quite rightly praises Spinoza's "atheistic religiosity" as an ideological framework designed to pit democracy against absolutism. But he poses this as a stunning shift in modern thought when it was really a philosophical choice—an alignment, in this case, with a paradigmatic position from antiquity that I have discussed above.[87] In a memorable and much-quoted formulation, Vico concludes that Spinoza speaks of the commonwealth as if it were "a society of shopkeepers [*mercadanti*]" (*NS*, 98, "hucksters"). To put this another way, Spinoza expressed a view, however radical in his time, that captured the incipient market interests struggling against absolutism, agitating for a form of reason that calculated action purely on the basis of advantages to life, to gain. Looking forward to the sentiments of eighteenth-century political economy, Spinoza declares: "For man, alike in the natural and in the civil state, acts according to the laws of his own nature, and consults his own interest" (*PT*, 302); and later, he proposes an ontological definition of freedom that merges with that of an incipient bourgeois political economy: "A free multitude ... aims at living for its own ends" (*PT*, 314-15).

Neo-Spinozism is forced to contend with a radicalism now safely entombed in an earlier age. When measured by twenty-first-century needs, Spinoza's goals were heroic when capitalism was still vulnerable and unstable; they now seem relatively modest and have even become in many ways comfortable and nonthreatening. Although a heterodox thinker, Vico was no radical, but his modes of literary sociology weakened the claims of technoscience and struck the notes of dynamic global contacts, insurrection, and self-making that later informed modern anticolonial movements. The different levels of acceptance of the two thinkers is related to this fact.

VICO'S CADRE

> The historical memory of mankind is full of such worn out ideological signs incapable of serving as arenas for the clash of live social accents. However, inasmuch as they are remembered by the philologist and the historian, they may be said to retain the last glimmers of life.
>
> V. N. Volosinov[88]

Althusser's celebrated break with Hegel over teleology, idealism, and system thinking could just as easily have singled out Vico. After all, Vico displays many of the same procedures and styles of inquiry. Had these affinities been marked by Althusser's readers, the hermeneutic stakes of reading *Capital* would have seemed very different. An antihumanism forced to reckon with Vico's literary coordinates and without the baggage of German idealism would have deprived Althusser of alliances among those already arrayed against dialectical thought and so opened his own work up to a different kind of scrutiny. The silent collision of Spinoza with Vico in postwar theory would have been much more audible.

But how could a Vichian tradition have come to exist? As Croce and Auerbach both pointed out, many who adapted his ideas remained ignorant of his larger project; others, while absorbing his lessons through intermediaries, had no feel for his adversarial encounters, his rhetorical personality, or the politics of knowledge implicit in his assault on scientism—that is, on the outlooks that would later permeate Althusser's writing and that were always evident in the larger turn to language. We need at least to clarify the trajectory of this war of positions. Up to now I have laid out several cases that establish that there *is* a tradition and that it is vital (in Herder, Sorel, Auerbach, and others). Here my aim is more focused: to give a sense of the form it takes in Marxism and in anticolonial theory.

If there is any interest in Vico today in either one of those two circles, it is mainly because of Said. But a lineage is always greater than a single life, and that principle applies to Vico as well, since by "Vichian" I am referring not to him alone but to a philological, antinomian, globalist outlook that he developed in a particular way in response to the scientific Enlightenment on the periphery of European intellectual life. He wrote and thought within a line of descent beginning well before him—before even Plato, his philosophical parent, to whom he pays homage frequently. Vico absorbed the lessons of Neoplatonism, as well—especially its reliance on Arabic learning, Egyptian sources, and Alexandrian hermeneutics. Vico's minoritarian intellectual position was, as I have said, modeled on Varro in Roman antiquity but also on medieval scholarly legacies, already implicitly secular, to which, as Martin Bernal has observed, Vico was heir. These in turn championed the legendary Egyptian founder of writing, Hermes Trismegistos (a.k.a. "Thoth," the etymological root of Greek *theos*, or "god"), as the founder of nonbiblical or "gentile" philosophy and culture.[89]

This lineage of thought, most clearly exemplified by Vico, developed and popularized, as I have said, a philosophy of language that was attentive to the demotic, the extramural, the foreign, and the vernacular. Literature as writing took on the air of a preserver of the brute illiteracy and prismatic imagery of everyday life in prehistory, which is perhaps to say that the Vichian lineage passes through a literary rather than a textual authority—one of Said's distinctions that is rarely foregrounded in comments on his work. His discomfort with the religious turn in criticism during what he called "the ascendancy of Reaganism" was directed against modern theories that were themselves uncomfortably aware that their own methods derived from an originally clerical, proprietary relationship to texts.[90] Wanting at all costs to cast off the dogmatic legacies of coercive "right readings," they flirted with semantic free play, eventually developing an aversion to interpretation entirely. Not-knowing became the warrant against imposing doctrines upon others—except the doctrine that there be no meaning as *intention* (to use Said's term from the subtitle to *Beginnings* [1975]).

Said's project was to a large degree about counterposing the literary to this version of the textual. He returns to this idea constantly, holding up the literary in an expansive sense (much like Vico's broad sense of philology) as referring to the curious, anti-utilitarian, imaginatively driven, idealistic critic drawn to ideas for their own sake, polymorphous in his or her intellectual wanderings and experiments. He wished to take an ethical stand against a technocratic commercialism gullibly awed by the claims of the applied sciences but, at the same time, to support suppleness in place of infinite open-endedness, a non-+utilitarian relationship to ideas in place of the suspension of all conviction, and an alert intellectual hunger in place of professional specialization. Said certainly did not invent this way of being an intellectual, but he translated it by way of Vico into an idiom that meant to address directly the culture of imperial resurgence that characterized Britain and the United States after the 1970s. For Said takes from Vico, among other things, the idea that he was (as we all are) really adapting and reassembling older patterns and was part of a conversation rather than a monologue of genius. Our beginnings are a beginning again in the sense that we do not set out from an absolute origin fashioned by a definitive break with everything past.

Conveniently placed outside the contemporary critic's range of reference, Vico became important for Said's veiled polemical purposes because he carried with him no offensive connotations and was therefore a perfect figure for Said's strategy of indirection. Like Vico, Said's philosophy was one of complementarity: the lateral as opposed to the linear and sequential, the beginning as a repetition of worthy precursors, language as "the rewriting [which is to say, the writing again] of history," and the unfolding of a thesis not in prophetic explosions but by way of "a gradually developing exemplary discourse."[91] Said deliberately summons Vico, in fact, as a counter–pole of attraction to postwar textualism. By doing so, he points to the uneasy truce between philology and anticolonial theory in its postcolonial form, one that remains as unexplored as Vico himself in this context.

That Said was not particularly invested in the philosophy of Hegel is undeniable; if anything, he was hostile. But he was immersed in the work of Marxist intellectuals, particularly during his formative intellectual period (1967–1978). Under the tutelage of intellectual companions and mentors such as Eqbal Ahmad and Ibrahim Abu-Lughod while still a graduate student, Said was pushed to draw on Marxist scholars from the Arab world, who helped shape his understanding of the ideological structures of imperial dominance in the Middle East and the difficulty of achieving independence given the terms of engagement.[92] This included the scholarship of Palestinian communist intellectuals who foreshadowed, and in some ways surpassed, his writing on the Arab-Israeli conflict.[93]

He read, frequently quoted, and discussed the works of Marxist thinkers throughout the 1970s and 1980s. That he did not only look favorably on them but consistently borrowed from them, reviewed their books, and taught them in his graduate seminars suggests the closeness of the relationship.[94] It may not be generally known, for instance, that in 1980, two years after the publication of *Orientalism*, Said's graduate teaching at Columbia University was taken up with seminars on the postwar British Left—not the New Left that would emerge in the '68ist sympathies of the Althusserian turn, but the Old

Left of former Communist Party members and public scholars who between 1950 and 1975 had altered the landscape of historical inquiry in Britain and laid the groundwork for what would later become known as cultural studies. They had charted a path of novel thinking that he sought urgently to bring to the attention of a new generation.

Another aspect of these years of apprenticeship leading up to *Orientalism* was less veiled and more genteel, although not discussed much nowadays. Drawing on the work of the now somewhat forgotten generation of broad-church literary critics of the 1950s and early 1960s such as Richard Blackmur and (Said's dissertation co-advisor) Harry Levin, Said found his way through their nonsectarian, broad-ranging interests to the work of the latter-day philologists such as Leo Spitzer, Ernst Robert Curtius, and Erich Auerbach. He took to heart Levin's counsel that "the open-minded critic cannot afford to be too much of a purist, since literature has a habit—which he must follow—of absorbing so much else, of involving itself in so many extraneous matters, of extending its purview farther and farther."[95] If the problem of "philology" informs the entirety of his work thereafter (it is the power and danger of philology that are as central a theme of *Orientalism* as the discursive creation of the Muslim or Arab "other")—that influence comes to him through Levin, which is significant as well as forgotten. But even then, when English departments were in general hostile to or uncomprehending of the transdisciplinary invasions of cultural studies, his reading tastes were not limited to this literary coterie, however urbane and worldly it might be.

For philology, the Left Hegelian tradition loomed larger in his orientation than has generally been considered the case; he explicitly saw, for instance, "German intellectual history and philology" as not being conceivable outside the tradition of "German romanticism and Hegel."[96] Philology in Marxism, then, which I have been exploring in this book from a number of angles, also reveals itself in these missed Saidian allegiances; and in Vico's cadre we are, in this way, re-introduced to a story we thought we knew. How did Said find his way to Vico to begin with? It may well have been through the most likely source, Auerbach—specifically through his *Dante, Poet of the Secular World*. It is from that book that Said adopts the terms "worldly" and "secular" in the specific sense of earthly or grounded (*irdische*).[97]

But there were ample Vichian resonances as well within the Marxist literature he was reading in the years before *Beginnings*. In a letter to Ferdinand Lassalle in 1861, Marx comments on Vico's "philosophic conception of the spirit of Roman law in opposition to the legal Philistines," going on to praise him for positioning himself at the "foundation of comparative philology" and recommending strongly that Lassalle read him.[98] In his treatment of Greek mythology in the *Grundrisse*, he follows Vico very closely: "All mythology overcomes and dominates and shapes the forces of nature in the imagination and by the imagination; it therefore vanishes with the advent of real mastery over them."[99] Even more explicitly, in "Reification and the Consciousness of the Proletariat" Lukács speaks of the "prophetic words" of Vico, the man who averred that if we are able to "regard the whole of reality as history (that is, as *our* history, since there is no other), we shall have raised ourselves ... to the position from which reality can be understood as our 'action.'"[100] Many forget that Lukács pits Vico against Spinoza in this passage, observing that Spinoza lacks a sense of dialogue or discursive negotiation; in Spinoza, Lukács argues, all givens—that is, inherited ideas considered conventionally true—are dismissed as though they were nonexistent: "every subjectivity, every particular content and every movement vanishes into nothing before the rigid purity and unity of this substance."[101]

By extension, it would be plausible to see the controversion of Marxist notions of language, labor, and "world" in Hannah Arendt by noticing that she singles out Vico for blame as the ideologist of a history that humans *make*, which is a concept, she suggests, that allows productive labor to appear a positive principle, a source of liberation—a Marxian maneuver she takes to be fatal to intellectual modernity. These Vichian innovations led, in her view, to the baleful concept of the "classless society."[102] As though anticipating the logic of Said's strategy of indirection, E. P. Thompson, in his remarkable polemic against Althusser in *The Poverty of Theory*, claims that Vico was "able ... to hold in simultaneous suspension, without manifest contradiction, a Hegelian, a Marxist, and a structuralist ... heuristic."[103] The meeting of these various elements no doubt had a great deal to do with Said's figurative deployment of the Neapolitan thinker during a period when his own politics and literary values were part of a diminishing minority.

Predictably, though, the juncture is most acute in the study of language as such. The significance for anticolonial thought of Marxist linguistics within the Vichian tradition is difficult to overstate, and I will explore the topic in more detail in the second volume of this study. But it is this connection in particular which clarifies a great deal about the misunderstandings that swarm around philology itself in the reception of the selective traditions of postwar theory. To gain a sense of this, we might look for a moment at Volosinov's *Marxism and the Philosophy of Language* (1929), since references to imperialism in that work have been severely underplayed. While criticizing what he calls "abstract objectivism" in the work of Saussure and the Geneva school, he attacks philologism from a unique angle:

> At the basis of the modes of linguistic thought that lead to the postulation of language as a system of normatively identical forms lies a practical and theoretical focus of attention on the study of defunct, alien languages preserved in written monuments. This philological orientation has determined the whole course of linguistic thinking in the European world to a very considerable degree, and we must stress this point with all possible insistence. European linguistic thought formed and matured over concern with the cadavers of written languages; almost all its basic categories, its basic approaches and techniques were worked out in the process of reviving these cadavers.[104]

Volosinov follows Vico very closely in connecting two senses of the word "alien" when studying dead languages: that which is not native (with an intimation of the esoteric) and that which cannot be understood by the profane in the national-cultural sense of being inferior to the native.[105] He compares philologists of the Saussurean persuasion to priests and actually links them as such historically. Just as philologists pore over "philosophemes of the alien word," they are really recapitulating, in Volosinov's terms—although perhaps without knowing it—the process by which earlier acts of foreign conquest brought the conqueror's civilization to subject peoples. They in turn come to associate that new civilization with their own, submitting themselves in effect to what they perceive as the power of the alien word. This whole style of thinking about comparative linguistics as the study of encoded acts of earlier conquest and linguistic revaluation is taken up later by Graziadio Isaia Ascoli, who deeply influenced Matteo Bartoli, Gramsci's teacher at the University of Turin.

In Volosinov, at any rate, we find a very clear statement of the uncertain, wavering relationship of philologism (that is, not philology in the Vichian sense) to imperial attitudes and civilizational prejudices at the level of language itself. He stresses, in fact, very different features from those of discursive, institutional authority found in Said's *Orientalism*, for example; it is much more about the impregnation of a very style of philological study—a content of form—by an imperial relationship that has stamped its attributes on the general linguistic medium of communication, and it is this style that he associates with the philosophical and linguistic schools (primarily Saussure) that dominated the cultural Left of Europe and Anglo-America throughout most of the postwar period. By contrast, Vichian philology is implicitly held up in this critique as an alternative to the fetishizing of form and the apotheosis of grammatical laws that Volosinov is so determined to unseat. By way of Volosinov and the Vitebsk circle of Mikhail Bakhtin and others (especially evident in Bakhtin's *Rabelais and His World* [1962]), this philosophy of language as politically specific, interregional, and secular undergirds a more general aesthetic distaste for textualist abstraction, formalist poetics, and literary modernism.

At this very juncture, Said's critique of modernism in *Beginnings* links him more firmly to the Lukács of "The Ideology of Modernism." Our sense of the divergent commitments of both thinkers may at first resist this conclusion, but it is remarkable how similar their critiques of modernism were. What Lukács dislikes in the tendency is picked up by Said as well, if more mutedly, for many of the same reasons: modernism's exaggerated concern with form; its elevation of the fragmentary, occasional, or temporary over anything monumental; its preference for disembodied sense data over ideas; its ontological view of humans as solitary, asocial, unable to enter into relationships; its phenomenological clichés—that is, the Heideggerian *Geworfenheit ins Dasein* (thrownness into Being) where it is impossible to determine theoretically the origin or goal of human existence.[106] Said's critique, one could say, is a translation of Lukács's argument for a post-1970s North American academic community. He is politic enough to insist that, despite his serious reservations concerning tendencies in modernism, he finds its "method" exhilarating. But he certainly does not mean those methodological elements targeted by Lukács: for example, its use of stylistic devices as a governing formal principle, its criteria for selection as a deprivation of perspective, its intentional distortion in representation as a way of embracing the pathological. Rather, Said is referring to modernism's global scope, its restructuring of historical time, its irreverence toward convention: all of the aspects that, with much more eloquence and force, he assigns throughout *Beginnings* to Vico.

When Said invokes the method of complementarity and adjacency in *Beginnings*, he has very much in mind Lukács's synthetic view of the totality. His symptomology of late nineteenth and early twentieth-century writing is meant to unearth traditions of humanism and rationalism in modernity that have been buried under modernism's cultural pessimism, irrationalism, and third-worldist invocations of the primitive. Any reference to "origins" in postwar theory had come to be considered a harmful fantasy of Western epistemological arrogance. Said pointed out that this reading of the term had to be rejected, since it served to delegitimize any reference to the past at all. In Vico's explicit terms: no origins, then no sense of the continuity with tradition either; in short, no history.

By introducing the term "beginnings" as a substitute for "origins," Said reinjected the historical sense into the inquiry surrounding modernism. If his audience could be expected to think of modernist experimentalism as the result of an artistic directive for making one's own rules and rupturing all contact with the rotten legacies of the human past, he uses "beginnings" in the Vichian sense of the making of our past. In other words, his emphasis is not on rupture but on agency and, at the very same time, on the idea that our obsession with causes, points of departure, and influences is inevitable and should not be evaded. What Said would say of Vico, he says of Lukács himself: "Theory for him was what consciousness produced, not as an avoidance of reality but as a revolutionary will completely committed to worldliness and change."[107] For Said, in short, the name "Vico" was a way of alluding to ideas that were under attack in the critical winds of the post-1970s when a Left Hegelian posture was as blasphemous as atheism in the Middle Ages.

Frontispiece for Victor Hugo's *Bug-Jargal*, Célestin Nanteuil (1832)

HEGEL AND THE CRITIQUE OF COLONIALISM

> Even the naturally grown variations of the human species, such as differences of race ... can and must be abolished in the historical process.
> Karl Marx (as quoted by Walter Benjamin)[1]

VICO'S HEGEL

> It is always time for Hegel.
> Ernst Bloch[2]

Hegel's importance to anticolonial thought is especially evident in those aspects of his philosophy that place him as an heir to Vico. Debates on the affinity between the two thinkers have raged among specialists ever since K. H. Müller translated parts of Vico's *Universal Law* in 1854, where he explored the connection at length in his notes to that work.[3] My interest, though, is not to defend or contest Müller's Hegelian gloss on *The New Science* or to claim Vico for Hegel, as Benedetto Croce had urged us to do. I am more interested in the inverse proposition: to mark their shared intellectual personalities by considering Hegel part of a larger Vichian family—something very different from and more approachable than the inherited image of him as the imposing edifice of absolute idealism.

Belonging to a constellation of thinkers who share a general theory of developmental history, civic institutions, human agency, class conflict, and labor does not imply equivalence. Vico's confidence in the poetic imagination has no counterpart in Hegel, nor does Vico's focus on metaphor and etymology as the master codes of prehistorical knowledge. The two wrote, after all, in very different regions of Europe, north and south, and with a dissimilar reception—Hegel rewarded by the academia of his day, Vico ignored by that of his. A full century of momentous social changes separate them, and the refinements of the natural sciences, the evolution of idealism in the language of Kant and Fichte, and the French Revolution all dictated that Hegel's style and methods would be more austere, disciplined, architectonic, and marked by a meticulous abstraction that he describes at one point as one of the by-products of modernity's self-consciousness—that is, the extinction of the colorful "picture language" (*Denkbilder*) one finds in early religious thought.

Although both situate thinking in its material determinations, their stories of development are very much at odds, even if they begin similarly. In his account of the early "comminglings and wanderings" of prehistoric peoples (precisely Vico's brief), for example, Hegel's words might have been taken directly from his Neapolitan predecessor:

> It is a fact revealed by philological monuments, that languages, during a rude condition of the nations that have spoken them, have been very highly developed; that the human understanding occupied this theoretical region with great ingenuity and completeness.... It is, moreover, a fact, that with advancing social and political civilization, this systematic completeness of intelligence suffers attrition, and language thereupon becomes poorer and ruder: a singular phenomenon—that the progress towards a more highly intellectual condition, while expanding and cultivating rationality, should disregard that intelligent amplitude and expressiveness—should find it an obstruction and contrive to do without it. (*PH*, 62–63)

But these words—which should make us pull back somewhat from the claim that Hegel is Euro-normative—deny in the end that early peoples were capable of writing history, since they were not sufficiently "self-conscious" or capable of acts of the "Will ... mirroring itself in a phenomenal form" (*PH*, 63).

This judgment Vico would have called the "conceit of the scholars" that assumes the ancients viewed history with eyes like our own. For the violent emotion of metaphor was the very means by which the ancients recorded the past for their offspring, drawing on the vivid colors and textures of the world itself and making the language of objects substantive. Hegel is even more explicitly at odds with Vico when he alludes to a standard Vichian theme, finding in the global migrations of early peoples the "obscurity of a voiceless past," an insufficiency of "intelligent amplitude and expressiveness" when compared to the hard work of the concept, which disciplines itself in the name of the actual and not only the imagined world. This, for Vico, would be not to see the rough reason in crude amplitude itself—the plebeian logic of the literary vulgate that later, as Vichian Marxism, would express itself in a fascination for populist genres like the notebook, *feuilleton*, and reportage. And it would be to ignore the vigorousness of the early heroic effort before books and libraries to carve out of the chaos of nature a meaning.

When I refer to the "personality" of the Vichian enterprise, I mean in part this gesture toward the sensuality of early attempts to achieve conceptualization. Vico defends the mental feats of human subjects in what must have been very cruel surroundings. This same attempt to project into, and to re-imagine, the relative clarity and ordering knowledge of vulgar art and thought under desperate conditions becomes a central feature of the Marxist attitude—most famously, perhaps, in Bertolt Brecht's love for *plumpes Denken* (rough or inelegant thoughts), in Paul Nizan's appeal to intellectuals to have the "courage to be crude" in the face of phony complexity, in Mikhail Bakhtin's praise for scatology and corporeal laughter, and in Ernst Bloch's continual return to colportage. In this light, Vico characterized modernity as a "barbarism of refinement"— a vital groundwork for the postcolonial critique of Western norms in what C. Wright Mills would later call the "overdeveloped" parts of the world.

By contrast, Hegel openly doubts that a sophisticated God existed in the earliest civilizations or that astronomical knowledge was developed under the early Hindus—both opinions that flatly contradict *The New Science* (*LPH*, 132–33). Vico's entire theory of prehistory, as we have seen, is based on rejecting the diffusion thesis of mankind's development; Hegel, however, affirmed the diffusion of nations out of Asia, seeing Germany as the offspring of, and intellectually dependent on, ancient Indian peoples. Unlike phenomenology and its avatars, which insist on the authority of Greece as absolute origin or find their settled confidence in early biblical terrain, Hegel follows the conventions of Indo-European philology in seeing Europe as the precocious child of the East, dependent on its earlier discoveries.[4]

Notwithstanding these differences, the consonances are actually more pronounced. Vico's scornful rejection of Descartes's arid dualisms of man and nature, body and mind, pitted human essence against social existence in a way exactly replicated by Hegel's correction of Kant's antinomies of phenomenon and noumenon, subject and object. The very sense of having the mission to correct by opposing the dominant discourses of their time envelops both thinkers and marks their writing with an incorporative movement—a sweeping attempt to fold into their respective projects the halting or partial attempts of others.[5] Both delivered their ideas to the world in the form of weighty masterworks (or in Hegel's case, several interlocking works that represented different stages of his elaboration) that each considered a complete system of the sciences, reclaiming "science" for their respective inquiries of philosophy and history and thereby denying the natural sciences a unique claim to the name.[6] Vico's famous theories of historical recurrence are, moreover, echoed in surprising detail in Hegel's *Lectures on the Philosophy of World History* (*LPH*, 127).

Hegel's affiliations with Vico also lie in areas even more characteristic of the latter's work as a whole—the idea Hegel expresses most clearly, perhaps, in the preface to the *Philosophy of Right*, namely, that "the Absolute is Subject," which is to say that humanity acts in us and as part of an effort larger than any one of us. The expressions of self are realized in the activity of a collective subject. The term "absolute" has led to misconceptions. "Absolute knowledge" for Hegel is not omniscience—not final, complete, or total knowledge—but knowledge absolutely given over (reconciled, one might say) to the collective nature of knowledge, to the contingency of any personal apprehension of it. The term is about the necessity of superseding the self in the recognition of the other, yielding a shared understanding of knowing as that which all humans have the capacity to possess. It is "absolute" because it is possessed by all and because it is the final phase of self-consciousness, where the self achieves actualization by the dissolution of the arbitrary side of its subjectivity.

Such correspondences aside, even the details of their arguments confirm the affinities. Like Hegel the ostensible idealist, Vico maintains that "Mind ... is the free and absolute sovereign of nature" (*NS*, 3), by which he proposes that culture is what is left over after we transform nature. History is the inventory of human labor congealed in cultural artifacts as the material warrant of Mind. Vico observes that humans have the capacity to see outside themselves but cannot see themselves without the help of others. When he argues that their innermost desire to become determinate presences in the world requires interaction with like beings in a social setting (*NS*, 97), he anticipates Hegel's account of the necessary mediation of subjectivity in order for consciousness to become *actual*: "Self-consciousness is merely a 'something,' it has *actuality* only in so far as it alienates itself from itself" (*PhS*, 297). If Hegel declares, in the *Elements of the Philosophy of Right*, that "the basis of right [*Boden*] is the *realm of the spirit* in general and its precise location and point of departure is the *will*," he is also repeating Vico's declaration that "the will is the fount of all that is just and of all the laws dictated by justice" (*PR*, 35; *NS*, 101).

For Vico the ethical leap that leads to the establishment of laws relies on the creation of settled communities, the tilling of land, and designating offspring through marriage, just as the *Philosophy of Right* observes that "marriage ... [is] the immediate ethical relationship" (*PR*, 200). Similarly, Hegel wishes to defend the existence of religion by saying that historically it amounts to the same codification of ethical behavior one finds in the laws of government. In this way he secularizes religion, as it were, just as Vico announces that prehistory teaches us that "religion alone has the power to make us practice virtue" (*NS*, 170). One of Hegel's most radical propositions is to renounce the idea that only property holders have the right to vote; he turns the tables on that idea by arguing that one cannot be considered free, and therefore a person, unless he or she possesses property. Hence, "everyone ought to have property" (*PR*, 81).

Here, too, Vico beats him to the sentiment: "Natural liberty is fiercer in proportion as property attaches more closely to the persons of its owners; and civil servitude is clapped on with goods of fortune not essential to life" (*NS*, 87). In other words, when wealth extends to the point where one possesses far more than one can actually use, part of the population will be thrust into servitude. Abundance for the few signals privation for the rest, just as contempt for property-as-use arises in this decoupling of ownership from utility. Both lead to an irrational logic of possession that extends in time to the owning of people. Vico projects this way of thinking into other aspects of the market economy as well when he remarks on the paradox that in "free commonwealths all look out for their own private interests" (*NS*, 378), a view that Hegel adopts and modifies by arguing that *bürgerliche Gesellschaft* (bourgeois market society) might serve the general interest if submitted to what we today call "regulation," although it is clear that he judged the society he saw unfolding as unlikely to be thus reined in. And so we find cautionary statements toward the end of the book, where Hegel speaks of "grave miscalculation" when the state identifies with business, making "its ultimate end ... the security of the life and property of individuals" (*PR*, 361).

While Vico and Hegel are not identical, there is more than a little evidence of common cause. Vico links the specific forms taken by language and thought to specific forms of government, finding the most progressive to be those founded on "intellectual wisdom." History is a coming-to-consciousness, a refinement of earlier civic instruments, although not without long stretches of backsliding, waste, and civilized savagery, an uncertain process but one that cannot simply be relegated to an undifferentiated series of acts that are either meaningless or infallibly representative of the corruptions of human nature or the gratuitous coercion of all law.

As I discussed in the last chapter, Vico gives voice to a protohistorical materialism when he traces (as Hegel would later) models of development within a universal mapping of "the course the nations run" (*NS*, 345), as well as in terms of the structural necessity of patterns he calls "the natural course of human institutions" (*NS*, 397). The 1744 edition of *The New Science* ends with a "Practic," where Vico modestly explains that although his work is "a purely contemplative science of the common nature of nations," and as such contains "no promise to help human prudence toward delaying if not preventing the ruin of nations in decay," his ardent hope is that it will be used by "wise men" and "princes of the commonwealths" as a practical instruction to create better states (*NS*, 427). This same political ambition for scholarship—Minerva's owl notwithstanding—would be expressed by Hegel in his early theological writings and in the *Phenomenology of Spirit* as "actualization." Vico's description of the science as a "rational civil theology of divine providence" (*NS*, 4) prepares us for his extended argument that institutions are created according to a plan that exceeds individual conception, which is what Hegel will later call the "cunning of reason."

Hegel never actually cites Vico, but he knew of his propositions, above all through Hamann and Herder, and in passages seems clearly to echo him. "To *explain* History," Hegel writes, "is to depict the passions of mankind.... and the providentially determined process which these exhibit, constitutes what is generally called the 'plan' of Providence" (*PH*, 13).[7] In another Vichian allusion, he speaks of "the plan of Divine Providence generally," where he discusses the reluctance of readers to associate his notion of Spirit with God himself on the grounds that, in the popular view, "the Divine Being is thus placed beyond our knowledge, and outside the limit of all human things"; for him, by contrast, it was important to posit a conception of God that is not "beyond our knowledge" but coincident with it (*PH*, 14). Like Spinoza in this respect, he does not consider philosophy the enemy of religion but the expounder of its intended truths, where Spirit represents "the process of working out the knowledge of that which it is potentially," realizing more faithfully what religion inadequately sets out to do (*PH*, 17). Ultimately Hegel would infuriate believers, since his concept of Spirit (*Geist*) is secular in the manner of Vico—the concept singled out by Marx and the Young Hegelians when they criticize this quasi-theological notion. But it is, for all that, only *quasi*-theological, and Hegel is consciously opposed to equivalence, for religious thought in general and Christianity in particular is suspect in Hegel's view. Religion and politics have conspired together," Hegel wrote to Friedrich Schelling. "The former has *taught* what the latter *wanted*: contempt for mankind, man's inability to achieve good, to become something through his own efforts."[8]

The point matters, since interrogating secularity itself today characterizes a number of influential movements in the humanities.[9] These challenges to the secular are often accompanied by references to Hegel in order to make the point either that he condemned religion to the realm of the irrational or held on to a particularly lifeless, official form of Protestantism. Either of these positions, though, ignores his lengthy exposure of the shortcomings of the Enlightenment's conceited dismissal of all religion in the *Phenomenology of Spirit*.[10]

The logic of burial in Vico is grasped well in a passage of Hegel's *Phenomenology* that foreshadows his Vichian argument about the family as a protostate in the making of laws in the *Philosophy of Right*. Although it would take too long for our purposes here to spin out methodically the parallels between the conception of the civic in the *Philosophy of Right* and *The New Science*—a task well worth doing—Hegel's treatment of burial, marriage, and religion in this concentrated passage summarizes the remarkable confluence of the thinking of both:

> The dead individual, by having liberated his *being* from his *action* . . . is an empty singular, merely a passive being-for-another. . . . The Family keeps away from the dead this dishonouring of him by unconscious appetites and abstract entities, . . . weds the blood-relation to the bosom of the earth, to the elemental imperishable individuality. (*PhS*, 271)

Here, marriage is required logically for parentage to be conceivable; the blood relation that results is the basis of family; and the passing of generations leads, given this intense interest in the bond and its implications for self, to a theory of the afterlife that is typically the province of religion. Hegel speaks of honoring the dead (in burial) by taking over the dead individual's action while protecting its material remains. This movement from inert (singular) being to (communal) activity is religious only insofar as it transcends the physical limitations of death.[11] But the spirit that lives on is the mundane life force of the dead individual's descendants. This is the kind of figural language and appropriation one finds throughout Vico and Hegel, subversive but without iconoclastic posturing.

What Vico and Hegel most shared was an abiding sense of belatedness and backwardness. Both had the ambition to deliver a riposte to their times, overcoming to that degree the marginality they felt in southern Italy and semifeudal Prussia. Their philosophies take the shape they do because of this fact, alerting them to the intellectual problem of centers and peripheries, despite the ambiguous elements in both that make aspects of their anticolonial thought more doubtful or less immediately evident. The misrecognized thread of philosophical thinking in Europe that they articulated resonated with postwar theoretical currents in Latin America, Africa, and Asia—in the work, to take only a few possible examples, of José Aricó (Argentina), Samir Amin (Egypt), and K. M. Panikkar (India). Our contemporary positions, at any rate, have a hidden life, and it is not possible to do *theory* without a better grasp of intellectual history. The re-emergence of these positions in a later time marks the contemporaneity of the past just as it challenges the almost canonical assumption that the selective traditions of postwar theory represented a Copernican break.

As I suggested in Chapter 1, the conservative aspects of tradition have at times been the only way to imagine radical change. To situate oneself within a lineage that sees the now as a rediscovery of what others already knew is a fundamentally Vichian point. Since Vico, so attentive to etymologies, would have known that *ricorso* is a legal term for reviewing a criminal case, the *corsi* and *ricorsi* of history, he implies, are a second chance to get it right. Vico's review as return (*ricorso*) is much more than a theory of history. It is a program for mobilizing the past to better ends.

AT THE COURT OF LIBERAL THOUGHT

> It is thus not too far-fetched to suggest that one could easily recast the story of post-war French philosophy (and recent American literary theory and criticism) as the story of Hegelianism by other means.
> Stuart Barnett[12]

Hegel, we now know, was deeply interested in economic questions from very early in his career, at least from the time of his studies in Frankfurt (1797–1801).[13] He was particularly concerned with conditions in England, the center of a vast empire. As Marx would do later, he followed parliamentary debates there, read newspapers daily, and commented at length in his notes on the Poor Laws of 1796 while remarking on their anticipation of public welfare policies arising from the reform of Prussian civil law (*Landrecht*). His self-training and habits of inquiry were not at all restricted, then, to what is customarily called philosophy. On the contrary, he aimed to moderate its abstractions by tracing the intertwinement of law and morality, commerce and art.

Emerging out of these encounters with the public affairs of his time, Hegel's thinking begins to bear on anticolonial concerns, expressing itself in philosophical form. For it is Hegel, we should remember, who first historicizes Kant's attempt to grasp the limits of reason and aims to turn the static, a priori categories that have such descriptive force in Kant into an intersubjective drama of the knowing self and the alien other.[14] Hegel deploys, and in this form actually invents, a language of movement and volatility that implicitly disrupts accepted categories of social and natural status, and refuses to accept the ontological authority of the powerful and the powerless locked in binary opposition.[15] In regard to social mobility, for example, although in the *Philosophy of Right* he appears to assent to the continued existence of the Estates, his argument moves away from inherited privileges and toward the ability to make oneself anew through education (*PR*, 232). This sentiment is consistent with his resistance to the segmenting force of class structures; the only universal class in his view—the civil service—is *not* based on inherited property. And it is Hegel who first brings a geopolitical consciousness into the discourse of philosophical modernity; his epistemology and ethics are valid on his terms only if they are shown to grow out of, and live up to, the converging streams of thought from abroad, and especially from the East, that he examines in his studies of world history. As we will see below, in the *Philosophy of Right* he explicitly yokes together the destinies of center and periphery and sees an economic motive behind the rhetoric of European "civilization" (*FPS*, 164–67; *PR*, 267–70, 372–80). But as he sardonically notes in the *Phenomenology*, this powerful combination of ideas did not simply spring to life by way of "pure insight" in the reclusive lair of the philosopher-genius (*PhS*, 349–50). It had a parentage—in Vico.

As Fredric Jameson has recently observed, we are experiencing a "Hegel revival, which seems as vigorous today as it will ever be."[16] We could add that this return itself is colored by specifically postcolonial imperatives, not only in Susan Buck-Morss's *Hegel, Haiti, and Universal History,* or in Slavoj Žižek's neo-Hegelian writings on terrorist violence, the bombing of Serbia, and Islamophobia, but also in a whole array of scholarship in the last two decades that sets out to establish the relevance of critical theory—and, of course, Hegel's central place in it—to the study of empire.[17]

But a revival presupposes that Hegel had somehow left. Seen across the disciplines or in the public sphere, this would be an odd point of view to take. On the one hand, along the lines of Barnett's epigraph above, Hegel lurks even in the theories whose purpose is to remove him as their medium and ground. On the other hand, one can point to the uses of Hegel in one of the most influential theories of the postwar period, Francis Fukuyama's "end of history" thesis, which pervaded work in the social sciences and government policy circles throughout the 1990s; to the continuing influence of the Frankfurt School in a variety of disciplines; and to the recent incursions of Hegel into even so unlikely a milieu as analytic philosophy and its offshoots, such as Roy Bhaskar's inauguration of "critical realism."[18] So I proceed on the premise that there has been not only a tendency to overlook the affinities between Hegelian philosophy and the problematics of anticolonial theory, but also an active effort to demote or marginalize the philosopher. These have taken various characterizations—from "overcoming Hegel," in Judith Butler's words, or a "detour" away from Hegel, as Louis Althusser put it much earlier, to Gilles Deleuze's succinct declaration, "I most detested ... Hegelianism and dialectics."[19] Perhaps a more telling—because more casual—example of this anti-Hegelian trend can be found in the book *Introducing Hegel*, one of a widely read series of philosophical primers in graphic guide form, which improbably declares that "one could write an intellectual history of our century without mentioning Hegel."[20] In a completely different register, Edward Said renders a revealing judgment that indicates another line of resistance to Hegel's influence, complaining not of failures but of successes:

> The irony is that Hegel's dialectic is Hegel's, after all: he was there first, just as the Marxist dialectic of subject and object had been there before the Fanon of *Les Damnés* used it to explain the struggle between colonizer and colonized. That is the partial tragedy of resistance, that it must to a certain degree work to recover forms already established or at least influenced or infiltrated by the culture of empire.[21]

Said partly exalts Hegel by considering him the principal founder of Western literary history and the animating spirit of comparative literature (an honor that probably belongs more to Herder).[22] He also recognizes that the cross-cultural sympathies and de-centering of Europe that characterize the work of Vico and Herder gave European scholarship the techniques for "breach[ing] the doctrinal walls" separating the Orient and Occident.[23] But in some of Said's statements there is ambivalence toward such intellectual generosity. Their unprecedented articulation of the view that all cultures have their own unique coherence, however much he endorses it, seemed somehow to constitute a rude epistemological monopoly—that it was not *their* point, as white Europeans, to make. This seems to me misplaced, not only because ideas should be judged by their effects and value rather than their place of origin (from affiliation rather than filiation, in Said's terms) but also because the creation of those ideas was not uniquely European. This borrowing, if that is what it was, is the logical outcome of the terrain one inherits—a terrain, we should not forget, constructed not within a hermetically enclosed, culturally uniform continent but by dissidents and conformists side by side, who came both from within and outside Europe. This is particularly the case, as we will see, in the early decades of the twentieth century, when Vico's influence again comes to the fore.

We are not, then, speaking of Hegelian nuances missed because of competing frames of reference or the elusive meanings of alien vocabularies or trainings. For that would assume a close familiarity with his oeuvre, as well as an attempt to genuinely think through his complexities, which most will admit has not generally been the case. What we have is more like a campaign to avert one's eyes from Hegel—an enterprise that Brecht, in a different context, called "organized silence." Clarifying inheritances, moreover, often involves factoring in such antipathy—and seeing antipathy itself as having a more than occasional relationship to theory and being in fact a defining part of it. This is what Domenico Losurdo has in mind when he writes:

> The political history of interpretations has nothing to do with the "history of effects" (*Wirkungsgeschichte*) so dear to Gadamer's hermeneutics. Yes, he does replace, by way of a truly priceless conciliatory strategy, the notion of a "misunderstanding" with that of a "dialogue" articulated between critics and text in various ways. However, the manner in which he disregards the notion of actual contradiction and the sociopolitical dimension of the hermeneutic debate is no less radical than the historiography we are criticizing here.[24]

In the end, political antagonisms add an additional dimension to the admitted complexities of productive misreadings. The willful occlusion of possibilities is one aspect of the hermeneutic process not captured (in fact obscured) by an aleatory reading based on semantic indeterminacy. In the effort to overcome Hegel in recent theory, moreover, there has grown up a prescription for reading the past that has become, for many, the philosophical lens through which imperialism must be seen and one of the preconditions for declaring, as some now do, that empire no longer exists.[25]

The reading I propose in this chapter draws on Hegel's oeuvre as a whole, though my specific focus is on the *Philosophy of Right*. I have several reasons for this choice. First, it was the most formative of Hegel's works for the thinking of critics of empire who followed in his wake.[26] Marx's written response to the book led to many of the analytical techniques of the first global movements against imperialism in the early twentieth century. Second, attempts at reviving Marxism in the postwar period tended to rely on the philosophy of antiquity or on the Dutch or English enlightenment.[27] Hegel, by contrast, is unthinkable without the French Revolution, the crucible of his system. The uncomfortable issues of popular insurrection, active organizational forms, and militant agency that inform that revolution are essential to any attempt to rethink Marxism philosophically. Third, it is most clearly in the *Philosophy of Right* that Hegel brings the quotidian, practical, visceral aspects of social life into philosophy, where all the dialectical language refined in his earlier theory reappears and where its stakes are most clearly evident as they are applied to problems of labor, ownership, law, slavery, colonization, and political organizations. My fourth reason has to do with the characteristic slippage in contemporary political discourse from the political to the ethical. Hegel anticipates this move, but calls ethics "morality" and distinguishes it from a higher order of political commitment to the social (which he calls "ethical life" [*Sittlichkeit*]). Fifth, the *Philosophy of Right* is a late work from the part of Hegel's career when he is widely seen to have become complacent and conservative, whereas it is his emphasis in this phase on the *civic*, in the quotidian sense of a politics of material effects, which in my view is particularly radical. Sixth, because in the *Philosophy of Right*, above all, one sees that what Marx is said to have superseded in Hegel can be found in Hegel himself, and that what are commonly seen as Marxist revisions of Hegel are often original Hegelian positions. And finally, I focus on this text because it offers an unusual and highly original defense of the state form divorced from any particular state (including, of course, the Prussian one). This nexus—of state authority, coercive means, and legal restrictions—more than any other vexes our current thinking about the political, in the humanities no less than the social sciences.

The concept of the state in Hegel, moreover, is closely tied to the fate of colonial and anticolonial discourse in at least two ways. The many arguments over the legacies of Fanon, who wrote in a Left Hegelian political idiom, divide the field down the middle.[28] These arguments revolve around the degree to which the formation of the postcolonial state qualifies as a form of independence, or indeed, whether it has anything at all to do with the liberationist goals of the postcolonial enterprise. The philosophical grounding for Fanon's influential theories of national liberation in the one book by Hegel dedicated to analyzing the authority and purpose of the state is therefore obviously relevant. But there is also a domestic and metropolitan sense in which the problem of the state has played the role of shepherd to the critics of empire within. This second issue revolves around the familiar, if somewhat normative, call to displace or relativize Europe itself as though it were a monologic entity. The abstraction "Europe," because of its older colonialist connotations, is in this way superimposed upon a territory and a community that are in reality increasingly interracial and international and subject to many pockets of underdevelopment and tense economic and currency crises, as well as internal forms of colonization.[29]

As a theoretical matter, the question of the state form is brought to our attention in yet another context. For many, annoyed by the accusation that postcolonial studies has little to offer a politics on the ground and has been strangely indifferent to national liberation movements, believe these complaints to be misplaced. The field, they argue, was never about agitating for the dismantling of colonialism's political structures but about the inscription of imperialism into philosophy; not about institutions but about the structure of colonialist thought; not about the mechanics of power but about the language of empire. Hegel, though, like Vico, tends to treat these two realms as one, considering the separation of the institutional and the philosophical to be a division of labor that tears into two halves what is in fact a totality.

Along these lines we might say that what appears to be a rejection of Hegel on the grounds of his conservative or Eurocentric aspects may be a flight from his radical political implications. For Hegel, theory is not really valid unless it is real. What he calls "actualization" is expressed in the form of an individuality that "cannot know what he [really] is until he has made himself a reality through action" (*PhS*, 240). As in Vico's proposition of the *verum/factum*, so too for Hegel: "In work, therefore, consciousness becomes what it is in truth, and its empty Notion of itself vanishes" (*PhS*, 244). Hegel deliberately posed this as a paradox that concisely summarizes the subversive core of dialectical logic: namely, that when reason does not conform to reality, it is not reason but reality that has fallen short. He subversively observes that if the subject and object do not correspond to one another, it is not that the subject should change his or her opinion but that the object should be transformed: "It would seem that consciousness must alter its knowledge to make it conform to the object. But, in fact, in the alteration of the knowledge, the object itself alters for it too, for the knowledge that was present was essentially a knowledge of the object: as the knowledge changes, so too does the object, for it essentially belonged to this knowledge" (*PhS*, 54). This is the curious bifocal energy of his objective idealism.

No effort to establish Hegel's centrality to continental philosophy or anticolonial thought, however, can ignore his relationship to non-European philosophy itself. Although he pays homage to philosophical precursors from the Far East, his gestures are more tentative than recent attempts by scholars to found their inquiries into peripheral value on non-European philosophical sources. These latter include, for example, African vernacular thought and religious iconography,[30] as well as the syncretic neo-African philosophy of the Americas.[31] Critics have with good reason also turned to the belief systems of the Far East, whose role in recent criticism should not be discounted (even when they are not immediately evident): the role of Eastern traditions of dialectics, for example, which influenced Mao's writings on peasant revolt; and the effects of *dvaita* and *advaita* philosophy, in their turn, which can be felt in the important thinking of Indian figures such as Mohandas Gandhi and Rabindranath Tagore. More recently, traditions of religious thought outside the continental tradition, or in tension with it, have become evident: for example, Hinduism (which plays a significant role in the late Heideggerian phase of subaltern studies); Islam, in today's interrogations of secularism; Zionism, in a variety of academic contexts; Jewish hermeneutic thought, in deconstruction; deistic Christianity, in the Jeffersonian mode of American studies; and so on. Even in Europe itself, the term "continental" ignores the significant Anglo-American contribution to our actually existing literary and critical theories. Here it would be relevant to mention, for example, the scientism of Althusser's work, the influence of British empiricist ideas on New Criticism, analytic philosophy's role in the turn to language, and pragmatism in the work of critics such as Richard Rorty and Cornel West.

We consistently find ourselves having to confront European thought not because of its inherent superiority but because of the structures of colonial influence that dictate its centrality. To argue, as some have, that postcolonial studies was not originally a metropolitan phenomenon at all, but rather the outgrowth of a set of purely indigenous concerns of native authors indifferent to the philosophies of the center and working in isolation from it, is to falsify the multiple historical and intellectual routes by means of which theories travel.[32] Recent critics such as Janet Abu-Lughod, Harry Harootunian, Fredric Jameson, and Edward Said are to me more persuasive when they argue that modernity was jointly conceived—that the name given to European modernity is the creation of many people working at times antagonistically, at times in concert, but always in relentless colonial fields of force, involving the European and non-European together, usually unequally.

To be sure, Hegel's liberatory implications in this light are double-edged. It is not only, as Jean-Luc Nancy puts it, that Hegel is "the inaugural thinker of the contemporary world"[33]—the person who first articulates the questions intellectuals are still compelled to ask about subjectivity and the natural world, about the relation of thought to politics, about the epistemology of the "other." Given the shape modernity eventually took, Hegel identifies within those issues a glaring paradox. It is Hegel, for example, rather than, say, Edmund Husserl or Friedrich Nietzsche, who gives an explicit theoretical space to non-Western thought and provides an opening for scholars to explore such sources seriously. He is not alone in Western philosophy in this regard; Arthur Schopenhauer in particular was deeply invested in Buddhism and wrote articles on Eastern philosophies for learned journals. But although it is considered settled in many quarters that Hegel was basically a theist—a position that would obviously militate against reading him as incorporative of other religions or sincere in his universal sympathies—it is difficult to support the claim. Being a proclaimed Protestant, after all, was a requirement for keeping his job in Berlin, and so foregrounding an antinomian position on God in published books or lectures would have been pointless. It makes more sense to look more closely at his theological writings, where he makes the concept of the Trinity a shadow of the workings of Mind in passages whose purpose is to reveal that what he means by "God" is human self-consciousness (*PhS*, 334–35). As we will see below, he is deeply critical of Christianity. As with Vico, though, it matters less what Hegel technically was than what his work led others to be: the new frames it built around stale debates and the logic it injected into the intellectual veins of freethinkers.

Many critics of Hegel's supposed Enlightenment complacencies seems simply not to know that he challenges the Enlightenment at length in the *Phenomenology* (he is thinking primarily of Spinoza) for its superficial rejection of religious faith as mere superstition. He asks us instead to appreciate the philosophical achievement of world religions (*PhS*, 297–355). He is opposed to the one-sided rejection of religion in this part of the *Phenomenology*, and if we examine his later arguments in that book about received religion, we can see why. Religion, for Hegel, also goes through phases—unhappy consciousness, cult of the dead, pure sunlight, the pictorial (animal shapes, human shapes), and then, finally, the self. Enlightenment neglects this development, driving a wedge between its own complacency and religion's original strivings. This is for him a mode of critique that is a "sheer negative," a "pure vanishing . . . devoid of content" in that it sets itself up against the "naïve consciousness of the general mass" (*PhS*, 330). It simplistically imagines that people's minds will be changed through a direct and immediate imparting of the pure insight of the Notion—penetrating others' truth as a "diffusion, say, of a perfume in the unresisting atmosphere" rather than as the result of a painful struggle (*PhS*, 331). Such static reason portrays religious belief in a life beyond as a mere "error and a fiction" without seeing the creativity of the concept or its own errors in denigrating it (*PhS*, 334). Despite their single-minded emphasis on utility, the Enlightenment thinkers he criticizes fail to see that "the *relation* to absolute Being, or religion, is therefore of all useful things the supremely useful" (*PhS*, 343).[34]

Similarly, in the *Philosophy of History* he reminds his readers that Spirit or Mind is only a development of an idea invented in the Orient during those millennia when Europe was irrelevant, and remarks that German culture relies for its thinking on the early metaphysics of Vedantic philosophy. These Herderian (and Vichian) observations provide some of the earliest justifications for treating seriously the noncontinental traditions of thought I outlined above, seeing them within a common vision of the imperial past.

The word "liberal" in my subtitle above connotes the sense present in a phrase such as "liberal compromise" or Clintonian "liberalism." In his own day, of course, Hegel was called a "liberal" in quite another sense. He was seen as the bane of conservatives, an enemy of the defenders of order, and hated precisely for this reason.[35] In the journal *Vormärz*, an author writes that those who attack Hegel are taken to be the "hangman's servant" and that his philosophy was seen as an oppressed spirit of freedom [*Freisinn*]. Losurdo remarks that "for a whole cultural and political movement, Hegelian is a synonym for *freisinnig*, that is, 'liberal,' and anti-Hegelian—or even non-Hegelian—is a synonym for 'servile.'"[36] Applied at the time to the poet and satirist Heinrich Heine and the militant activist Georg Forster (who as a German fought on the side of the invading French forces of Napoleon) as well, the term referred to a dangerous proponent of constitutional government and a Jacobin sympathizer.[37]

As such, Hegel disrupts the sensibilities of political liberalism.[38] The world of commercial negotiation or sanguine compromise is inimical to his sense of law, and he explicitly decries the rise of the unelected arbiter known as "public opinion," which, then as now, is a frequent factor in the justification of liberal policies. Both his specific statements about social authority and (even more) his emotional and rhetorical makeup are in conflict with the liberal personality. The implications of his thought, and certainly the story of its dissemination in the late nineteenth and early twentieth centuries, make it impossible to see the middle ground between the twentieth century's "two totalitarianisms" as a place of good sense and the only comfortable site to occupy in an age of extremes. Hegel in every way challenges this middle position—one that preoccupies, often quietly, most of contemporary Left political and cultural theory.

AN OTHER STATE

> The German Idealist tradition ... reached its culmination in Georg Hegel, the master of Karl Marx. It consists of the rejection of any transcendentalism and the identification of philosophy with history, with the act of thinking.
> *Antonio Gramsci*[39]

The conceptual terrain of all anticolonial thought begins with the actuality of the other. It is in the *Philosophy of Right* that the concept of the other is most fully elaborated in Western philosophy. There it takes the form of a political realism that is at the same time both ethically ambitious and optimistic: "While I *preserve* my subjectivity in implementing my ends ... in the course of thus objectifying them I *at the same time* supersede this subjectivity in its *immediacy*" (*PR*, 139). One's own subjecthood is at best a premature entity unless it grounds itself in the world independent of will: "In the moral sphere, the will ... is thus the point of view of *difference*" (*PR*, 137). Hegel had put the matter even more clearly in the *Phenomenology*: "this new shape of knowing ... the knowing of an other" (*PhS*, 104–5).

From this claim, Hegel derives a series of subjunctives about the "good," the "bad," conscience, obligation, duty, and responsibility. These are, however, not normative. They are not based on religious or traditional moral grounds or (at the other pole) by the impositions of the sovereign. Instead, he situates these oughts in what he calls the truth of the concept of will. The persuasive links Hegel establishes between apparently unlike dimensions (politics and ethics, self and other) depend on his argument's systematic character—that is, on the chain of incremental steps through processes of Mind outward to law, communities, and associations. Self-realization is both a coming-to-understanding of what I am and a realizing (that is, making real) of the self in the act of making it determinate and external (*PR*, 79). Quite unlike Spinoza's geometric method, the logical progression of the argument deduces nothing that is not socially observed or historically worked through.

It is difficult in this light to see Hegel as an advocate of an authoritarian state. For him the state is not simply a mechanism for enforcing abstract rights; rather, it is obliged to agree in content with the "inner necessity" of the good. In his analysis of the German constitution (1798–1802), for example, he explicitly decouples the actual German state from its laws, demanding that the former be made to answer to the latter: "Anyone who tried to understand [*kennenlernen*] what normally happens in Germany by looking at the concepts of what ought to happen—namely the laws of the state—would be utterly mistaken" (*HPW*, 9). What the reader gradually realizes is that the entire motivation for Hegel's methodology of proceeding from the abstract to the concrete (rather than the reverse) is to give authority to political opposition. For if our collective concept of right does not accord with the practical effect of the laws, the laws must be made to conform to that concept rather than to the state's practice. Concretely, for Hegel, the poor are not poor naturally but as a result of having been abused. They are the victims, as he says in so many words, of a wrong.

It should be clarified that the term *Recht* (right) means variously (a) an entitlement to freedom (as in the phrase "human rights"); (b) law; and (c) a distinction between what is right as opposed to wrong. The *Philosophy of Right*, then, is at once about establishing the basis for social interaction as such—the rules and self-limitations of individuals in a collectivity; the political and juridical forms possible when subjects attempt to make sense of, arrange, or codify this basis for social interaction; and the abstract principles that undergird these attempts. These three dimensions mutually bind Hegel's inquiry and are inextricable from one another.

In a setting like our own that is often invested in challenging norms and the very validity of *nomos*, it is consequential that Hegel firmly rejects the commonsense assumption that politics is an imposition of external entities onto the natural embodiment of self-expression and freedom. For this reason, his provocative challenge to our contemporary assumptions lies most in that he refutes the claim that one can choose *not* to be social, or that society can exist without political order. As law, *Recht* in Hegel, unlike in previous political philosophies, is neither natural (Jean-Jacques Rousseau), contractual (John Locke), nor positive (Jeremy Bentham). Rather, it is the right that I give myself through my own determination in the presence of the fact of others. The consequences of this view of the state for anticolonial thought are profound. For Hegel articulates a political freedom that is not simply posited; it is instead struggled over, politically. In fact, "positivity" (a negative for Hegel) neglects the truth of what Schelling had, from Hegel's point of view, rightly pointed out in his study of natural law: that "the Absolute, the Unconditional, can never be an object."[40] For Hegel it is rather always a relationship, a negotiation. Here the term can be seen as well to prepare the way for the critique of positivism that, as Gillian Rose maps out in *Hegel contra Sociology*, characterized the neo-Kantian displacement of Hegel in the mid- and latter nineteenth century in the Marburg and Heidelberg schools, and that so forcefully reappears today in a variety of recent attempts in the humanities to emulate the natural sciences.[41]

The crux of the encounter between will and sociality arises in this portrait of the historical actor or agent as a "subjective will" that "determines itself as correspondingly objective, and hence as truly concrete" (*PR*, 135). We have here, it seems to me, a welcome deepening of Spinoza's insistence on the objective character of the Subject, now made more flexible by the concession of its place *in* (rather than outside or above) nature, and yet without sacrificing its freedom to change, transform, construct. The subject is "the series of its actions" (*PR*, 151). Here, it is relevant to mention that the very title of the *Philosophy of Right* appeals to a ground distinct from mere individual or constituent-based interests as well as to the power manifested in the might that enforces laws civically. In other words, Spinoza's qualms about the myth of the absolute individual entrepreneur and master of nature are fully taken on, but much less one-sidedly in this image of a collective subject that proves its freedom only by acting. The critique of teleological thinking in Hegel is related to this confusion between right as posited and as made. For example, the notion from the *Philosophy of History* that history has its ends in self-consciousness has been criticized for proposing that this progressivism always takes the same form. But this is a very different teleology from the one resisted in Spinoza's *Ethics* or Kant's *Critique of Judgment*. The primary meaning of teleology in Hegel concerns the idea of will. *Telos* is not a fixed and inevitable outcome but an intention that one cannot not have without dissimulation.

Along the same lines, "Spirit," which can only sound crypto-transcendent to most readers today, has more to do with desiring, planning, and striving. It accomplishes for Hegel the task of indicating a nonarbitrary arbitrariness, a limit of real and possible history. There is no "out there" of natural law that steps in to provide an unshakable ground or to deliver a chiseled tablet of divine commands, thereby establishing our mode of existence. The idealism of Hegel lies in that he stipulates that this basis for right has no external source for its validation. We make it by insisting on it, producing it immanently from within; the will is dialectically free only insofar as it demands freedom as its *right*. What makes it free is that it has chosen freedom as the nonnegotiable ground of all social interaction. For Hegel, "the will is a particular way of thinking—thinking translating itself into existence [*Dasein*], thinking as the drive to give itself existence" (*PR*, 35). Hegel is actually not far here from Spinoza in the *Theologico-Political Treatise*: "The will and the understanding of God are in reality one and the same" (*TPT*, 62). Where they part company, with crucial consequences for the contemporary humanities, is on the effacement of the subject in the Spinozist tradition, which finds itself expressed, telegraphically, by the term "immanence." Hegel's ingenious response to the Spinozist position (which was common in his own time, as in ours) is to render the ontological *thing* inaccessible and therefore nonexistent from the perspective of the human beings involved in the debate, unless there was mediation—that is, the conceptual seizing or grasping of the object by thought:

> Thus *pure being* is immediately *nothing*. Quite in general, everything real is at its beginning only an immediate identity of this sort, for at this stage it has not yet opposed and developed its moments. . . . It has not yet *inwardly recollected* itself from externality [and] . . . has not yet *relinquished* its inwardness, not yet produced itself out of it." (*SL*, 462)

Even though Althusser made it popular to think of theory as itself a material intervention, Hegel the "idealist" actually prefigures what Marx later said in his own revision of Feuerbach: namely, that we come to know by a thinking that coincides with our activity in the world and that constantly modifies itself by engagement with sensuous materiality. There is in this recursivity between thinking and action a noncontemplative rejection of what Hegel condemns in Plato's dialectic as "empty ratiocination" (*PR*, 20). It is a plea on behalf of the ideal, but in a way that reinforces the notion that the messiness, difficulty, and conflicts of actual life are the medium through which thought achieves its rationality as part of a hard-won effort to make sense of that reality's confusing particularities. In Hegel's words: "The theoretical is essentially contained within the practical" (*PR*, 36)—not, as in Althusser, the other way round.

Hegel's idealism, although evident, is of a special type that, however paradoxically, has at times been called "materialist." Its features are clarified in several moments of his work—for example, in the "Sense Certainty" section of the *Phenomenology of Spirit* ("The Notion of the object is superseded in the actual object" [*PhS*, 104]), where it is clear that Hegel wants to hold in tension concepts and their objects. Accordingly, in his lexicon the term "Idea" (as distinct from "concept") is used to refer only to concepts that have been actualized (*PR*, 25–26), where the latter term does not simply mean acting upon an idea, or turning the idea into a physical presence, but bringing an idea to its completion by allowing its inner necessity to express itself. His method in this sense anticipates the structural movement of *Capital* even if Marx reverses its direction, beginning with the commodity (a "hieroglyph," in Marx's words) and proceeding to the system of capital. Because Hegel views thought itself as a product of mental labor, he considers it concrete to an extent that Marx could not:

> One might accordingly ask at this point why we do not begin with the highest instance, that is, with the concretely true. The answer will be that we wish to see the truth precisely in the form of a result, and it is essential for this purpose that we should first comprehend the abstract concept itself. (*PR*, 61–62)

Hegel is referring here not only to sense-making in the process of forming concepts, but also to *Verkehr* (traffic, intercourse) among individuals struggling to bring into alignment freedom and the imposed limitations of a governing authority.

Hegel's response, then, is not to recoil from the state form because of the excesses of states but to demonstrate the inescapability of government along with its potential to be other than it is. His early enthusiasm for the French Revolution moved him to conclude that there will inevitably be a state and so one must participate in shaping its outcomes ("even if no state is yet present, reason requires that one be established" [*PR*, 106]). Even if the language of the *Phenomenology* is more mediated, it expresses throughout a similar rejection of the "arbitrary will of . . . individuals" when it deals with the immature view that individuals can make laws that apply only to themselves (*PhS*, 262, 266). The state's highest purpose is not to protect individuals, nor is it an institution that can be judged by the morality of individuals, nor is it capable of a unity based on emotional bonds like the family, nor does it work according to a commercial contract. In short, Hegel's point is explicitly to oppose the bourgeois form of the state. Without mobilizing the terminology of the people, masses, or multitude, he lays out what is, in effect, a position that at the very least underwrites any possible revolutionary posture.

Hegel, as I said above, like Spinoza and Vico, tactically supported constitutional monarchy in his time. Why he did so is implied by his statement that "subjectivity attains its truth only as a *subject*, and personality only as a *person*" (*PR*, 317). A monarch, rather than the Junkers or the emerging commercial bourgeoisie, would be easier to appeal to and more exposed to public judgment; a single arbiter of the laws is likely to be less under the sway of sectoral interests. That the monarch is raised to his position in an immediate, natural fashion through birth (*PR*, 322) may be disadvantageous from the point of view of civic equality; nonetheless, at a time of aristocratic intrigue it obviates conspiratorial activities on the part of special interests by introducing a completely arbitrary rationale for leadership. The charge that Hegel is coercively normative or that he polices desire in some respect is almost exactly inverted. For the human being is, in Hegel's terms, "wholly indeterminate" (*PR*, 45). On the contrary, it is Spinoza who conceives of the subject as helpless in the presence of natural drives toward the enhancement of life.

To turn now to consider Hegel's perspective on colonization, we find, first, a technical and brief account in the *Philosophy of Right* that vividly condemns the *Machtpolitik* of market forces seeking a deus ex machina to resolve domestic overproduction (*PR*, 268–69). "Despite an *excess of wealth*, civil society is *not wealthy enough*," he laments. Laborers robbed of self-sufficiency and dignity are forced to seek them beyond the confines of the home country and "look for consumers" as well as "the means it requires for subsistence" (*PR*, 267). Earlier in the text he had voiced his opposition to slavery for its contravention of the right to possess oneself as one's ultimate property. The emphasis on ethics requires him to spend almost half the book exploring, under the name of *Sittlichkeit* (*PR*, 86–87, 96), the system of ethical life.[42] The deprivation of the self is thus the ground on which Hegel lodges his objections to both colonialism and slavery. As we can appreciate in our own times of stock market crises and financial fiascos, the state (however paradoxical this may seem) appears as the only leverage against the excesses of private calculation. This is the proleptic point in the *Philosophy of Right* when Hegel discusses the growing dangers to life and art posed by an unregulated market (*PR*, 231–34; *HA*, 193–94).

We should recognize that Hegel anticipates here what later commentators would take for granted—that even if one held the doubtful position that colonialism was not a direct source of European enrichment (as many critics of imperialism, including Marxists, have at times contended), it undoubtedly brought out the worst in the home country.[43] There is no question, he remarks, that the "fluidity, danger, and destruction" of traders crossing the seas invigorated the colonizers, but "*this specific society* [namely, capitalism]," he stresses, is driven fatally by two motivates: eliminating the "rabble" at home and "look[ing] for [new] consumers" abroad (*PR*, 267–68). Despite the apparently endorsing language of Hegel when he speaks of the "creativity [that] has flourished" as a result of these trade-induced cross-cultural contacts, he portrays colonial territories as a kind of cynical leverage for avoiding the consequences of "disproportionate wealth . . . concentrated in a few hands" (*PR*, 266). For Hegel, unemployment and the poverty that results from it might be solved by job creation were it not for "overproduction and the lack of a proportionate number of consumers who are themselves productive." This is wherein the "evil" (*Übel*) consists, he writes, and "this is merely exacerbated by the two expedients in question" (one of which is colonialism) (*PR*, 267). This novel analysis that colonies come about because the endangered market seeks a way to survive by extramural means will later be made famous by Carl Siger in *Essai sur la colonisation* (1907).[44] In part because of this intertwinement, and because "bourgeois society" (as he calls it) is for Hegel the malign author of the alienation of labor, he concludes his brief comments unambiguously: "The liberation of the colonies itself proves to be of the greatest advantage to the mother state, just as the emancipation of slaves is of the greatest advantage to the master" (*PR*, 269).

Liberal forms of theory have often balked at Marxism's apprenticeship in Hegel's thought on the very grounds of his defense of law, order, and the potential of the state to provide safe harbor for the weak and dispossessed. Indeed, the state's capacity to curb excess is of course what we would today call "regulation," which Hegel saw in staunchly ethical terms. Government for Hegel, as for Vico, is a remarkably difficult and fortunate human achievement, not unlike the invention of fire by early Homo sapiens. Only by tracing its gradual coming-to-form can one understand its necessity, or to put this in a related way, why this problematic imposition on freedom was collectively created in the first place. To express this idea in the manner most fitting for postcolonial theory, his position is that freedom must be able to *defend itself*. Hegel is in this respect akin to Spinoza in believing it pointless to outline a political theory without recognizing power as the guarantor of right; for this reason, he declares that the "absolute right of the Idea" is based ultimately on violence [*Gewalt*].

Writing about the destiny of the German constitution, Hegel reinforces this point early in his career and in an evocatively colonial context: "It has been the fate of Italy to come for the most part under the authority of foreign powers. ... If Germany is not to suffer the same fate as this after a few wars, it should re-organise itself as a state."[45] This sovereignty-as-state nevertheless raised an ethical conundrum that Hegel proceeds to work out in the course of the book. The *Philosophy of Right* is among other things a book of ethics, though it does not displace politics by ethics—instead demonstrating the impossibility of being ethical without being political. After all, to be good one must also be effective in an action-oriented sense. According to such a perspective, politics ceases to be written off, as it sometimes is today, as just another name for the "police." On the contrary, communal constraint, even coercion, on behalf of the common interest becomes theoretically viable.

Almost every aspect of this philosophical instinct is likely to disturb liberalism. The intent to disturb was, as Lukács methodically shows in *The Young Hegel* (1938), part of Hegel's intellectual disposition from a very young age. By way of a sustained study of theology and the history of religion in Bern and Frankfurt, Hegel probed the dispiriting logic of Christianity, setting it against pagan antiquity and seeing Christianity, in fact, as being the fruit of the despair brought to every corner of the Mediterranean world by the Roman Empire, whose brutal violations of civic right left the people little option but to seek a redeemer. And yet this savior launched a project that can only be seen as imperialist. It is true that he reigned not over this life but the next, not over things but the transcendental spheres; nevertheless, he also shifted, with fatal consequences, the social ideal resting on public and civic virtue (as in antiquity) to the personal, the private, and the individual.[46] Christianity took the Roman repression of foreign races and turned its silencing impulses "inward."[47] In Hegel's account, therefore, Christianity comes very close to being seen as a kind of monstrous internalization of a historical defeat and retrenchment whose seeds were sown by the occupying armies of the Romans. This explicitly imperial problematic, however limited its scope, formed Hegel's thinking as a young man.

Another line of attack summons the "apolitical" Hegel, emphasizing his ponderous abstraction and idealism. If Hegel has been accused, wrongly, by some postcolonial critics, for example, for "confin[ing] philosophy to an exclusive sphere," the charge can certainly be found to hit its mark when directed at anti-Hegelian legacies.[48] Heidegger makes this clear in his own lengthy study of

Hegel's *Phenomenology*, where, without saying so, he disputes Hegel's argument in the preface that philosophy is epistemologically superior to the sciences. Hegel had there contended that speculative philosophy's strength was, among other things, its understanding that "Substance is essentially Subject" (rather than matter inertly observed under "objective" conditions) (*PhS*, 14).

> One cannot decide whether or not philosophy is *the* science by considering some epistemological criterion or other. This decision can be made only from out of the actual content and inner necessities of the first and last problem of philosophy—*the question of being*. If we suggest that philosophy cannot and should not be *the* science, then we are also not saying that philosophy should be made a matter of whim. Instead we are saying that philosophy is to be *freed* for the task which always confronts it whenever philosophy decides to turn into work and become actuality: It has become free to be what it is: philosophy.[49]

This warrant for philosophy's autonomy, a variant of art for art's sake, becomes clear in Heidegger's demarcation of the gulf between him and the Hegelian principle of actualization. Seeing it as the essence of his opposition to Hegel, Heidegger directs us here to the paradox that philosophy must be relieved of the task of knowing; its relationship to actuality will always be moot and a detour from its true self, which is to be a form of writing. This position will become an important support for counterphilological reading.

The antistate position (above all, its Left variants) is for Hegel the complacent option, overlooking that freedom requires "some kind of order, a particularization both of institutions and of individuals" (*PR*, 38). But even more, the rationality of the state in Hegel speaks to the unevenness and underdevelopment that mark the colonial relationship. Colonialism is portrayed by Hegel as having an economic logic based ultimately on the family. It is given an anthropological inflection, exactly as in Vico, to account for the movement from prehistory to history by way of the creation of civic institutions whose earliest forms were based on family alliances. Territorial conquest, Hegel writes, is considered necessary by civil society to acquire the land that all families need for sustenance and for the inheritance owed to one's progeny.[50] What we must recognize, though, is that colonialism is in this way also cast as an act of self-entrapment whose dissolution can only come about by universalizing the other. Put differently, colonialism reflects a structurally identical relationship to that of intersubjective negation and supersession in the *Phenomenology*, and Hegel understands it this way.

THE TALE OF HEGEL, AFRICA, AND SLAVERY

> Hegel was... a German philosopher whose fundamental vision was determined in every respect by the backwardness of Germany.
>
> Georg Lukács[51]

Hegel's critique of colonialism was certainly limited, of course. He never publicly agitated against colonialism, nor did he attempt to work out its specific and expanding theoretical logic in the course of his system. He is capable, also, of talking about the "stagnation" of peoples who had been cut off from its dynamic contacts, and considered global trade itself an "educational asset" (*PR*, 268–69). For all that, the parts of his writing that are open to the harshest criticism of this sort also happen to be subject to philological skepticism.[52] Although during his lifetime he never discredited the versions of his lectures that his students delivered to the printers, it matters that the *Philosophy of History*, the most maligned of his works, is made up of passages that combine his written lecture notes with student summaries and commentaries, presenting both together as the Hegelian text.[53] The student notes are always blunter, less developed, and more conventional than his own words, which were themselves assembled from often-conflicting notes for lectures delivered over several years. Hegel was by this point in his career a movement as much as an author, overwhelmed by duties and so sought after that almost anything he uttered in a lecture hall was assiduously taken down, interpreted, and presented to the public. To ignore this setting is also to disregard the fact that the lectures themselves were works in progress. He saw them as elements of a course undergoing at times significant revisions in each new presentation of it, and some of his statements were deleted in later versions of the lectures.

The hostility to Hegel in postwar theory is at first bewildering, given the enthusiasm he generated in anticolonial circles of the early twentieth century. Explaining why this antagonism arose after World War II is not easy, although the timing is meaningful, as we will see. What is more interesting, perhaps, are the very recent efforts to construct positive linkages between Hegel and postcolonial thinking. Featured in the writings of Kevin Anderson, Susan Buck-Morss, and others, such linkages, while welcome, are not all that new. They are consistently thematized in the scholarship of Frantz Fanon, Aimé Césaire, and C. L. R. James, through world systems theory, and into a rich and growing strain of critical, materialist postcolonial studies of the 1980s and 1990s. The importance of Hegel was also an implicit motif running through the projects of interwar thinkers such as Bloch, Gramsci, Brecht, Marcuse, and of course, in the most pronounced way, in Lukács—all of whom also had things to say about emancipatory movements around the globe.

This interwar era was a transition between, on the one hand, the nineteenth-century Hegel resonant in the public, nonacademic critiques of the philosopher by Bruno Bauer, Ludwig Feuerbach, and Max Stirner (who together made philosophy "worldly" in Marx's terms), and, on the other hand, the rise of social democracy and, later, communism as organized movements in the context of the Great Imperialist War of 1914–18 (as World War I was known at the time). Both contributed greatly to the explosion of anticolonial liberation struggles following World War II. This transition and its associated linkages, however, have remained poorly explored in writing on and against empire in recent decades. The chronology nevertheless suggests that what we might call the postcolonial Hegel comes to us today by way of the Left Hegelian Marxism of the 1920s and 1930s—which, for a variety of reasons, was embroiled in debates over the peasantry, national culture, ethnic autonomy, the languages question, uneven and combined development, and international forms of protest and organization. The parentage of the postcolonial is, ultimately, a communist one.

The resistance to Hegel in postwar anticolonial circles takes many forms. It is argued, for example, that the master/slave dialectic is a metaphor of class struggle without any particular reference to actual slavery and therefore a diminishment of the specificity of racial oppression; second, it is said that Hegel's view of history as following predetermined stages suggests that the institution of slavery had by the mid-nineteenth century come to be seen by his followers as a problem modern capitalism had already outgrown.[54] It is hard to give credence to these complaints. Slavery was a contemporary problem in the 1840s, not only for Marx and the incipient labor movement but for anyone who read the newspapers. It had been outlawed in the British colonies but continued in the major Spanish and Portuguese colonies and of course throughout the American South. Far from banning slavery from their narrative or metaphorizing the master/slave dialectic, early twentieth-century Marxists were the most persistent interrogators of its colonial logic—a position amply shown in the writings of (white) Marxists such as Rosa Luxemburg, Nancy Cunard, and Maurice Thorez, among others. The innovative case of primitive accumulation that Eric Williams examines in *Capitalism and Slavery* (1944) would be unthinkable without the writings of the *Grundrisse* and *Capital*, Lenin's *Imperialism: The Highest Stage of Capitalism*, and the existence of the lines of solidarity and popularization of the Third International, as Williams himself freely acknowledged.

Along similar lines, C. L. R. James repeatedly testifies to the formative influence of Lenin's late work on black liberation (for example, in his essay "Lenin and the Problem" [1964]) and in *The Black Jacobins* [1938], a study modeled on Trotsky's *History of the Russian Revolution* [1930]). James would never have considered Marxism mechanistically driven by a uniform *telos* nor divisible along a spurious epistemological axis ignorant of race. On the contrary, his *Notes on Dialectics* (1948) draws on Lenin's study of Hegel's *Logic* to argue against false universals and the sovereign subject, as well as for the need for a conception of totality that forges the link between European revolutionary theory as it grew out of Hegel and subsequent anticolonial thought.[55] In mainstream postcolonial theory, these kinds of emphases are seldom discussed in any detail, as a result of which Hegel's reception is mostly incidental. Said argued that Hegel believed that history "run[s] unilaterally... becoming more sophisticated and developed... as it goes"—which is not untrue except that nothing in Hegel is "unilateral" and the statement fails to capture the retreats, atrocities, and political failures in such "sophistication" in Hegel's view.[56] In time, this rhetoric in the field would escalate significantly, drawing on philosophical sources that were quite alien to Said—ones, in fact, that he openly criticized. Nevertheless, a series of positions appeared in postcolonial essays throughout the 1990s and 2000s, declaring (among other things) that Hegel believed Africa had no history, that the binary logic of dialectics formalizes the racial divide of white and nonwhite,[57] and that Hegel is the author of "Western European... modernity in its double face: the economic and political configuration of the modern world as well as the theological and epistemological space."[58] We are told that Hegel applauds the British as "the missionaries of civilization to the world'"[59] and that Hegel's thought is "implicated in the link between the structures of knowledge and the forms of oppression of the last two hundred years: a phenomenon that has become known as Eurocentrism."[60]

Although most of these judgments are rendered without a close reading of Hegel's work or textual support, there are two attacks within postcolonial studies that are worth exploring in more detail. Tsenay Serequeberhan has explicitly taken up the *Philosophy of Right*, for example, proposing that Hegel's epistemological enthusiasm for the Idea "justifies the enslavement of 'Negroes'" as distilled in the equation "the Idea (*Idee*) = colonialism." He goes on to argue that Hegel believed in the "inherent desirability" of Western "colonial expansion."[61] Unlike the more common procedure of alluding negatively to Hegel only in passing, Serequeberhan methodically works through the logic and arguments of the text's account of property. He concludes that colonial expansion, which Hegel saw as a "paradoxical contingent effect of the inner workings of Modernity," is "nicely dressed up and packaged as the ontological necessity inscribed in the self-actualization of *Weltgeist*."[62] Hegel, he concludes, believes that "a person has the right to take possession of 'any and everything.'"[63]

I have already discussed why this reading is contrary to Hegel's meaning. Hegel inveighs against ownership for its own sake. But it might be helpful to go beyond refuting this particular idea and cast the argument in its broader context. "Civil society" as Hegel meant it was the parallel power and authority of the market, the world of business, and the organizations that attend them. In this context, he analyzes what he calls the "system of needs"—that is, the arena of work, the Estates of trade and industry, colonization, law, police, and the corporation. Organizing his entire argument about the state under these categories, he describes an operation of dual power, the market and the government. However, it is the market that has acquired the power, outside of government, to undermine values and destroy lives:

> [As] the *accumulation of wealth* increases . . . the *specialization* [*Vereinzelung*] and *limitation* of particular work also increase, as do likewise the *dependence* and *want* of the class which is tied to such work; this in turn leads to an inability to feel and enjoy the wider freedoms, and particularly the spiritual advantages, of civil society. When a large mass of people sinks below the level of a certain standard of living . . . that feeling of right, integrity [*Rechtlichtkeit*], and honour which comes from supporting oneself by one's own activity and work is lost." (*PR*, 266)

It is not only, then, that Hegel brings labor into his epistemology, ethics, ontology, and aesthetics; he is also the first to analyze the "alienation" (*Entäusserung*) of labor.

Accordingly, he sets out in the *Philosophy of Right* to revise the terms of business life. Inaugurating a generalist and nonspecialist form of inquiry, he redirects the emphases of economists—denying, for instance, that property is sacred or that it must be protected even over human life; on the contrary, he argues that everyone must have property, especially the propertyless, for without it their personality cannot be realized.[64] To possess objects as one's own is to hasten a reckoning with what one is not and therefore to define will negatively: that which has no will is owned. We should note how this argument is logically derived from earlier parts of Hegel's system and for that reason is not merely declarative. The system nature of his argument—that is, the way will, self, and labor are tightly linked with foreign expansion as intertwined elements—is what allows us in the passages that treat colonialism to read them as referring to the incompatibility of bourgeois ideals with its own practice. According to those ideals, one does not have the right to appropriate all things (as Serequeberhan suggests). Hegel's point instead is that others' "things" include their possession of themselves, and what makes them free and a person is their possession of property. If the bourgeois norm is to be consistent, Hegel cleverly argues, one cannot own another person or take his or her property. This may amount to a defense of bourgeois property, but only tactically; for it is also a defense of regulation. It sees Spirit as itself contingent on self-possession, where the word "possession" has been subverted and turned into something other and higher than ownership of mere status objects.

My stress on the value of systematicity in Hegel's thought is in marked contrast with recent readings such as Fredric Jameson's *Valences of the Dialectic*, where the system character of his work is sharply criticized.[65] But ignoring Hegel's systematicity in the *Phenomenology* is to miss that when Hegel writes what appears as true in one phase of the process of thought, he often controverts it upon its later development. The view often attributed to Hegel in liberal legal theory that poverty is the necessary consequence of the workings of civil society and that certain individuals must be reduced to poverty is accurate. But he is not justifying civil society but leveling a charge against it.[66] When Hegel writes that colonialism is the inevitable outgrowth of capitalist modernity, this is not an apology but an accusation, although only taking account of the systematic presentation, which begins with a phenomenology of Mind and proceeds to the system of ethical life, will make this clear. Serequeberhan avers that Hegel wishes to exclude the poor from society, making them ineligible for justice, and yet Hegel defends theft by the poor (*PR*, 154), placing it higher than the right of secure property because the poor have been done a wrong and because "what is law may differ in content from what is right in itself" (*PR*, 243). A person's own body and the means to keep it alive are possessions for Hegel, the very paradigm of property, in fact. So he curtails the right of the powerful to possess another's, immanently undoing the existing conception of property.

At one point, Serequeberhan remarks that his reading of Hegel is "de-structive," in the sense of the term *Destruktion* from Heidegger's *Being and Time*.[67] Why, though, is it necessary, if one is only revealing what is hidden in the text, to have recourse to the idea of "destruction"? Regardless of the claim that one's reading "undermines the text from within," the term suggests a prior disparagement and therefore an invitation to emotional misreading. Why, also, in a book that rightly speaks of "the *beguiled* and *beguiling* service rendered European colonial expansion by the occidental tradition of philosophy,"[68] would one apprentice oneself to Heidegger or take him as one's guide in exposing the complicit Hegel, when Heidegger felt Europe encircled by enemies in the colonies, joined a party based on racial extermination, and displaced humans from an active conceptualization of their being?

Similar problems arise in what is perhaps the best-known confrontation with Hegel within postcolonial theory—Robert Bernasconi's "Hegel at the Court of the Ashanti."[69] I should begin my consideration of his argument by saying that some of his charges are accurate and that Bernasconi is effective at demonstrating Hegel's (or his students') redeployment of the offensive language and attitudes of sensationalist travel literature of the time. But Bernasconi does not raise the interpretive problem surrounding a text partly composed of student lecture notes, nor does he clarify that the available editions of the *Philosophy of History* (he mentions three) are all posthumous. He notes that not all of the versions mention Africa but says nothing about why this is so. According to Duncan Forbes, Hegel taught the course that constitutes this book five times and kept gathering historical materials, revising his views, and simply dispensing with sections of his earlier lectures when he considered them insufficiently informed.[70] Without any special pleading, we might be able to grant that Hegel's efforts at revision suggest an understanding of the limits of his own knowledge; they are, at any rate, consistent with his skepticism about available information. For instance, he questions the motives of Catholic historians from France and Germany, whose reports on China he distrusts because they were funded by state powers with vested interests. Two other aspects of Bernasconi's essay seem even more doubtful. The essay is unremittingly critical, proceeding without a word on the dimensions of the *Philosophy of History* that demonstrate Hegel's cultural relativism (rather than racism) and lend support to his emphasis on de-centering Europe. One does not have to go far to see that Hegel's commentary on German culture proceeds by showing its reliance not only on Vedantic philosophy but, interestingly, on Egypt—whose unparalleled civilization in antiquity arose, Hegel notes, from the inspirations of a kingdom founded by the Nubians of present-day Ethiopia.

Let me amplify this point by referring as well to *The Science of Logic* (*SL*, 14), where Hegel grants Egypt the distinction of having developed the mathematical sciences earlier than anyone else. Bernasconi claims that Hegel establishes an anomalous relationship between Africa and Egypt, pointing to the fact that in the *Philosophy of History* Egypt is not treated as part of Africa at all but rather as part of Persia in order to deny African cultural achievement. This is a mistake on Bernasconi's part, however. Hegel's comments on Africa (as opposed to *parts* of Africa such as Egypt) are restricted to the introduction only because the introduction is dedicated to analyzing *continents* geographically (he goes on to discuss North America and Asia, for instance, as a whole, without distinguishing among its various peoples or traditions). When he discusses Egypt in the next section, it is because the organizing principle there is different. The purpose in that section is to explore what survived and what did not from past empires (he argues that Egypt's "marvels" survived, while Persia's did not). His discussion of Egypt in the company of other civilizations from the eastern Mediterranean world (Judea, Syria, Greece) is no more an attempt to sever Egypt from Africa than to sever Greece from Europe or Syria from the Near East. As I mentioned above, Egypt's civilization according to Hegel was prefigured and influenced by the Nubians to the south, which is still another way to appreciate that his point is not what Bernasconi ascribes to him.

In other words, Hegel explicitly locates distinct cultural values in sub-Saharan Africa, not merely in the racially mixed societies of the eastern Mediterranean. His emphasis throughout the *Philosophy of History* is that the Oriental world devised a philosophy of change, rebirth, and renewal that provides a place for the notion of Spirit. What he rejects is the Orientalist habit of superimposing moral reflections or sentimentality on history by attributing superiority to the Indian epics over Homer or arguing that Chinese stoicism anticipates the Eleatics and Spinoza. He took this to be overcompensation by Orientalist scholars. Some readers object to the element of theodicy in the text, and detractors have regarded this to be an apologia; in point of fact his formulation is rather more modest: not to condemn individuals, states, or providence in history without recognizing their import or value. Often cast as a supercilious or condescending text, its emotional tenor is on display in his defense of Thersites, the object of ridicule in the *Iliad* for daring to complain in the presence of his royal betters—a striking moment of plebeian sympathy that reflects his more general attitude in this and other texts.[71] The trope of the "court" that Bernasconi invokes in order to suggest Hegel's arrogance, as though Hegel pretended to sit in judgment over Africa and found it wanting, is misapplied. It is taken from the *Philosophy of Right*, first of all, not the *Philosophy of History*, and in a very different context: "World history is a court of judgment" (*PR*, 372).

The court (*Gericht*) that Hegel refers to there is, precisely, not one delivered by one people upon another as an exercise in spurious evaluation. His whole point in summoning the term is to distance himself sardonically from the contingent tastes of specific nations or races. They assume the right to judge others, he is saying, but a valid assessment can emerge only from the eventual outcomes of historical action, which is not apparent to those locked within their own moment: "This history of spirit is its own *deed*; for spirit is only what it does" (*PR*, 372)—a point that will become central in postwar existentialism, above all in Simone de Beauvoir's *The Second Sex*. It is also misleading to imply that there is unanimity among scholars of African descent regarding Hegel, since many embrace his philosophy.[72] But more than anything, it is problematic to pretend to act as an attorney for the Ashanti, in part because the dispute, in the end, is not based on race or nationality but on political position. Let us then look more closely at those positions.

Perhaps the most sensitive point to raise in this context is that while Hegel certainly believed that there were advanced and backward cultures, so did many of the intellectuals from Africa, Asia, and Latin America who were actively involved in struggles for political independence or who assumed roles in government after taking power. Their accounts bristle at the hypocrisy of the term "backward" used by the European powers when poised on the spearpoint of intervention, but they understood that living with an undeveloped infrastructure, spotty education, inept technical knowledge, and illiteracy was a much greater scandal. In their view, there could be no sovereignty without development.[73] This is not to say that this position made them Hegelian, necessarily, or that his philosophy guaranteed their understanding of this issue. Far from it. Throughout the twentieth century, intellectuals involved in liberation movements from the periphery were uniform in avowing the need to overcome what they themselves called "backwardness."

The delicate balance to be maintained between modernization and the progressive promotion of indigenous forms obsessed, for instance, the late nineteenth-century social activist and rationalist Vedantist Swami Vivekananda, who in 1898 criticized India for having lost touch with internationalism and becoming "stagnant and mummified." He wrote: "The fact of our isolation from all other nations of the world is the cause of our degeneration and its only remedy is getting back into the current of the rest of the world. Motion is the sign of life."[74] This view is exactly the same as Hegel's in the *Philosophy of Right* (*PR*, 269). The Indian prime minister Indira Gandhi, somewhat later, was not alone in saying that "every State has special problems, and special difficulties, and no State can really be called advanced. 'Advanced' and 'backward' are relative terms. Our greatest enemy is poverty and economic backwardness. Until we can defeat this enemy, our country cannot be really strong."[75] Despite current sensitivities, then, we should acknowledge that outside the West the term "backwardness" was not shunned because of its implicit insult; on the contrary, rather than being viewed as an index of imperial slander, it was taken up enthusiastically as a reprimand and seen as the consequence of coercive colonialist policies.

There is no better example of what I am saying than the Guyanese activist Walter Rodney, whose classic study, *How Europe Underdeveloped Africa*, is not insensitive to the vicious comparisons lurking in the term. He observes that "it is in line with racist prejudice to say openly or to imply that their countries are more developed because their people are innately superior, and that the responsibility for the economic backwardness of Africa lies in the generic backwardness of the race of black Africans." And yet Rodney mobilizes it to articulate a more offensive fact: "Today, our main preoccupation is with the differences in wealth between, on the one hand Europe and North America, and on the other hand Africa, Asia, and Latin America. In comparison with the first, the second group can be said to be backward or underdeveloped. At all times, therefore, one of the ideas behind underdevelopment is a comparative one."[76] The stigma attached to the term, with its devastating psychological effects, does not lead him to assume that it is simply a rhetorical dodge. In fact, for Rodney (as for W. E. B. Du Bois, Mulk Raj Anand, Luis Inácio Lula da Silva, and others), to dispense with the term "backwardness" would amount to euphemizing exploitation.[77]

A demurral in the face of the term "backward," in fact, contains risks all its own. In certain contexts, it can be taken as expressing a desire to preserve backwardness by refusing to name or oppose it. What is there left to do but, in the name of consistency, actively deride popular, indigenous movements on behalf of new states, civic freedoms, and economic development such as those in contemporary Venezuela, Bolivia, West Bengal, Nepal, and Chile? What can their strivings appear to be from this perspective except the results of malign Western influence? As Harry Harootunian points out in *History's Disquiet*, a "temporal lag" is not necessarily a "qualitative difference." His argument negotiates the two positions above, accounting for different senses of time and cultural conventions, stressing that modern cultures and economies in both the center and the periphery share a common reference point coercively provided by the colonial inheritance.[78]

It is more balanced to say that Hegel, at a time when it was much rarer to do so, sought an appreciation of difference, rather than that he imposed an unwavering European norm. "The Absolute," argued Hegel, is "world-historical." "Genius, talent, moral virtues, moral sentiments, and piety," he writes in the *Philosophy of History*, are found in "every region, under all constitutions, and in all political circumstances" (*LPH*, 140). That he at times shared the cultural disparagement and even racism of other thinkers of his era is undeniable. Spinoza, for his part, declared that "the Turks . . . consider even controversy impious, and so clog men's minds with dogmatic formulas, that they leave no room for sound reason, not even enough to doubt with" (*TPT*, 5). That the project of reformers such as Descartes, Hume, Kant, Hegel, and others was to fixate on reason in opposition to the primitive or "uncultured" mind is very true, although it is important to remember that they wanted to overcome the superstitions, blood privileges, and carnivalesque violence of a fading European autocracy in doing so. This does not excuse their extension of this principle to invidious comparisons between Europe and non-Europe, of course, although it makes such comparisons seem more the result of ignorance and insensitivity than the impudent logic of the conqueror. Still, given the ubiquity of these prejudices at the time, when comparatively assessing philosophical schools we are really forced to abandon illusions of purity and simply ask, with what resources, if any, has one or another legacy endowed the anticolonial project?

But it is important, finally, not to be merely defensive. Bernasconi's critique appeared originally in a volume titled *Hegel after Derrida*. Today's reputedly post-Hegelian environment is alive with challenges to the integrity of the subject, the viability of humanism, and the false and illusory presence of speech. As a philosophical matter, privilege is given to the written and to a peculiar, even imperious, authority, where theories of knowledge based on textuality want to place the critic in a position of political prominence. An anticolonial reckoning with these ideas is long overdue. Can it really be denied that these familiar tenets of deconstruction derive ultimately from the early clerical writings of the great monotheisms (Judaism, Christianity, Islam)—the people of the "book"— and find their initial authentication in the early Christian era among exegetes such as Philo of Alexandria, rabbinical scholars, and the early fathers of the church in the eastern Mediterranean, the very laboratory and testing ground of what later became Europe? How can we not recognize the devastating consequences for nonwestern cultural values that this sublimation of writing, together with the priority given to the written, the clerical, the rabbinical, and the hermeneutical (what Gramsci called the "bookish") over the oral and the vulgate, have had? After all, these forms effectively diminish popular nonliterary modes of artistic expression, literary realism, the vernacular, and directly didactic or educational cultural practices: in short, they undervalue the aesthetic core of the majority of work produced in the formerly and still colonized world.

DIALECTICAL OBLIVION

> It is true that stabilities are always provisional, and that they have critical moments. It is true that every structure collapses, or has the potential to do so. These considerations do not eliminate the very general and creative problem of stability and (relative) constants in the process of becoming.
>
> Henri Lefebvre[79]

Hegel's *Phenomenology* is the result of a dialogue—a term latent in the very name "dialectics" from Plato onward. Because of the encyclopedic sweep of Hegel's ponderous body of work, we forget how much of his writing—beginning with the *Phenomenology* itself—is a conversation, at times angry, with colleagues and rivals. I take this point to be crucial in the larger movement of the present book, which has as much to do with what Amanda Anderson calls "the way we argue now" as it does with making visible a philosophical tradition of modern intransigence against imperial culture.[80] We learn what Hegel believes by learning what he opposes. In the preface to the *Phenomenology*, he rejects what he identifies as the views then circulated by Friedrich Heinrich Jacobi (a famous contemporary commentator on Spinoza) as well as by Novalis, Schlegel, and others—all in the air and of his time, though he does not name them. His problem with these thinkers is that affect dominates their philosophies and that knowledge is made the vassal of intuition. Hegel's reservation concerning intuition is that it is "immediate knowledge of the Absolute," whereas he identifies his own mediated conception of knowledge to be "the opposite." Knowing for him can only be the result of analytical labor and self-questioning, wherein one watches one's own thinking as it gets around earlier misconceptions, placing itself in contact with an external ground (*PhS*, 4). Nor is he shy about ascribing a personality to what he opposes. He links it with a reactionary utopia longing for a time when one directed one's "gaze to the stars" and to the "lucidity ... of heavenly things" to find foolproof revelation, rejecting "ordinary affairs" and the experience of the "here and now" as unworthy enterprises (*PhS*, 5).

I would like to begin this part of the discussion of Hegel's thought-as-critique with this opposition—the *Phenomenology*'s inaugural gesture—and particularly the word "opposite," not only because it foreshadows perfectly the war of positions that now prevails in postwar theory but also because it becomes a decisive mode of anticolonial thinking of the early and mid-twentieth centuries. This antagonism that characterizes dialectics has aesthetic implications, and not merely rhetorical ones. It leads in the periphery to an art that not only recollects as realism Hegel's sensuous world of ordinary affairs and the here and now he alludes to but also finds aesthetic value in the polemical attitude itself.

Opposition as negation is also to be understood as an epistemological principle in Hegel, and not simply as a description of his arena of debate. His summary point in the *Phenomenology* is deceptively simple: that "truth has only the Notion as its element of existence." He is saying that after a process of conceptual confrontations with what we are trying to grasp, a form of thought (we could say, a certain stage of achieved thinking) contains truth and is inseparable from it. The conceptual architecture of what is called—and really is—truth for Hegel is the result of a sensuous encounter whereby the Notion (*Begriff*) adequates itself by painful stages of opposition to the inner necessity of otherness (*PhS*, 32). By negating our earlier, merely inward selves in a dynamic encounter with existent things, we are not simply applying concepts to objects from outside of them but, self-reflexively, coming to understand their reality by witnessing the work of our own.

My contentions about the centrality of antagonism in Hegel's thinking are offered in the context of two recent influential expressions of a general agreement about the nonoppositional character of Hegelian dialectics. In *Outside Ethics*, Raymond Geuss puts the position plainly:

> Hegel's general philosophical approach is an assimilative one. Instead of trying to refute and reject all other philosophers' views outright, he claims to supersede them by incorporating all of them as partial, subordinate components in his own system.[81]

The idea of enveloping all difference, subsuming it within one's own, now-altered perspective by grasping its inner truth, has a good deal of textual support in Hegel, as we will see shortly. It is therefore the note that Jameson reasonably strikes as well in his own ambitious attempt in *Valences of the Dialectic* to expand the meaning of dialectics so that it includes openly post- and even anti-Hegelian thinkers such as Jacques Derrida and Gilles Deleuze.[82] In this way, Jameson actually exhibits, through his own critical method rather than in the form of a declaration or quotation, the Hegelian ideal of encounter as Geuss, at least, conceives it.

The art of confronting positional differences is memorably described in *The Science of Logic*, where Hegel proclaims that "we must get over the distorted idea that system has to be represented as if thoroughly *false*, and as if the *true* system stood to the false as *only opposed* to it" (*SL*, 511). Here he parts company with the "one-sidedness" of what he calls "argumentative thinking" in the *Phenomenology*—thought that simply rejects what it opposes, a "negative insight" and "dead end," a "reflection into the empty 'I', the vanity of its own knowing" (*PhS*, 36). In determining whether another's philosophical system is true or false, Hegel continues, we cannot regard it as a mere opinion to be discarded, since it has developed itself into a totality that involves a form of speculation that, on its own grounds, is true. He would contend only that "it is not the highest standpoint." As a primer intended for students, and as a way of explaining plainly what he had said more poetically and with a great deal more difficulty in the *Phenomenology*, *The Science of Logic* repeats key arguments found in the early chapters of the earlier work.[83] Since this point is crucial to what follows in my argument, we need to look at some of them. In the preface to the *Phenomenology* his meaning could not be clearer:

> "True" and "False" belong among those determinate notions which are held to be inert and wholly separate essences, one here and one there, each standing fixed and isolated from the other, with which it has nothing in common. Against this view it must be maintained that truth is not a minted coin that can be given and pocketed ready-made. (*PhS*, 22)

My hesitation comes only gradually when dwelling on the phrase "against this view," which implicitly holds out for a choice between two possible positions. This seems at odds with the rest. But as he pursues the point later in the preface, he appears to return to a more incorporative gesture that obviates taking sides:

> That something is *not* the case, is a merely negative insight, a dead end which does not lead to a new content beyond itself. In order to have a content once again, something new must be taken over from elsewhere. Argumentation is reflection into the empty "I," the vanity of its own knowing. This vanity, however, expresses not only the vanity of this content, but also the futility of this insight itself; for this insight is the negative that fails to see the positive within itself. (*PhS*, 36)

But can one be opposed to the fixation on the negative isolated from its accompanying positive without falling into the "dead end" of a "merely negative insight"? Or to put this another way, how can one be for anything without situating oneself as being against others? The entirety of the *Phenomenology* might be said to work its way through this conundrum. A glimpse of the kind of answer Hegel provides in the form of a slow-motion emergence is found in the passages on perception. He is not prescribing a brand of thinking but rather seeking to capture in words how thought proceeds as such, even when it is unaware of doing so or when it insufficiently grasps the dialogical character of its own processes, settling too often for one-sidedness and what he calls "fixity." Just as important, he wants to push this descriptive element to its limits, showing that along these paths a more developed, realized mode of thought moves beyond simple sense-certainty and understanding. We should keep this in mind as he returns to the problem of opposition:

> Two contradictory extremes are not merely *alongside each other* but in a single unity, or in other words, the defining characteristic common to both, viz. "being-for-self," is burdened with opposition generally, i.e. it is at the same time *not* a "being-for-self." The sophistry of perception seeks to save these moments from their contradiction, and it seeks to lay hold on the truth, by distinguishing between the *aspects*, by sticking to the "Also" and to the "in so far," and finally, by distinguishing the "unessential" aspect from an "essence" opposed to it. (*PhS*, 77)

As so often in Hegel, though, the statement unfolds in a process, and so leaves suspended for our purposes whether he is for indecisionism or only for a more careful negotiation of contrary tendencies. We are unsure in this passage, read in isolation, whether he takes his stand with a momentary protest against the one-sidedness of mere perception and its impatient (and therefore false) sense that it has achieved an objective stance, or whether he is declaring that the finished process of dialectical negation is itself founded on the suspension of any resolution of opposition, which at this point is held together in a contradictory unity.

This dilemma underlies Jameson's remarkable effort in *Valences* to find a point of contact between Hegelian Marxism and contemporary theories of discourse and difference on the grounds that the quarrel between them (when it comes, say, to temporality or the idea of contradiction) is itself dialectical.[84] To "deconstruct each side," for him, is not to weaken the dialectic but to strengthen it, and to show, in fact, its realization in difference. The first step in his attempted negotiation (one might even say, reconciliation) is to grant freely what the anti-Hegelian philosophical schools of the postwar period have often claimed: namely, that theory is not philosophy—that all philosophy is (bad) "system" philosophy and that theory, by contrast, finds its mission in the anti-singularity of the perpetually open-ended and unresolved, thereby representing a different, though related, utopia from the one described by Hegel above.[85] For this reason, Jameson keeps invoking the third step, or synthesis, of what he observes is the popular misconception that Hegel advocated a three-part syllogism of thesis, antithesis, and synthesis. As Jameson expresses it: "To resolve [opposition] one way or another is the non-dialectical temptation. . . . The deconstruction of each side . . . ought to offer a perspective in which the problem becomes its own solution."[86]

Let us leave aside for the moment that theory derives its ideas from philosophers who found their own involvement in philosophy unproblematic. And let us look past the fact that Adorno (whose *Negative Dialectics* Jameson is in many ways emulating in *Valences*) wrote frequently about the necessity for philosophy in a technocratic age. None of the twentieth-century critical opponents of metaphysics would have understood, much less been sympathetic to, the assertion that "theory" is a new genre of critical thought.[87] By contrast, I speak of theory in its equivalence with philosophy, "theory" being from this vantage point distinctive only in the eclecticism of its scattered, often idiosyncratic borrowings from or recombinations of earlier philosophical positions now freed from their textual specificity and content. Nevertheless, the rapprochement between apparently hostile positions in Jameson's gesture exceeds issues of terminology and should at this point simply be noted.

Apart from Žižek, no active critic in the humanities demonstrates as much depth and originality as Jameson when reading Hegel. Several of the chapters in *Valences* (for example, "Hegel and Reification") and a much earlier essay from 1993, "Persistencies of the Dialectic: Three Sites," are brilliant and illuminating. Although the overall project of his career may be described as dialectical criticism or cognitive mapping—and as such suggests traditional literary criticism or intellectual history by arriving at its positions in the form of commentary on others' work—it would be a mistake to suppose that Jameson was not himself a philosopher of consequence. More successfully than either Sidney Hook, C. L. R. James, or Herbert Marcuse, Jameson has taught many American intellectuals—against all apparent hope—to think dialectically and has kept a Hegelian outlook alive in the era following the Frankfurt School without slavishly following their high philosophical style or hostility to popular culture.

I would like to confine my objections, then, to the first, long chapter of *Valences*, the part of that volume written (apparently) last, which may even signal a new direction. At any rate, I want to focus on this single point about opposition, together with its primary corollary in Jameson's rejection of the polemical intelligence, because it is the axis around which so much of what I am arguing here about the Vichian traditions of anticolonial thought revolves. It seems to me that a conflict of interpretations is at stake here, and not merely a matter of style, impulse, or tactical means where the aim of demonstrating the superiority of the dialectic means extending the intellectual territory over which it reigns. But this, in turn, involves his arguing not that its claims on the real or the good exceed those of deconstruction or of Deleuze's invention of modalities, but that they in fact precede them: that Hegel, as it were, was deconstructive and Deleuzian *avant la lettre*—a view that recalls Jameson's related strategy in *The Political Unconscious* of incorporating theory into Marxism by mobilizing the phrase "always historicize" after many pages that set out to demonstrate the basic indistinction between Althusserian Marxism and poststructuralism. As Jameson argues:

> [The dialectic] proceeds by standing outside a specific thought—that is to say a conceptual conclusion about a problem ... in order to show that the alleged conclusions in fact harbor the workings of unstable categorical oppositions.... The dialectic belongs to theory rather than philosophy: the latter is always haunted by the dream of some foolproof self-sufficient autonomous system, a set of interlocking concepts which are their own cause.... Theory, on the other hand, has no vested interests inasmuch as it never lays claim to an absolute system, a non-ideological formulation of itself and its "truths".... It has only the never-ending, never-finished task and vocation of undermining philosophy as such, of unraveling affirmative statements and propositions of all kinds. (*V*, 26, 59)

The difficulty—one might even say the thankless task—of such a reconciliation as a strategy of enfoldment lies in the points of fracture or dissonance that in an unwelcome way keep forcing their way into this carefully worded appearance of similarity between dialectical mobility and deconstructive remainder. To place "truths" in quotation marks (as here), for instance, would seem to be a nonstarter to those who had actually grasped the novel way in which Hegel defines truth. Hegel's objective idealism ingeniously posits a qualitative nuance of beings, each one of which has its own self-identity and distinct thought. To cancel itself out, to become a mere moment in a wider whole, requires not some imposition by thought on the object but contrivance by the content itself. Thinking for Hegel must immerse itself in its object's own development. The key move here is that the Understanding is an aspect not only of self-conscious subjectivity but also of existent being. As being, it has its own "qualitative nuance," its own distinction in quality—namely, the Understanding of existence (*nous*) or, when taken together, the Hegelian Idea. In other words, Mind is itself part of the reality it seeks willfully to grasp, which is what allows Hegel to supersede the Kantian antinomy of essence and appearance and to evade the subsumption of freedom by the merely material mind/body of Epicurus. This is what is involved in the subject's own dissolution by reference to another, for in that moment Understanding becomes Reason. This return by Jameson to the notion of suspended, or merely perspectival, "truth" is a departure not only from the text but from the feel of Hegel as well, and it provokes an initial skepticism about his reading. It was Hegel himself, after all, who emphatically denounced this position of the suspension of truth while driving a wedge between his own work and those who espoused it:

> This self-styled philosophy has expressly stated that *truth itself cannot be known* [*erkannt*], but that truth consists in what *wells up from each individual's heart, emotion, and enthusiasm*. . . . What has not been said in this connection to flatter the young in particular? (*PR*, 15)

The repeated moments of subtle reservations on Jameson's part toward the Derridean project (his disagreements with Deleuze and, above all, Foucault are even more evident) are a substantial part of his negotiation. His strategy is one of coaxing and deft ideological splicing in the name of theoretical flexibility. But his is also an attempted infiltration and encirclement worthy, in his eyes, of Hegel's own prismatic intelligence. Both, though, are overcome by the adulation that is the price of entry. For he cannot make headway by arguing that Hegel, against all odds, is friendly to theory; he must go further by saying that the early Hegel of the *Phenomenology* is theory before theory: "It remained for Derrida to propose a temporalization of this non- or antidialectic . . . a reincorporation of the dialectically inassimilable back into some new and enlarged dialectic as such" (*V*, 25). But if this "non" or "anti" is to become one with its prior unity, then "the elimination of opposition as such is not always desirable" (*V*, 21). Opposition in this case must rather be thought deconstructively, argues Jameson, as a productive "dissymmetry . . . to be preserved." Even these "arrested asymmetrical oppositions" can be thought of as dialectical, he suggests, because they "solicit a puzzlement which alternates between separation and conflation, between the analytic work of the negative and the temptation of synthesis" (*V*, 21). This, Jameson suggests, is how to finesse this almost chemical abreaction of two positions.

"Arrested"? A dialectics without movement? This would surely be an anti-Hegel designed to elude his requirement that Mind establish itself by way of a contrast in difference. The escape is effected, in this case, by Derrida's assertion of a "third way" that plays according to new rules and watches the real from the outside, as it were, as a supplement to the real, positing the nonbeing of what *is not* by way of a god that never actually arrives but whose coming is announced by the traces it leaves behind.

This engagement with Derrida by Jameson is more consequential than it might appear if we did not recognize the influence of the former on a number of circles relevant to my larger argument. Apart from being the philosophical inspiration of the most well-known postcolonial theorists (with the exception of Said), he is drawn on actively by Bernasconi and by contemporary posthumanism. Jameson's ingenious compromise, though, in order to seem plausible, must detach itself from the practices of Derridean thought in its unfolding. It seems much less tenable when we recall its characteristic moves. For the Derridean text, from *Of Grammatology* through *Monolingualism of the Other*, tries less to free prose from its evidentiary referent than to taunt that referent with the mimicry of correspondence (the pretense to meaning) that can then, when the prose reasserts itself as object, be revealed as a ruse. In this way, the versatility of the prose, the machinery of erudition, arises as its own ground. This is a mode of theorizing that means to run and dodge around any alterity that can be held as productive of the singularity that alterity, in opposition, creates. The philosophical claim of the Derridean text operates according to the model of appositional statement and restatement. Its writing is therefore an attempt to approach (asymptotically) the always fleeting third element, the spectral presence of the nonpresent, or at least to force the reader to submit to that which cannot be seen but which, by being surrounded and pitilessly pursued by phrases, slowly emerges as thing. The great triumph of Derrida's ontological lessons from Heidegger is that both have succeeded, while questioning Being, in inducing readers to write long books about nothing. It is, however, a very precise nothing described at some length by Heidegger in "What Is Metaphysics?" as the essential absence overlooked by the methods of the natural sciences (an Epicurean point, originally).[88] In effect, Derrida significantly re-introduces a static element into Hegel's post-

Kantian notion of the contradictory, doubling character of thought. In fact, while mimicking Hegel, Derrida transforms that thought into the inflexible features of a reading practice. He takes us to a mental space where one can always display proof of what is not because what is not, as lack, is. Any text is an authority for his positions, for it either will support them by embracing them or support them by contradicting them.

This desire to move past conflict is, of course, not a stylistic matter alone. It is rather a declaration of theory's political *immediacy* in the sense that theory is by these means presented as the practical world, the place where "possibility" presents itself in the form of previously unthought thoughts, new constellations of meanings, percipient exercises of insight. This prose of immediacy tends to generate protective force fields of countervalue to prevent co-optation, a circling, retreating motion. Within this protected but surrounded space, the theorist sees him- or herself departing sharply from the tenuously civic and ameliorative emphases of the liberal humanist. Rejecting liberalism for not going far enough, this mode of argument nevertheless shares a similar aesthetic value, expressed as an endless cycle of refutations in the form of revisions and appropriations. These, in turn, stand for the interpretive act, happily unresolved, displaying a pluralist sublime that enshrines the open-ended as its end and complexity as its primary aesthetic ideal. Not having a *telos* is its *telos*. Or, to put it another way, its *telos* is irresolution.[89] Derrida's position, then, can be stated thus: an opposition to opposition.

The "logic of the supplement" is certainly, as Jameson suggests, a version of dialectics, but *different*—in other words, self-alienated, indecisive, seeking a state of deferment as salvational irresolution.[90] With an urge for political effectivity belied by an active flight from traditional forms of political organization and action, theory is in this way confounded. Associating itself for reasons of political authenticity with the dissident mode of an originally Left Hegelian critique, theory nevertheless rejects that tradition's commitments to civic action and flees from most of the latter's political conclusions on principle, as well as from its attempts to systematize thinking. As a result, theory is compelled only to signify on that tradition, to achieve in form what dialectics achieved by the flight from mere form.

Despite having arrived at this place in the discussion, we have not reviewed how Hegel himself handles the problem of reconciliation. And this omission is perhaps the result of talking about dialectical thought in the static terms of "the dialectic"—which is not merely one of the ways Jameson says dialectical thinking has been wrongly cast (one of the "three names of the dialectic" he invokes in his opening chapter) but also his own way of casting it. It is hard, then, to concede the saliency of his distinction between "the dialectic," "a dialectics," and "dialectical thinking," since he reverts to using the concept he has earlier undermined. Why not in each case say "dialectical thinking," which is not simply his third instance and is certainly not always an accusation against lazy commonsense thinking? We would then have a term that more accurately evoked the manner in which thought compares itself to itself and to its other in the act of conceiving objects (in a dialogue with itself).

There is an inability here to escape the habit of treating dialectical thought as a thing—an item in the theory toolbox—that one can either deploy or not deploy according to one's taste or outlook. In Hegel, "dialectical" is rather a quality of thought as such: a phenomenology of mind. From the false starting point, Jameson then moves on to speak of the choices of deployment: the dialectic cannot be a "system," he argues, because the "self or subject is structurally disunified or dispersed," and it cannot be a "method" because this would lead to instrumentalization (V, 3–8).[91] Within this orbit, and only there, is it possible to take the Archimedean view, as Jameson does, that "the dialectic proceeds by standing outside a specific thought." In Hegel, however, the Subject thinks dialectically when it learns to see itself objectively inside the very process of thought. And only within Jameson's antisystem view can conceptual conclusions be said to "harbor the workings of unstable categorical oppositions" (V, 26), whereas for Hegel these would not be conclusions at all.

This emphasis on resisting the temptation to resolve dilemmas, encouraging us rather to leave them open-ended, which is forced on Jameson by the logic of his appeal to the common family of dialectics and theory, does not capture Hegel's words very well—or at least essential parts of them—and seems instead to set off for another encampment. In the *Philosophy of Right*, Hegel could not be clearer about distancing himself from the position that Jameson adopts:

> A will which resolves on nothing is not an actual will; the characterless man can never resolve on anything. The reason [*Grund*] for such indecision may also lie in an over-refined sensibility, which knows that, in determining something, it enters the realm of finitude, imposing a limit on itself and relinquishing infinity; yet it does not wish to renounce the totality which it intends. Such a disposition [*Gemüt*] is dead, even if its aspiration is to be beautiful. . . . Only by making resolutions can the human being enter actuality, however painful the

process may be (*PR*, 47).... [Or later] the opposite of determinacy—namely indeterminacy, indecision, or abstraction—is only the other, equally one-sided moment. (*PR*, 50)

It is likely, though, that Jameson would see this as the late, conservative Hegel, after the revolutionary spirit of the *Phenomenology* had dimmed, when the dialectic "paused too long, and became another ideology in its own right" (*V*, 27). The problem is that identical sentiments are found throughout the revolutionary *Phenomenology* as well:

> The scepticism which only ever sees pure nothingness in its result and abstracts from the fact that this nothingness is specifically the nothingness of that *from which it results* ... [wants to throw everything] into the same empty abyss.... But the *goal* is as necessarily fixed for knowledge as the serial progression; it is the point where knowledge no longer needs to go beyond itself, where knowledge finds itself, where Notion corresponds to object and object to Notion. (*PhS*, 50)

As though commenting on the theory that Jameson seeks to reconcile with dialectics, Hegel later remarks: "The sceptical self-consciousness thus experiences in the flux of all that would stand secure before it its own freedom as given and preserved by itself.... But it is just in this process that this consciousness, instead of being self-identical, is in fact nothing but a purely casual, confused medley, the dizziness of a perpetually self-engendered disorder" (*PhS*, 124–25).

More telling, the process of negation in Derrida is not conceived as an active process of Mind but as an evolutionary inevitability of powerless transformation into the very target of one's earlier critique. To suppose, for example, that the detective will not necessarily become a murderer, the feminist a misogynist, or the exposé journalist a corrupt politician is, by the logic of Jameson's argument, to be "undialectical." The very ground of taking a position is foreclosed, since it must become a mockery of its earlier self. But it is reductive, I would argue, to conflate the un-ironic with the empirically naïve, and less an epistemological than a rhetorical matter: a chosen mode of engagement that brings the sincere and the ingenuous into play as a means of empathy, and empathy in turn as a means of education and ethical action. What it comes down to at this juncture is that Hegel stood for straight sincerity. He worked hard to show, with philosophical precision, that to do so was not romantic—that a valid epistemology and politics stood behind the gesture.

POLEMICAL INTELLIGENCE

The moderation of genius does not consist in the use of a cultivated language without accent or dialect; it lies rather in speaking the accent of the matter and the dialect of its essence. It lies in forgetting about moderation and immoderation and getting to the core of things. The underlying moderation of the mind lies in reason, that universal liberality which is related to every nature *according to* its essential character.

Karl Marx[92]

Throughout Jameson's incorporative reading, we find the projects of theory outlined in the crevices of Hegel's system. Primarily this is expressed in Jameson's habit of seeing the dialectical moment as the holding-in-stasis of "two distinct dimensions" (46), but also in the anonymity he injects into the process by draining the subject of anything more than a spectatorial role. Theory, he avers, has instilled in us two, by now almost unconscious, lessons: the fear of semantic closure and the evasion of the subject. Not surprisingly, then, in the course of his presentation, "perspectives" (as he puts it)—ones that remain unattached to any particular author or person—are said to "demystify" each other by their very adjacency. They critique each other ideologically by their very presence in the space of the text, so that these two forces, having sapped each other's vigor, accomplish conceptualization only by achieving a stalemate, which is, in fact, the goal sought.

Forgotten here is the early emphasis of the *Phenomenology* that the Absolute "is a Subject," not only a substance (*PhS*, 10), and that Reason is not a set of strictures on thought but "purposive activity" (*PhS*, 12). By contrast, Jameson, acutely aware of the vernacular of theory and the fluency of the idiom his audience speaks, cannot reach it tactically in his attempt to contribute still more to the Hegel revival without borrowing its premises. He simply takes for granted that we all share theory's views of language, hermeneutics, the ethics of difference, and the end of the will-based Subject of the *Phenomenology*. The sublimity of the infinite, another of his tropes, surrounds Jameson's argument in order to ensure the indifferent equality of singularities, along with the habit of speaking about criticism as an autonomous activity of juxtaposed "codes": "To this proposition we can now add the imperative that the two codes must criticize each other, must systematically be translated back and forth into one another in a ceaseless alternation" (47). Here, however, he enters territory that, whatever its merits, has simply lost contact with the *Phenomenology*, neglecting, for instance, that book's attacks on the Skeptics, the Stoics, and Enlightenment rationalists: the Stoics, who "could only appear on the scene in a time of universal fear and bondage, but also a time of universal culture" (*PhS*, 121); the Skeptics, whose talk is "like the squabbling of self-willed children ... who by contradicting *themselves* buy for themselves the pleasure of continually contradicting *one other*" (*PhS*, 126); and the rationalists, who consider all faith merely "error and prejudice" (*PhS*, 333).

Hegel was a gifted polemicist when he wanted to be, adopting the confrontational style that Herder displayed when dismantling Condillac in his "Treatise on the Origin of Language" and that Vico, as we have seen, exhibited in his battles with Bossuet and Descartes.[93] Passages of Hegel's work are often emotional and at times even sarcastic. At such moments, the voicing of his comments seems almost contemporary. Hegel's remarks on classical Stoicism, for which he reserves barbs of Vichian force, outline positions on indeterminacy, irony, and fatalism that prophetically challenge, often in striking detail, similar attitudes in contemporary theory. Hegel's strategies of encounter, then, are in basic ways unlike the enfoldment-as-supersession described by Geuss. Not only here but in many places, he mocks his contemporaries in German romanticism: "The same old brew is reheated again and again and served to all and sundry" (*PR*, 11). There is in general a remarkable contrast between the vividness and health of debate in Hegel's time and our own. For today, disagreement itself is required by theory to cast itself as a deeper "synergy," as ultimately the same essential insight as its other, in the name of dialectical depth.

Polemical intelligence is not only rhetorical. It is a theory of understanding that stipulates as a contrast to itself the object of analysis to be overwhelmed and subsumed so that it might be internalized. What seems mere contrariness, and for that reason offensive, appears from this perspective rather as the foregrounding of one's own interested knowledge, now freely submitted to another's oppositions and, crucially, vice versa. It is the meeting of the other view on an open terrain, honestly. The standpoint of polemical intelligence rejects the discourse of negotiation as another version of the acclaimed doubling rhetoric of the positionless position explored above.

But without the conceptual requisite of antagonism, polemic has been seen as a critical indulgence, unbalanced and impetuous, and in this way dehistoricized—as though philosophers of the past who defined our current styles of argument were not polemicists in their time (Galileo, Freud, Foucault were all considered "polemical" in the positive and productive sense that I am here avowing). The epistemological stand of claiming that Hegel is against opposition is, among other things, a way of expressing one's distaste for polemic. By the same token, the rhetorical mode of polemic, now in disfavor, is expanded beyond its normal range of meaning to include anything that challenges the findings of theory on matters of language, subject, and will, as though disagreement on these issues was belated or simply contrariness.

But all of this is to forget the polemical moments throughout Hegel's writing—when he ridicules the "shallow-minded" Herr Friese in the preface to the *Philosophy of Right*, or the equally mocking tone he adopts toward an unnamed Schelling in the preface to the *Phenomenology*, or his blunt words in his early theological writings for the romantic Anglo-Saxonism of the Teutonic movement—a vitriol that looks forward to Bloch's satirical outbursts in the 1930s (which are very similar in tone and type) against the ecological fitness fanatics of the pre-Nazi youth movements. Even in more sober moments, there are sharp and emphatic denunciations: Skepticism is "sophistry" (*PhS*, 124); "As for hypocrisy this includes above all those religious hypocrites (or Tartuffes) who comply with all ceremonial requirements" (*PR*, 183); "[Romantic] irony was developed by Friedrich von Schlegel, and many others have babbled about it or are now babbling about it again" (*HA*, 66). To show the limitations of mere opposition, as he did, is not after all to forgo all opposition. He makes it clear that it is for him a crucial feature of the process of dialectical negation.

In his theological writings, looking to Luther, who summoned faith and feeling to express his rebellious spirit, Hegel says it is time now, in late modernity, to reclaim that sort of passion for the concept, though without giving space to mere lukewarm testimonials. Whatever is "neither cold nor hot" (that is, middle-of-the-road, temporizing), Reason "spews out of its mouth," (*PR*, 22). In the *Philosophy of Right*, only a page after the much-misunderstood line on the rationality of the real, he writes that Reason is "the rose in the cross of the present" (*PR*, 22)—that is, the bright side of depressing actuality and the polemical means of transforming religious symbols of torment into political regeneration. His position and language, in other words, are radical vestiges of the more emotive and condemnatory style of the *Philosophy of Right*'s earlier drafts before they were toned down under the censorship that prevailed during the Restoration that followed the death of Frederick II, who had presided over a more tolerant intellectual landscape.

To conceive of dialectics as itself dialectical—which is Jameson's central trope—is in the end a confusion of categories. Its apparently inescapable consistency obscures a slippage among the phases of the process of negation, which has, again, been de-subjectivized so "*the* dialectic" (a thing) can be spoken of as though it possessed a *property*: the dialectical. But this is never how Hegel conceives of dialectical thinking. For to say that dialectics is dialectical (in the spirit of Jameson's argument) is to say that dialectics can only remain true by consuming itself. No method, then, could from this perspective ever stand for itself, ever content itself with the characteristics that distinguish it. It would have to demonstrate its reality by becoming every other method in an undifferentiated unity, dissolving itself into what Hegel derisively calls throughout the *Phenomenology* "self-identity." That, however, is what Hegel considered a "monochromatic formalism which only arrives at the differentiation of its material since this has been already provided and is by now familiar" (*PhS*, 9).

The introductory essay of *Valences* itself, to this degree, is troubled by the same strategy of equivalence: deconstruction simply is dialectics; the return to the Bergsonian *durée* and to *élan vital* in Deleuze is nothing but a more contemporary form of dialectical thought. Even Adorno, with his great antisystem critique in *Negative Dialectics*, would never have thought to demonstrate the power of Hegel by seeing the debates of his age as a mutually enlightening oscillation between complementary extremes. On the contrary, the entire first part of Adorno's study—over thirty pages long—is an extended polemic against the stagnant pseudorealism of Heidegger's dispiriting ontology. In this pursuit, Adorno repeatedly attacks all conceptual efforts at self-identity, showing their inadequacy when confronted by contradiction. Only by opposing opposition—that is, only by denying the law of contradiction (in Robert Pippin's judgment), does theory believe it escapes teleologism.[94] The theory that Jameson counterposes to system philosophy, it seems, demands that everything be dialectical (in the improvised, non-Hegelian sense of self-defeating) except, of course, the tyrannical starting point of theory that no system philosophy be permitted in advance and no success trusted unless it is at the same time, and equally, a failure. This is dialectical oblivion.

In contrast to Jameson's philosophy/theory binary, the Vichian tradition tends to link system thinking not with a normative deficiency but with intellectual generalism. Outside theory's ominous tones, we recall nothing so much as Vico's celebrated "unitive method" (*NS*, 167). His techniques are those of montage, encyclopedia, circling around, repetition, cumulative force, and above all (after Bacon's *Novum Organum*) "uniting particulars to obtain universals." Hegel's philosophy, as Lukács points out, is a mixture of economics, political reflection, historical prediction, and speculative descriptions of how subjects think—not the first but the most systematic attempt to bring diverse intellectual inquiries together in a structured whole. "System" for theory, of course, implies an exclusionary imposition of brittle form onto an aleatory plenitude. This ethical or normative demur, though, decontextualizes Hegel. His statement that "knowledge is only actual, and can only be expounded, as Science or as *system*" (*PhS*, 13), means only that for argument to develop, it must grow in each step out of the ideas established in an earlier phase, holding that earlier finding before it as a remainder, staying faithful to it throughout. What matters is the internal consistency of the movement, where each part contains the whole and forever returns to itself. This is precisely what Vico refers to when he uses the word "philological."

On the one hand against the impatience of merely argumentative thinking, Hegel is on the other hand for opposition, which demands that we immerse ourselves in the content of thought while developing it in dialogue with the world and other, differing subjects. These distinctions are not considered by *Valences*, where the essential guilt of system thinking is taken for granted as the common knowledge of theory. Stressed instead are the claims of the inaugural antisystem polemicist for whom, according to Jameson, "the ideal of the philosophical system has been seriously called into question" (3). It is Nietzsche who forever destroyed the "unassailability of philosophy" (as distinct from theory) (5).

But it would seem important here actually to demonstrate that Nietzsche is not a system thinker. This too cannot just be assumed. After all, he reminds his readers in *On the Genealogy of Morals* (1887) that his themes are already found in the "collection of aphorisms" of a much earlier book (*Human, All-Too-Human*, 1878). Comparing the two, and remarking on his trajectory over the previous decade, he insists that nothing has changed: he "still cling[s] to them even now":

> They must have been originally neither separate disconnected capricious nor sporadic phenomena, but have sprung from a common root . . . that ever grew more definite in its voice, and more definite in its demands. . . . With the necessity with which a tree bears its fruit, so do our thoughts, our values, our Yes's and No's and If's and Whether's, grow connected and interrelated, mutual witness of *one* will, *one* health, *one* kingdom, *one* sun.[95]

He lays out with astonishing brevity the themes that make up his system in a letter to Franz Overbeck in 1881, where he concedes that he is not unique, that his philosophical parentage is found in the great systematizer, Spinoza:

"[Like me] he [Spinoza] denies free will, purposes, the moral world order, the nonegoistical, evil" (*SLN*, 177).[96] Although famous for his broadsides against philosophy and philosophers, he does not always undermine philosophy's cohesive strategies in pursuit of what he is not ashamed to call, from time to time, the "real."

Repetition, granted, is not necessarily system thinking. But we have to take note here of how emphatic Nietzsche is that his entire philosophy revolves around a single, universal principle: "life." It is actually not the case that he always stresses fragmentary or spontaneously invented truths; just as often he insists on the interconnectedness and organic totality of the truth he seeks to invent: "We have no right to *isolated* acts of any kind: we may not make isolated errors or hit upon isolated truths."[97] The corollaries of this proposition, though obviously not expressed by Nietzsche in the form of an ordered, logical treatise or in syllogistic form, are extraordinarily consistent from book to book. I will explore the consequences of this more fully in the next chapter.

MARX, HEGEL, AND BACKWARDNESS

> And just like the rest of Continental Western Europe, we suffer not only from the development of capitalist production, but also from the incompleteness of that development.... We suffer not only from the living, but from the dead.
>
> Karl Marx[98]

Apart from the *Philosophy of Right*'s innovative treatment of the state as the only political structure that allows freedom to defend itself, the book's greatest contribution to anticolonial thought, as I have been saying, lies in what it made possible in the work of others.[99] Some of the explosive anticolonial implications of the *Communist Manifesto*, *Capital*, and the *Grundrisse* were taken up both within and outside Europe by those who worked in anti-imperial movements—especially in the first decades of the twentieth century. Many of these ideas, I would argue, are already found in gestation in Marx's critique of the *Philosophy of Right*—the only one of Hegel's works that Marx explores at length. They include startling observations whose significance became obvious only when Marxism began to preside over states and to make policies, particularly in the periphery. Among the original ideas, now commonplace, that can be found inchoate in Hegel and in Marx's reading of Hegel are the problems of new taste markets in the colonies, the intentional underdevelopment of peripheral economies, the idea that wage slavery is linked to racial slavery, the cosmopolitan character of world literature, and the war between country and city.

Marx foregrounds the importance of the *Philosophy of Right* to his philosophical formation: "The first work which I undertook to dispel the doubts assailing me was a critical re-examination of the Hegelian philosophy of law; the introduction to this work being published in the *Deutsch-Französische Jahrbücher* issued in Paris in 1844."[100] The "doubts" he refers to are about what he took to be the "dilettantism" of the philosophically weak versions of French socialism and communism then circulating. As Marx expresses it, in other words, it is by way of working through this book that he first came to understand that "political forms" are rooted "in the material conditions of life"—a view he counterposes to what he takes (wrongly) to be Hegel's position, which supposedly roots them in the "general development of the human mind."[101] In a letter to R. Kreuznach the year before, however, in outlining his position, he can do little more than summarize Hegel's arguments that the political state is a kind of inventory of all the struggles of mankind, its truths and needs and hopes, all expressed in a partial, usually failed fragment of a passing dream. But its various trials and momentary successes and failures nevertheless chronicle the reason that exists within it, although "not always in a reasonable form."[102] This was, of course, exactly Hegel's original point.

Without appreciating it, Marx was inspired by the chain of ideas and associations in the political-ethical realm of the *Philosophy of Right* that regarded Europe as stamped by its colonies and as negatively affected by this exploitative relationship. In his response, European expansion abroad is for the first time seen in some detail as being intertwined with European underdevelopment at home. This aspect of mutual entanglement and shared destiny permeates the writings of both Hegel and Marx and helps define their thinking. Lukács had earlier alluded to this "unequal development in the field of ideology" in his *Goethe und seine Zeit* (1947):

> It was precisely the fact that [in Germany] the foundations and consequences of certain theoretical and literary questions were not immediately clear that gave the spirit, the concepts, and the representations a wide margin of freedom that seemed practically limitless: at the time, this freedom remained unknown to the more developed Western societies.[103]

That is to say, Germany's sociopolitical backwardness in the eighteenth and nineteenth centuries was inversely related to its innovations in philosophy. This inversion was seen by both Hegel and Marx as mutually constitutive, and this sense of the perceptual advantages of unevenness is one that Roberto Schwarz has forcefully explored in recent writing on the literature of colonial Brazil—the development, that is, of a conceptual trope found in the Marxism of a much earlier period.[104]

By way of Marx's readings of Hegel, anticolonial sentiments are given a basis that is neither immediately linked to movements fighting for political independence in the colonies themselves nor, in Europe, focused on colonialism as a moral taint or self-defeating economic strategy of short-sighted, one-sided enrichment. Instead colonialism is seen as the global expression of the same destructive market logic that prevailed domestically.[105] The practical emphasis of the *Philosophy of Right* binds dialectical abstractions of thought in movement to a pragmatic theodicy of everyday government and economic affairs. In Hegel, one can begin to see affiliations between the impulse to self-realization as a species form and political independence as a social need—that is, between the alien and the alienation of labor. Not every critique of the market is anticolonial, of course; but Hegel's explicitly was.

In his introduction to the *Critique of Hegel's Philosophy of Right* (1843), Marx dwells on the belatedness of Germany in a form that prefigures the language of uneven and combined development in Leon Trotsky before and after World War I. His focus would express itself again in the repeated return within Marxist theory to the problem of the country and the city—notably in Gramsci's analysis of the "supercity-supercountry" motif in Italian historiography; in Henri Lefebvre's series of sociologies, first urban then rural (a project that extended over decades); and in Raymond Williams's classic literary sociology, *The Country and the City*, which was a major influence on *Orientalism* as Said reports it. It is in Marx's Hegelian critique of Hegel that the relationships among the state, colonialism, and underdevelopment are further clarified and begin to find a mode of articulation that would be widely followed in later decades. Marx's emphases in the introduction may be puzzling to readers who do not appreciate his critique's rootedness in the Hegelian contexts that I have been tracing; it would not at first be clear to them why Hegel's study of the universal basis for politics and law might generate in Marx reflections on a specifically German intellectual stasis.

Without going into a lengthy excursus, let me respond by suggesting some possibilities in Marx's condensed, paratactical, and highly figurative introduction. His argument is that because Germany is still in the grip of the stale and superseded political culture of the ancien régime, it has not yet caught up with the advances of England and France and lives largely off the crumbs of their economic and political futurisms: "For we shared the restorations of the modern nations although we had not shared their revolutions."[106] The dismal pressures this exerts on intellectual life are profound and illustrate a particularly depressing situation of intellectual complicity with the state. German criticism, such as it is, is restricted to impotent indignation and denunciation. A meeting of "uneasy consciences" with "brutal mediocrity" had been the result, which meant that "the struggle against the German political present is the struggle against the past of the modern nations" (*CHPR*, 178). He goes so far as to identify the new "barbarism" of capitalist Germany with the barbarism of Old Testament law, which he then grafts onto an image of an emergent capitalism: "the monstrous image of an egoistic individual engaged in the satisfaction of his own material wants."[107]

Essentially, Marx goes on to say that this profound feeling of belatedness has moved German dissident intellectuals to seek a specifically national-cultural (German) contribution to modernity. They seek to identify what Germany may be perceived to do better than England and France on behalf of the contemporary and the forward looking. This avant-gardism in thought is the rear-guardism of the historically belated, and, he concludes, it is the role specifically played by philosophy: "As the ancient peoples went through their pre-history in imagination, in *mythology*, so we Germans have gone through our post-history in thought, in *philosophy*. . . . German philosophy is the *ideal prolongation* of German history" (*CHPR*, 180). Although some of Marx's misreadings of Hegel have been discussed by others, the anticolonial impulse embedded in his reading has been overlooked, as has the reliance of his reading on Hegel's own system. Marx understands the *Philosophy of Right*'s brilliant contemporary undercurrents, including its world-historical dimensions: "The relation of industry, of the world of wealth generally, to the political world is one of the major problems of modern times. . . . People are therefore beginning in Germany to acknowledge the sovereignty of monopoly within the country by lending it *sovereignty abroad*" (*CHPR*, 179). But in Marx's view, Hegel does not quite escape the tendency to apotheosize criticism in Germany—a national defect forced upon it by conditions that prevent its claim to equality in the realm of industry, literature, or architecture. To him, Hegel appears to benefit too directly from the illusions fostered by Germany's major export, philosophy: "Germany was [the] *theoretical consciousness* [of modern nations]. The abstraction and conceit of its thought always kept in step with the one-sidedness and stumpiness of its reality" (*CHPR*, 181). Hegel is therefore allied in Marx's mind with the "real abstraction"—that is, the process of making the Subject abstract—embodied in the German state. But Marx misses, I think, that it is his mentor who had already made Marx's own, supposedly clinching point: "*you cannot supersede philosophy without making it a reality*" (*CHPR*, 181).

The Communist Manifesto's brilliant and often-observed descriptions of capitalism as inherently imperialist ("the discovery of America, the rounding of the Cape . . . ") are a continuation of his observations in the earlier engagement with Hegel's political theory, where he describes the inextricable mutuality of the colonies and Europe.[108] As Marx analyzes it, capitalism is from the beginning global in its aspirations and contacts. Colonialism, similarly, is by nature intrinsic to capitalist development rather than simply a stage of it. As such, he portrays the wealth of Europe as founded not only on the labor, raw materials, cultural practices, economic techniques, and aesthetic ideas stolen from abroad but on what that process of plunder inspired and even made necessary *at home*. These included a revolution in the modes of production and the organization of society into new institutions to reflect the new constituencies, a combination of technical progress and social retardation. And it meant, as well, an enormous importation from the colonies of new ideas, practical techniques, intellectual perspectives, and cultural innovations.

Seeing Hegel as the negation of anticolonial thought (as postcolonial studies does, for instance) has as its counterpart seeing Marxism as an anti-Hegelian project. If in some contemporary versions of the latter, Marx is seen as a Spinozist, in others he is seen as a Kantian.[109] But this move, too, in a pattern we now recognize, has interwar echoes. Lukács's 1938 study on Hegel, for instance, was composed in part to offset the claims of scholars such as Herman Nohl, Georg Lasson, and Johannes Hoffmeister, all of whom had published accessible editions of Hegel's early and, at the time, unknown writings. But Lukács resisted their framing of Hegel and wrote in part to counter what he took to be their tendentiousness.[110]

It is, though, Alexandre Kojève's famous reading of Hegel, of course, that brings us most directly to the meaning of the conflict over Hegel in current theory.[111] Kojève's *Introduction to the Reading of Hegel* (1947) not only set the tone for all of postwar theory's improvisational Hegel (which is known), but inadvertently chronicles the anticolonial setting of the *Introduction*'s quasi-Hegelian motifs (which is much less well known).[112] The book concludes with somber allusions in its closing passages to colonial revolution and, in that context, to the United States, Japan, and the "Orient." On the basis of the traumas of the war and this postwar sea change in the periphery, Kojève predicts there that our historical destiny is to reach a stage where the boundaries between the human and natural worlds are erased. At that point a final social harmony—displacing communism but not in his view contradicting it—will emerge: the end of that "negativity" that separates humanity from its natural, animal self. Death is "dialectical" in the sense that, like freedom, it is a mere appearance that entails its other and is enhanced by its presence. One finds freedom in death, and death and freedom are but two ('phenomenological') aspects of one and the same thing."[113] In a long footnote, he clarifies what it is about the postwar setting that impels this turn to the essential mortality of nature:

> The two world wars with their retinue of large and small revolutions had only the effect of bringing the backward civilizations of the peripheral provinces into line with the most advanced (real or virtual) European historical positions. If the sovietization of Russia and the communization of China are anything more than or different from the democratization of imperial Germany (by way of Hitlerism) or the accession of Togoland to independence, nay the self-determination of the Papuans, it is only because the Sino-Soviet actualization of Robespierrian Bonapartism obliges post-Napoleonic Europe to speed up the elimination of the numerous more or less anachronistic sequels to its pre-revolutionary past.[114]

Leaving aside the fact that his invocation of the human-animal awkwardly, and even embarrassingly, summons memories of earlier European discourses about the savagery and bestiality of colonized peoples, Kojève's position here is disturbing for other reasons as well. He considers Nazism a form of democratization, considers revolutions in Russia and China reactionary "Robespierrian Bonapartisms," snidely dismisses the independence struggles of small countries, and relieves the Western powers of any guilt in their response to these challenges ("obliges"). The entire comment is steeped in a progressivist narrative about the reprehensible backwardness of the third world and the need for the West to eliminate anachronisms. It is a classically Cold War discourse that, as we have seen, is at odds with the spirit and letter of Hegel's undertaking.

What I would foreground here, though, is the image of *reading* central to Kojève's improvisation, one underlined in the very title of his famous lectures. Kojève's exploration of the "Being" of the human-animal, he makes clear, is predicated on a theory of "discourse"—or as he rather clumsily puts it, "thought or discourse."[115] For Hegel, of course, thought is not coincident with discourse as language (as Kojève misunderstands it) but arises out of the process of a dialogue of objects who become subjects. It is true, however, that although Hegel's investigation of language per se is understated in the *Phenomenology*, on the few occasions when he turns his attention to the problem, he expresses himself in ways that seem at first to support Kojève's phenomenological reading: "In [language]," writes Hegel, "we ourselves directly refute what we *mean* to say" (*PhS*, 60). Indeed, Jameson picks up on this aspect of Hegel's thought as support for his position that Hegel treats language as little more than "an index of error or contradiction" and that this outlook marks his kinship with later literary modernism.[116] But as I said earlier, this is rather Spinoza's (and Hobbes's) position—distrusting the truth content of language aided by literary figures. There is not enough space here to explore in sufficient detail Hegel's aesthetic hostility to saying what one does not mean (as irony or interiority)—which would later be so central to modernism—but there are multiple other reasons for rejecting Kojève's view, and doing so allows us once more, from another angle, to see the Vichian character of Hegel's thought and its relevance to the thought and art of the non-European world. For Hegel's entire "Preface" to the *Phenomenology* sets out to demonstrate the truth uniquely available to the *form* of philosophical writing he creates.

Hegel's statement above implies only that thought is not discourse, since he believes (unlike Herder) that thinking can take place without language. This is not the only place where Hegel's strangely understudied theory of language is in conflict with Kojèvian "discourse." The point is vital. For in Hegel's *First Philosophy of Spirit* (1803/4)—which is all the more interesting for being written in a more awkward, rough, and for that reason, transparent way—he lays out what can only be called a populist linguistics quite at odds with literary modernism and many contemporary trends in literary theory. Vividly revealed there are hints of what was on his mind as he began to map out the *Phenomenology*. His emphases in this draft resemble closely what will become self-defining for interwar Marxism's Vichian currents: the prioritizing of speech, the social scene of the utterance, and language as a meaning-act connecting individuals in the social ensemble:

> Speech *only is as the speech of a people*, and *understanding and Reason* likewise. Only as the work of a people is *speech* the ideal *existence of the spirit*, in which it expresses what it is in its essence and its being; speech is a universal [mode of expression], recognized in itself, and resounding in the same way in the con-

sciousness of all; every speaking consciousness comes immediately to be another consciousness in it. (*FPS*, 244)

If speech is evanescent, melting into "the aether" (as he puts it) at the very moment it is coaxed into existence, it is nevertheless sounded into life by sensuous bodies filling the air with tones. Here he repeats a theme found widely in Herder: "The vowel distinguishes itself because the organ of voice indicates its articulation as an organ [of conscious spirit] in its distinctions" (*FPS*, 222). This tactile, physical evocation of speech as an utterance in space, by persons who feel things and who urgently wish to communicate, is very far from the disembodied futurism of Kojèvian discourse (and, of course, its philosophical descendants in Althusserian structuralism and deconstruction).

Hegel's strategy of conceptualizing the human was, I have been arguing, unique. Despite first appearances, his depiction of what it meant to be a person was devoid of moralizing or religious transcendence; its colloquial idealism grounded itself in the self-circular, willful act of subject making. It is difficult to see at first why he, rather than Kojève, arouses critical suspicions of ethnocentrism, given the bluntness of the latter's views. But it is not just the question of a footnote; it is the direction of the entire "reading" that should make us pull back. In Kojève, after all, we are no longer simply talking about a coercive European universalism but the ability to imagine humans at all. It would be more logical to see Kojève's writings on Hegel as themselves a new universalism—a global negation of the self, which while displacing an unwelcome hierarchical ordering of human types, also eliminates every distinction among ideas, positions, beliefs, or situations. Nature emerges as the ultimate quietism. When sensing the coming displacement of Europe, theory reclaims its supremacy in an act of prophetic suicide by obliterating the human altogether. Hegel offers one kind of response to these non-options—an intellectual portrait of the one power that can resist global inequality and ecological catastrophe: the subject as agent, the human.

"Barbares," František Kupka (1906)

3 NIETZSCHE AND THE COLONIES

> The philosopher who is in some sense [Hegel's] antipode, Nietzsche.
> *Raymond Geuss*[1]

CLASSICS AND CLASS WAR: VICO AND NIETZSCHE

> It is another vulgar tradition that those were created the
> first kings who were the worthiest by nature.
> *Vico*, The New Science

> Just the "good man" of the other morality, just the aristocrat,
> the powerful one, the one who rules.
> *Nietzsche*, The Genealogy of Morals

Nietzsche became famous at the very moment that European colonialism reached its apogee. With a few exceptions, all of his books were written between the time that Germany entered the race for colonies in earnest in 1871 (roughly the start of his public career) and the holding of the Berlin Conference in 1884, only a few years before he collapsed in a public square in Milan to begin a decade-long physical decline that led to his death by 1900. And yet, his complicated response to the debates over European colonialism that raged in Germany throughout his *anni mirabili* rarely find their way into appreciations of his work. These questions, all the same, reverberate throughout the body of his signature concepts. His impact on those who took up his ideas in the first decades of the twentieth century, when revolts on the periphery were making the colonial question more obvious and urgent, is still being felt.

In the vast literature on European colonialism, race, and postcolonial emergence, he has usually been seen as the scourge of Europe, bitterly and eloquently protesting its poses and arrogance. But this widespread view, for which there is, after all, considerable evidence, looks very different if we consider Nietzsche's formation as a classical scholar—as a student at Pforta and Leipzig, later as a philologist and professor at Basel. A number of authors are aware of these beginnings, of course, and make note of them, but few attempts have been made to work out their implications.[2] Although it may seem a non sequitur at first, my view is that this apprenticeship shaped his later views on colonialism and cultural otherness in ways that cast this familiar reading of Nietzsche in doubt.

This philological training—and indeed, all the methodological and terminological trappings of philology—remained with him throughout his career. It was present not only by way of his investments in certain classical literary figureheads—his polemics against Plato, say; his self-confessed stylistic debts to Sallust; his affection for Heraclitus; his famous portrait of the Dionysian—but in his proposals for how to *read* genealogically, which may be the deepest of his influences today. Nietzsche's particular spin on the problem of origins, his attempt at offering a new theory of historical memory and recurrence, his doctrine of truth as a matter of will and utility rather than worldly correspondence—all of these classical lines of inquiry amount to the very intellectual environment of his thought: but antagonistically, that is, counterphilologically.

Nietzsche, in effect, struggles against philology, but is so immersed in its language and premises that his rejection is often hard to distinguish from approval. His rhetorical genius—the *aere perennis* of his style, as he puts it—became, as it were, his philosophy; in his mind the two were the same. His reproach of opponents, such as David Friedrich Strauss in *Untimely Meditations*, reminds us that for him, to revile an adversary's ideology is the same as disliking his or her style.[3] We could, in fact, simply set aside his views on the non-Western world, Bismarck's imperial policies, and so on when assessing his views on colonialism, since the matter of style is itself directly related to colonial discourse. That relationship is most apparent where the oriental texts of antiquity come to signify for him the colonial conflicts of his day—in, for example, his admiration for the Bible's populism; his embrace of the demand of the *Laws of Manu* to "name your enemies," as well as his concession that the Greeks stole writing from the Phoenicians—that they were a derivative, adaptive race like the Germans—and that this belatedness and mimicry made both stronger. Each of these was, on occasion, summoned by him in the context of his comments on contemporary political events.

The literariness of Nietzsche's philosophy, in other words, is itself philological. He carries on, by way of a confrontation with Hegel's thought, an ongoing relationship with Vico. The careers and personalities of the two thinkers were, of course, very different. Nietzsche was an award-winning essayist, a highly rewarded academic at a young age, who retired early, spending his creative life writing in southern European tourist destinations. He became a best-selling author while still living. In contrast, Vico slogged through the composition of fawning volumes on the exploits of aristocrats who paid him to praise them, was passed over for a decent academic job, and wrote his masterwork while toiling as a humble teacher of rhetoric in relative obscurity.

Not surprisingly, as philologists Nietzsche and Vico shared obsessions: both sought to refine their styles by drawing on models from Latin rhetoric; both propounded theories of cyclical history; both took up the cudgel for their disciplines, writing inaugural lectures on the crisis of humanistic education; and both displayed a passion for origins in the etymological sense of *birth*—a point whose biological connotations will become important for the discussion below. Nietzsche, moreover, followed Vico's innovation by thinking of Homer not as a single person but a collection of Greek authors, although he did not cite Vico on the issue. In fact, he rejected Vico's principal point that Homer was not simply a man of the people but the Greek people. Nietzsche avers rather that the idea of popular poetry was a "dangerous assumption" and that the worst superstition of "philological science" was this "soul of the people" (*WFN*, 3:159, 147). He remarks on the next page: "The masses have never experienced more flattering treatment than in thus having the laurel of genius set upon their empty heads." It is precisely in these points of indirect contact that their antipodal attitudes toward empire are revealed. The symmetrical disparities between them are expressed in Nietzsche's more or less systematic revision of classic Vichian themes on the demotic, the primitive, the barbaric, and the modern. These departures, I am arguing, helped set a tone and provided a specific language that was taken up in later colonial discourse.

For both Vico and Nietzsche, to understand the essence of a thing is to know its beginnings. Origins tormented the mythologies of antiquity, offering a terrifying glimpse into the nature of human beings at the dawn of language and before recorded history. This dark phase when humans wandered in the woods, preying and being preyed upon, is the stuff of intense interest to both authors. In *The Birth of Tragedy*, Nietzsche paints a memorable portrait of naked, chanting dévotés raising their voices in song before a bonfire in the depths of the woods. This was his image of an original unity—the *Ur-Eine*. On his part, Vico depicts a very different scene: freely defecating, copulating brutes living in misery without fear or shame, lacking any sense of time or obligation. The heroic age that brings this long stretch of unrecorded time to resolution is characterized by both as barbarism, although with a different ethical valence.

Nietzsche disowned the ideal Greece of Johann Winckelmann, composed of beauty, balance, and light, in favor of the *real* Greece prior to the age of Athenian tragedy, which was clever, savage, and versatile.[4] For the Homeric nobility, no superlatives in Nietzsche are strong enough: "The happiest people, in the happiest period of its existence, in the highest activity of fantasy and formative power. . . . The unutterable simplicity and noble dignity of the Hellene" (*WFN*, 3:156). Two centuries before, however, Vico had gone somewhat further. He questioned not simply the idolization of Greek classicism and Roman order but the myth that in Greece and Rome one found the origins of a "West" to be emulated. "Roman history," he observes, "will puzzle any intelligent reader who tries to find in it any evidence of Roman virtue where there was so much arrogance, or of moderation in the midst of such avarice, or of justice or mercy where so much inequality and cruelty prevailed" (*NS*, 254). The fascination Nietzsche had for the intrepid disrule of prehistoric times is cast by Vico in much less alluring colors: "Luxury, refinement, and ease were quite unknown" (*NS*, 255); "boorish, crude, harsh, wild, proud, difficult, and obstinate in their resolves" (*NS*, 267).[5] Given his thesis of humanity's multiple origins, Vico views Greece as a conduit rather than an innovator (*NS*, 279), although it was the decisive link that brought Europe into contact with everything it comes to know later about the gentile world. Nietzsche agrees.[6] Still, Greece comes off in Vico's account as an exalted record keeper rather than, as in Nietzsche, the wily adapter that invents the sort of wisdom that Germans later manifest.

In Vico and Nietzsche, then, there is a politics of the literary that is more wide ranging and form driven than what is usually meant by "literary politics." Inasmuch as the two thinkers are in dialogue, they mark a deep division within contemporary theory, for instance, over the uses of etymology. When one recalls how central etymologies are to the Nietzschean methods of Martin Heidegger, Hannah Arendt, and Giorgio Agamben, or on the other side, to the Vichian techniques of Antonio Gramsci, Edward Said, and Martin Bernal, this division—which has been relatively neglected—appears immensely important. In Nietzsche's celebrated treatment of the origins of the terms "good" and "bad" in the opening sections of *The Genealogy of Morals*, there are crucial differences from Vico's practice. *Schlecht* (bad) for *schlicht* (plebeian), *gut* (godlike) for the noble Goths, and his other examples from Latin and Greek are meant to show the validity of an original judgment embedded in language. They stand as documentation of discovered character. Here the archaeological decoding of archaic words has nothing like the aura of distant contact with an outmoded ethos. Rather, it is like a fossil in language mapping a deviation from an earlier and preferable norm.

Arendt, Heidegger and Agamben follow Nietzsche to the extent that they see in antiquity the ideological kernel of unfolding political forces in the present fully embodied in the Greek and Latin textual mind. Here the gesture is to the careful archaeological act of sifting through the sedimentary layers of semantic subtleties in ancient languages in the name of shedding modern scales from our eyes. It is about recovering the lost clarity and resolve of an age when philosophy and simplicity were one with balance and station. The future one desires to effect is expressed as a past passively found, posed in the neutral terms of a buried archaeological treasure and a specialist hermeneutics.[7]

In Vico, etymology is, by contrast, a different kind of decipherment entirely: "words are carried over from bodies and from the properties of bodies to signify the institutions of the mind and spirit" (*NS*, 78). By providing a record of earlier, now alien meanings, etymology charts latent meanings and missed connotations, not to refer the present to the past but as a sign of the long road traveled. Words are always utterances (written, of course, but reanimated in their original spoken form) devised for particular purposes in specific encounters. There is no longer sanctity to the dead languages. They are only a way to reconstruct a lost everyday life—to recover the ways of seeing, and just as often the manias, of peoples who left behind records that we read as literature rather than as history.

Vico's excitement when unraveling verbal codes is usually civic and republican. *Ious*, an early rendering of the god *Jove*, he observes, is how we get *ius* (right, law, justice), just as *urbs* (the moldboard of the plow circumscribing the first agricultural encampments) becomes *urbs* (city)—and, he speculates, perhaps also *orbis terrae* (the circle of the world). Vico's is an etymology that records social reform as lying at the very heart of all imaginative life—the political and the civic as a deeply personal, sacred mythology. The *famuli*, the forerunners of slaves captured in the wars, "were called *vernae* by the Latins; with them came the languages called vernacular" (*NS*, 197). As for Dante before him, "vernacular" is positively inflected, although, unlike Dante, in a specifically revolutionary sense. The sons of heroes were, by contrast, called *liberi* (the free ones), but, Vico is quick to add, it was a "distinction without a difference," for the master is not distinguished from the slave by being brought up with greater delicacy" (*NS*, 197). Status distinctions, in other words, are not natural but the violent outcome of a kind of killing-as-naming. The associations of good and bad embedded in language are, in this way, revealed to be themselves aspects of the violence perpetrated by those who are no better than their servants. In remarkable detail he anticipates the language of class war.[8]

I have said nothing so far about the most obvious link between the two thinkers—Nietzsche's theory of eternal recurrence and Vico's *ricorsi*—since the discordance between these two views of history is formally identical to that of their views on etymology: the coming round again of an originary home in precivilized vitality (in Nietzsche's case) versus a second chance to learn from history when setting up political institutions (in Vico's). Even this brashly political collision between the two thinkers, however, had its counterpart in form. If Vico had treated oral cultures with respect for their rich symbolic life and the gloriously crude poetic imagination of pre-antiquity, Nietzsche disparages the oral in favor of the hermeneutics of the written text.[9] He develops the idea in the longer fragment from the early notebooks of a somewhat later period, "On Truth and Lie in an Extra-Moral Sense" (1873). There we find an anthropological conjecture about the adaptive advantages of dissimulation for humans as a weaker species that relies on trickery for its survival. With a perspective no doubt conditioned by his own years learning philology in the highly scientized ways in which it was understood in the late nineteenth century, he chooses as his point of departure conventional speech, which he describes as lying "herd-like in a style obligatory to all." Speech, for Nietzsche, is always described as a primitive instinct accessible only by way of philological reading (*WFN*, 3:145–46).[10] In views that would become more familiar in turn-of-the century linguistic circles, he considered it illogical to believe that there is anything but an arbitrary relationship between words and things or that the inventors of words even have correspondence as their goal. Words then become "concepts," he argues, by being applied outside the original contexts of their use, a situation common above all to writing. It is through Nietzsche, in other words, that the connection between postwar theories of discourse and an anthropological skepticism toward oral language becomes evident—that is, we see that contemporary "discourse" has a biological and hereditary origin.

The most distinctive and influential of all of the instances of form in the meeting of Vico and Nietzsche is that of genealogy. For Vico, the concept of nobility was originally based on the ability to engender a new social capacity—the tracing of one's genealogy and the establishing of one's parentage. This rendering is less catachrestic than Nietzsche's much better-known concept of genealogy, which probes the origins of its own political life in the invention of birth privilege and outlines a strategy for identifying with this invention ironically. In Vico we have a civic hermeneutics, a vernacular theory that will go on to inform the aesthetics of interwar Marxism and much of the writing of the global periphery. In Nietzsche's genealogy we have a new way of arguing, a way of reading *around* meaning that is built on reversals. Thus, the contradictory banner of the Nietzschean avant-garde: "into the past." Genealogy is not a theory of history but a theory of reading, as I will explain at more length below.

NIETZSCHE IN COLONIAL DISCOURSE

> This axiom ... convicts of fraud the oracles of Zoroaster [a.k.a. Zarathustra] the Chaldean.
>
> *Vico*[11]

Nietzsche is seen by many today as a combative, restless soul, ill at ease with European dominance. But in making this point, few seem interested in his extensive use of non-Western sages, eastern Mediterranean religious movements, and Oriental imagery. The very fabric of his argument is unusually reliant on tropes of the Far East, North Africa, and Central Asia. We would expect him to draw on such sources from his philological repertoire, since in antiquity in the regions we today call "Europe," intellectuals looked east rather than west for civilization. The boundary lines cutting off the Levant and Asia Minor from Greece were, in his original field of study, still indistinct. How, then, can it not matter that in the book of his that he liked most (*Thus Spake Zarathustra*) he places his own words in the mouth of a borrowed persona—a Persian religious savant whom he wanted to take the place of the Jesus of the New Testament in a new holy book? Or that his best-known coinage from his early study of tragedy (the "Dionysian") is drawn from an Egyptian fertility cult that, according to Nietzsche, would eventually become the malign origins of Christianity itself and proof of its Oriental ground (*WFN*, 13:168)?

Epicurus, notes Nietzsche, in combating Oriental paganism was really attacking what he, Nietzsche, would later call "Christianity." For Epicurus, this meant the subterranean cults of Osiris (a.k.a. Dionysus), Mithras, and others. The genius of St. Paul, the "eternal Jew par excellence," remarks Nietzsche, was to address this motley assemblage of dévotés as equals, folding together their various versions of the revolt from below of Mediterranean riffraff when inventing his Christian God (*WFN*, 16:197, 223).[12] The abhorrent slave mentality of Christianity is referred to repeatedly as "Chandala values," after the name for the untouchable caste in India. It was not the German barbarians with horses and spears, he observes, who really conquered Rome, "it was the Orient, the *profound* Orient, it was the Oriental slave" (*WFN*, 16:48, 105; 12:65).

Throughout Nietzsche's writings, the non-Western can be either desirable or repellent depending on the valences of his argument, just as the terms "Jew," "nihilism," "Wagner," "mixed-race," and "barbarian" shift from positive to negative and back again without affecting the consistency of his politics or the concurrence of his philosophical themes. Complaining bitterly that in the West we cannot imagine anything but obeisance before the divine, he applauds the Indians, Persians, Greeks, and Scandinavians, who were virile enough to devise mythological systems where humans could kill gods when they failed to deliver (*WFN*, 9:136). Similarly, he repeatedly praises Islam for being a religion of real men: "If Islam despises Christianity, it is justified a thousand times over; for Islam presupposes men" (*WFN*, 16:226). He comes back again and again to the *Laws of Manu* and the Koran as representing the best of the "*affirmative* Arian religion which is the product of a *ruling* class" (*WFN*, 14:126). Arthur Schopenhauer, moreover—one of Nietzsche's principal mentors—was deeply invested in Indian and Chinese philosophy, especially Buddhism, where he found resources for his philosophy of resignation. Schopenhauer was impressed by the large number of Buddhism's believers and its geographic coverage, its atheism, and its stipulation that suffering is a normal human state, that humans are not morally superior to animals, and that its founder did not claim to be a god.

On the face of it, then, and against this background, the resources Nietzsche seems to offer anticolonial thought are substantial. He advocated cosmopolitanism, rejected nationalism, and considered homelessness a "distinction and an honour" (*WFN*, 10:342). He insisted on the virtues of nomadism and found a historical "coming later" to be inviting. The "self," he insisted, in a motif that would become widespread in a postcolonial politics of identity, is a recent creation, based on historical forgetting. Given these themes, it is not surprising that in the academic field of postcolonial studies, many critics have seen themselves in Nietzsche, finding in him a kind of home. The field's leading intellectuals, according to Leela Gandhi, "invoke the ... figure of Nietzsche to bolster their onslaught on the epistemological narcissism of Western culture."[13]

Edward Said puts him in the company of Marx and Freud, arguing that all three with "remarkable symmetry" argued for the "interpretive leeway" of texts, for the dialectic of originality and recurrence in historical emergence, and for the critical dissection of the "reified data of bourgeois society" and the "subterranean foundations of the edifice of Western reason."[14] As Gandhi observes, Nietzsche lent authority to the field's reservations concerning Western humanism, especially its belief in origins as a "place of plenitude, presence and truth" rather than a "mythical compensation for an originary lack."[15]

Surveys of the field written for broad audiences continue in this vein, extolling "Nietzsche's realization that the Enlightenment replaced divine providence with the equally transcendental providence of reason. . . . In effect, providence was replaced by the temporally and spatially empty dominance of the European subject."[16] Nietzsche was instrumental in these circles for turning the emphasis away from the subject to the body: "The philosopher," wrote Nietzsche, "cannot do other than convert his physical condition into the most highly intellectual of forms—this act of transformation *is* philosophy. We philosophers are not at liberty to distinguish between soul and body."[17] Seized upon by Georges Bataille (and after him Michel Foucault), this principle laid the groundwork for an eventual postcolonial epistemology of the body.[18] As Jacques Derrida asks, for example, "Is not all of Nietzsche's thought a critique of philosophy as an active indifference to difference, as the system of adiaphoristic reduction or repression?"[19] Here Derrida means not only epistemological but physical differences—that Nietzsche gives support to movements of racial and sexual recognition. Foucault adds an even more liberatory edge by claiming that Nietzsche belongs with Marx: "It was Nietzsche, in any case, who burned for us, even before we were born, the intermingled promises of the dialectic and anthropology."[20] So Nietzsche burrows within terms such as "deterritorialization," "imperial power-knowledge," "refusal of dialectics," "subaltern consciousness," and "indigeneity"; for the postcolonial critic, he inspires this language, lending it a distinctive authority.[21]

As others have shown, the stage was set for this enthusiastic reception much earlier. Declared the ally of youth, he emerges in postwar France in the image of a radical who, unlike other revolutionaries, resists all domestication or institutional taming. The fronts of his war were too dispersed to be withstood; they ranged from the corporeal to the ethical to the genetic and the linguistic and rose above the squabbles of the vulgar political world. His appeal was not simply intellectual and artistic—the fabulous writing style, his claim that he wanted to turn "ugly" German into the beauty of French, the unpredictability, the chiding, the riddling and irreverence—but antipolitical. He penetrated thought patterns and dictated forms, moving beyond mere contents. The appeal of the combination is not at all difficult to understand or sympathize with, and regardless of one's position, he has always been the kind of author one had to read and learn from.

In the Anglo-French intellectual scene, this story about Nietzsche the sovereign trickster extends over so much territory and in so many directions that it is hard to find a critical space outside it.[22] Its influence has been greater for joining, with slightly different emphases, an already established consensus about the post-European, anti-German Nietzsche crafted by his Princeton-based émigré translator from the 1950s, Walter Kaufmann. He, more than anyone else, tirelessly agitated for the now well-known view of Nietzsche as apolitical, not anti-Semitic, a wearer of masks—essentially the victim of his sister Elizabeth's redactions. The near uniformity of the view, however, has lately met a series of challenges. Even if it were understandable before, there are now massive revisionist intellectual biographies of Nietzsche written by scholars in Germany, Italy, and Sweden that call this older story into question.[23] This work, which has gone more or less completely undiscussed in Anglo-American circles, displays an impressive, global knowledge of the main texts and sources. These rereadings of Nietzsche's corpus are now too visible to ignore.

Before looking at them, we should recall that there had already been in place for decades a powerful anti-Nietzsche discourse within anticolonial circles. With shocking harshness, in *Discourse on Colonialism* (1955), Aimé Césaire denounces the "hoodwinkers" he considers Africa's false friends—the "chattering intellectuals born stinking out of the thigh of Nietzsche."[24] Colonization itself, Césaire argues, worked by first "decivilizing" the colonizer in order to "awaken him to buried instincts"—precisely Nietzsche's project from his own point of view. In *La consagración de la primavera* (The rite of spring, 1978), Alejo Carpentier portrays French interwar bohemia in terms that closely match Césaire's description and come from an identical sensibility. Similarly, in his novel *The Lost Steps* (1953), he dispatches Nietzsche with bitterness, seeing him as a comical prophet of the demimonde:

> Some high priest of delirium would initiate them in the cult of Dionysus, "god of ecstasy and fear, of brutality and liberation," . . . though without telling them that the one who invoked this Dionysus, the officer Nietzsche, had been photographed on one occasion in *Reichswehr* uniform, sword in hand, and helmet on a console table of Munich style, like a prophetic figuration of the god of horror whom reality would unleash in the Europe of that *Ninth Symphony*.[25]

And once more, in the novel *The Chase* (1956), the protagonist—a political rebel hunted by the police—overhears a scholarship student speak of "the superman . . . the will to power," hearing only "shreds of sentences interrupted by angry grunts and confused insults aimed at unnamed people."[26] It is striking that postcolonial theory did not carry on the critique, or at least aspects of it, since it was so pronounced in the anticolonial circles that preceded it.

Even prior to Nietzsche's appearance, the emotional tenor of these challenges is present in the Vichian tradition. If we can posit, as some have, a Marx before Marx in the figure of Spinoza, perhaps a Nietzsche before Nietzsche is equally plausible. In his critique of "representational thought" [*Vorstellung*], for example, in the *Phenomenology*, Hegel observes that such thought "transform[s] the evil will into a semblance of goodness." In this relying on semblance, Hegel concludes, "good and evil in and for themselves have disappeared, and it can pass off as good or evil whatever it wishes and its ability dictate"—a view he calls "absolute sophistry" (*PR*, 183). I am not saying the comment captures Nietzsche before the fact or that it addresses every complexity in Nietzsche's transvaluation of values, but that it expresses a culture of belief—one shared by an important later tradition that has been more or less ignored on these terms. Marx, for instance, had complained of a brand of socialism that was "half lamentation, half lampoon; half echo of the past, half menace of the future; at times, by its bitter, witty and incisive criticism, striking the bourgeoisie to the very heart's core" but unable to "comprehend the march of modern history."[27] In Nietzsche's wake, Walter Benjamin writes from exactly the same sensibility and with surprising contempt:

> This passage of the planet "Human" through the house of despair in the absolute loneliness of his trajectory is the ethos that Nietzsche defined. This man is the superman, the first to recognize the religion of capitalism and begin to bring it to fulfillment. . . . The paradigm of capitalist religious thought is magnificently formulated in Nietzsche's philosophy.[28]

The postcolonial Nietzsche, just like the postwar French Nietzsche before it, interrupts, and even effaces, the judgments of theorists whom it considers authorities on almost every other question. Theodor Adorno and Max Horkheimer's observation, for example, in the "Juliette" chapter of *Dialectic of Enlightenment* (1944) draws, perhaps for the first time, explicit connections between Nietzsche and colonialism. For them, he "maliciously celebrates the mighty and their cruelty when it is directed . . . against everything alien to themselves."[29] Preferring this to the fake compassion of bourgeois sentiment, Adorno and Horkheimer nevertheless see Nietzsche as being caught up in a "bourgeois" (their word) contradiction based on "biological idealism."[30] His vaunted praise for the "beautiful terribleness of the deed," they add, ends up "elevating the cult of strength to a world-historical doctrine." The German philosopher's "master morality," perhaps against his intentions, "places itself entirely in the service of the civilizing powers" by being unable to "shake off the idealistic habit of wanting to see the petty thief hanged while imperialist raids are transfigured into world-historical missions."[31]

Others with radically different political intentions had no trouble identifying in Nietzsche an identical conviction—for example, Carl Schmitt, whose writing in 1950 on the concept of "just war" looks admiringly to Nietzsche's arguments of the 1880s on behalf of "the battle for the domination of the earth ... in the name of fundamental philosophical doctrines."[32] The charge is, in fact, glancingly made much earlier in Wilhelm Carl Becker's *Der Nietzschekultus: Ein Kapitel aus der Geschichte der Verirrungen des menschlichen Geistes* (1908) (The cult of Nietzsche: A chapter from the history of the aberrations of the human spirit).[33] In 1931, in a study by Alfred Bäumler, Nietzsche is shown entering "into battle riding with the German *Wehrmacht*, fighting against the legalist, institutional, 'Roman' state in the name of a 'warlike' and German-Nordic world revolution."[34]

To rethink Nietzsche this way, though, is unwelcome in many quarters, Right and Left. They see him not simply as a major figure, but as the inventor of an entirely new moral and affective world—too ethereal for criticism actually to harm him.[35] A philological reading of the philosopher, then, has potential for at least two reasons: first, because most of the writing on his life and work has almost nothing to say about what made Nietzsche, namely, philology; and second, because we are forced to ask how his work appears differently when we read all of it, rather than just parts of it, and do so paying attention to textual consistency, sources, and historical situatedness. There is a necessary perversity in this plan. For even if not at first, Nietzsche's whole philosophical momentum led eventually to an inversion of philology. Truth, he would come to believe, may be noble, but it is without use; archival recovery is mainly rumination; language is an evolutionary form of dissimulation. All of these provocations began, tentatively, when he was in his twenties and a gifted professor at the University of Basel, but only slowly found expression. There he produced studies on Democritus, who inspired (paradoxically) his later antimaterialism;

on Sophocles' *Oedipus Rex*, which began his anti-Sophoclean assault on rationalism in *The Birth of Tragedy*; on Diogenes Laertius, the model for his extensive use later of epigrammatic poetry; and, of course, on Homer, the source material for his war on morality and his politics of aristocratic virtue.

This strategy seems stalled from the start, though, by the doctrine of undecidability that forms a protective network around Nietzsche's writing today. In his introduction to the *Writings from the Early Notebooks*, Alexander Nehamas expresses the prevailing view:

> Nietzsche's almost irresoluble ambiguity and many-sidedness are partly generated by his style of writing—playful, hyperbolic, cantering and full of twists and turns. . . . Nietzsche was intentionally a philosopher of many masks and many voices. . . . Most of his writing (more than two thirds of his total output, not counting his voluminous correspondence) has come to us in the form of short notes, drafts of essays and outlines of ideas and books he never published—fragmentary texts that allow great latitude in interpretation.[36]

It is important to recognize that this view is not so much an opinion as a philosophical doctrine. In his four-volume study, *Nietzsche*, Heidegger had already foregrounded the idea that reading for definite meaning in Nietzsche was a nonstarter. The theme was repeated by Derrida in *Spurs: Nietzsche's Styles*, which resists even the possibility of coherence in the body of Nietzsche's work.[37]

There are at least two objections to this common claim. First, as Pierre Bourdieu and Geoff Waite have shown, the louche quality woven into the texts by Nietzsche (and later emulated by Heidegger) is part of a deliberate strategy of esotericism.[38] He devised *Geheimschrift* ("secret writing") consciously to attract adherents from a select group of poets and intellectuals who would be inspired by decoding his messages, as it were, at the expense of the public.[39] Clearly, the illocutionary in Nietzsche, his rhetorical feints, make multiple readings of passages inevitable, and even more interesting. They are what he describes as "wounding and torturing by word and look. . . . All that is *well said* is believed" (*WFN*, 10:64). All the same, one can never quite get around the problem (as Waite goes on to say) of "making use" of Nietzsche without some level of textual support. For doing so simply keeps critics "safe in the *a priori* belief that *their* 'recontextualization,' at least, is inoculated from any possibly hallucinatory effects."[40]

Claims about Nietzsche's dizzying interpretive levels, at any rate, elide a distinction between a controlled genre (prophecy, paradox, epigram) whose semantic slidings are meant to take the elect toward their destination by indirect routes and, by contrast, something very different: a searching, manifold query attentive to dialectical reversals. While it is certainly true that individual epigrams or short, independent entries, say, in Nietzsche's less narrative books or in the unpublished writings can be cryptic, and while he carefully crafts them to dodge any overly obvious renderings, this cannot really be said of any global analysis of the Nietzschean corpus. Over its many pages, there emerges, in fact, a constant return, from new angles, to the same four or five positions. To read Nietzsche from beginning to end is to get the sense that the writing is not marked so much by ambiguity as by obsessive reformulation.

Recently, these continuities have been mapped with precision, and the interlocking categories of the Nietzschean system have been persuasively laid out. Domenico Losurdo's monumental undertaking in *Nietzsche, il ribelle aristocratico* (Nietzsche, the aristocratic rebel) is simply unanswerable in most respects, and although it leaves important issues of language and style untouched, it still seriously weakens the idea of Nietzsche's shifting, elusive intentions. Losurdo re-poses the common sense surrounding Nietzsche among Left intellectuals between the wars which was first challenged, from the opposite side of the political spectrum, in the period just before and after World War II. The current scene represented by Losurdo, then, is a revision of an earlier French postwar revision. And as I indicated just above, he is not alone. A battery of scholarship in the last three decades has reconstructed the logic of Nietzsche's imagery, affects, and location. Thomas Mann's widely quoted statement that Nietzsche was an apolitical philosopher, "remote from politics and innocently spiritual," no longer seems even remotely plausible.[41] A standard edition of Nietzsche's complete works, including the unpublished notebooks, was not completed even in German until 1977. For that reason and others, the door seems more open than before to doing what Losurdo in his own way has done: to let Nietzsche speak for himself.

We are operating, nevertheless, in an interpretive space where affective desire meets the demand that it have a substantive ground, and a tension arises between the two. There is a coercive aspect to the elaboration of this tension that deflects questioning and reaches for mesmerizing effects. These effects themselves are what Nietzsche did not simply exemplify or theorize but in fact prescribed. To say, then, that Nietzsche is uninterpretable is really to say that a Nietzschean conversion has to take place prior to any assessment of his work. It is to say that inquiry should employ the means it interrogates, which would, of course, make the object of inquiry impervious in advance. The resistance to readings (like Losurdo's and others') that do not submit to these demands are of two kinds: either that Nietzsche does not really mean what he says, or that it does not matter. In the latter case, what appears to be his political extremism is taken (inaccurately, I think) to be common knowledge, and in any case, it can always be read against the grain. Enthusiasm for Nietzsche in this way can continue unimpeded, pushing aside these "already known" facts even as the attempt to problematize or expose them is immobilized by a claim masked as a question: "Who doesn't know?" For the implication is that what really counts is not the political views, whatever they might be, but the genealogical brilliance, which opened up entirely new ways of conceiving disagreement, proof, and history.

We will have to see whether his politics of form does not itself deserve to be resisted. But I recognize that I have adopted an approach similar to this one when dealing with certain dubious aspects of Hegel and Vico in preceding chapters. My interest above all is in philosophical legacies—what enables and disables, and with what consequences for our politics and our thought. Demanding that claims about Nietzsche be forced to look at evidence may in the end be unconvincing to many theorists today, since textual findings matter less to them than the politics of form. But, on the one hand, the posited slippery or playful Nietzsche has begun to buckle under the archival weight of the revisionary studies I mentioned above, and a once subtle appeal to irony and double entendre has come to seem more and more like simple denial. On the other hand, why not simply agree to let the case for revision be built not only of statements but of forms? Pursuing the content of form would be an acceptably Nietzschean way into the philosopher's place within colonial discourse—one that still relied on the historical thereness of textual proof. I would like to look especially at two forms: the epigram and genealogy. But first I would like to recall how he came to them, and why.

THE WAR ON PHILOLOGY

The many readings of the philologists: hence their poverty of original thought.
Nietzsche[42]

Nietzsche was proud of philology, envied it, mocked it, and was bored by it. But he could not leave it and finally built a philosophy by parodying it. His complicated relationship to the discipline was expressed with characteristic bravura: "People in general think that philology is at an end—while I believe that it has not yet begun" (*WFN*, 8:142)—at least the philology he would remake, which turned out in time to be more like a *counter*philology. All of his writing through *Untimely Meditations* bears witness to his immersion in the history, debates, and afflatus of the field, mostly in the form of highly technical studies for philology journals or the Basel classroom. To these, however, are added self-conscious theorizations of philology itself, where he sought to settle accounts with what this interpretive practice, in the larger scheme of things, signified: namely, high-stakes theoretical problems of scientific method, historicism, authenticity, and the autonomy of the written word. How does one say anything about Nietzsche without reading his first major philosophical statements, "Homer and Classical Philology" (1869) and "We Philologists" (1874)? All the later writing is colored by them.

In terms almost identical to Vico's in the early pages of *The New Science*, Nietzsche declares that "philosophia facta est quae philologia fuit"—that philology needs to take account, like philosophy, of the whole of a text, not simply its isolated elements. Done properly, argues Nietzsche, philology represents "a philosophical view of things" (*WFN*, 3:170). In his introduction to the study of classical philology (1871), he advocates students spending a year studying philosophy (*NGW*, 2:344–47). In short, his later declaration that "it is only as an aesthetic phenomenon that existence can be justified," as well as his devising a kind of philosophy as creative writing, evolves from this moment of philological apotheosis. His counterphilology is antiphilosophy.

In 1869, at least, he is still feeling hurt on the field's behalf, wanting it to be given more respect. Even though it was the most prestigious discipline in the humanities at the time, he worries that the public has become skeptical. Commentators have begun to mock it, calling it "dust-eating" textual regurgitation, an "inoffensive pastime." He comes off in this early work as a beleaguered loyalist struggling to make a public case for the humanities because of its important role in preserving the "everlasting standards" of antiquity. In these early lectures, he bucks up his colleagues against their enemies, the industrialists and commercialists who consider rummaging around in ancient Greece irrelevant to practical life. Goethe and Schiller may have been right, he notes, to upbraid philology for contributing nothing to artistic invention, and yet from the time of the Alexandrian grammarians, it brought the likes of Homer's poetry out of obscurity.

As a young professor, he is still conservative regarding the truth of the literary text. Nietzsche repeatedly comes back to the dilemma of how to derive a comprehensive, unified picture of meaning from a bewildering assortment of unearthed archival details, corrupted as they often are by errors and emendations. He is not at the outset as skeptical as one would expect of arriving at a reliable case in such a search, and even appears to adopt a position contrary to the one commonly attributed to him. In an early review of G. F. Schoemann's *Die hesiodische Theogonie* in the *Literarische Centralblatt* (1868), he is quite snide, objecting to classicists' obscurantism. When seeking textual sources, they feel the need to introduce an "element of fantasy" into their "methodical research":

> Methodological research in the field of Hesiod studies on the *Theogony* is nowhere more brought to a halt, indeed thrust into temporary obscurity—than by a fantastical element that our modern Pythagoreans and Orpheans, with a great deal of wit and ease, have introduced. The former seek with their magic wands a cipher for a single, unified ur-text of *Theogony*—very doubtful—and take this as being demonstrated if they smash the present text loudly into three- or five-membered pieces. (*NGW*, 2:221; my translation)

Nietzsche will later consider a wand less useful than a philosophical hammer, but his tone suggests the intensity of his feelings when it comes to the ur-text of Hesiod's epic.

At this point he is not at all indifferent to philology's claim to science. He wants, in fact, to insist upon it, while at the same time combining this rigorous strength with a "concealed" inner artistic "imperative." This beautiful science, he believes, must be saved from irrelevance by recognizing that even though its métier may be to bring myriad data under "morphological laws," one cannot lose sight of a loftier goal: the "creative force, the real fragrance, of the atmosphere of antiquity." His whole point is to superimpose over what he calls the "ideal antiquity" of the "Teutonic longing for the south" a real antiquity, with a precisely scientific insistence on the real as supported by the evidence of texts.

What I am calling his war on philology begins to take shape only in the writing of "We Philologists," although, again, not along the lines we might expect given his reputation as an inventor of textual play. Even in a late work like *The Antichrist* he defines philology in a manner out of step with what most criticism attributes to him: "What I mean here by the word philology is, in a general sense to be understood as the art of reading well, of being able to take account of facts *without* fasifying them by interpretation, without losing either caution, patience or subtlety owing to one's desire to understand" (*WFN*, 16:206). Inasmuch as he modulates (without rejecting) the view, it is partly because textual science is too hard for its initiates to live up to; the discipline is too demanding, he laments, for all those drawn to its prestige. In time, the scholarly grinds fall under the weight of specialist demands and become "skeptical and melancholy" toward the past. This adopted solemnity only makes antiquity seem dead and alien. Genuinely imitating the past, then, seems in their hands an unrealistic task. Nietzsche's program, by contrast, is to be "more like the ancients."[43] Philology's proper mission is to teach us how. As the field's would-be redeemer, he sets out to fuse an artistic inner life with a scientific textual practice.

Science should not be pedantry, though; who cares, he asks, about the fine points of "Greek particles" when there are bigger issues of "valuing" at stake? Being a grammatical mole of that sort only "bungles life." The problem with philology is not so much its historical methodology as the modesty of its operation. The more the field's lost promise sinks in, the angrier he gets, until the insults fly. He attacks the research habits of the field's untalented majority: "the disgusting erudition, the lazy, inactive passivity, the timid submission . . . a hobby of hair-splitting" (*WFN*, 8:140). And the fruits of this distraction are where the real fissure lies. He rejects the idea, promoted by most philologists of his time, that Greece was humanitarian and enlightened—a view, he adds derisively, that fits much better the "Chinese or the Hindoos." Science as datamongering yields a misbegotten reverence for a Greek antiquity that, if men could only see it as it truly was, they would "shrink from it horror stricken." This is a horror by which Nietzsche is exhilarated, a reprimand to the blandly modern: "My aim is to bring about a state of complete enmity between our present 'culture' and antiquity. Whoever wishes to serve the former must hate the latter" (*WFN*, 8:120, 118).

It is significant that his portrait of this fearful Greek character, "bungled" by overidealization, prefigures his affectionate assessment (in *Beyond Good and Evil*) of the mixed German character. This first articulation of the figure of the nomad and cosmopolitan dissident so central in the rhetorical imagination of later colonial discourse is carried out, then, on behalf of a didactic *Bildung* based on mores whose values are not post- but antimodern. He too feels himself a victim of being from backward Europe. But his deployment of the theme heads in the opposite direction. The real Greeks, Nietzsche asserts, were (like the Germans later) "geniuses among the nations." They had a "childlike nature" which involved "credulousness"; they were "passionate . . . enemies of shyness and dullness"; they had "intuitive insight into misery, despite their bright and genial temperament"; they were "mendacious, unhistorical," with "individuality raised to the highest power" and with "envy, jealousy, as among gifted people ... lacking in sobriety and caution" (*WFN*, 8:156–57).

That this character portrait found its counterpart in his later sizing-up of Germans is not hard to show; that the one led to the other is also likely. In his late career, he alludes to Germans as "a people made up of the most extraordinary mixing and mingling of races, perhaps even with a preponderance of the pre-Aryan element, as the 'people of the centre' in every sense of the term" (*WFN*, 12:197). This allows Germans to be contradictory, to remain unknown, frightening, surprising—they "escape *definition*"—all characteristics we know from other contexts Nietzsche celebrated. In fact, his portrait of Germans is not at all contradictory, the confusion coming from his assigning customarily pejorative traits to them that he then transvalues. The German has the "charm of the mysterious ... [and is] an expert on secret paths to chaos." He is boorish, *bieder*, but also noble, occult, both "good natured and vicious." A "deceiver people" and bad stylists—no music or rhythm to their prose, no understanding of tempo, their profundity comes from mists and indigestion. But they are profound, and Nietzsche admires the influence of their philosophy, which, with "German beer and German music is labouring to Germanize all Europe" (*WFN*, 12:198–99).

He stresses that the Greeks too were dabblers and "dilettanti" who stole their alphabet, the *polis*, and even the goddess Aphrodite from the Phoenicians; similarly, "the truly scientific people, the literary peoples, were the Egyptians, and not the Greeks," living like immigrants with "adopted institutions and an acquired language." The strength that comes to a people from mixedness is a prominent trope throughout his work, derived from then-popular Darwinian notions about the vitality of hybrid offspring as well as from the ancestral history of Germans (to which he incessantly refers) as the sackers of Rome, the scene-setters of its eventual Christian unity, and the motley tribes of central Europe where interbreeding thrived: "the terrible consistency of Darwinism, which, incidentally, I regard as true" (*NPW*, 19).

What is evident above are the actual contexts (which is to say motives, as well) for his philosophy of language as we have come to know it—one that, according to the consensus, signals a repudiation of almost everything philology stands for: historicism, textual proof, correct and incorrect interpretations. But Nietzsche's campaign against his own field, exemplified by his resignation from the post at Basel after committing professional suicide with the writing of *The Birth of Tragedy*, was nothing like a departure from it. The logic of his journey was to travel from philological classicism through the Darwinian body to modern race theory while superimposing a philological terminology and method upon both. This interpretation may seem forced until we review the trajectory of this movement fully. As we remember from *The Birth of Tragedy*, Greek classicism for Nietzsche was not static. The changes roughly correspond to an early instinctual society symbolized by the forces the Greeks designated by the god Dionysus; next, a period of epic naïveté corresponding to the time of Homer, when the art of "illusion" holds sway and a comforting brace is built against the real so that people may tolerate existence (the Apollinian); then, a period in which the orgiastic, Oriental cults of revery and cruel nature (the Dionysian) reassert themselves, demanding that the wisdom of suffering and the knowledge of irrationalism be heard. It is in the meeting of the second and third phases that Attic tragedy achieves its heights.

The final period, which signals for Nietzsche the decline of ancient Greece, is represented by the teachings of Socrates, who argues that art is bad illusion. He advocates methods of measure, balance, restraint, and reason that are represented in the art of tragedy by Euripides, who, in Nietzsche's view, had the bad judgment (in *The Bacchae*) to dramatize the Dionysian orgy as uncivil, as though civility, and the civic, mattered. Euripides loses touch completely with the necessity of tragedy, which is always about losing one's individuality, returning to our original state. From this point of view—and it is one Nietzsche comes more and more to adopt—"truth" is finding our way back to this original state—through illusion, through art.

In the fragment "On Truth and Lie in an Extra-Moral Sense" he develops further the "concealed inner imperative" of art in philology by emphasizing the adaptability of mixed peoples, the virtues of recidivism, and the redemptive qualities of lying. The underlying biologism of his thought is suggested by his pitting the bogus raptures of knowledge against bestial instincts—the world, as he puts it, of the "coils of the intestines, the quick pulse of the bloodstream, and the involved tremors of the fibres" (*KGW*, 3.2:371).[44] His investigation, importantly, is not about truth and falsity as in traditional philology but about truth and lie. He argues that humans, less robust than other species, rely on dissimulation to survive. How then, he asks, given the biological imperative, could the idea of "truth" have arisen among us at all? If he goes on to say, famously, that truth is only a "lie one has gotten used to," he has not abandoned truth. It is important to see that something of his early attachment to philological science is retained here. The frightening and shameful primordial reality of the human is the "truth"—a doctrine that he elsewhere calls "life-enhancing pessimism." Knowledge is not learning myths one forgot were myths but learning to accept who we are. One must "lie" on behalf of truth, and to accept is to understand.

This tension in his work is generally overlooked. In *The Birth of Tragedy*, he favors the Apollinian and Dionysian in equipoise, even if the latter is all that most readers remember as his preference. As the principle of dissimulation is developed in his system, it acquires new logics and fields of force. *Geheimschrift* as a language of the elect is not quite the same thing as the adaptive verbal camouflage of the "On Truth and Lie" fragment, although they are related; so too is another avatar he calls the "holy lie" (*WFN*, 14:121). History's great prophets all presumed to have the right to lie: "Manu, Plato, Confucius, the teachers of Judaism and Christianity have never doubted their right to falsehood" (*WFN*, 16:49). Lying is "a prudent measure of revelation that belongs to the priestly type" (*WFN*, 16:213–14).

The genius of the Jews as the panegyrists of Chandala culture, after all, was for him that they conquered the Roman Empire by *writing a book*. Their scribes and scholars concocted a story that perfected the fictive arts. The Bible in German, Nietzsche thought, was the only real masterpiece of the country's literature. Nietzsche sought, of course, to reverse that accomplishment by employing the same means and found classics of the epic-religious genre to emulate in many cultures: "The most elaborate of lies ... [a] double lie, developed by the typically Arian philosophers of the Vedanta.... The lie of the one has to create a condition in which the truth of the other can alone become *intelligible*" (*WFN*, 14:120). He is referring here to himself as that "other" of the earlier founders of religions and wishes to play their role in the future in respect to other others.

His attempt to supersede philology would end up borrowing many of its principles, and certainly he leaned heavily on its repertoire of standard texts and readerly techniques. Wanting to improvise in those areas where there was only a lack of original thought, and wanting to move past its timid dust-munching, he sided all the same with its primary directive: the discovery of the truth of earlier peoples by means of texts. Even though he re-imagined it, he did not at first disparage that truth. His position was not semantic indeterminacy or plenitude but anthropological reversal, where lying (not falsity) became the truth that had to be preserved. The science of textuality no longer denoted the linguistic confidence authorized by usage or consensus but the science of the species in struggle with other beasts. Art became the evolutionary weapon of lying.

ODYSSEAN IMPERIALISM

> There is a handwritten draft in which Caesar instead of Zarathustra is the bearer of Nietzsche's tidings.... That is of no little moment. It underscores the fact that Nietzsche had an inkling of his doctrine's complicity with imperialism.
>
> Walter Benjamin[45]

Readers of the *Odyssey* will likely not notice too much its blithe accounts of the rapine and plunder of Odysseus's band as it roves the harsh Aegean.[46] The adventures have about them an air of the routine, and apart from the Oxen of the Sun (whose killing was proscribed by divine decree), there is not a hint of disapproval by the poem's author, who sees theft and the killing of foreign peoples to be little more than a sign of its hero's prowess.

> What of my sailing, then, from Troy?
> What of those years of rough adventure, weathered under Zeus?
> The wind that carried west from Ilion
> brought me to Ismaros, on the far shore,
> a strongpoint on the coast of the Kikonês.
> I stormed that place and killed the men who fought.
> Plunder we took, and we enslaved the women,
> to make division, equal shares to all.[47]

When the much-maligned Cyclops, not without reason, asks the Achaeans, "Who are you? And where from? / What brings you here by sea ways—a fair traffic? Or are you wandering rogues, who cast your lives / like dice, and ravage other folk by sea?" (*O*, 164), he is right to suspect the pirates of ill intent, eyeing as they had just done his "drying rack that sagged with cheeses, pens / crowded with lambs and kids ... and vessels filled with whey" (*O*, 163). War is a craft; Odysseus declares, "Carnage suited me" (*O*, 266), throughout the poem's ports of call: Egypt, Phoenicia, Libya.

Good Antinoös is literally the offspring of a father who "joined the Taphian pirates" (*O*, 303).[48] Nothing so mercenary is praised in other epics, such as the Mahabharata or the Popol Vuh (a point Nietzsche noticed), and we have to wait for the literary epics of the European colonial era to find anything comparable in the way of praising the patriotic slaughter of other peoples in a quest for riches: for example, Tasso's *Jerusalem Delivered* or Camões's *The Lusiads*. We need not see Nietzsche's attraction as being only to Odysseus the imperialist adventurer, with widespread fame "for guile in peace and war" (*O*, 158), since there is an entrepreneurial energy in Homer's text that Nietzsche did not miss—which is the kind of bourgeois sensibility that Benjamin found lurking in the philosopher. Material, physical conquest is tightly linked in the poem with the idea of Odysseus's resourcefulness. "Cunning" is his answer to being a "sorrowful man" (*O*, 165: "my life is pain"; or *O*, 104: "born for trouble") who solves problems, finds solutions, knows many "techniques" for doing things (*O*, 125), while refusing to let moral compunction get in the way.

The imperial attitude is woven into other predominant themes of the *Odyssey*, including its principal one having to do with the proper manners of guests and hosts in nobiliary culture. The "barbarous" and the "foreign" for Homer have to do with transgressions of etiquette in the eating of food (*O*, 130–31); with those who are rivals in matters of trade; and significantly, as in the Cyclops story, with agriculture versus pastoralism. The Cyclops is evil because he is a bad host, is crude, keeps an uncomfortable house, cannot converse, lives a solitary life. He is detestable because he is a shepherd rather than a farmer like the lords of Ithaca (*O*, 112–23). Homer has the advantage, then, like Vico, of granting a higher value to the very caste that is reviled by the Bible (which favors shepherds over farmers) but embodies the same mobility and shifting sense of "home" as the nomad, since this lord of an agricultural estate arrives in his proper place only at the point where the story breaks off.

When Homer portrays Odysseus as beloved of Athena, he is saying that his heroism is inseparable from his talent for dissembling. That is what Odysseus primarily means for Homer, and this is the heart of the particular brand of his wisdom or intelligence—the sacred gifts that Athena bestows on him. Thus, in classical Greek, *homêrizein*, "to Homerize," can mean "to lie"—not only because Plato charges art with distorting truth by crafting fiction to assume its appearance, but because Homer embraces lying without shame and places it in the very foreground of his poem as a divine virtue.[49] And so in *Beyond Good and Evil*, in a false etymology, Nietzsche beckons Germans (*deutsche Volk*) to "do honour to our name—we are not called the 'tiusche Volk' (deceptive people) for nothing" (*WFN*, 12:200).

The confidence games of the maritime tradesman and the stealth of the military spy are the virtues of conquerors in the arena of eastern Mediterranean antiquity. The aristocratic audience of this epic were crude enough to relish such qualities. Bronze Age lords gobbled lamb shanks and washed them down with wine as they listened to the bard sing his verses at their banquets. After the dancing girls had left the stage, on came the professional flatterers of the aristocracy, praising Odysseus as the nobles' heroic forefather. The poem known as the *Odyssey* was composed by many poets and for many reasons, but there is no question that one of its purposes was to aggrandize noblemen. It was likely sung by hired performers at opulent banquets with a seductive naïveté enabled by the hermetically sealed aristocratic world of self-regard that it depicts. The charm of the poem today is that it lacks any modern anxiety, self-interrogation, or the doubts of free personality; it is without the ability even to imagine a challenge to social hierarchy. This social setting is hypostatized by Nietzsche as *das vor-Homerische* (the pre-Homeric) in the essay "Homer's Contest" in 1872.[50] When Marx in the *German Ideology* considers "communal life" to be a truth in antiquity, whereas in modern times it has become an "idealistic lie," he may not share the antipathy of Nietzsche toward equality, but he does share the later philosopher's German love affair with Greece—one that Vico went a great distance to explode before the fact. Even Lukács, in *Theory of the Novel*, before he joins the Vichian traditions of Marxism, depicts as an enviable social wholeness and aesthetic bliss this Argive society marked by the suffocating absence of alternative visions or plebeian claims as well as the complete inaudibility of any opinions other than the rulers'. Their wedding of art and reality, desire and realization, derived from complacency, shallowness, and tyranny. Rebellion, which occurs in the poem only in the form of the hapless servants of Odysseus's house who are forced to tend to the suitors, registers only as ingratitude—as, in the *Odyssey*'s terms, failing to observe the laws of hospitality. How can we square such moments with the awed veneration that attends the epic as the literary foundation of Western civilization, except to say that imperialism, via Homer, is inscribed in it: that the poem that founds Western literature immortalizes slavery and conquest? But more to the point, how can we square the portrait of Nietzsche's alleged antipathy to late nineteenth-century European power when colonialism was at its height, without noting that this same Homer is enlisted by Nietzsche to de-idealize Greece on behalf of Germany? At the time, his portrait of Homer as the minstrel of imperial barbarism was scandalous. It was also accurate.

To say that Nietzsche's Odyssean strivings are imperialist—in their romantic attachment to a roving, warrior ethos of foreign conquest and pillage—is to say that his politics were derived from a philological relationship to classical texts. *Ressentiment*, Promethean virtue, *Spiel* (play), will to power, and of course, the grounding of philosophy in aesthetic redemption, can all be encapsulated as a revival of the ideals of pre-Athenian Homeric antiquity. His own taste for trickery was, as he saw it, a contemporary reinvention of the Homeric figure. This arises very early and unmistakably in Nietzsche's retrospective judgment on the author of *The Birth of Tragedy* as *der Grübler und Rätselfreund* (the ponderer and friend of enigmas). Here is where we might return to the content of form and to the politics referred to above as a philosophy based on style. Entire books and sections of his books were given over to the genre of aphorism. In fact, his first truly original book, *Human, All-Too-Human* (1878), was of this type. With the same investments in textual arcana and Hellenic wisdom as in his Odyssean musings, he turned in an early study of 1870 to a critique of the source materials of Diogenes Laertius, the *Epigrammendichter* (poet of epigrams). There he placed his emphasis again on the possibility of definite interpretations, seeking to exclude all unstable conjectures that mar inferior textual approaches. Operating still as the faithful philologist who believes in the accuracy of semantic recovery, he concludes that his best chance to locate the authentic source of the poet's work is in his epigrams. This would seem counterintuitive, since they are by their nature fragmentary, impassive, and without any setting or authorial personality.

That he does so, though, suggests that his early transition from philologist to antiphilologist was the formative moment of a negative obsession. Laertius and others from the classical canon moved him to redeploy the epigrams found widely among the authors of antiquity. This manner of expressing himself had a practical side, of course. It accommodated his frail health and allowed him to compose books by writing short, overlapping, often repetitive entries involving intense spurts of inspiration that did not have to be sustained when his headaches or stomach ailments returned. Form as utility (and lying as an adaptive tool) is a principle applicable not only to his epigrams and aphorisms but also to his prose after *Untimely Meditations*, divided as his books are mostly into short, detachable paragraphs assembled under a loose thematic organization. This early study on Laertius bears witness to a wider reading experience for any aspiring young classicist trained, as Nietzsche had been, at a school like Schulpforta. While mastering Latin and Greek in his teens, he would have been accustomed to the assignment of translating Greek and Roman apothegms (*sententiae latinae*), typically used by teachers for this purpose because of their brevity. "My sense of style, for the epigram as style" came from Sallust, he at one point reports—that is, from Latin, not from Greek, which is "too strange" to modern ways of thinking" (*WFN*, 16:113). The form would become his choice for enacting a counterphilology—a revenge on years of schoolboy exercises.

The many generic names given to what we loosely call the "epigram," however, are often used interchangeably without paying attention to their differences.[51] Axiom, maxim, aperçu, apothegm, analect, adage, precept, proverb, aphorism, parable are not the same, although they share the features of pithiness, brevity, and a stand-alone summary judgment crucial to Nietzsche's self-presentation as well as his methods of working under the duress of ill health. We saw in an earlier chapter the distinction that arose over the understanding of "axiom" in Spinoza and Vico, an author who (like Nietzsche) wrote cumulatively, building his argument through an assemblage of archival facts and declarative outbursts. Vico's quarrels with Spinoza over the definition of science depended on Vico's redeployment of the term "axiom," now reclaimed from geometry and ironically named to mark off the difference between two kinds of science, natural and humanistic. His findings were nevertheless "axiomatic" as he saw them, because they were based on the evidence of thousands of archival fragments reassembled like shards of pottery from an archaeological site.

Nietzsche's playing with genre takes a different turn. His mastery lies in a compelling fusion of the aphorism and the parable which he usually called (after Laertius) "epigrams" (*Epigrammen*). He means to bring into contact two genres automatically associated with certain audiences, settings, and occasions that typically do not belong together. What he communicates in the fusion has as much to do with what the two, in combination, mean formally by themselves as with the content of his sentences. Although similar in structure (terse, elegant), the aphorism and the parable traditionally belonged to different sensibilities—the aphorism to the comedian of manners, the parable to prophets or saints. The one is satirical, pulling back the curtain on hypocrisy and social pretension; the other is deliberately enigmatic and pitched to initiates. Aphorists are usually world-weary and above the fray, like the caricaturist of *Human, All-Too-Human*, *The Dawn of Day*, and *Beyond Good and Evil*, making fun of human nature. Writers of parables, on the other hand, do not assault their audience or laugh at its limitations but speak in code because what they have to say is shocking and socially dangerous. Theirs are the amoral and irreligious lessons of *Zarathustra*, *Twilight of the Idols*, and *The Anti-Christ*. But in fact, the first set of books have all the features of the latter, and vice versa. They are all to varying degrees a comedy of manners in the service of an irreligious redirective.

Obviously, this mock-religious element in Nietzsche is never entirely ironic. Despite his irreverence toward the Bible and the Lutheran catechism, his parodies want less to do away with religion than to take its place. *Beyond Good and Evil* and *Human, All-Too-Human*, moreover, are divided into sections that Nietzsche called *Hauptstücke* (major parts) rather than the more conventional term *Kapiteln* (chapters) because, among other things, *Hauptstücke* commonly refers to the divisions within Lutheran prayer books. Unlike the reassemblage of fragments, as in Vico, the short and uneven blocks of prose are independent pieces (*Stücke*), each supposed to be oracular. They are neither parables nor aphorisms but both at once. For the message was both temporal and transcendent, about the immediate politics of his time as well as a new prophetic cult.

In Nietzsche, weighing in on a matter of pressing political concern takes on the coloring of an ethical revelation: for example, "The lawyers defending a criminal are rarely artists enough to turn the beautiful terribleness of his deed to his advantage" (*WFN*, 12:91) Here the stock Nietzschean reversal of moral law creeps toward an obsession that in other epigrams becomes more openly biologistic, revealing itself repeatedly in his epigrams as the natural basis of evil's inner goodness: "A nation [*ein Volk*] is a detour of nature to arrive at six or seven great men.—Yes, and then to get around them" (*WFN*, 12:84). The politically charged nationalism of the term *Volk* at the time is deflated here in service to an equivalent, though antithetical, rejection of democracy along social-Darwinist lines. The focus is on the prophetic few: "Pity has an almost ludicrous effect on a man of knowledge, like tender hands on a Cyclops" (*WFN*, 12:100). Classical allusions, the fixation on learning as a way of setting oneself above commoners, are intertwined here with the godlike right to control life and livelihoods.

UNTIMELINESS IN REAL TIME

> The notion of eternal return appeared at a time when the bourgeoisie no longer dared count on the impending development of the system of production which they had set going. The thought of Zarathustra and of eternal recurrence belongs together with the embroidered motto seen on pillows: "Only a quarter hour."
>
> Walter Benjamin[52]

My argument would not be, as Geuss puts it in the epigraph at the beginning of this chapter, that Hegel and Nietzsche are "in some ways" opposed, but that Nietzsche defines himself against Hegel and that his whole philosophical project cannot be seen outside that attempt. The form of this encounter is clearest in Nietzsche's participation in debates over colonialism and empire that took place when he was emerging as an author and celebrity.

Many of Nietzsche's most vivid remarks on colonialism have circulated in underground circles for some time, so there can be no question of surprising his readers by pretending here to expose them. On the contrary, these remarks are often eagerly seized upon by followers as evidence of his antinomian spirit. A recent example is Massimo Cacciari's *Geofilosofia dell'Europa*—a book whose point of departure is to chart the displacement of Europe and the emergence of a new and welcome concept of the West. In the book's opening epigraph, he summons Nietzsche's words in prophetic support: "I have internalized the spirit of Europe—now I want to strike back."[53] Nietzsche is taken to be an ally, before the fact, of a new dispensation, and like many other commentators before him, Cacciari cites passages from Nietzsche's work to demonstrate the latter's proleptic anticolonial sympathies. He is the philosopher dissatisfied with all endpoints, incapable of the fixity of the arrogant imperial postures of "Western Man."

But Cacciari stops short of finishing the idea—strike back, Nietzsche meant, against the deadwood of Europe, on Europe's behalf, in the name of what Europe might become. His antagonism toward Europe was, rather, like that of the prophet Jeremiah, who was "against" Israel as Nietzsche was "against" Europe, wanting to reform, shock, and berate it in the name of seeing it ascend to a higher station. An opponent of the nationalism of Bismarck, he was at the same time *for* Germans, whose crudeness and natural taste for deception, he argued, were their peculiar historical signs of prowess. His intentions are expressed most clearly perhaps in his admiration for Napoleon, whose greatness for Nietzsche lay in the general's hatred of modernity and his bringing back a "slab of antiquity" so that Europe might resume the decisiveness and will of ancient conquerors. Nietzsche explains that "Napoleon . . . as one knows, wanted *one* Europe, which was to be *mistress of the world*" (*WFN*, 10:321).

From the mid-1870s to the late 1880s—the time both of Germany's advances in South-West Africa and of Nietzsche's growing prominence—Nietzsche wrote of the need for a united Europe to recover its vital life by territorial expansion (*WFN*, 13:224). He urged Europe to take over England's role as global sovereign, though not in the name of German nationalism but in that of a new European "cosmopolitanism," and declared the spiritual imperative to slough off *Recht* as "justice" (in Hegel's sense in the *Philosophy of Right*) in the name of a more basic *Recht*, seen now as the right to resume the role of heroic predator and so displace a degraded democracy run by a Europe of timid shopkeepers (*WFN*, 12:196).[54] Although his involvements with German colonialism were indirect—he was the brother-in-law of a fervent German colonialist who set up business schemes in

Paraguay—there is ample evidence of his enthusiasm for the colonial project as a "fundamental philosophical doctrine" (in Carl Schmitt's words). The debates over emigration, race, and colonial conquest that raged in Switzerland and Germany during the 1880s find many echoes in the writing of Nietzsche—the free spirit who (as Peter Bergmann has shown) closely followed and fell prey to the political fashions of an era for which he claimed to be "untimely."[55]

Even more consequential was the manner in which Nietzsche's enthusiasms created an ambiguous Left/Right amalgam that, as with almost everything else Nietzschean, would become a model for contemporary theory. Colonialism as an unfettering of the European spirit and a vital reawakening of "life" was enmeshed in his mind with the early socialist movements, whose assertive rise took place during his most productive decade of writing.[56] This is not to say that the other great political pole of attraction at the time—the mobilization of the European citizenry of various national states seeking the imperial expansion of borders—was for him anything but a new fettering. Imperialism of this sort was the dangerous expression of a premature *große Politik* (great politics) that he would regard with enmity until his own *große Politik* could supplant it.[57]

But the influence of early social democracy on Nietzsche's reading and thinking has mostly been ignored. In his preoccupation with socialist thinkers and anticolonial movements, there is startling proof of a larger rhetorical posture on the European Right. For them, these two constituencies—socialists on the one hand, colonial natives on the other—were interconnected, raising similar theoretical questions and demanding related solutions. "The Socialists and state-idolators of Europe," Nietzsche wrote, "could easily bring things to Chinese conditions and to a Chinese 'happiness,' with their measures for the amelioration and security of life" (*WFN*, 10:67). The new politically active laborers placed alongside the "barbarians" of the global periphery were in this discourse interdependent, though not interchangeable. Imaginatively merging them was prompted by the considerable rise of social democratic parties as well as vocal public claims made by other radical tendencies (above all, anarchism) during the period in which Nietzsche's influence on European philosophy was consolidated.

As I remarked earlier, the main currents of writing about colonialism seem either unaware of or uninterested in the origins and setting of Nietzsche's type of antihumanism. From the start, his encounter with socialist ideas sharpened and gave direction to his posthumanist convictions, which found expression not in the name of combating the false universalism of European Man, as colonial discourse has supposed, but because humanism was afflicted with the disease of moral restraint. He constantly calls out the socialists of his era: "We are no humanitarians; we should not dare to speak of our 'love of mankind'; for that, a person of our stamp is not enough of an actor! Or not sufficiently Saint-Simonist" (*WFN*, 10:344).

In precisely this vein, there are extensive parallels between Nietzsche's philosophical themes and political causes célèbres found in popular political books and journal articles of the time—in the newspapers of the 1870s and 1880s, for instance, as well as in academic movements such as anthropological antihumanism in Germany. These obsessions included problems of German emigration, the threat (or promise) of socialist government, and German competition with other European countries, especially Britain. Anthropological antihumanism was a cultural dominant in the late nineteenth and early twentieth centuries that harmonized with aspects of Nietzsche's critique. Loudly charging academic humanism with enshrining the "positivist, ratiocinating West" and excluding Africans and Asians from the human as such, an insurgent anthropology arose with a countermethod that was both intellectually appealing and commercially viable. It produced a large number of popular museum exhibitions and pamphlets: "Rather than excluding the colonized other, anthropology would focus explicitly on societies that, all agreed, were radically separate from narratives of Western civilization. Instead of studying European "cultural peoples" (*Kulturvölker*), societies defined by their history and civilization, anthropologists studied the colonized "natural peoples" (*Naturvölker*)."[58] As a populist discourse with the aim of displacing academic mandarins, anthropology promised Germans that they could re-invent themselves along the lines of the country's new imperial ambitions. The conquest of foreign territories provided antihumanism with its "ethnographic performers, artifacts, body parts, and ... field sites that provided the empirical data" and so linked the imperial, the natural, and the German in a style of thought that led directly to theories of "racial hygiene."[59] One particularly well-known anthropologist, Leo Frobenius, argued that "Germans like Africans were people of emotion, intuitive reason, art, poetry, image, and myth," thereby establishing an antihumanist affinity with the peripheral subaltern that had the great merit of making Germanness unique within the family of Europe.[60]

In this context we can appreciate why the political radicalism of the early Marxist Wilhelm Liebknecht was, as Peter Bergmann notes, "a foreign curiosity for Nietzsche."[61] The word "foreign" is important, for it brings together what he conceived as the twin threats to Europe, socialists and Christians. The latter had always been linked in his mind with an asceticism derived from St. Paul's taming of the cults of the eastern Mediterranean and was for him an Oriental ideology. Everywhere in his thinking the politics of a more flexible egalitarian social station—democracy and socialism—bleed into his observations on breeding, blood, and ethnos:

> Whether we call it "civilization," or "humanising," or "progress," which now distinguishes the European; whether we call it simply, without praise or blame, by the political formula: the *democratic* movement, in Europe—behind all the moral and political foregrounds pointed to by such formulas, an immense *physiological* process goes on, which is ever extending: the process of the assimilation of Europeans; their increasing detachment from the conditions under which climatically and hereditarily, united races originate. (*WFN*, 12:195)

Elsewhere, he had grasped the "value of having enemies" and the need (for clarity's sake) of having powerful opponents against whom he could define himself; in this way, Nietzsche learned how to "spiritualiz[e] enmity," and one of his principal targets, for both practical and philosophical reasons, was German social democracy.

In 1866, he attended a mass rally of the party of Ferdinand Lassalle—a member of the Communist League and the founder of the *Allgemeiner Deutscher Arbeiterverein* (later to become the Social Democratic Party of Germany [SPD]), who had died two years earlier. He was deeply moved by the "powerful words" of the speakers but recoiled from the "impotent and unreal things" Lassalle had advocated, such as a "European workers' state."[62] Nietzsche was caught up, as many were, in the excitement surrounding the socialist and anarchist challenges during the 1870s and 1880s. In 1868, he rented a flat in the home of Karl Biedermann, the founder of the Leipzig Workers' Educational Society, which August Bebel (the future leader of the SPD) had joined, before representing the party's Marxist wing at a later date. It was in the Leipzig organization, in fact, that Bebel received his training and orientation. Biedermann was more of a moderate, but deeply embroiled nevertheless in the controversies surrounding Marxism in the 1860s, attempting to fend off the influence of Liebknecht, who had been expelled from Prussia earlier for his political activities.[63]

The atmosphere of revolutionary thinking was pervasive, and Nietzsche was deeply aware of the fact. Even Richard Wagner was entranced for a time with the revolutionary ideals of Mikhail Bakunin, whose words he rapturously recited in conversation. Nietzsche, at any rate, was intrigued enough to work systematically through the writings of Eugen Dühring (the target of Engels's famous polemic *Anti-Dühring*, where Engels calls him, among other things, "the Richard Wagner of philosophy").⁶⁴ It was Hegel's ex-student Ludwig Feuerbach, Nietzsche notes, who profoundly inspired Wagner with his "healthy sensuality" (*WFN*, 13:125). Dühring had more influenced than been influenced by German social democracy, especially in his writings on socialism and the national economy, which August Bebel had positively reviewed in the party paper in 1874. When socialism became strong enough under Bismarck to prompt repressive legislation, Nietzsche wrote his friend Franz Overbeck "requesting the address of a Zurich book dealer from whom he could obtain a catalogue of banned socialist literature."⁶⁵ But even apart from his hurried look through Bebel's *Woman under Socialism*, Nietzsche kept abreast of events by way of both liberal and conservative writers, reading John Stuart Mill's "Socialism" (1879) and Albert Schäffle's *Quintessence of Socialism*, as well as some of Dühring's works.⁶⁶ He recognized that in order to become effective, he had to define himself in terms of the new movement; this he did resolutely by adopting its language of rallying the disaffected in a bid for power.

In his writings, he is obsessed with the rise of socialism, whose philosophical prop he finds in Hegel, the thinker who has "corrupted" German philosophy and who dominates the nineteenth century (*WFN*, 17:38). In the late 1870s, he goes so far as to call the democratization of Europe a "resistless force." Its enemies (among whom he counts himself, one of a select group of "spirits of upheaval") "seem only to exist in order, by the fear that they inspire, to drive forward the different parties faster and faster on the democratic course" (*WFN*, 6:329). He feels powerless to stem the tide. He laments the fact that workers have become a cause célèbre and attributes it to modernity's "degenerate instincts" (*WFN*, 16:98). His accusations against socialism are relentless, often even artless, and signal his fear of its dominance over the late century's imagination: the Left is made up of "howling ... anarchist dogs"; socialists are tarantulas—"wherever thou bitest, there ariseth black scab"; socialists and nationalists alike are driven by "envy and laziness"; socialism is a "decrepit despotism" that annihilates the individual and deifies the state; because of socialism, we act slavishly while "anxiously eschewing the word 'slave' ... and talk[ing] of the 'dignity of man' and the 'dignity of labour'" (*WFN*, 12:127; 9:116; 6:352, 343–45; 2:3–4). In a view that Arendt would later amplify in the United States, he denounces the interests of labor because to the Greeks, "labour is a disgrace."⁶⁷

Even his grudging praise is meant to undercut its object. Socialism has a right to exist like any other natural object, such as steam, insofar as it has force:

"With every great force—be it the most dangerous—men have to think how they can make of it an instrument for their purposes. Socialism acquires a *right* only if war seems to have taken place between the two powers, the representatives of the old and the new" (*WFN*, 7:322–23). It keeps the "democratic herding animal" from getting too weak; it forces them to be craftier and more warlike; it keeps them from becoming like women (*WFN*, 14:103). Closer to the end of the century, in a startling prediction, he expresses his respect for the morbid power against which he summons his will. As though anticipating the Russian Revolution—an event that coincided with the institutionalization of his philosophy in Europe—he proclaims that "the coming century is likely to be convulsed in more than one spot, and the Paris Commune . . . will seem to have been but a slight indigestion compared with what is to come" (*WFN*, 14:102). He singles out Russia as its probable source, calling it a "gaping Asiatic maw" that threatens to "swallow our little Europe" (*WFN*, 6:314). He goes on to speak in terms that, again, explicitly unite Oriental foreignness and socialist insurgency: "that immense middle empire where Europe as it were flows back to Asia—namely, in Russia. There the power to will has been long stored up and accumulated" (*WFN*, 12:146).

An enthusiastic supporter of the Prussian royal house in his youth, by the late 1860s and early 1870s Nietzsche felt profoundly threatened by the rise of social democracy in the electoral sphere. This movement was then joining forces with the philosophical authority that Hegel had given civic melioration and to which his own field of philology contributed by promoting the vernacular "spirit of the people." What he targeted in the persons of Bebel and Liebknecht was only the spiritual offspring of a Hegelian germ. If one of Nietzsche's sternest reprimands to Europe was that it indulged in a merely "reactive" attitude to what endangered it, forgoing in this way the more effective glancing blow, the dodge, the maneuver ("*Looking aside*, let that be my only negation," as he put it), nevertheless Nietzsche's enterprise is profoundly reactive when it comes to Hegel and his political legacies (*WFN*, 10:213). One of Schopenhauer's early attractions for Nietzsche was the former's mission to obliterate the philosophical triumph enjoyed by Hegel and his school, which Schopenhauer associates with the coming to power of the "abject class . . . the scum of society."[68] Tormented by nostalgia for "the *schole* of classical antiquity," Schopenhauer sought to undo all the effects of modernization, believing that the merging of the idea of culture with profit in modern life was mainly Hegel's doing. Hegel, by way of "Taine—the *first* of living historians—exercises an almost tyrannical influence" (*WFN*, 12:214). The "amazing skill" of the Romantics with their Goethe cults "was passed on to the disciples of Hegel, the real educators of the Germans" (*WFN*, 6:86).

In *Ecce Homo* (1888), Nietzsche looks back on his *Birth of Tragedy* (1872), writing that "it smells offensively Hegelian, and it is only in a few formulas affected by the cadaverous perfume of Schopenhauer," referring to the fact that Dionysus and Apollo are there "sublimated [*aufgehoben*] into a unity" (*WFN*, 17:69). When in "The Use and Abuse of History" he complains that a person is "condemned to see 'becoming' everywhere," he is explicitly referring to the philosophy of Hegel and to dialectical thinking in general. Seeing everything "fly past in an eternal succession" is to stop believing in one's own being, he argues, and it is this mobilization of being as against becoming that would later become the watchword of Heidegger's own reaction against the Hegelian tradition (*WFN*, 4:8). He continues to dwell on Hegelian "becoming" in his very last work, clearly disturbed and intrigued by the concept (*WFN*, 15:177). Yet another and perhaps clearer way of grasping the reactive quality of Nietzsche's philosophical imagination is to note that his intellectual career was launched in *The Birth of Tragedy* by pitting Dionysus against Socrates—that is, by pitting intoxication against dialogue, the first dialectic. The polemical dispatching of Plato was the first step in the attempted supersession of dialectical thought that preoccupied him thereafter.[69] In *Futures Past: On the Semantics of Historical Time*, Reinhart Kosellek highlights Nietzsche's appropriative displacement of borrowings from Marx, who in "Contribution to a Critique of Hegel's *Philosophy of Law*" used the categories *Übermensch* and *Unmensch* in an ideological critique to "destroy the doctrine of the two worlds." The "religious reflection of *Menschen* [humans] in the image of heavenly *Übermenschen* [supermen]" was, Marx argued, a degradation of *Menschen* "to the status of *Unmenschen* [inhumans]"—a line of thought that Nietzsche famously sought to reclaim.[70]

That Nietzsche was embroiled in European colonial and socialist politics, despite claims even now of his apolitical untimeliness, is a view significantly reinforced when one looks at his extensive critical treatment of these questions. *Beyond Good and Evil* is, in this context, programmatic. By his own account, the book was an attempt to translate into a more publicly accessible form the parables of *Thus Spake Zarathustra*. The unfolding politics of Europe are very much in evidence throughout the book. At times he is quarrelling with social democrats, at times with anarchists, at times with French radical thought, at times with British reformers, and at times with reactionary militaristic nationalists in Germany itself. When describing what he means by the will to power as an expression of Darwinian "life," he passionately defends "exploitation," a term that against the backdrop of social democracy is almost certainly picking up on the vocabulary of the insurgent labor movement.[71] Although not always consistent in matters of detail—in one passage in his early career, for example, he condemns the exploitation of Europe's workers as a "folly" and a "robbery"—his perspective is unwavering enough (*WFN*, 6:341). In general, he summons the term in order to overturn its pejorative connotations, countering that "'exploitation' does not belong to a depraved, or imperfect and primitive society: it belongs to the *nature* of the living being" (*WFN*, 12:226).

His doctrine of "slave morality," similarly, is not only a bold philosophical dictum founded upon the earlier Jewish and later Christian transvaluation he both emulates and despises; it is a specific contemporaneous reference. This morality is objectionable to him not simply in the general sense that a slave is unfulfilled, compelled to follow orders, captive, defined by limitations, unfree, and unable to express will. Nietzsche is also conjoining the word "slave" and European workers. He means, among other things, to impugn the morality of those political movements representing workers that, while pretending to support them, keep them enchained with strategies of petition, redress, and equality, which sap their vitality. Recognizing that slavery is not desirable for oneself or the truly talented or ambitious, he explicitly defends the institution of slavery for inferiors both at the very beginning and end of his career (*WFN*, 2:7; 12:59).[72] His view is that one finds slavery more tolerable "provided that the superior class above them constantly shows itself legitimately superior" and is not like the flabby, commercial bourgeoisie (*WFN*, 10:78). With the ghost of Greek antiquity hovering always in the background, he predictably takes the view that by opposing slavery—the institution that enabled Athenian creativity—communists, socialists, and liberals are really just opposing the arts and classical antiquity (*WFN*, 2:7). So, logically, he comes to endorse a project he expresses, significantly, in imperial terms—he and his disciples as "lords of the earth," a new, vast aristocracy of "artist-tyrants" (*WFN*, 15:365).

Along these same lines, an argumentative thread in *The Genealogy of Morals* psychologizes economic arguments based in antiquity as a way of explaining how the concept of "debt" became the idea of "sin" (both meanings found in the German word *Schuld*). Over several pages he attempts a new gloss on theories of labor, credit, debt, value, and exchange (*WFN*, 13:69–70, 79–80). It would not be overreading to see this as Nietzsche's fixation on the new prominence of economic arguments in Marxist political challenges to the state. It is in these very passages, after all, that he mixes with this etymological explanation of the origins of morality the idea that horrible "Judea" (as he puts it) was one of the forces behind the (to him detestable) French Revolution, identifying the poisonous plant of anarchism and socialism as being the logical outgrowth of Judeo-Christian *ressentiment*. Dühring is once again brought in—the man Nietzsche dubs one of the two "lions of Berlin" but, at the same time, a "paramount moral blusterer" who promotes a "communistic model of treating every will as equal ... a principle hostile to 'life'" (*WFN*, 12:135, 160; 13:160, 88). He inadvertently defines the term later when he remarks how disgraceful it is that socialist theorists want to "put an end to all vice, illness, crime, prostitution, and poverty, ... but that is tantamount to condemning *Life*" (*WFN*, 14:33).

Riding the publicity coattails of social democracy, his hope was to outmaneuver it. His directive is evident already in his early polemic in *Untimely Meditations* against David Friedrich Strauss, whose undoing of the mythical Jesus in his hugely successful *Life of Jesus* (1835–36) scandalized Germany after its publication and set the tone for Nietzsche's later and more radical assaults on Christianity. Here, too, Nietzsche is following a social democratic lead while attempting to surpass it. His scathing critique of Strauss, which was as impudent as it was unyielding, given Nietzsche's youth and the disastrous reception of his only previous book, *The Birth of Tragedy*, was also an attack on the Young Hegelian movement with which Strauss had earlier been strongly identified. In the essay, Nietzsche associates what he calls "the Hegelian school of reasoning" with philistinism and considers Strauss its most egregious exemplar.

Given the philological basis of Nietzsche's thought, it is interesting that when Hegel is invoked in the essay, the philosopher is lumped together with Friedrich Schleiermacher, the biblical scholar and founder of modern hermeneutics, whose efforts to reconcile Enlightenment critique with Protestantism Nietzsche found as reprehensibly optimistic as it was marked by the repulsive "glistening idealism" of Hegel (*WFN*, 9:188). The most vitriolic part of his broadside has to do, as stated previously, with Strauss's style—the dark inheritance of all those who wallow in the "Hegelian mire":

> [Strauss] sins against style in the black book, the sable mantle of twilight is falling upon his fame. For he who has sinned against the German language has desecrated the mystery of all our Germanity. Throughout all the confusion and the changes of races and of customs, the German language alone, as though possessed of some supernatural charm, has saved herself; and with her own salvation she has wrought that of the spirit of Germany. (*WFN*, 4:95)

Hegel proves to be more than a philosophical adversary; he is the inexorable force behind everything dangerous to German culture in Nietzsche's view—politically, aesthetically, and stylistically. His own work—as the early unpublished notebooks of the *Nachlass*, among other sources, drive home—can be said from the very outset to set up Hegel's undoing. As one of the inaugural moments of his public career, then, the Strauss essay is all about exposing "the horrible destruction caused by Hegelianism!," a theme that rings throughout Nietzsche's oeuvre, most often in the early notebooks and the late posthumous collection *The Will to Power*. Even those who knew how to free themselves from Hegel, as Strauss eventually did, "never can be fully cured," trying as Strauss had in vain to "jettison Hegel and everything theological."

The Strauss broadside opens significantly with a declaration that its composition is occasioned by the German reception of the Franco-Prussian War. The military victory of Germany, heralded at home as a triumph of the German spirit, was for Nietzsche a danger sign—the advent, in fact, of a philistine complacency. He is not at all opposed to celebrating Germany's triumph, but he thinks this postwar discourse has turned "our victory into a signal defeat... into the uprooting of the 'German Mind' for the benefit of the 'German Empire'" (*WFN*, 4:5). He looks instead to "the creation of a genuine German culture," which he does not want to be mistaken for an "alien 'cultivatedness'" that he associates with the French, commenting that "Germans have never lacked clear-sighted and courageous leaders and generals," only those willing to follow them. His task, as he sees it, is to "redirect German bravery"(*WFN*, 4:6).

The degenerate "symptoms of the age" that he complains of as early as 1874 took a definite shape and color for him early on as a volunteer hospital orderly in the Franco-Prussian War—a conflict he joined with enthusiasm. He himself characterized the war, as many other Germans did at the time, as a death struggle between French and German civilization. In his youth, Nietzsche had been a fervent Prussian patriot. In 1873, at the close of the war, we find him drawing his lessons from that traumatic experience, in which (as he relates in his letters) he lived among mangled bodies, struggling not to faint: "My starting-point is the Prussian soldier: here we have a true convention, we have coercion, earnestness and discipline, and that also goes for the form.'"[73] What France represented for him in this conflict is made explicit in a letter to Carl von Gersdorff in 1871:

> If in peace there is one thing remaining for us from that savage game of war, it is the heroic and at the same time reflective spirit which, to my surprise, like a beautiful unexpected discovery, I found fresh and vigorous in our army, full of

old Germanic health. We can build on that: we may still have hope! Our *German* mission is not yet past! I am in better heart than ever, for not everything has been ruined by French-Jewish superficiality and 'elegance' and by the greedy turmoil of the present age. There is still courage—and German courage—between which and the élan of our poor neighbors there is an inward difference. Over and above the struggle between nations the object of our terror was that international hydra-head, suddenly and so terrifyingly appearing as a sign of quite different struggles to come. (*SLN*, 80)

The "international hydra-head" refers to the popular insurrection in Paris that, under the pressures of the war, brought to power that provisional government of laborers and intellectuals that was the Paris Commune. This has traditionally been seen as a watershed in European socialism, the moment when the movement becomes conscious of its ability to compete for control of the state and to be acknowledged seriously as a rival in the creation of a new political direction for Europe. In an almost perfect symmetry, then, Nietzsche found his voice precisely as the anti-Commune, the philosophical warrior against popular insurrection. His intellectual youth was in this way characterized by a fear of usurpation couched in civilizational terms.

Nietzsche saw socialism and anarchism as rivals to his status as the subversive scourge of old Europe. In place of its barricades and congresses, he proposed a subterranean politics of immoral redefinition.[74] His attitudes toward the workers' movements were indelibly marked by the rumors in 1871 that the Paris Commune had burned down the Louvre (a slander, it turned out, but one that moved Nietzsche to think forever after of the lower classes in terms of cultural barbarism). He recoiled in horror when friends thought they detected in his concept of the Dionysian the spirit of revolution. He was quick to correct them by associating all political conflict of this type with the Apollinian, reserving the Dionysian for a sublime Hellenic affirmation of an older aristocratic agon and aesthetic brotherhood (*WFN*, 10:333–34).[75] Socialism meant "the state" for Nietzsche—the destroyer of great intellects and individuality. Yet he in no way wished to be seen in the costume of the more predictable opponents of socialism at the time—the Basel industrialists, for instance:

> The manufacturers and great magnates of commerce have hitherto lacked too much all those forms and attributes of a *superior race*, which alone makes persons interesting; if they had had the nobility of the nobly-born in their looks and bearing, there would perhaps have been no socialism in the masses of the

people. For these are really ready for *slavery* of every kind, provided that the superior class above them constantly shows itself legitimately superior, and *born* to command—by its noble presence! (*WFN*, 10:78)

He made Switzerland his home in exile because of its reputation as the refuge for all that was dangerous in the late nineteenth century, the place where radicals of all types congregated; and Basel was, after all, the very center for a while (1869) of the international socialist movement. His strategy is appropriative: to possess the power he opposes by first adopting it, then "signifying on" it in the sense of subverting it with insincere imitation.[76] Noting with displeasure that democracy had flattened out differences in Europe generally, he observed that "equality" might nevertheless be useful if it were refashioned. The new reality imposed by the *demos* provided the grounds for superseding nationalist divisions and of creating a unified, cosmopolitan Europe.[77] The spiritual unity of the continent was impossible unless one could liberate it from its nationalist fervors. The new bloc was vital, for it could then combat the utilitarian mentality of an accretionary imperial Britain (a country he did not consider European). He geared his repeated phrase "We Germans" against the cant and "moral Tartuffery" he linked specifically with England, English morality, and English psychologists (utilitarianism particularly), for they were the ones who had popularized the idea of "the general welfare" (*WFN*, 12:174–75).

It has become conventional to see Nietzsche, on both the Right and the Left, as a philosopher "ashamed of Germans" and as acerbically critical of the very idea of Europe.[78] But his position on both is of a different order entirely.[79] He instead sought racial mixtures as a future source of European strength, one of those threads of his highly performative philosophy that begs to be misread as a post-racialist, pre-postcolonial discourse.[80] It is not that he did not also condemn the mixing of races "indiscriminately," since the human products "have in their bodies the heritage of multiple origins . . . that fight each other and rarely permit each other any rest" (*WFN*, 7:347). But the inconsistency is only apparent; it was a sacrifice in which we must all learn to "wag[e] war against [ourselves]," just as the ancient warrior Germans who conquered Rome, given their home at the crossroads of Europe and Asia, were highly mixed themselves (*WFN*, 12:122–23).

One of his more forceful arguments against Bismarckian nationalism, then, was to propose that its blunt oppositionality was no match for the superior virtues of subterfuge and evasion. "Cosmopolitanism," as he promoted it, was attractive precisely because of this tangential, maneuvering quality in which the boring legal and civic dimensions of political nationalism gave way to a miasmic cultural cohesion marked by strong personalities. What Europe is infected with, he suggested, is nevertheless productive—creating a "magnificent tension" that "had never yet existed on earth." For Nietzsche, Europe was central, unique (*WFN*, 12:3). The great Europeans of the past (Goethe, Beethoven) teach us that their genius had nothing to do with nationalist manias. Instead, they stood for "world literature." They "lust[] after the foreign, the exotic, the crooked, the successful plebeians" (*WFN*, 12:219–20). They were "virtuosos through and through, with uncanny access to everything that seduces, allures, compels, overthrows.... It fell to them to first teach their century—and it is the century of the *crowd!*—the concept 'higher man'" (*WFN*, 12:220).

In this context, too, it is important to note that his references to the "nation" are hardly all negative or mocking. Again, he very often cajoles his nation as cultural ethnos, expressing his frustration over its not being smarter when pursuing its own interests. What never leaves his discussion is the emphatic language of what is possessively "us" and "ours." His rejection of nationalism is imperially specific: "I see over and beyond all these national wars, new 'empires,' ... [based on a] "United Europe." This was the "only real work" of the "deep-thinking men of this century." In order for it to achieve the "mastery of the world" it must come to an understanding with Britain and will need her colonies as well as the colonial possessions of Holland (*WFN*, 13:225).

He was to conclude that philosophy itself needed to speak in the "vanishing voice of olden times," which meant that those like himself of the higher cultures would need to establish "the caste of compulsory labor and the caste of free labor"—to embrace an inequality that would ensure the dominion of the arts and the intellect (*WFN*, 7:319). For Nietzsche, philosophical depth is itself associated with social hierarchy: what he calls the "pathos of distance," the ingrained differences of strata that are necessary to produce "the ever widening of distances within the soul itself" (*WFN*, 12:223). Employing an imperial rhetoric that was fully resonant with the time, he implores his fellow poets and savants: "Send your ships into unexplored seas! Be robbers and spoilers, ye knowing ones, as long as ye cannot be rulers and possessors" (*WFN*, 10:219). It is tempting to see this, and some do, as sarcastic metaphor, but in the flow of his prose, as it actually moves from thought to thought and book to book, the broader undertaking behind these lines eventually becomes clearer, as does its direct dialogue with the newspapers. Accordingly, to avoid rancor within Europe and to retain the project of (European) equality that gives socialism its appeal, he concedes that "backward peoples would have to be imported to undertake society's more menial and unpleasant tasks."[81]

No German, at any rate, could have been immune to the debates around the German quest for colonies in the years of Nietzsche's most prolific decade. By 1885, Germany had taken control of four African territories—South-West Africa, Togo, Cameroon, and German East Africa—as well as several smaller territories in the Pacific.[82] The large-scale emigration of Germans to the Americas for want of opportunities at home further fueled the colonial impetus and was already considered a national scandal by the 1860s.[83] Nietzsche's frequent phrases "We Europeans" and "We Germans" must be seen in the light of both developments.[84] In this context, it is worth mentioning that Bernhard Förster, who married Nietzsche's sister Elisabeth on May 22, 1885, and moved with her to Paraguay in February of the next year, was one of the promoters of colonial emigration to the Americas and sought Nietzsche as an investor in his enterprise. Nietzsche in the end declined for financial reasons. The colony, Nueva Germania, was founded two years later in 1887 in the Paraguayan outback (in the province of San Pedro) with fourteen German families, based on the principles of "anti-semitism, aryan supremacy, anti-animal vivisection and vegetarianism."[85] Like Nietzsche himself, Förster was not interested in the German state's owning colonies for its own national glory or to compete with its European rivals. His project was only that colonies establish Germanness abroad.[86] This is the setting in which we can appreciate Nietzsche's words from *Dawn of Day*, which, like Cacciari above, some on the Left have misread as a call to proletarian action:[87]

> The workers in Europe should declare that henceforth as a class they are a human impossibility, and not only, as is customary, a harsh and purposeless establishment. They should introduce an era of vast swarming out from the European beehive, the like of which has never been experienced, and with this act of emigration in the grand manner protest against the machine, against capital, and against the choice with which they are now threatened, of becoming of *necessity* either slaves of the state or slaves of a revolutionary party. Let Europe relieve itself of the fourth part of its inhabitants! . . . What at home began to degenerate into dangerous discontent and criminal tendencies will, once outside, gain a wild and beautiful naturalness and be called heroism. . . . Perhaps we shall also bring in numerous *Chinese*: and they will bring with them modes of life and thought suitable to industrious ants. Indeed, they might as a whole contribute to the blood of restless and fretful Europe something of Asiatic calm

and contemplativeness and—what is probably needed most—Asiatic *perseverance*. (*WFN*, 9:215–17)[88]

Not an Aryan supremacist (a weakness based on *ressentiment* that kept Europeans from being "warriors," in Nietzsche's view), not an anti-Semite (since one had better learn from the Jewish genius for creating a new morality by telling a good story) (*WFN*, 13:29–31), Nietzsche was not a colonialist, either, if by that one means an official supporter of German policies or economic goals in Africa. But this was because the European was supernational—a race suited to fill the role of the Nietzschean "free spirit."[89] The harsh conditions of workers in Europe in the 1880s led Nietzsche to conclude that the remedy lay in emigration: "Outside of Europe, Europe's virtues will accompany these workers on their wanderings." With a Homeric tinge, he explains that the workers' "inclination for crime will, once abroad, acquire a wild beautiful naturalness and be called heroism."[90] He does not flinch from the brutality of the operation, and his references to "predatory nature" (*Raubtier-Natur*) in this context are entirely positive. His writing during the last years of sanity just prior to 1890 becomes increasingly biologistic, so that although he flatly opposes nationalism and class conflict, he preserves the notions of both domination and difference, advocating a hierarchical order (*Rangordnung*).[91]

His return to the theory of "Great Politics" in this period was a program to establish his philosophical system founded on a European underground elite. What the next two generations of European intellectuals and activists would make of these prophetic leads is only vaguely known. The invention of what I have been uninventing was, as Steven Aschheim has shown in his meticulous tracing of Nietzsche's many readers between the wars and after, the work of the political Left and Right alike. Few of them, however, paid attention to his classical sources or appreciated the stakes of his ongoing war on philology or the philological evidence of the corpus itself as the precursor and enabler of a complicated, and not altogether novel, discourse of imperial sovereignty.

As we will see, though, intellectuals of the interwar Left (Benjamin, Lukács, Sorel, Adorno, Gramsci) had inklings of all three in their readings of him. Only in the early decades of the twentieth century did their international resistance to the European imperial project gather momentum, drawing on the very social democracy and communism with which Nietzsche had been at war. The interwar years saw, as a direct result of these developments, a popular genre of racial and civilizational fear-mongering that brings to life Nietzsche's early-century reception.

THE INTERWAR FEAR GENRE

> For the French monarchists, history is not development, but natural evolution:
> the pseudo-concepts of race, origin, soul, order, hierarchy, heredity are the
> principal factors, in their view, in causing and consolidating events.
>
> *Antonio Gramsci*[92]

It is in the first decades of the twentieth century that a portrait of Nietzsche as an opponent of Eurocentricism begins to emerge. The ascendency of intellectuals of the interwar German Right who came of age under Nietzsche's guiding hand—Heidegger, Ernst Jünger, Schmitt—were building on earlier incarnations of this story of his unique and complicated acts of subversion. In fact, unlike Heidegger and Schmitt, some in the 1920s wrongly identified him as a vital enemy of European imperial priorities, but in a manner that vividly shows how misrecognition could lend support to the view of Nietzsche as the prefiguration of postcolonial thought.[93]

As early as the turn of the century, only a few years after Nietzsche's death, wars and uprisings in the colonies led to a growing mood of alarm expressing itself in out-of-the-way corners of the European imagination. Working as a popular illustrator in 1906, the Czech émigré to France, František Kupka, for example, composed a series of illustrations for a multivolume work titled *Histoire Moderne* (Modern history). There he captured sentiments that were circulating more widely after two deeply traumatic events for the European establishment on the eve of World War I: the stunning defeat of Italy by the Abyssinian king Menelik at the Battle of Adwa in 1896, followed by the victory of Japan in the Russo-Japanese war in 1904–5. Kupka's cycle of pictorial studies titled *Divisions et rhythme de l'histoire* (The divisions and rhythm of history, 1905–7) record, among other things, the connections that he and others felt between the growing socialist movement (with which he sympathized) and challenges to the tired rhetoric of Western civilization. His depiction of barbarians in one of these drawings as prehistorical, blond Europeans (see frontispiece to this chapter) seemed to be an answer to Nietzsche's "aristocratic races, the beast of prey; the magnificent *blonde brute*, avidly rampant for spoil and victory" (*WFN*, 13:40).[94]

Dubious interpretations of Nietzsche's infamous "blond beast" have appeared on both sides of the political ledger. In sorting out the various readings, it is advisable to begin by remembering the setting of the passages of *The Genealogy of Morals* where the image first makes its appearance. At that point in his presentation, he is demonstrating how etymologies reveal that our current vocabulary of virtue is derived from words that referred simply to the aristocracies of the past, and that our pejorative vocabulary, by contrast, derives from associations with the lower classes and the darker races. His whole discussion leading up to the mention of the "blond beast," therefore, is racialist, and we must conclude that "blond" refers specifically to race, as indeed he makes clear when he notes that "the pre-Aryan occupant of the soil of Italy ... was distinguished most obviously from the blond, that is Aryan, conqueror race by his color" (*WFN*, 13:25). His phylogenetics were complicated, however. It is true that they were not garden variety racism, but that does not mean that they were not premised on hierarchies of race. For the blond beast is based, in Nietzsche's thought, on the ideal of the ancient, supposedly Aryan peoples who wreaked havoc throughout Europe and conquered Rome. The twist is that Nietzsche wants to deny that Germans of his day have any claim to being the pure progeny of these ancestors—that they are not unmixed descendants of this blond type as the Bismarckian nationalists were, in his view obnoxiously, claiming.

Moreover, in his theory this noble savagery can be found in many other peoples; racial mixture is a modified good forced upon free spirits by democratic leveling. It is true that these peoples include Europe's colonial others in his account—he mentions the Chinese and the Japanese, for example—but one should be careful not to make too much of this fact. Nietzsche is just as likely to explain the decline of humanity by its becoming "more attenuated, more inoffensive, more cunning more comfortable, more mediocre, more indifferent, more Chinese, more Christian" (*WFN*, 13:44). He took the position that these intrusions from the East (near and far) amounted to a "dwarfing and leveling of the European man [which] is *our* greatest peril" (*WFN*, 13:44). His most emphatic point is to promote Europe, but only by giving it a more expansive definition: "We understand by 'Europe' a far wider region than is embraced by the Europe of geography, the little peninsula of Asia." It is based on the "common past" of Greece, Rome, Judaism, and Christianity; it includes America and excludes parts of eastern Europe (*WFN*, 6:306). In that light, it is important to remember that German colonization schemes in this period recognized that with much of the global periphery already under the control of other European powers (especially the British), Germany's major colonies would have to be its immediate neighbors to the east—particularly the Slavic countries.

As the most eloquent rallier of Europe to find again the right to its privileges, Nietzsche saw very early that socialists, on the one hand, and the insurgents of Asia and Africa, on the other, were related challenges to the systems of

European rank that he fought to redefine. They were not on the same track, but as "slaves" they possessed a strong family resemblance, amounting to the same dangerous power of resentment that brought them naturally into each other's camp. Classical antiquity had a patrilineal bond with Europe itself and was the proper conduit of all political wisdom.

This was discourse borrowed by Nietzsche from literary modernism but then borrowed back again by late-century literary movements inspired by Nietzsche's theories. In late nineteenth-century Russia, for example, the symbolists—as Irina Gutkin points out—proposed a historical imagination centered on apocalyptic premonitions. One of its poets, Dmitry Merezhkovsky, "prophesied the threat to civilization from 'the coming boor,' a mythic savage, who was in fact somewhat of a cross between the petty bourgeois and the proletarian." Vladimir Solovyov's poem "Panmongolism" (1894) predicted the "destruction of the existing civilization" by "'the yellow peril'—the eruption of dark, savage, nomadic, heathen forces of chaos from 'Asia' (which could also be interpreted, of course, as the non-Europeanized elements of Russia) who would triumph over European culture." Gutkin goes on to observes that the Apollinian/Dionysian opposition was a "synthesizing strain in the symbolists' eschatological imagination . . . place holders for a series of traditional oppositions—the rational and the irrational, the forces organizing 'logos' and 'chaos' and the largely uneducated and impoverished 'spontaneous' masses and the Westernized educated and propertied elite." Both the Russo-Japanese War and the strikes and demonstrations during the Russian Revolution of 1905 were read as the "pagan-Asian-Dionysian forces . . . historically present in the Russian masses."[95]

It was during the interwar era that any number of thinkers began to copy, quote, and creatively misapply Nietzsche along these same lines. Many took his arch-aesthetic loathing to be at one with socialist critiques of an instrumental cultural and economic system. Traditional conservatives and popular journalistic commentators of the interwar era, many of them frankly racist, considered Nietzsche to be, along with Dostoevsky, a metaphysical sniper giving aid and comfort to the Bolshevist enemy. These conservative defenders of the West, frightened by the spreading interest in Asian religion and philosophy among European intellectuals drawn to the East by Russia, invoked Nietzsche's phrase 'We Europeans' as their rallying cry.

Despite their prima facie characterization of Nietzsche as an inspirer of Bolshevism, there is a convergence between his and their own thinking about otherness. It is in Nietzsche's writing on the barbarian, in fact, that we find the first hints of a coupling of the image of the socialist and that of the uncivilized colonial masses, a strategy that inspired a hugely popular interwar genre of fear-mongering tales of the "death of the white race" among writers such as Maurice Muret, Henri Massis, Lothrop Stoddard, and (somewhat later) Herbert von Beckerath. The fact is, the conservatives of the interwar era shared many of Nietzsche's positions, although they expressed them much less skillfully and without the reversals that make them philosophically interesting and less easy to domesticate. What was and was not barbarous became, as a result of a now real colonial emergence crowding in at the edges of the European family, a question on everyone's mind. The prevailing obsession was succinctly captured by Oswald Spengler: "The occidental civilization of this century is threatened not by one, but rather by two world revolutions of gigantic proportions. One comes from below, the other from outside: Class struggle and racial struggle."[96]

The socialist threat, even more acute in the interwar years than in the 1880s, had made people suddenly conscious of the power of the world outside Europe to overwhelm the center by the sheer chaos of its cultural panoply, its strange and ungraspable gradations of self-confidence, and its estrangement from seeing modernity (as it so often was among European intellectuals) as something to be lamented. It is here, I am arguing, that the rejection of social democracy took on its sharpest philosophical features and became fused at a conceptual level with a lineage of European and American writing that sought to represent the Left as a new barbarian wave. What Nietzsche originally devised—the image of the Left as a racial and genetic miscreant—is taken up by Stoddard in his twin popular studies, *The Revolt against Civilization: The Menace of the Under-Man* (1923) and *The Rising Tide of Color* (1926). With a bigotry rampant in the era, Stoddard flags the "mongrel's political ascendancy" and bodies that are "a battle-ground of jarring heredities," and calls on "race duty" to "resolutely oppose . . . Asiatic permeation of white race-areas" to defend Europe as the "white homeland."[97] As for the *Unter-Mensch*, he finds the uppitiness of workers emulating Bolshevik impudence the corollary of a malignant Russian stock: "The Russian people is made up chiefly of primitive racial strains . . . [that are] 'wild'"; revolutionary doctrines from Rousseau through Lenin are a type of "destructive criticism" based on the "lure of the primitive."[98] As a lot of people have pointed out over the years, these kinds of ideas are not Nietzsche but half-read, misunderstood Nietzsche, without irony or the usual doubling back that accounts, unpersuasively, for the view of his ambiguity and uninterpretability. But the coupling—this image of the barbaric Left—was Nietzsche's creation, and it led, through many mediations, to a popular genre perfected in the interwar era and still lively today.

Confusions of attribution abound on both sides, in any case. Georges Sorel's *Reflections on Violence* (1908)—a work that was written in the milieu of an intense Nietzscheanist excitement in the first decade of the twentieth century—is frequently characterized as a book that counts Nietzsche among its major inspirations. By the time of its appearance, a generation of French Nietzscheans had been spawned, among whom was the essayist and author Daniel Halévy, to whom Sorel wrote an open letter beginning the book. A year later, Halévy published a biography of the philosopher (*La vie de Frédéric Nietzsche*, 1909), counting as one of his closest associates Édouard Berth, who drew excitedly on Nietzsche in his writings for *Le mouvement socialist*, the principal organ of Sorel's "new school." The allusions to the philosopher in Sorel's great study, however, are sparse, and where they appear, damning. Sorel notices right away that Nietzsche's talk of the "masters spoiling for privilege" grows out of a particular take on Homeric heroes and demigods as a result of his classical training, and he may be the first to make this connection. But when he dissents, it is not so much to insert his own proletarian virtues in place of Nietzsche's aristocratic ones as to point out (like Benjamin later) that Nietzsche's ruthless, bold, enterprising type has not vanished from the earth as Nietzsche claims. It is perfectly embodied in the Yankee entrepreneurs of the United States, who inscribe into a new ethics older racialist hierarchies. Nietzsche's ideal type, in short, is for Sorel the unfettered American capitalist.[99]

In his *Defense of the West*, written in 1927, Henri Massis sets out to attack what he calls the "Asiatic influences on the intellectual life of contemporary Germany." He specifically dedicated a final appendix to Rabindranath Tagore, who shortly before the appearance of Massis's book had completed a widely publicized speaking tour of Europe and had recently delivered a lecture in Paris which was, according to Massis, "attended by intellectuals, scholars, professors and society people" and was "heard religiously" and with "submissive admiration."[100] For his part, Massis insists, "I was indignant. I recalled our saints, our heroes, our citizens of Europe; I thought of all the work, all the discoveries, all the institutions, which their will had created, and it did not seem to me that we should bow down before the mystical, dreaming, lousy and ever idle East" (*DW*, 247).

Massis was writing in a setting when the fear of a rising Asia was prevalent in Europe among British and czarist military propagandists who had in 1904–5 fought on both sides of the Russo-Japanese War. He does not want to be confused with the hammer-pounding sort of rhetoric characterized by the likes of Stoddard and others and so clarifies his position by stating that "when we speak of an 'Asiatic peril,' we are not accusing the East, in general, but denouncing the philosophic, moral, and social errors and the dubious idealism which Oriental propagandists educated in our schools and served by certain European idea-mongers, set up in the name of the East against the West" (DW, 27). The war of ideas, in his mind, centers on Germany, which in these years is "perpetually hesitating between Asiatic mysticism and the Latin spirit, and which seems to be in a state of permanent protest against the Roman idea" (DW, 29). Defeated in World War I, Germany looked confusedly to the East and "began to prophesy, in dark apocalyptic tones, the final bankruptcy of the world, the mastery of which had escaped her." Massis's allusion here may be to Spengler's *Decline of the West*, with its dire prophecies for Europe's future set alongside its monumental praise for the revelatory aesthetic counterlogics of the non-Western world. But he would also have been thinking of the popular film *Die Leuchte Asiens* (*The Light of Asia*, 1924), directed by Franz Osten and Himansu Rai in a German/Indian co-production, which narrated the life of Buddha, whose story left Europeans with the lesson that enlightenment comes only after renouncing one's kingdom. And closer to home, he may also have had in mind the extraordinary work of René Guénon (a.k.a. Shaykh 'Abd al-Wahid Yahya). A French occultist, Freemason, and metaphysician who himself converted to Sufism, in *Orient et occident* (1924) Guénon directly addressed himself to the fear-mongering literature prevalent in the era in order to pull Europe back into a more self-reflective comprehension of its own inadequacies. He questions the "superstitions" of Western science, concentrating on Western illusions of moral progress, and urges Europe to learn from the philosophies of the East, particularly Hinduism, Taoism, and Sufism.[101] In 1921, he had written a well-received book for general audiences, *Introduction to the Study of the Hindu Doctrines*, which joined the works of other Orientalist scholars in providing a primer on what Europe philosophically lacked, dwelling on the West's "ignorant knowledge" and its confusion of science with industry and attacking Madame Blavatsky's theosophism for injecting the interests of the British Empire into its pseudo-Hinduist notions.

Massis's book may be seen as setting out to block these currents, which he and others saw as defeatism and sentimentality. His task was to remind his readers of Europe's accomplishments. His ends are very similar to Edmund Husserl's in *Phenomenology and the Crisis of Philosophy* (1935)—surprisingly ignored in postcolonial studies—which emanates from the same epochal anxieties. In every sense part of the interwar genre of fear, its significance lies not so much in the guilt by association implied by his mentorship of Heidegger or his influence on Derrida as in its contrasts, from the colonial point of view, with the traditions of Hegelian thought. In this lecture, delivered in Prague, Husserl speaks—quite unlike Hegel in *The Philosophy of History*—of the new "epoch of humanity" that alone pertains to an immanent "spiritual image of Europe." All "other human groups" understand this about "us," he maintains, and as a result they are Europeanizing themselves in a way that can never happen, for example, by our "Indianiz[ing] ourselves":

> In our European humanity there is an innate entelechy that thoroughly controls the changes in the European image and gives to it the sense of a development in the direction of an ideal image of life and of being, as moving toward an eternal pole.... Let us as "good Europeans" do battle with this danger of dangers with the sort of courage that does not shirk even the endless battle.[102]

Although very likely alluding to Nietzsche directly with his phrase "good Europeans," he finds in European reason and in philosophy itself the "West's mission to humanity," rousing his audience against the irrationalism that he finds seeping into the edifice of Western knowledge from the East (that is, Russia and India).

For his part, Massis, in his attacks on the India-loving German youth movements, conducts his study on the plane of the universal, writing as a loyal Frenchman fresh after world war diagnosing the febrile sickness of the German psyche. But his discourse does not remain there; it becomes more interestingly focused on the unique politics of the moment. The "German mind," he writes, had to seek energies outside itself, which it did by turning to Russia, India and China: "The sympathy shown to Bolshevism by a section of our younger generation is only one of the outward signs of this tendency" (*DW*, 60). He is worried less by the political outcomes of Bolshevism than that sympathy for it suggests "a change in the tendencies of the Western mind.... The German mind has ceased to gaze with any interest towards intellectual France" (*DW*, 61). Against "the materialistic West, which is all Machine," the Asiatic mind poses its own spirituality "with frantic insistency." Gandhi and Tagore preach tolerance of all religions "only to reawaken its own beliefs and better to dissolve ours" (*DW*, 135–36). The enablers of this assault? Massis has no trouble locating them. They are Lenin and Zinoviev, who shall overcome the West "by way of the East" (*DW*, 102). Russia is the "Orient of Europe" and has swept into its camp certain "young men of education" who now invoke the Bolshevist ideal in the form of Nietzsche and Dostoevsky.

But by associating Nietzsche with a "German intoxication" that prepares the gullible intellectuals of Europe for the dance of Shiva, Massis seriously misreads his opponents. If the reception of Nietzsche in interwar Europe associated him with Asiatic weakness and the gullibility of the Orientalist sentimentalist (à la Tagore), the picture is actually inverted. In lines that could have come from Massis or Muret themselves, Nietzsche claims that European "nihilism" comes from Europe's enticement and seduction by the will to nothingness, which he calls a "new Buddhism" (*WFN*, 13:8). This was not a passing theme. Two years earlier, he had made an identical claim: "[They are] at one in their involuntary beglooming and heart-softening, under the spell of which Europe seems to be threatened with a new Buddhism" (*WFN*, 12:128).

While Nietzsche's concept of noble virtue does not derive from any love for the trappings of medieval royalty, the figments of a warrior caste were fashioned, as so much else in his work, after an image of the epic demigods. So, when Nietzsche issues his call in *The Birth of Tragedy*—"You [readers] are to lead the Dionysian celebratory procession from India to Greece!"—his intent is to claim across the stretch of the Orient the unacknowledged influence and hidden power of that antihumanist side of Greece that humanist philologists suppress (*WFN*, 1:157). By widening the scope of his inquiry to those texts and traditions outside the Bible and the Greek and Roman classics—to take it instead to that other sphere of philology occupied by the Orientalists—Nietzsche developed an extratextual (indeed, inventive and idiosyncratic) theory that plays with models drawn perversely from well-known philological scholarship. In this way, he does not challenge Orientalism but joyfully accepts as givens those claims about despotism, inscrutability, and the baroque excesses of its dynastic forms of art that later scholars from Egypt, Syria, and elsewhere would consider slanders, and that Spengler immortalized in *Decline of the West*.

In *The Genealogy of Morals*, Nietzsche drives home the idea that the dangerous emergence of the colonized in Europe and the rise of socialism are the same problem (and opportunity) and that German patriotism is doomed if it continues to rely on a simplistic hatred of all difference:

> On the contrary, it is the *pre-Aryan* population that makes itself felt . . . [in] almost all of Europe. . . . The conquered race has there succeeded in getting the upper hand in color, in shortness of skull, perhaps even in intellectual and social instincts. Who will guarantee that modern democracy, and anarchy (which is

still more modern), and especially the hankering after *la commune*, the most primitive form of society—which is held in common by all our European socialists—do not represent in the main an immense *atavism*, and that the conquering and *gentleman race*, the race of Aryans, is not among other things physically succumbing? (*WFN*, 13:25–26)

The language of racial pollution is by no means absent here, only expressed in favor of atavism and mixture, the planks of his platform. He counsels that we learn from the enemy and not succumb to *ressentiment*, that we adopt its themes and language in order to simulate an alliance that is really an effort to destroy, and dissimulate our own position. In a passage from his notebooks the following year, he clarifies what the step after dissimulation might be:

> A man should have to choose between either going to the dogs or *prevailing*. A ruling race can only arise amid terrible and violent conditions. Problem: where are the *barbarians* of the twentieth century? Obviously, they will only show themselves and consolidate themselves after enormous socialistic crises. They will consist of those elements which are capable of the *greatest hardness towards themselves*, and which can guarantee *the most enduring will-power*. (*WFN*, 15:308)

We can see, then, given the context above, that "socialist crises" means something like "threat to our existence"—the crisis that prompts us to strike back. The word "barbarian" is another double entendre—not the image of what "we" seek to conquer or repel in this case but the image of what we need now to make our model.[103] He had earlier written a great deal about the barbarians of modern culture, but here he rather imagines a "conquering and ruling nature" of "*another kind of barbarian* who come from the heights.... Prometheus was a barbarian of this stamp" (*WFN*, 14:329). As I have shown, he had already painted the socialists of his day as hordes on the edge of the European encampment. It was a short distance to travel to jest that the noble had to cleanse slavish democracy with a barbarism of its own. This is why when discussing Cesare Borgia in *Beyond Good and Evil* as the "healthiest" of all aristocrats, he calls him a "tropical man" and taunts the moralists by saying "they harbor a hatred of the primeval forest and the tropics" (*WFN*, 12:118). The noble men will learn their colonial mission, moreover, by practicing on the socialists at home. The one will sharpen the weapons for use against the other. What is arguably ambiguous in the above rendering (are the socialists the barbarians he speaks of, or the latter's victims?) is clarified in a note from the same year: "What means one has to employ with rude peoples, and that 'barbarous' means are not arbitrary and capricious, becomes palpable in practice as soon as one is placed, with all one's European pampering, in the necessity of keeping control over barbarians, in the Congo or elsewhere" (*WFN*, 12:487). "Socialist crises" will inspire us to act as we know the "tropical" barbarians of old acted: with terrible violence and furious strength, exterminating the enemy. He approaches the intermeshing of the destinies of the colonies and European socialism from a different angle by proposing to crush the "pampered" and the "weak." The language of eugenics and colonial control over natives is implicit in the late Nietzsche, consistently wavering between fantasy and literalism, but always keeping in mind the target of social democracy:

> A teaching is needed which is strong enough to work in a *disciplinary* manner; it should operate in such a way as to strengthen the strong and to paralyse and smash up the world-weary.... The annihilation of declining races. The decay of Europe. The annihilation of slave-tainted valuations. The dominion of the world as a means to the rearing of a higher type.... The annihilation of universal suffrage—that is to say, that system by means of which the lowest natures prescribe themselves as a law for higher natures.... Constitutional plenitude should be aimed at by means of the coupling of opposites; to this end race-combinations should be tried. (*WFN*, 15:298)

Aggressive and blunt, these words seem very far from the playful or transgressive acts of signifying with which his writing is so often associated.

It is not enough, though, to trace Nietzsche's complicated response to the movements and moods of the German 1880s. For one thing, despite the labor of working through his volumes' words, triangulating them with letters, contemporaneous accounts, biographical details, and so on, it will inevitably be seen as too easy, as though the literal itself were not onerous. But even if we focus only on Nietzsche's rhetorical resources, dissociating his influence from mere contents in the name of the artistry of method, there still remains the fact that forms have political contents. The greatest of these problems is found in his most enduring formal influence, genealogy.

WHAT NIETZSCHE MEANS BY GENEALOGY

> The peasant is the commonest type of *noblesse*: for he is dependent on himself most of all. Peasant blood is still the *best blood* in Germany, e.g. Luther, Niebuhr, Bismarck.
>
> Nietzsche[104]

The term "genealogy" usually appears in essays and books today as a simple substitute for the word "history"—a term many consider compromised because of the supposed confidence of historians that archival data yield an original truth. It tends to be used as though it were a genre that Nietzsche invented, with a set of features that he specified or set out to demonstrate. He never did, however. We owe this confusion, in part, to Foucault's attempt to systematize Nietzsche's critique of history and his new methods under the rubric of genealogy in a widely read essay from 1971, "Nietzsche, Genealogy, History."

Although brilliant and original, like so much of Foucault's writing, the essay introduced a number of thematic threads that have been hard to disentangle. Right at the start, for example, it is arresting to find Foucault declaring that genealogy "opposes itself to the search for 'origins.'"[105] Nietzsche, though, announces in the opening pages of *The Genealogy of Morals* over a stretch of ten or so entries that he intends to pursue the "origin of our moral prejudices," the "origin of the morality of asceticism," the "origin of justice," the "origin of punishment," and the "origin of language."[106] The more one knows about Nietzsche's training, his place and time, the more one would expect this emphasis; and we can see from his career trajectory that it would be logical for him, especially in the counterphilological mode, to insist only on a better mechanism than textual recovery to arrive at the truth of origins. His entire political program regarding antiquity's real character depends on them. All the same, Foucault is not exactly wrong, at least in any simple way. He is right to point out, for example, that Nietzsche uses two words interchangeably for "origin" in the text: *Ursprung* (source) and *Herkunft* (stock, birth, descent). He does not notice, or at least does not mention, that *Herkunft* also means the "derivation" of words and that this is, in fact, its primary meaning in Nietzsche's text, which is all about exploring how words ("good," "bad") relate to physical and social "stock." Nietzsche casually blurs these various meanings throughout, first using the term generically in the phrase "*origins* of morality," second in reference to his own *upbringing*, and third as a synonym for *genealogy* itself: what he calls his *Herkunfts-Hypothesen* (genealogical hypotheses).[107] He does not see these meanings as distinct.

Foucault's point, though, is very different. He wonders whether Nietzsche did not want to colonize the first term, suspending our confidence in it, gradually pushing *Ursprung* to the side for its associations with the lofty solemnities and metaphysical poses of the traditional historians. In Foucault's account, Nietzsche was eager, when coining the term "genealogy," to get away from any hint of uniform sources or unilinear chains of causation. The idea was to get us thinking, Foucault implies, along the lines of the second term, whose biological overtones brought us less to the history of events than to the body. In place of "go[ing] back in time to restore an unbroken continuity that operates beyond the dispersion of forgotten things" (*Ursprung*), Nietzsche wished to strike a more intimate, aleatory note (*Herkunft*): "the body ... [as the] stigmata of past experience" that "gives rise to desires, failing, and errors" (*NGH*, 146, 148). Naturally, given the weight of Germany's own specific history in regard to higher and lower *races*, Foucault is wary at this point of the likelihood that some will see a reference to "stock" or "descent" in Nietzsche as suspicious. So he explicitly redeems *Herkunft* by stating that it has nothing whatever to do with race or nationality: "Genealogy does not resemble the evolution of a species and does not map the destiny of a people" (*NGH*, 146). In fact, though, this is exactly what the term "genealogy" is meant to do.

It is difficult to tell from Foucault's rendering, but Nietzsche is simply not involved in *The Genealogy of Morals*, at least in any primary sense, in an attack on historical sense-making. He dwells instead on others' misprisions, bungled etymologies, bowdlerizations—all, as we have seen, the métier of his years at Pforta. Yet this becomes for Foucault evidence of a new principle for Nietzsche of doing history, a new method called "genealogy," which lays out a preference for small-scale histories of everyday life, subaltern wanderings, and the embrace of the indeterminate and unfinished—above all, the reliably false past of our reconstructions, memories, and the traces left on our individual bodies. But all this is to overlook the gist of *Herkunft* in the contexts we explored in the previous sections, as well as the fact that one of Nietzsche's major goals in *The Genealogy of Morals* (and he states this in so many words) is to lay out a method of "exegesis" of the aphoristic form, which is the subject of the entire third essay of the book. As we have seen, Nietzsche was signifying on well-known philological techniques with the aim of undermining only one kind of history writing: monumental history (we know that he earlier identified at least three other kinds, about which he says nothing here). He did this because he found a necessary value in other ways of doing history (its uses rather than abuses). The criteria Foucault outlines, although all of them ring true, never amounted to anything like a program: "to identify the accidents, the minute deviations ... the errors, the false appraisal and the faulty calculations that gave birth to those things that continue to exist and have value in us" (*NGH*, 146).

In fact, though, the two major emphases that Nietzsche announces in the book go unmentioned in Foucault's account.[108] First, in his polemic with "English psychologists" in the opening pages, he advocates a rhetorical model of dealing with intellectual opponents by not arguing with them. He proposes instead that we dodge interlocutors, mocking them but above all ignoring them, creating instead a different and more alluring story to persuade audiences emotively rather than substantively. He is clearly upset by his detractors and writes very emotionally, but he pretends to be unmoved, asking sardonically, "What have I to do with refutations?" In other words, he dissimulates intellectual and emotional disengagement. Second, he dwells not only on origins but the utility of origins, which he understands in physical terms. This is evident when, for example, he speaks of the "physiological depression" of modernity being the result of "the crossing of too heterogeneous races (or of classes—genealogical and racial differences are also brought out in the classes)" (*WFN*, 13:169). What he wants the term "genealogy" to suggest atmospherically (since he never exactly lays it out as a new method) is very much a part of the evolutionary vitalism of his career generally. *Menschliches Natur* (human nature) is, unlike a history of dynamic agents, a fluctuating sameness that may traverse time but without voluntary practice or guiding intelligence. It is a legacy in blood, recorded inexorably in language—the etymology as a word's parentage. The term's usefulness is that it allows him to partake of both sides, stipulating historical change without admitting to human agency. Indeed, he is arguing on behalf of *utility* to a degree—an ironic riposte to the utilitarianism of the English psychologists. We do not, after all, choose our parents, our sex, or our nation. So he wants to be able to portray the narrative counterpart of this inheritance; he wants a form of history writing that creates a sense of causation but without the attribution of a cause. Nietzsche's politics of style, then, is to devise the technique of adjacency, where the juxtaposition of events that are not causally linked forces readers to supply, without realizing that they are doing so, the connections that have been left out on principle (although, in another feint, made inevitable by the placement itself).

Let us return, then, to Foucault's view that genealogy is resolutely opposed to absolute origins despite Nietzsche's words to the contrary. As a critic who agrees with Foucault on this point, Raymond Geuss argues that genealogy points to a "historically contingent conjunction of a large number of such *separate* series of processes that ramify the further back one goes. The key point is that they present no obvious or natural single stopping place that could be designated 'the origin,'" as opposed to what he implies are the more mono-causal explanations of "traditional" history-writing.[109] But this ignores Nietzsche's apprenticeship as well as his sallies into European colonial politics. It is confuted by an earlier observation from "We Philologists," which at first seems to support Geuss's position: "Careful meditation upon the past leads to the impression that we are a multiplication of many pasts. So how can we be a final aim?" Nietzsche does not stop there, however: "But why not? In most instances, however, we do not wish to be this." His point is not that historical causation is simplistic or that it needs a theory of multiple causes, but that our singular aim is the desire to escape demonstrable causation in the name of the openness or indetermination that one, extra-ethically, seeks (*WFN*, 8:118). If anything, his sense of causation is strict. For, in another biologism, he proclaims at the outset that ideas and values grow out of us "with the necessity with which a tree bears fruit ... connected and interrelated" (*WFN*, 13:3).

All the same, there are good reasons for making Geuss's (and Foucault's) arguments in a more limited sense for certain passages.[110] But their approaches are selective: how miss, for example, the performative contradiction when Nietzsche argues that origins tell us nothing about a thing's value while at the same time attempting to reroute our thinking about the transvaluation of all values by exposing its origins in early Jewish scripture? He wants to adopt his anthropological view on the necessity of enhancing life without moral restraints. But Nietzsche is very far from trying to establish historical accuracy in the manner described by Geuss. Although inevitably, by talking about the past, he offers forms of evidence (this principally is the role of his deployments of etymology, in fact), yet he explicitly rejects the idea that evidence substantiates a hypothesis. He makes this point emphatically in "On Truth and Lie in an Extra-Moral Sense."

The many layerings of his account of the usefulness of lying are impossible to reproduce without simply repeating his collected works, since the point is so central to the entire operation. When he writes that truth is "a sum of human relations which have been enhanced, transposed, and embellished poetically and rhetorically," he is, of course, not lamenting hypocrisy but establishing its purpose in the form of a discovery of the human animal. Although Nietzsche toys with the word "science" in his early lectures on philology, from a very early date in his training he had urged instead an aesthetic, intuitive approach to the reconstruction of origins in *Quellenkritik* (source criticism) (*NGW*, 1:429–32). The stemmatic graphs of genealogical recension (illustrated in the accompanying figure) vividly mirror the genealogy as family tree. There is a biological dimension that Nietzsche has grafted onto textual recension. In both cases, at any rate, we can see that the multiple origins Geuss holds firmly on to in his reading are upside down, since a genealogy actually ramifies only as we descend through time from a single source.

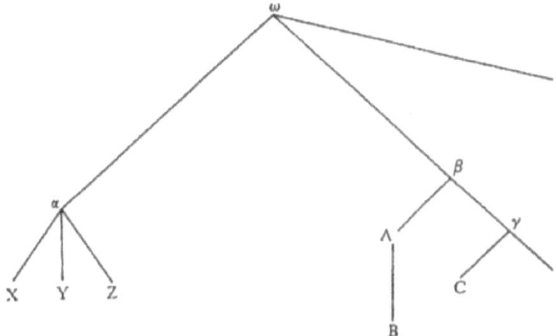

Stemmatic graph of textual recension
From L. D. Reynolds and N. G. Wilson, *Scribes and Scholars:
A Guide to the Transmission of Greek and Latin Literature* (Oxford UP, 1991) 211.

Geuss's position might still be maintained if Nietzsche were setting out to reverse the graph in line with his war on philology, except that Nietzsche had no such intention. He says very clearly in a fragment on the "Method of Philological Source Criticism" that one arrives at a variety of hypotheses after the fact, intuitively, and based on a fundamental picture "in which a long array of specific and previously unified phenomena are seen together and where they are understood to be diverse effects of a *single* cause of various materials."[111] This might be only the difference between early and late Nietzsche, and we could imagine that here where genealogy as a concept is developed he wants to overthrow an earlier philological mania with his own theory of multiple origins. But then the image he adopts is incoherent. For a genealogical tree, after all, begins with a single parentage and achieves its multiple branchings and unpredictable combinations only in later generations—just the opposite of the point alleged by Geuss, who sees more ramifying the further one returns to the past.[112] The methodological centrality of etymology, ignored by Geuss and others, has to be taken into account here and theorized in order to reveal the secret of origins as sources (*Quellen*), which plague Nietzsche throughout his apprenticeship.

Although Nietzsche is capable of sarcasm, there is no hint of it in the passages on origins. He follows up his list with an explanation of his mode of operation: "There is needed a knowledge of the conditions and circumstances in which they grew" (*WFN*, 13:9). Or later, when he underlines his intention of exploring "what is documented, what can actually be confirmed and has actually existed, in short the entire long hieroglyphic record, so hard to decipher, of the moral past of mankind!" (*WFN*, 13:10). His principal charge against the

English psychologists of morality in the book is that they are *not* historical (instead of the other way round). He needs this to explain how what seems so natural today is rather very recent and only gradually came to be with the waning of aristocratic privilege. Among the origins he seeks to clarify is the "origin of language," because, for Nietzsche, to seal a thing or event with sound (that is, to name it) is to take possession of it (*WFN*, 13:17–21). Those of rank gave themselves the right to state values and to coin names for them, and this is how they came to originate. Naturally, too, in the ongoing indignation of Germany toward imperial Britain and its collusion with France in spreading the virus of democracy, he locates etymologically the spuriously heroic connotation given to "plebeianism" as being "of English origin"—a theme, as we have already noted, with colonial overtones given the rivalry between Germany and Britain. His assault on utility as a precept among the British is not an assault on utility as such but on social usefulness, anything that gives the weak a say in determining the valences of the word "good." By urging that we see the origin of goodness as a matter of rank, he asserts a utility of a different sort—one found in the act of naming a new ethics and by naming, creating it. This is why Nietzsche shifts the discussion from what these dispositions (judgment, punishment, conscience) are, or how they arise, to an inquiry into their value, that is, use. Every disposition is measured against the standard of whether it is "useful to life" (the basis of his solidarity with Spinoza's *conatus*).

Geuss and Foucault are silent about three features of genealogy that Nietzsche himself highlights and which, as we have seen, bring to culmination the intertwining themes of his career. In Nietzsche's actual presentation in *The Genealogy of Morals*, first of all, genealogy is in part what it literally denotes—that is, the descent of family as a filiative group set off from those outside its bloodline. This line of thinking, as we saw, animates a great deal of his work on the instinctual bonding and inherited character of the ethnos, even if he allowed for those not born into the group who could be, in his words, "cultivated for it." Second, it is biological inheritance: in place of historical actors, genealogy describes a progression of time without progress; in place of historical causation, inactive actors whose work is to recognize that they are natural carriers of an instinctual and impulsive life. Nietzsche's way of expressing this principle is to "become the one you are."[113] Third, and most important, genealogy is a technical term in the philological circles of his time.

Nietzsche's own teachers had contributed significantly to the concept of genealogy before him. At the University of Bonn, for instance, Nietzsche studied under Otto Jahn and Friedrich Wilhelm Ritschl; Jahn's training had been under Karl Lachmann (1793–1851), the philologist known both for his editions of Lucretius and for having developed the genealogical method of textual recension. Lachmann's principle was that agreement in error implies identity of origin, which might fairly be taken with a few changes as the motto of *The Genealogy of Morals*. Lachmann's influential method was a technique employed in classical and biblical textual scholarship for examining variants grouped into types to determine the original text; it was widely embraced and produced its most enduring scholarly triumphs in the 1830s. By invoking the term "genealogy," Nietzsche was playfully mimicking a well-known practice of textual recension—a method of determining precisely the original form of a text on the basis of flawed or corrupted later variants. He may have thought this allusion self-evident to his readers, but it was, in any case, altogether obvious to him—a direct inheritance, in fact.

What Nietzsche hammers away at as the myths and delusions surrounding the origins of morality are versions, in his metaphor, of the paleographic corruptions and erroneous transcriptions of ancient texts. In this figural rendering, which is really an extended act of ironic distancing from the philology he was busily adapting and changing, there is no question that an authentic original text exists. Indeed, Nietzsche counts on this in order to effect the re-transvaluation of all values that he struggled for in his career in order to mimic Jewish genius in having invented the idea of good and evil as against good and bad.

Lachmann's vocabulary was appropriately suggestive: traditionally, the text as it passed from one version to another was known as the "vulgate"; philologists also used the term "filiation" to describe the relationship between manuscripts based on their errors and corruptions.[114] Textual critics were not allowed to take as authentic the manuscripts as transmitted. Instead, the expectation was to read what was not there—the embedded, implied "vulgate" that formed the connective basis for all the written records that actually survived.[115] As a scientific response to creative conjecture, Lachmann's method stressed the highly mechanical nature of most errors, their unthinking repetition in the act of copying, in order to remove questions of scholarly improvisation or taste in determining ur-texts, basing the finding rather on rules and probabilities. It is widely accepted that the method of nineteenth-century linguists in reconstructing the mother tongue of Indo-European was directly modeled on the archetype established by philologists in classifying classical manuscripts on the basis of Lachmannian "stemma." We also know that this model of comparative linguistics was adopted by Nietzsche's teacher, Ritschl, informing his own textual criticism.[116]

Thus it is Lachmann who has already introduced the idea that "textual corruption too is an innovation compared to the previously transmitted text, just like a linguistic innovation" and that "a linguistic innovation, once it has achieved success, ceases by that very fact to be felt as an error."[117] From the 1860s onward, throughout the time Nietzsche was writing, Lachmann's method was still the standard, but it was under assault. We can begin to understand what must have been on Nietzsche's mind in adapting the term "genealogy" from within a chorus of scholarly debates that he joined in his own peculiar way—one that embraced a new comparatism, emphasized the horizontal rather than purely vertical transmission of textual errors, and reacted against positivism. Sebastiano Timpanaro describes the prevailing mood:

> As is well known, this was a reaction that combined some justified elements (an impatience with hasty schemes and generalization, the need for greater faithfulness to the complexity and variety of historical facts) with other more dubious ones (a return to the spiritualist metaphysics far older than the old positivism, a sophistic rejection of empirical classifications in the name of the uniqueness of the individual phenomenon, irrationalist and anti-historical tendencies now named "historicism."[118]

Much of Nietzsche's undertaking was to that extent already familiar in others' returns to the past, but he was also original in some respects: his genealogy turns historical actors into textual surfaces and active interpretation into textual errata. Lachmann's textual recension refers to "witnesses," although a "witness" in hermeneutic terminology does not refer to a person but to earlier versions of the text itself or its citation in works by other authors. Even the very language and terminology—taken inaccurately by many of Nietzsche's postwar French readers to be signs of deliberately aleatory acts of subversive creativity—are derived from textual recension itself more or less unchanged. But he then figuratively, even sarcastically, applies it to the world of beliefs and values rather than the graphemes of biblical texts, suggesting that the resulting origin would be a matter, above all, of textual desire. This allows him to fold into a theory of history—or rather, a contravention of the writing of history as a past that enabled the present in contingent ways—a biologistic emphasis on instinct embedded in the everyday meaning of genealogy as family tree, along with ideas based on a shared philosophical secret to which he, cryptically, spends a good deal of time at the beginning of the book drawing our attention. This secret—one interpretation of which may explain Foucault's otherwise unmotivated emphasis on the body—seems to refer to Nietzsche's sexual preferences. Whatever these were, Nietzsche makes a very sustained point about it in the opening pages by stressing that this secret was given to him by birth, by genetic inheritance—his "a priori" as he playfully puts it—and yet he realizes how much it informs his impulse to demolish late nineteenth-century morality.[119]

This last point helps explain why in *The Genealogy of Morals* Nietzsche ridicules the English moralists as "genealogists" (a point that Geuss and Foucault, for instance, say nothing about). Why would Nietzsche employ "genealogy" while mocking genealogists? It can only be that he is signifying on philology, jesting with those who still restrict philology to historical recovery work and the correct rendering of verbal texts rather than, like him, vastly expanding the claims of philology to embrace the lineages of peoples, politics, and values operating according to the logic of words. Nietzsche's system, in fact, relies heavily on establishing *what really happened in the past*, and he is consistently involved in correcting his contemporaries' historical illusions by providing an alternative reading based on etymologies and a more bracing and honest insight into human nature. Among these key claims, for example, are that the Bible invented evil, that Homer is a collective noun for aristocratic warrior poets, that Germans labor under the historical myth that they are pure Aryans, and so on—all of them key historical points of departure and correctives essential to his project of reorientation and revaluation.

Genealogy, then, for Nietzsche is not a new way of writing history but the transformation of history writing into a philological—that is, textual—operation. But along these lines, and as an extension of them, genealogy (being primarily literary and textual) involves a theory of rhetoric. There is no reorientation without persuasion, so how does one persuade? With more evidence? Nietzsche does not think so. What the entire opening of the book is attempting to lay out is a rhetorical strategy of anticritique. He is very clear about this. What he is trying to explain is how to handle disagreements when confronted by antagonists such as the English genealogists. Step one, he writes, is to know the value of the "perverse" (in his words). Tap into "that magnetic attraction, inherent in that which is diametrically opposed and antithetical to one's own ideas" (*WFN*, 13:5): shock, outrage, the antinomian, the absurd, the tasteless—stylistic techniques of amplification that seduce an audience with images of its own imagined iconoclasm. Next, free persuasion from evidence (his refusal, as I said, of involving himself in "mere refutations"). He counsels like thinkers to avoid facing opponents or trying to defeat them in argument, opting instead to use texts as raw material—for lying, essentially. There is no subject who wills, only a will to truth, and why settle for a mediocre truth when an exhilarating one is more attractive? Be relentlessly positive; never negate, in the sense of denying the truth of, or demonstrating the incompleteness of. Provide instead a rhetorical lure that is always tangential to the position you want to overcome. Change the subject (in every sense). And finally, he counsels, replace the "improbable with the probable"—that is, appeal to convention and so win arguments phatically. Ask your audience not to worry about what you are insinuating because you are, after all, providing them with a mirror of their own prejudices. You are asking them less to weigh evidence than to look within themselves to discover what they think they always already knew. Every argument is really a posing of the question, "this is so, is it not?"

The genius of the strategy is that anyone who disagrees with a genealogical assertion is not so much defeated as forced to occupy a terrain whose verbal signposts have been rendered momentarily unintelligible. The genealogist moves in the realm of the "as if" of his or her original positing. The prominence of etymologies in the genealogy is the genetic theory underlying the larger biological metaphor: our truth comes encoded in words transmitted over the generations without agency. Truth does not have to be shown, or established, or grounded, because it is felt as an inheritance. In place of the ethical or epistemological, Nietzsche created the affective milieu of a prose persona. The *what* becomes the *how*, and if skeptics insist on returning to the *what* in order to submit it to scrutiny, they are simply seen to be lagging behind the "argument."

The challenge genealogy poses to any theory of reading—in fact, to any searching, caring, or knowing—is one operating at the level of *form*. These techniques of lofty nonargument and insouciance have been hugely influential and in many ways characterize entire schools of thought today. In the humanities, they may even be dominant. If knowing the beginnings of a thing is to know its essence—and I have been trying to map in some detail the beginnings of Nietzsche's concepts in their own settings—that fact should trouble those for whom things like justice, kindness, the poor, help, colonial subjects, improvement, society, and conscience still matter. Nietzsche circles around his targets with a ring of phrases echoing and mocking them in order to pounce on meaning from an unexpected angle in an assault whose distress, fury, and envy pose as indifference.[120] The legacy of his terminology—"ressentiment" is an obvious case in point—is difficult to re-enlist on behalf of palatable social programs or even coherent analytics, since he wants to label as a psychological crime any feeling that elite privileges have ever been ill gotten or undeserved. There simply can be no social victims according to Nietzsche; there can be no anger against oppression. And so the moving appeals of the likes of William Hazlitt, Rosa Luxemburg, Nelson Mandela, Camila Vallejo—all anticolonial, democratic outrage—count as nothing but the envy of others' intelligence and power. Even if one set aside the racialism, misogyny, and militarism—believing that the case, despite all the evidence, had not been made or did not matter—they would still be left with the dissimulating style, which loses none of its contempt or elitism in others' hands, and turns any politics, whatever its contents, into a kind of aristocracy of virtue, both there and not there at once, ironically receding.

Germany's significance in the history of colonialism, as we have already seen with Hegel, may have less to do with its misadventures in South-West Africa or eastern Europe than with the global popularity of its exported philosophical concepts. In that constellation, Nietzsche managed a mixed and stylistically novel fantasy of conquest and European triumphalism that has skillfully come down to us as its opposite, more or less unscathed by criticism.

"Modern Condition" [etching on paper], Lucy Valkury (2009)

4   BORROWED LIGHT

BATAILLE AND THE PARTY OF DE SADE

> Nietzsche's position is the only one apart from communism.
>
> *Georges Bataille*[1]

Georges Bataille's *La part maudite* (*The Accursed Share*, 1949) is, among other things, a midcentury conduit for everything troubling and transformative about Nietzsche in interwar thought. The book that in one way or another preoccupied Bataille until his death in 1962 was, however, much more as well. It offered a new economic theory that managed to read like a novel, couched in digressions on the sacrifice of kings and autobiographical confessions about the masochistic pleasures of marital sex. For all its underground fame in English-speaking circles since the 1990s, it is not especially revered for what makes it in the end so central to the argument in this book. For the important occasion of its appearance has been largely forgotten.[2] The very study that would later underwrite the reinvention of the Left Nietzsche in the 1960s and 1970s was composed in a period of intense metropolitan fear in the face of the postwar redrawing of the imperial map. Bataille's remarkable performance lay as much in its echoing of interwar anxieties over international communism in the colonies (especially the influence of the Soviet Union on the political restructuring of the periphery) as in its new economic theory about the utility of disutility and the productivity of waste.

The medieval trappings of Bataille's modernism of kings, knights, and village carnivals in *The Accursed Share* found early traces in his graduate thesis in 1922 at the École nationale des chartes. Celebrated by his teachers at the time and winning him admission into the prestigious Society of Ancient French Texts, his dissertation had been nothing less than a critical edition of the thirteenth-century manuscript *L'Ordre de la Chevalerie* (The Order of Chivalry), which he reconstructed from eight manuscripts found in the British Library and Bibliothèque national. The librarians of the École des chartes especially praised his labors on the "historical sources of the poem."[3] A tale in verse about the knight Hugues de Tabarie, who is taken prisoner by Saladin and eventually induced by Saladin to knight him, *L'Ordre de la Chevalerie* is a story decorated with the ceremonial iconography of knightly investiture. What particularly fascinated Bataille was the way in which the poem had been used by preachers in sermons where it was linked intertextually to St. Paul's Epistles to the Ephesians (6:11–17: "Put on the whole armor of God ... "). And yet, despite assurances from his superiors, his thesis was never published, being deemed too derivative (a complete critical edition had appeared in Oklahoma only a few years earlier) and too plagued by what his judges deemed "uncertainties" regarding its textual authenticity. Crushed by the failure, Bataille gave up hopes of a career as an archivist, and began to undergo psychoanalysis. His love of the medieval would survive, of course, in his late novelistic book on the trial of Gilles de Rais, for instance—but more as a fascination with depravity than as a performance of textual science. His model remained the sovereign might and extravagant spending of knights who fought crusades, as he explains in a letter in 1918: "In earlier times, men of war lived the glory of pillaging. Their campaigns were for them the true field of exuberance in their lives. O good old times!"[4]

These philological beginnings left their stamp on Bataille's work, and their relative neglect might be taken to foreshadow the careful omissions and amplifications that characterize Nietzsche's postwar reception, which for the most part has been indifferent to philology or unmindful of the shared pattern of the two thinkers, originally dedicated to the field but then, after a personal crisis, eager to push it in new directions. We can see in Bataille's thesis, ultimately, an act of sympathetic understanding. For he might have felt that he did not need to recapitulate every stage of his mentor's journey, beginning instead where Nietzsche had left off in a genealogical mode of antipathy toward political reform. A major undertaking, Bataille's three-volume tome (volumes 2 and 3 remained unpublished at his death in 1962), *The Accursed Share* ambitiously extended the concerns of the book he published four years earlier, *Sur Nietzsche* (1945), and is almost entirely dedicated to him.

A tour de force, Bataille's study is not just a summary statement of a new philosophical movement that translated the tenets of interwar Nietzschean thought (including his own) for the altered conditions of postwar Europe. The book's antinomian distaste for democracy, and its immodest longing for a return to the ethos of an earlier time when being was allowed to *be*, found some of their inspiration in the interwar German philosophical right: Martin Heidegger, Ernst Jünger, Karl Jaspers, and others who supported the same German state that had occupied and humiliated France only a few years earlier. Bataille's three-volume "essay" (as he put it) announced a coming theory built on the vision of a prophetic Nietzsche, a new "Jesus" in his terms. It established many of the themes and gestures of what came to be called "theory" after the 1970s in Anglo-America and Europe. We can say that it is this book more than any other that provides postwar theories of discourse and psychoanalysis with their insurgent tone and transgressive affect. His theory of sovereignty—to which all of volume 3 is dedicated—anticipated the language and direction of contemporary neo-Spinozism, for instance, as well as the political theories of Hannah Arendt on sovereignty, labor, aesthetic disutility, and imperialism and, after her, Giorgio Agamben. Although well aware of the legions of interpreters of Nietzsche before him, Bataille declares that the German philosopher "died without descendants," his "mobile, concrete thought . . . vanished with him." He adds, in fact, that only he really understands Nietzsche because he has not simply learned from him. He *is* him: "I am the only one who thinks of himself not as a commentator of Nietzsche but as being the same as he" (*AS*, 367).

It would be impossible to overstate the formative influence of Bataille's *impersonation* of Nietzsche on the latter's welcome in cosmopolitan circles, or to find a book that more suggestively mobilizes what we have been exploring in earlier chapters. Although not directly about Hegel or Marx, for instance—in fact it goes to great lengths to avoid mentioning them, except here and there—the book is at every turn addressed to them, setting out to revise their economic concepts by destroying their capacity to attract. In fact, the governing thesis of the entire study is to give shape to what Bataille calls "general economy," an argument that economic behavior is characterized not, as political economy tells us, by accumulation and profit but by purposeless destruction and excess. Striking the anthropological note of the early writings of both Marx and Nietzsche, his study is a cross between an ethnography of religion, a literary theory based on the Marquis de Sade, and a public events commentary on the new postwar political landscape.

The first volume, then, which was composed over the four years immediately after the war, dedicates its chapters by turns to Aztec sacrifice, Mexican potlatch, Islam, and Lamaism. These studies lead up to and punctuate later chapters on Weberian Protestant capitalist ethics and (not unexpected in the pattern we have set up here) Soviet industrialization and the Marshall Plan. Up until this point, I have been exploring the career of a similar genre of literary anthropology—for there is a strong anthropological element in Vico, Herder, and Marx as well. Any science of the human, after all, must establish what humans are, where they came from, and what they are capable of when compared with other animals. Classical political economists in general—this is certainly true of Thomas Hobbes, Adam Smith, David Hume, and Samuel Pufendorf—would have found it strange not to begin their studies with a theory of human nature, and in fact all of them do.

Bataille in this case summons a trove of ethnographic examples as evidence for his bid to revise political economy. But in effect, in his treatment of Aztecs, Islam, and Lamaism, he conjures a metaphorical *Geist* of emergent third-world polities in (respectively) Latin America, the Middle East, and Asia. What makes the study crucial for anticolonial and postcolonial theory is that Bataille, in the hovering image of Nietzsche, deliberately ties these latter chapters on the spirit of capitalist accumulation and the logic of Stalinist centralization to the problem of the political emergence of the non-Western world. The anticolonial implications of interwar Marxism are completely obvious to him, and he calls them out with remarkable candor and specificity, building as best he can a reactive bulwark against its past triumphs and, from the perspective of 1949, the likelihood of its future global success. That Bataille's study relies on the sardonic reversal of the language of communism is beyond doubt; to know this, though, is also to appreciate his indifference-in-hostility to the political aspirations of decolonization, whose liberatory concepts he expropriates and, in effect, makes fun of. The degree to which theory is given its original shape in Bataille's deliberately posed binary between Sade and Marx is altogether evident in the reading of this book. From the vantage point of the time, at least, the imminent independence of the global periphery, with or without Soviet aid, implied the formation of a vast economic power bloc outside the ambit of Western sovereignty. This is the context that made this epochal choice he poses between Sade and Marx, Nietzsche and communism, so urgent for him. Along with everything else, the book is grounded in a theory of appropriative reading that returns us, once again by this route, to the counterphilological that I am identifying and challenging in this book.

The Accursed Share not only enlists Nietzsche as a model—the final section of the long book, some sixty pages, explores "Nietzsche and Communism," "Nietzsche and Jesus," "The Example of Zarathustra," and so on—but gives novel shape to a Nietzschean synthesis. Bataille creates a Left-Right amalgam that will become a paradigm for cultural theory after the 1970s in Europe and the United States. Themes originally formulated by the interwar political Right (themselves a reaction against the growing authority of Marxism in those years) are taken on by the Left as its own, but without fundamentally altering their contents or reckoning with the adoption itself. This was a process Antonio Gramsci pejoratively called "transformism."[5] Bataille does this, moreover, by explicitly highlighting the philosophical collision of Nietzsche with Hegel that I have been tracing (to different ends)—a collision he presents as an expression of the threat of decolonization (*AS*, 368–71). Sovereignty is such a prominent issue for him in the book because it echoes what, on the other side of the dissimulation, is really at stake: the anticolonial independence movements ushered in by the war, many of them with communist sympathies and Soviet material encouragement. In part to preempt this outcome, and emulating Nietzsche's counsel, he does not refute or oppose but changes the conversation, transforming the sovereignty of states in the book into the sovereignty of subjects as a kind of solemn pun.[7] Similarly, the weapons of Marxist political economy, enthusiastically tapped for their militancy and their embedded historical memories of real-world material effects, are parodically refashioned as an ethnography of sadism, perversity, and death. By these means he enriches and deepens them out of existence.

This particular coupling, as well as its coded formulation, closely follows the suggestive contours of Nietzsche's own career-long obsessions. Bataille politicizes his hybrid discourse by constant reference to current events, which, as we have seen, was Nietzsche's practice as well. In this case, his dilemma is posed by the victors left standing after the war's destruction: those vast centers of "production" and "labor" in global geopolitics, the United States and the Soviet Union. He discusses both, especially the latter, at great length throughout the three volumes of the book, recognizing that communism is now the likely political option not only in the emergent global periphery but in Europe itself. As Bataille succinctly puts it, "Communism is the basic problem that is posed to each one of us, whether we welcome it or reject it: communism asks us a life-and-death question" (*AS*, 366).

I want to underline this point, since it has so much to tell us about the form that postcolonial and Left cultural theory takes in a variety of academic disciplines and artistic milieux in the following decades—views that speak, among others, to youth subcultures under the imprimatur of a literary philosophy estranged from itself as "theory." The very thinker who defines Nietzsche for postwar France (Foucault took more from Bataille than from any other French source) does so with the emergent sovereignty of former colonial possessions in mind.[6] The binary "Nietzsche/communism" expresses an epochal alternative to global socialist prospects. In Bataille, the "anti" theory derived from Nietzsche—one that stressed the mere utility of knowledge and the disreputable nature of manual labor for all "free spirits"—is deftly improvised upon.

Although Bataille's study comes off to most readers more as literary theory than analysis of production, its claim to offer a novel economic theory is defiantly clear: wastefulness is a hidden, natural, and *universal* economic law. The strategy of reversal is all the more effective in that it seems to mark the civilizing limits of Europe by looking to non-Western cultures for its proof of economic excess and disutility. These must be brought to bear, he suggests, and enhanced by following the lessons of primitive (his word) societies. Only in this way can one avoid enslavement by the new, modern regimes of economic sovereignty. His term *la part maudite* (the accursed share) should be understood as referring to the surplus arising from exchange that must be spent uselessly in order to demonstrate one's sovereignty over bare life.

In one sense, we should understand this mode of thinking—and this is true of so much of the contemporary theory he anticipated—as a quasi-philosophical genre switch based on the styles and attitudes of early literary modernism. In this light, Bataille's study can be seen as a translation into the genre of ethnographic/economic theory of those same sentiments found in the modernist authors who provided Nietzsche with some of his key content. Nietzschean core concepts—nomadism, the wearing of masks, effete taste as the "highest tribunal," "secret writing," an idealism of the "mud," the parody of the gospels—were taken *directly* from Dostoevsky, Baudelaire, and Poe.[8] Baudelaire goes so far as to extol the "founders of colonies, shepherds of peoples, missionary priests exiled to the ends of the earth, [who] probably know something of these mysterious intoxications"—that is, the "craving for disguises" and the "hatred of home and a passion for roaming."[9] He is the one who means to scandalize first with the claim that "cruelty and sensual pleasure are identical."[10] One recalls Poe's "The Man of the Crowd," with its cryptic judgment at the end (in German) "er laßt sich nicht lesen" (it does not allow itself to be read) and his remark shortly after that "there are some secrets which do not permit themselves to be told." In a kind of anticoncession that plays down these influences, Nietzsche admits that Dostoevsky was "the only psychologist from whom I had anything to learn."[11]

It is significant, then, that Bataille's concluding section dedicated to Nietzsche is titled "The Literary World and Communism," as though the literariness of Nietzsche's philosophy was already assumed. In a typical double entendre regarding the uses to which the aleatory and the nonteleological might be put in a new postethical world, Baudelaire was the perfect model. Anticipating Bataille's economic principles, the poet castigates utility: "To be a useful person has always seemed to me something hideous."[12] The homages to Baudelaire in the book, if not as sustained as to Sade, are lengthy. And so it is no surprise to find passages in *The Accursed Share* that read as if they had been cribbed from *Paris Spleen*. In that work, too, Baudelaire struggles to craft a poetic capture of the unruly view of the demimonde, taking over the mission of an underclass that is precisely not proletarian in pursuit of the powers of abjection. Bataille's language and style appear at times to be direct quotations of Baudelaire's prose poems:

> The true luxury and the real potlatch of our times falls to the poverty-stricken, that is, to the individual who lies down and scoffs. A genuine luxury requires the complete contempt for riches, the somber indifference of the individual who refuses work and makes his life on the one hand an infinitely ruined splendor and, on the other, a silent insult to the laborious lie of the rich.[13]

This act of supposed insolence, though, suffers from late arrival. In 1765, Herder wrote that "the art of squandering is a necessary part of the household regime of a rich man who does not wish to be too full or too poor." In Herder's anthropology we actually find Bataille's central term already articulated in the former's argument that the character of humanity comes not only from "societal forces" but from "the *general economy* of animal life."[14] It is always possible that Bataille missed the fact that some of his main ideas, and apparently even the banner under which he carries out his economic revision ("general economy"), had preceded him by almost two centuries. But how could he have overlooked Thorstein Veblen's spirited take on Herder, since it was much closer to him in time and stood right in the middle of any project of reviewing earlier maverick economic theories? In his chapter on conspicuous consumption in *The Theory of the Leisure Class*, Veblen treats at length this same "contempt for riches" that Bataille takes as his primary theme. There Veblen makes the point that it is precisely the rich who show "contempt for riches," given the utility of doing so in the atavistic warrior culture they inhabit. "Costly entertainments, such as the *potlatch* or the ball," observes Veblen, "are peculiarly adapted to serve this end," that is, the end of comparing the one doing the entertaining and his competitor who is "made to serve as a *means to an end*." The competitor at the opulent feast "is witness to the consumption of that *excess* of good things which his host is unable to dispose of single-handedly, and he is also made to witness his host's facility in etiquette."[15]

Everything Bataille takes to be transgressive, Veblen brings down to a human scale, describing in every detail the gist of Bataille's future argument while giving it a more persuasive, class-inflected gloss. And everything Bataille takes to be contemptuous of economic utility, Veblen shows to have a social function. Disutility is, for the nonworker at any rate, a utility. In Veblen's terms, Bataille has not zeroed in on an antibourgeois ethos but recycled as dissident a traditional ploy of the gentry. For it does not need to work, and therefore heroizes its own refusal to work as a mark of its superior status.

Bataille's achievement is also put in perspective by the work of his near contemporary, Henri Lefebvre. The latter's *Frédéric Nietzsche*, published before the war in 1939,[16] came on the heels of his pioneering study with Norbert Guterman, *Cahier sur la dialectique au Hegel* (Notebook on Hegelian dialectics; 1938) and was followed in 1947 by his magisterial *Logique formelle, logique dialectique* (Formal logic, dialectical logic). Unlike other studies on Hegel in France both before and after, his was untouched by Kojèvian improvisations. Alexandre Kojève's famous prewar lectures on Hegel would not appear until 1947, and then only with a number of Nietzschean emendations—for instance, the species crisis of the "last man" at the end of history, the idea that freedom is a function of appearances, the idea that Totality is not a social concept but "the existence of Man's very being."[17] The lectures appeared, in other words, alongside Lefebvre's and Bataille's books as a companion piece—the contemporary symbol of a seething but silent debate. Lefebvre's studies anticipated work on Hegel that, in the postcolonial moment, has recently begun to find its articulation but at the time was largely overwhelmed by the Kojèvian wave.[18] The *Cahier sur la dialectique au Hegel* was grounded in a study of Lenin's notebooks on the philosopher, which along with Marx's 1844 manuscripts were (according to Lefebvre) "crucial to the more humanistic, Hegelian Marxism that he [Lenin] began to develop."[19] Among other things, Lefebvre and Guterman had argued that Lenin discovered in Hegel certain buried tendencies such as the idea of development in spirals (an image we may recognize as coming from Vico). It is

Lefebvre, at any rate, who inaugurates a study of Hegel face-to-face with Nietzsche, a figure to whom, against all expectations, he is far from hostile even if the latter plays almost no role in Lefebvre's immediate postwar study, the *Critique of Everyday Life*, volume 1 (1947). At the same cusp, this latter book would provide for the first time a distinctive disciplinary perspective and a systematic new terminology to a cultural theory that was neither sociology, anthropology, nor literary theory but a unique synthesis of all three. Its methodological insights and new directions brought myth, image, and language together in a political sociology not seen since Vico. His project would not be seriously taken up again until Raymond Williams's *Sociology of Culture* (1981)—and then only within an English-speaking milieu largely unfamiliar with Lefebvre's earlier innovations, not to mention the decisively anticolonial moment of its composition. Lefebvre had taken his leads from interwar debates over the Russian word *byt* (everyday life), a central slogan within Soviet cultural organizations. In those circles, it meant drudgery, unwelcome errands, dirty and uneventful work, or an aimless, joyless, and unthinking passing of time. Unlike today's triumphant understanding of the everyday as a revolt from below, *byt* was for Lefebvre's milieu the very condition to overcome—the *un*imaginative, dronelike existence forced on laborers and the poor. It had to be addressed emotionally and aesthetically and from within if one was to redraft the political contract, or find the right principles from below for redistributing wealth and social access or reorganizing production. The symbolic potency of culture, its semi-autonomy in regard to politics and the economy, was Lefebvre's very point, but unlike for his counterparts, not in a purely ontological (that is to say, anthropological) sense but rather as a kind of politics of working-class form.

The Accursed Share, by contrast, carried on Bataille's interwar preoccupations with a "sacred" sociology inspired by surrealism—one based on violent and intentionally haunting third-worldist imagery. Its illustrations were drawn from the art objects and photographs of the ethnographic-imperial archive. In contrast to Lefebvre, it sought to get beyond the everyday—which it associated with bourgeois hypocrisy and banality rather than the tedium of productive labor—by way of extremes of experience outside reason, explorations of perversity, pain, and ecstasy that confer aesthetic legitimacy on a body past utility, morality, sense, or meaning.[20] Lefebvre is consciously addressing these trends in the *Critique of Everyday Life*, where he draws a sharp distinction between different kinds of cultural theorist. Pointedly, as though he had Bataille in mind, he calls Baudelaire a "half-starved bohemian clown" and "a Second

Empire bourgeois ham."[21] There are those, he explains, who try to decode social mystery by building a new vocabulary and a generalist method in order to penetrate the complexities of the "obvious"—one example being his own brilliant and elaborate investigations of "transduction," the "idea of level," "social space," the "micro and macro," and the "idea of ambiguity."[22] He invents an entirely new philosophical sociology of the invisible practices of working-class experience and of the felt ways in which ideas and values are formed outside official institutions. The other kind of cultural theorist, though, is drawn to the anomie that grips him or her in the face of the bizarre.[23] On the one hand, there is socialist wonder; on the other, a taste for magic—Baudelaire's drug-induced comas, the street cred of hanging out with prostitutes and johns, the sacral air that hovers over Poe's judgment that those who play by the rules are part of "the crowd" living in a zombie world.

The Collège de sociologie, as Bataille's interwar circle was called, sought out mystery not as a problem but as a destination; they ransacked medievalism and revived an interest in the modernist primitive of early twentieth-century Cubism. Now, however, the primitive was not a repertoire of sculptural form or the immediate thrill of the human being in nature but a more detached, patient ethnography of the posthuman. Their instruments were less the African exotic than the voyeuristic cruelty of public torture in China, documented in "realistic" grainy black-and-white photographs. The Collège applauded cultural differences, for in variety one finds antipodal evidence of the general impossibility of transcending the animal's inner coils. The "everyday," as it had been worked over by Georg Simmel at the turn of the century, in Freud's early writing on psychopathology, and in the cultural journalism of the Soviet sphere could only seem tedious when measured against the ecstasy of Christian mystics. The ethnography of the Collège is conceived as taking place outside of history in a double sense: at home, where the perverse is invisible because taboo; abroad, where it is safely consigned to a foreign lure. They pinpointed in particular the futility of the Hegelian citizen, targeting his attempt to fill a negativity or void with action, planning, and knowledge.

For Bataille, negativity ceases to involve becoming or communal self-understanding. Rather, it takes the form of a dwelling—a place from which to express the nothingness of the human being. The critique is not about the individual versus the collective as in other forms of liberal thought. It subverts this expected riposte, speaking instead (as Nietzsche had) in collective terms, although not of society but of the species. This permits a rousing political rejection of the capitalist individual in a language that, while replacing the Left, is confused with it. *Being and Time*'s "being toward death"—the waking-up of experience in the face of inevitable extinction so that it can be truly felt and lived—is picked up again in dramatically new ways. For Bataille, negation becomes the ultimate affirmation. The realization of the human is its oblivion, and death is not so much a final limit as a *telos*. Carrying on the antihumanist themes of interwar phenomenology, Bataille perfects a manner of bringing its discordant tendencies into a pattern of shared antipathy toward the Vichian civic.[24]

SIGNIFYING ON HEGEL

While tracing elements of the dialogue between this postwar Nietzsche and Marx, what I really want to convey is that *The Accursed Share* is a systematic, point-by-point mimicry of the latter. As the work of a maverick economist, the book enlists the prestige of *Capital* by portraying itself as equally lonely, dangerous, and heterodox. For what figure more powerfully embodies the intellectual renegade and founder of new historical values than Karl Marx? And we can recall here Nietzsche's worry that emergent social democracy was stealing his thunder, staking out the territory of the heterodox that he wished to occupy. As though following a road map through *Capital*'s table of contents, readers are led by Bataille from one section of his book to another, dedicated (in turn) to use value (as "utility"), to totality, and finally to state sovereignty. Just like Marx, he grounds his theory on an anthropological claim about "species-being" and proposes that social alienation—in the sense that Hegel first theorized it while critiquing modern manufacture—derives from the estrangement of one's own powers projected onto the divine.

If Bataille modifies these well-known Marxian themes even as he recapitulates them, his recyclings do not always subvert their original. At times they simply repeat them. The back-and-forth appears uncertain about the valences of its own apprenticeship and renegacy. He excoriates the bourgeois subject, for instance, and speaks of duty to a natural collective as though he were at peace with his mentor. But then, turning on a point, the mood shifts. In the opening pages of the book's first edition, he remarks that the title of his book, although "it might seduce, does not inform." With deliberate vagueness, he hints at what all this apparent emulation is about. "No one can say without being comical," he continues, "that they are setting out to overturn something: just subvert, that is all."[25] In other words, just as genealogy referred, among other things, to a way of arguing without appearing to argue, he feels no need to refute Marx or to acknowledge his negative reliance on him. He takes him over, in fact, by ignoring him so that he can wear his mask.

The shadowing of Marx, term for term, is too sustained for us to see the performance as anything but a mimicry-as-mockery of the Left Hegelian tradition. The detoxification is homeopathic. In place of revolution, Bataille proposes "transgression"; for materialism, corporealism; for political sovereignty, the sovereignty of sexual cruelty; for dialectical negation, the pursuit of nothingness; for communism, annihilation; for the future human being, the archaic protohuman; and so on. His point is very much about a new political direction, but he wants us to dwell on the calculated impudence of the presentation as well, the vacant double image of concepts whose substantiality needs the skeletal structure of the Marxian originals to have meaning at all. As a revisionary political economy, Bataille's, it must be said plainly, lays out the general strategy (and many of the specific points) later adopted with almost no modification by Hannah Arendt in *The Human Condition*, Jean Baudrillard in *For a Critique of the Political Economy of the Sign*, and Italian autonomist notions of the "refusal to work" and "affective value." Each of these strands can do little more than repeat *The Accursed Share*'s substitution of "works" for "work," for instance, in a passage that imagines that for "archaic man" works "had as their final and inaccessible end that miraculous element that illuminates being, transfigures it and grants it, beyond the poverty of the thing, that royal authenticity which never lets itself be reduced to the measure of humiliating labor" (*AS*, 226–27). This neo-aristocratic disdain for labor is very closely repeated by all three tendencies, each of which in its own way wants to paralyze the analytic of Vichian historical self-making.

The Accursed Share, in that sense, exemplifies the "adult play" that Bataille theorizes at length in the third volume of the study dedicated to sovereignty. There he looks over his shoulder at the model he was busy undoing, finding an ethereal substitute that dangles its alternatives before the audience with a sincerity that is always in doubt. In the overall book's attack on the slavery of utility (as in Nietzsche, with the same result), his own work is suspiciously enslaved by its mimicry of an antagonistic master. For even aspects of his alleged corrective were anticipated by the Marxist intellectuals from whom he departs by writing *The Accursed Share*. His bold reanimation of the insurgent aura of Marx that is supposedly exemplified by his move from a base-and-superstructure economics to a more potently symbolic culture was already well underway in the French Communist Party of Henri Lefebvre. It was, of course, thoroughly worked out as well in the Frankfurt School and in the *Notebooks* of Gramsci.

The burden of Bataille's re-presentation, then, is to write in this double register in order to make dependency equivalent (negatively) to originality. Politically incompatible, Bataille and Lefebvre as contemporaries are divided not by the fault lines of orthodoxy and renewal but by an anthropological quarrel over the meaning of the human species.

Mimicry as mockery, in this precise form, is one way of understanding what I mean by the phrase "borrowed light." Bataille's genealogical strategy is to re-possesses ideas in the Marxist lexicon in order to inoculate readers against them, which is to say not only that it is antipathetic but also that it is derivative. This, I would argue, is the sublimation paradigm of theory after the 1970s. The whole scope of the new departure stalks the categories, modes, and language of its original. This is made to appear less important because the intellectual grounds are no longer fought over by Bataille, and because they have supposedly been rendered obsolete by imploding intellectuality itself. With the pretense of not caring—or of finding more of interest elsewhere, in a new configuration simply indifferent to what it opposes—Bataille's struggle, as he sees it, is no longer over the realization of human subjects but over the viability of the concept "human." It is the genealogical tangent at its most basic—moving the *place* of argument so the antagonists never touch.

That being said, *The Accursed Share* is a captivating, lengthy book with an unusually relaxed, anecdotal prose structure. It is deliberately idiosyncratic, immensely repetitive, utterly unashamed of lacking a scholarly apparatus, and prone to make pleas to its readers to keep their minds open so that its story might be allowed to unfold gradually. It cannot really be capsulized easily or perhaps at all, and it is hard to give readers an accurate feeling for it—composed as it was over so long a stretch of time—since so much of the book's effects depend on getting to know Bataille's confessional mode and his many side roads and meanderings into the magic of everyday life. Since it would take a study with a different theme than the present one to explore the work adequately, let me try instead to give a sense of one dimension of it by considering, term by term, Bataille's unfriendly appropriation of the Hegelian features of Marxism.

Sovereignty

Marxism at least in part adapts Hegel's point in the *Philosophy of Right* that making one's own freedom relies on a government of laws. As a doctrine of revolution—rather than social theory or literary criticism—Marxism surrounds sovereignty with a dialectical interplay of self-making and rule-as-force. Anarchism is an obstacle every bit as much as autocracy, and the two are in fact intertwined. With all of its promised personal and cultural deliverance from the state, communism, as Marx speaks of it, is attainable only after political arrangements of sovereignty that shift the coercive power of the state to a broader and more representative constituency. Understanding the centrality of this problematic in its source, *The Accursed Share* devotes almost half its pages to sovereignty—the final half, and the book's last word. What he means by the term, though, is understandable only by way of the shorter volume that precedes it on the history of eroticism. There we find a long analysis of the medieval festival.

True to his guide in these matters, Bataille, like Nietzsche, knows that going back to a time before the intelligibility of the other's claim even existed is often a riposte that requires no actual argument. From the perspective of Homer, after all, what sense does it make to disapprove of "Jewish slave morality"? It had not been invented yet. Similarly, Bataille claims (without explaining why) that sovereignty always has "something archaic about it" (*AS*, 225). This allows him to seek its purer forms in a once-familiar European ritual in the foreign country of the past, rather than the Brazilian rainforest or aboriginal territories of a standard ethnography. In this Bataille resembles others in the *Collège*: however much the writing of Roger Caillois and Michel Leiris had unearthed materials in Polynesia or the Andaman Islands, their ethnographies always had in mind an implicit comparison with savage Europe.

It is clear in the flow of the argument that Bataille's deliberately impertinent displacement of Marx requires that he mimic that element of Marx's political theory that had come to the fore in decolonization. The immediate ends of philosophy for Marx were ultimately the creation of polities (as can be seen clearly, for example, in a work such as *Critique of the Gotha Program*), and no other period saw as many successful bids for national sovereignty as took place in Africa and Asia during the postwar years of *The Accursed Share*'s composition. Bataille's investment in third-world imagery was, as I said above, not only ambiguous but a metaphor of this political challenge, just as his allusions to European barbarity took on the features of pastiche. For if the gestures seemed at first to de-center Europe, that was not at all his reason for adopting them. He wanted two things: first, to restore Europe to primitive vitality in the name of a new image of the human as an animal whose sexuality in its highest sense involved cruelty and domination, whose appetites were non-normative, and whose taste for power was without political purpose; second, to be able to speak of sovereignty as what is embodied in a single person rather than a modern party or government. The festival was here an apt image, since they were presided over by kings who allowed the enactment of the subversion of hierarchies as part of their ritual play. This habit of seeing the overturning of entrenched elites as a game and of personifying governmental power as an individual (a king, queen, or president) has become conventional today and is widely repeated in neo-Spinozism, for instance, and in the work of Agamben and Derrida on law. The complex mechanisms of actual rule (as true of the Middle Ages as now) becomes in this way a synecdoche. But the simplification has another logic as well. It is necessary for Bataille to speak of unequal social status as spatial—that is, as situated in a body—just as Nietzsche had wanted to dispense with speculative logic and intellectual agency in favor of the "truth" that for him was to be found in the entrails and genitals. If sovereignty can be personified, the emotional agon of ressentiment acquires more narrative immediacy, clearing the way for Bataille to declare—in one of his many exhilarating assertions—that power belongs to those who merit it (*AS*, 250). The natural body's drives penetrate social hierarchy as an equally unchanging order.

The enactment of subversion in the carnival performance is, he writes openly, not a sign of the common people wanting to overthrow the sovereign but of their wanting to be more like him (*AS*, 247). His hypotheses, then, rest essentially within a literary trope (synecdoche), where even revolution is a performance with an archaic intention—one that precludes the independent thinking of the collective and that makes the monarch a *personal* destination for society. Of course, as we have seen, Spinoza too, as well as Hegel, gave a limited defense of constitutional monarchy (explored in Chapters 1 and 2). But Bataille's move is quite different—not the tactical maneuver of a faction attempting to arrest aristocratic privilege with a kingly authority to which one can more readily appeal, but the enthroning of every powerlessly natural human being as a private king. His "party," in this playful mismatching, is Sadian. As Bataille moves beyond the example of the medieval festival, his ethnographic fieldwork is culled from more literary sources—in long readings of Racine's and Euripides' dramas on the myth of Phaedra as well as Sade's *Justine*. The incest, rape, and sexual torture that fill those works are presented as anthropological proof of the only truly honest subversion—honest because it is what the human animal really wants, subversive because it conforms to what we really are (and what the normative intolerably disallows). Suddenly, in this company, "la part maudite" takes on a different meaning. It is no longer simply wasteful expenditure, as in volume 1, but that damned part of lust and aggression abhorred by humans when they try to set themselves apart as a species. To be sovereign for Bataille, then, is (in a compelling reversal) precisely *not* to have power—that is, precisely not to rule over *conatus*.

Transgression

Since Bataille dispenses with political revolt—indeed, he stresses that the "inner truth of the sovereign moment" is that rebellion "negates" subjectivity (*AS*, 252)—he is left in a precarious position in regard to the dissidence he announces as his own. It is in this spirit that he enlists the idea of transgression. A conventional term in ethnography for the violation of prohibitions, "transgression" refers to what is spiritually or morally revolting, not simply illegal. To be political, he seems to say, means to be apolitical, since the political on its own is not radical enough. Revolt is extragovernmental, not outside looking in but tangential or (again) indifferent to it. Revolt is anthropological in that its meaning coincides with expressing what has been proscribed—namely, the desire latent in the festival: exhilarating horror, frenzy, orgiastic fury, or in his own words, "new forms of ruination, forms that redouble the transgression, beyond complicity, through a boldness that increases in cruelty and crime" (*AS*, 174–75). Mocking the force that, at the time of his writing, was clearly the preferred alternative to a discredited bourgeois order (Marxism) placed Bataille in an uncomfortable position. His allies were certainly not his contemporaries Winston Churchill or Harry Truman, after all, even if their political targets were, in this restricted sense, identical to his own. All the same, it is only the force of transgression that prevents us from concluding that they were actually to the left of Bataille politically. For they, at any rate, had no interest in moving back from a modern to a medieval etiquette or in wielding a language reminiscent of the natural beast apologetics of late nineteenth-century social Darwinism.

This colonization of the image of rebellion left unasked whether certain prohibitions against desire might be worth keeping or whether the violation of norms was always against the present power rather than—in a period of revolutionary transformation in the colonies—a defense of it.[26] "Cruelty," in the service of transgression or not, must have sounded in 1949 a little too much like what the war had supplied in abundance in the form of interrogation chambers, death camps, and incinerated German and Japanese cities. Bataille, however, could not be clearer about his meaning. He embraces Sade's "fundamental discovery" that other people's suffering counts less than "my pleasure" and exalts rape as a fundamental component of Sade's system (*AS*, 176). It is difficult to appreciate now after many decades how foundational this armed occupation of the concept of revolt would prove to be in the 1960s and 1970s—how thoroughly it anticipated the later equation of non-normativity with a subversive assault on knowledge in the name of attaining power through abjection, or how completely it predicted the confusion between not following rules, on the one hand, and creativity, on the other.

His program—which he states at one point as "to be the cause of disorder" and to induce a "general corruption and derangement"—is paradoxical. For what kind of program is it that retains its force only if unachieved? Its fulfullment would mean the end of all transgression, for disorder would then become the new order, and as Marxism was forced to do in the early twentieth century, one would then simply have to take responsibility for power. This is an impasse: that even transgression can be conformist, that even the antiteleological can have a *telos*, a claim to disutility a use (*AS*, 181). To catch out contradiction this way by calling it circular, though, would not be enough. It would, for one thing, ignore Bataille's parody of Hegelian overcoming, where it appears now as an overcoming based on an opposition that does not confront. This dissimulation, as Nietzsche first invented it, is what antiquity identified as irony and what Bataille in his study calls simply the game (*AS*, 377). The political consequences of this move, crippling to the Left, have been far-reaching.

Negation

Bataille's speculations in *The Accursed Share* capture the attractive force of a style freed from philological commitments. Seeing them here in their origins, we can appreciate, among other things, how the body became in theory an anti-intellect. There is no necessary reason why intellect and body would not belong together (is not the mind in Lucretius and Spinoza part of the material of the body?) except where understanding is not considered the result of the labor of thought but the product of the revelatory experience of tragedy (based, in Bataille, on the Catholic mass). The anti-intellect is in Bataille a style. It is not just the claim that we are impulses plagued by the illusions of reason. His point is rather to protest philosophical complexity in the name of the purer register of a nondialectical singularity—to persuade by simplifying. By these means, Bataille reverses the poles of Hegelian negation, which is no longer, as in Hegel, a critical engagement that *adds* to the self after its transformation in dialogue with the object but a pure negative. He defines it as the original attempt by humans to consider themselves as not being animals. In short, negation as he means it is saying no to an obligatory assent. He arrests the movement of negation, restoring it to an antinomy, preventing the obvious dialectical questions from being posed: what animals except for humans toy with theories about their own natures, suppressing that part of theory that—in its very inquiry—exceeds that of other animals? He arrests self-reflexivity—the kind that observes that it takes unusual will and a unique perversity for humans to call into question the human. Bataille's negation eliminates this tension and seeks its reward in a rhetorical plan of persuasion by means of simplifying—of restoring an unbreachable two-part division whose truth is self-evident because it is felt, is already known, is always to be found within. His pun is that true autonomy tends to the automaton.

Abstraction

In the Hegelian tradition abstraction was the purely mental exercise that failed to bring thought into conformity with its object; it had to do ultimately with the division between mental and manual labor, and the problem of thought falling short of actualization. Here, though, Bataille would have it that thought itself is abstract—all thinking, discerning, beholding. He plies the language of a phenomenology of mind—an arena where thought is forced to dwell on its own abstraction and where the philosopher sees abstraction as an unfortunate necessity that must be kept in check by comparison to the world of objects to avoid thought for thought alone. Bataille, though, turns the ambivalent energies of abstraction into a simple pejorative. His life-affirming assent, seen from within as pure positivity, rests on the single side of an opposition sublimely indifferent to its other.

Totality

In Hegel "totality" had referred to the fluid movements and mutual entanglements of the apparently discrete categories of the social world. It precluded a notion of society as mutually unintelligible to its different, often isolated constituents, or as a system made up of atomized units with their own incompatible logics. As a counter, Bataille redeploys totality to mean the "not partial" of a more specific sort—the world beyond mere objects, the mystery of what remains outside usefulness: "Nowhere do we find a *totality* that is an end in itself" (*AS*, 112). Explicitly for Bataille, totality implies losing oneself: it is the oblivion of death—the universe "swallows me" (*AS*, 115); I cannot distinguish myself from it; I was outside of being until the moment of orgasm (*AS*, 118). To deny one's nature is to be separated from the totality in this revised sense of the nondifferentiated being of life in a universal void.

As borrowed light, Bataille's parody has to be seen differently from the revisions of others in the past who wanted to forge new paradigms by clearing a path through fundamental, usually institutional obstacles. Spinoza, for instance, set out to weaken official religion, obliterating its theoretical basis. His rational proof of God's existence by way of extension (matter) dispelled both tendentious scriptural authority and Descartes's a priori self. Similarly Rousseau, in order to undermine the forces of divine right, pursued a vision of endowment or entitlement by natural right. In both cases, these motives placed these philosophers in opposition to other thinkers before them—in Spinoza's case, the Scholastics, and in Rousseau's, Hobbes and Locke.

In the interwar philosophical descendants of Nietzsche, though, including Bataille, we find something more along the lines of ventriloquism. We find an appropriation that sought to supplant what it was forced to copy, subtly altering its terms while sapping light from its source. For example, in *Being and Time* (1926), Heidegger seeks to immobilize inquiry into events, actions, and consequences during an era of growing communist influence and even prestige by outmaneuvering Lukács's famous protest against reification in *History and Class Consciousness* (1923), which was widely read throughout Europe. Heidegger alludes at least three times to Lukács's arguments in *Being and Time* without naming him. "Reification" as the turning of social processes into things sets the tone for Heidegger's ingenious return to first philosophy as a meditation on things. *Alltäglichkeit* (everydayness) in *Being and Time* was likely derived from Lukács's exploration of the concept in his *Metaphysik der Tragödie* (1911).[27] He prioritized ontology over epistemology in part to offer an alternative pole of attraction to the critique of capitalism's assault on lived experience at the site of labor and cultural consumption. In place of a situated encounter with the world, his own resistance to capitalism (which was just as sincere) offered a meditation on "world" as the experience of materiality itself, saved from reification by an opening out to appearances. In place of (tactile, conjunctural) history we are given (atmospheric, pervasive) "time." Philosophy comes to elude all closure, all determinations of meaning, not because the inquiries are complex but as the principle of experiencing being. The process of thought takes on the features of a loop, watching itself think about itself in the (pleasing) consternation of never grasping the real but making of it an impenetrable *novum*.

My point here is not simply about influence, in other words, but about genealogy in action, although the lines of influence themselves have been vastly understated.[28] Few critics today take on Maurice Merleau-Ponty's declaration in 1946 that "all the great philosophical ideas of the past century—the philosophies of Marx and Nietzsche, phenomenology, German existentialism, and psychoanalysis—had their beginnings in Hegel."[29] In a similar vein, Jürgen Habermas's observation in *The Theory of Communicative Action* that "systems theory and action theory are the *disjecta membra* of a dialectical concept of totality employed by Marx himself and then by Lukács" is not generally considered, much less pursued. How is it that a philosophical lineage now so widely despised, attacked, or dismissed as belated has never stopped being the point of departure for those busily rejecting it? It is striking the degree to which Arendt's *The Human Condition* (1958) subverts a reading of Aristotle first put forth in Herbert Marcuse's influential essay "The Affirmative Character of Culture," which appeared in 1937 in the *Zeitschrift für Sozialforschung*. Daniel Bell's *The Cultural Contradictions of Capitalism*, similarly, is a sustained, if conservative, reworking of Marcuse's *One-Dimensional Man* without saying so. In *Conditions*, Alain Badiou—not at all a Hegelian Marxist—goes even further: "Nietzsche's genealogical method, just like Heidegger's hermeneutical method, were [sic] no more than variants of the Hegelian apparatus."[30]

Although my focus in this chapter is on Bataille rather than Heidegger, the latter carried on his own dialogue with Hegel in a closely argued book on Hegel's *Phenomenology of Spirit* that does not at all simply reject either the book or the philosopher. As Christoph Demmerling has argued, "homelessness" in Heidegger's essay on the "world picture" is a direct translation of Marx's concept of alienation.[31] Such an argument obviously cuts both ways, however, suggesting why Marcuse and others found it congenial to wed the philosophies of the two, and why Lukács himself was influenced by Heidegger in turn in his late study *The Ontology of Social Being*.

Demmerling's observation, though, can be put more forcefully. Heidegger's relationship to his own past reveals an altogether parodic relationship to Marx's notions of "man," "language," "nature," and "alienation" that is similar to Bataille's. Every key element of this series is treated by Heidegger in turn and then re-dressed in camouflaged form. Reification as the petrification of thought becomes the alertness of thought in the form of a meditation on things; consciousness (*Bewußtsein*) finds its doppelganger in conscience (*Gewissen*); "negation" (*Verneinen*) is impersonated first as "annihilation" (*Vernichten*) and later "nihilation" as the redemptive prompting of anxiety toward the nothing that is. Agency (*Wirkung*) becomes that which delivers itself to us through mood (*Stimmung*), of which *Angst* and boredom are the most revealing according to Heidegger. As Lucien Goldmann points out, Heidegger crafts *Zuhandenheit* (the state of being "at hand") to approximate Marxian *praxis*.[32]

Heidegger's inventive queries and reversals regarding "totality" in "What Is Metaphysics?" rest on the remaking of a well-known Hegelian category that, as we saw above, is highly reminiscent of Bataille's later effort along similar lines: "As surely as we can never comprehend absolutely the whole of beings in themselves we certainly do find ourselves stationed in the midst of beings that are revealed somehow as a whole."[33] If totality is essential to Heidegger's assault here on the particularist empiricism of science (which he names at the essay's opening as his primary target), he achieves his subversion of the master by rendering totality inert: an atmospheric awareness that emerges from an intimation of what lies behind shimmering appearances rather than an immanent immersion into the material by way of the Notion (*Begriff* in Hegel, rather than *Vorstellung*). It is hard not to see this contravention of Hegelian thought, which was at the time wed to powerful civic movements both at home and in the colonies, as being in every sense deliberate.

Is there a politics to Heideggerian form, though, along the lines of genealogy? A major theme of the interwar *Kriegsideologie* of Heidegger, Jünger, and Schmitt, for instance, was to rescue the white races of Europe from the insubordinate lower orders closing in on the center from the colonial periphery.[34] This was an explicit and sustained fear on their part, and they wrote about the defense of European *Zivilasation* persistently. It would be unpersuasive, at least to me, to argue that taking on a philosopher's style of argument or terms placed them necessarily within his politics. It is not the belligerent racism of these thinkers that is so widely emulated today, only their spiritual disgust and civilizational indignation.

But what the epistemology of this way of arguing passes along is more than merely a mood. Contemporary theory shares a number of the interwar Right's positions: the promotion of culture over an always compromised politics, an antipathy to socialism, valuing the indigenous over the universal, believing that Christianity is the West's original sin, and adopting a subaltern nativism based on a rural ideology of soil and people.[35] Although obviously not sharing its sources' ideology of racial war, cultural theory has (in the above examples, at any rate) adopted a discourse of subversion borrowed from the murkier side of that same Europe it wants to provincialize—one based on claims either to the unique rationalism of the West (a view that moves critics Eurocentrically to condemn rationalism for being, ipso facto, Eurocentric) or, in a variation on the same idea, to an antirationalism borrowed "subversively" from the anthropological other. Already formulated in its essentials by Bataille, the clearest contemporary version of these attitudes can be found in posthumanism, which itself began to be elaborated in *The Accursed Share* against the backdrop of decolonization.

PROPHETIC SUICIDE: READING

Genealogy circles around argument, stalking it at its perimeter. Its play (as pun, as mimicry) wants to singularize binaries, arresting all oppositions. Here, though, it gets caught in a contradiction. Parentage, after all, is destiny. A bloodline (figuratively as ideology, or literally) is not rupture but continuity, and so one helplessly returns to older contradictions, repeating them in a slightly altered form, with mimicry as the rehearsal of an earlier dependency. The unsettling historical origins of certain signature ideas in theory retain, by way of their genealogy, a guilty residue that calls forth play as a necessary dissimulation. The cosmo-European (that is, Homeric) substrate must reappear as the interrogation of European Man. Since a contextual, historical reading would place genealogy in contact with a past it feels it has to disguise, it develops a theory of reading based (after Bataille) on a principle of perversity. Disguise comes to be misrecognized in time as an inventive, nonsectarian, open and more democratic process of reading against the grain.

The way in which these varied negative attractions to interwar Hegel have expressed themselves in our own theories matters a great deal. Positions within the humanities are primarily divided today over the practice of reading itself. As I have been arguing, the intellectual history of these divisions is one of philology and counterphilology alternating and displacing one another, although not equally, since the derivative labors under the impersonation of the novel. At the very least, Althusser's and Macherey's methods of, respectively, symptomatic and productive reading, which played a decisive role in the creation of "Spinoza" (as we saw in Chapter 1), closely followed Nietzsche's lead by cutting interpretation off from the tribunal of the text in the name of political effectivity. Directly or not, they took on board Nietzsche's claim that the knowing of great philosophers is always a "*creating*, their creating is a legislation . . . [a] will to truth." If one's claims are legislated by a sovereign intellect whose truth is its ends, there is no reason to work on the correspondence between text and author, author and world, for there is no longer a motive for entering the field of ideological conflict in an open attempt to face and to persuade with better correspondences.[36]

The figure of productive reading comes to form a brash photo-negative image of productivity in the economy, as though the former took on the material groundedness of the latter by way of a shared adjective. Although in dissimilar ways, Bataille too enters the debate over reading by displacing the economy of food, shelter, and clothing in favor of consumption and the thrill of waste (which at every level of his argument alludes to its primary instance: the spent energies of orgasm). Bataille's chiasmus is too compelling not to reappear in a number of contemporary guises. The most remarkable and influential theory of reading it generates is laid out in some detail by Gilles Deleuze, for example, in a confessional mode in "Letter to a Harsh Critic"—a modern variant of genealogy and one of the most lucid expositions of its method. Deleuze here responds to the doubts of a young correspondent who thinks his recent writing willful and pretentious—the structural extravagances and sweeping neologisms of *Capitalism and Schizophrenia* (which Deleuze refers to as exemplifying the "new rules"—or rather, the not following of rules—his generation came to trust). He puts his interlocutor at ease by assuring him that these rhetorical excesses were no caprice, that others attempted similar experiments and that doing so was a generational imperative.

Some could not see their way out of the inherited boxes, he recalls, and could never quite break away from staler forms of inquiry and expression. But among those who could, few actually did the hard work of traditional philosophy, mastering the tradition on its own terms. Deleuze himself, however, had had this philological preparation, he relates, and it made his break from it more profound. He worked slowly, gathering knowledge for his project. And it was only by way of this protracted apprenticeship that his discovery of Nietzsche acquired its poignancy. He explains to the harsh critic how traumatic it was at this moment, but also how liberating, to realize by reading Nietzsche that this laborious archaeological recovery of meaning in the texts of the past had been misconceived. In the end, there are no means to keep one tethered to foundational ideas in the texts of earlier philosophers, since reading is an appropriation. One cannot escape this process of the "making-mine" of meaning, and so one must simply give up the attempt.

And yet, Deleuze explains, he did so only after having compiled a formidable arsenal of knowledge. Again, the juxtaposition of the narration of apprenticeship and the narration of traumatic "letting go" makes the following progression clear in his account: inventing new rules as generational directive + a scientific apprenticeship + the trauma of recognizing that truth is a creation = the invention of antirationalism as a secret (Deleuze's word) tradition. He does not feel in retrospect that his time pursuing an objective of reading for content and context that he later rejected as foolish was wasted. For he had learned to turn it into a utility. The issue was not the internal coherence, systematic structures, or contextual imperatives of earlier statements by philosophers. He had "freed himself" of this, he explains. So not making sense could now be presented as a form of originality, and breaking the rules of sense could be seen as the politically radical:

> I saw myself as taking an author from behind and giving him a child that would be his own offspring, yet monstrous. It was really important for it to be his own child, because the author had to actually say all I had him saying. But the child was bound to be monstrous too, because it resulted from all sorts of shifting, slipping, dislocations, and hidden emissions that I really enjoyed.[37]

The opening image, which not coincidentally reads very much like Bataille, is one of edgy transgression—where buggery is calculated to shake out, as it were, the reader's timidity by means of his own bold vitality. Less prominent, but still potent, is the residual sense of violence and mastery ("taking from behind"), partaking, in fact, of Bataille's common trope of substituting the manual creation of productive labor for procreation and of seeing transgression (as in Bataille's Sade) in terms of a sanctioned rape. Intellectual bravery—and it is very frankly presented in just these terms—joins ideological violation. By Deleuze's account, the authors he buggers do not necessarily have to "actually say all [he] had him saying," which is suggested by his use of the terms "shifting, slipping, dislocation" and later, his supplementary "emissions." It is true that the literal words of the authors he is reading may have been written as he quotes them, but there is every effort on his part not to place these statements in the overall organization of the piece, much less to pay attention to the conditions of their composition. The text is rather an occasion, as it had been for Althusser, for example, who tends to misquote, quote out of context, or reverse chronologies in his effort to make Gramsci an antihistoricist or to make the good Lenin appear to take nothing from the bad Hegel. At times Althusser turns statements into their opposite, arguing that "it makes more sense that way."[38]

Deleuze here gives a distinctive spin to a postwar science of semantic indeterminacy that derives from Nietzsche via Bataille and has found a number of contemporary variants. Object-oriented literary criticism and surface reading, for example, are two recent versions from this general lineage, although now the tropes already well developed in Nietzsche regarding a conspiratorial elect and the will to power give way to a complete denial of the human as an active, thinking, making being; if in Nietzsche and Bataille, the medium is the literary figure, in these two recent movements it is that of applied technologies and the natural sciences. They are not simply skeptical of humanism but (in Jane Bennett's words) "cut against the hubris of human exceptionalism" as such—the principle, that is, so clearly anticipated after the war by Bataille.[39] As though granting Hegel's observation, without wanting to, that consciousness and will are really two words for the same thing, they get past the human by imploding the oppositional intelligence as such—anything that might grasp meaning (*greifen*, *Begriff*). In a prose reanimated by counterphilological motifs, object-oriented criticism brackets hermeneutics, seeing texts as objects not to be read at all. As objects, they are (like Lefebvre's "magic") "weird entit[ies] withdrawn from access, yet somehow manifest"—happily uninterpretable, in short, and therefore not understood so much as experienced, sensed, lived.[40] For its part, surface reading is even franker about being against the "hermeneutics of suspicion" or anything that pretends to penetrate the manifest appearance of texts or to move from perception to understanding. Those who promote surface reading explain their position by declaring that "[a] surface is what insists on being looked *at* rather than what we must train ourselves to see *through*."[41] We might wonder what it means, for example, to "perceive"—a key word for them that is never defined—or to promote "the experience of art in its pure, untranslatable, sensuous immediacy."[42] For how is it that aesthetic apprehension is not itself an experience? But if it is, then it would have meaning and would require interpretation.

The larger point is that these variations on a theme, although related, are not the same. Surface reading stands against Althusser, yoking together Freud and Marx as guilty forerunners of ideology critique and of "depth models" in reading. Again, what strikes one is the convergence around (and against) philological reading as an unnamed constant. If surface reading is evidently exhausted by critical thinking and defiantly opposed to making distinctions, attributing motives, situating events or artifacts, these positions are not those of Althusser or Deleuze necessarily. But all of them, to various degrees, want to return meaning to a network of impulses—on the one hand, to feelings (as in affect theory); on the other, to a curiously insensitive anonymity of the human machine. The unexpected benefits of the anti-intellect is that it rids them of any demands to explore interested knowledge, precursors, favored constellations, or political affiliations. The point for surface readers, in short, is to descale the human by obliterating philological meaning, looking instead to the objectivity of the natural sciences and throwing in their lot with "computers, databases," and other machines in order to "bypass" subjectivity.[43] Although motivated by different ends, the neopositivism of "distant reading," to take a second example, is inspired by similar developments and joins the same mainstream. Its attraction to the computerization of aggregate data, nodal networks, team reading, and other attempts at removing the human actor from analysis derived from a school of positivist Italian Marxism exemplified by Galvano Della Volpe that took the developed philological school in Italy of Gramsci and later Sebastiano Timpanaro and others as its foil.

In many of these trends (although not in distant reading) undecidability has become a principle in its own right, where it is mobilized as a redemptive feature of writing that denies in advance any hermeneutics that pretends to render the signified comprehensible. To arrive at a meaning at all—let alone the question of alternative readings—is seen as a foreclosure of possibilities. This is a position, in fact, that has even overtaken some critics within so-called neophilology.[44] A number of current theorists, for example, who are not especially invested in posthumanist agendas—Jacques Rancière, for instance—are nevertheless caught in these tides. He insists on the freedom of the poet and critic to "withdraw from the duty of representation" and on a politics that dwells "in the non-signifying." Rancière seems to be on the defensive, as though wanting to defend the aesthetic as too precious to be sociologically deciphered or historically explained. Instead, he demands the inviolability of the "body of incarnation" of the text that "escape[s] the fate of the letter released into the world," as though the world might harm it, or as though critics might suppose it, wrongly, to be reducible to the mere world.[45] Although his project points in exciting ways to the everyday, democratic experience of art, his allusions to the Gospel of St. John ("the Word became flesh"), along with the doctrine from "The Origin of the Work of Art" that truth is a happening, forestalls interpretation and joins many others in veering toward an ontology of sensation.

What I have been exploring from different angles in parts of this book—through such examples as Nietzsche, primarily, but also Deleuze, Derrida, Macherey, Althusser, and now Rancière—is a convergence around an "Anti" philosophy that opposes without openly opposing anything that involves self-interrogation or comparison of one's positions to a ground. Despite their immense differences, what is being insinuated is that theory or the arts (or art as theory) are where possibility presents itself in the form of previously unthought thoughts, new constellations of meaning, percipient exercises of insight. The rejection of all correspondence to experience, evidence, or proof is seen as a necessary precondition for the creation of openings to new modalities of perception, since any politics based on the merely existing would, in this view, degrade the political as such. It is in the guarded terrain of a carefully prepared lexicon that a utopian space is carved out. And indeed, the utopia cannot survive outside the medium of that lexicon, and so it flees from any debate that would require translating ideas into the idiom of skeptical interlocutors. The verbal space of this kind of theory allows readers to transform themselves into global agents who do not act agentially (persuading, unifying, organizing); rather, their agency is to escape agency. In this mode, the reader exists immanently in an oppositional space, refusing to grant the merely real its reality.

In surface reading as in symptomatic reading, freedom from critical thought relies on a definition that conflates two interpretive ideals. For if it is easy to expose the narrowness of Church hermeneuts insisting on a single, canonically approved meaning of texts, it is another matter to confuse this kind of dogmatism with the philological claim that it is possible to be wrong—that some readers do not do adequate research, read sloppily, or make things up. The inversion of productivity in Bataille is similarly inverted in counterphilological reading by the figure of will. Since the human being in Spinoza and Nietzsche is without will, the mind can only express what wills it, and objectivity becomes subjectivity (as it does in surface reading). The complaint that humanism is arrogant for supposing that subjects act and plan freely and masterfully is easily reversed. For the subject made "objective" in this way—an object or thing of nature—becomes in these schools of reading an instinctual willfulness: an absolute voluntarism. For now it is not a mere subject doing the willing, but the subject in the guise of nature itself.

Confronted by a similar polarization in his battles with Friedrich Schlegel over romantic irony, Hegel observed that there was no articulation of an idea without conceiving of it. The suspension of meaning finds its meaning in the suspension, which is of course willed. It is an observation that is difficult to get around. Any idea that is held as being beyond conception finds its meaning in the nonconceptuality with which it has been endowed by the conceiving mind that wills it into existence. To put this another way, for critical theory (unlike, say, surface reading or posthumanism) the concept of the posthuman would be a nonconcept—an artificially constructed place-holder idea with no other content than the will to nonconceptuality itself. So it is not a thing or entity that has not been grasped; it is not even a concept that cannot be thought. It is, rather, an idea that stipulates a powerlessness in principle that its articulation reveals it has the power to express.

POSTHUMANISM AS IMPERIALISM

One of the obstacles when revisiting thinkers like Vico or Hegel is the assumption that they no longer matter—that their fights have nothing to say to a lightning-fast contemporaneity of computerization, biotechnology, compulsive television watching, and the surveillance state. The Vichian tradition, though, has from the start offered alternatives to the scientism that takes shape these days as the techno-obsessions of popular culture, academic research, and corporate funding. It did this by directly addressing and contesting the narrowing of the concept "human" in early Enlightenment engagements by philosophers with mathematics and physics. Opened up by those inquiries, as Vico and others could see very early, was a line of thinking that shares features with what is today called "posthumanism."

Posthumanism can mean either skepticism toward traditional humanism or the positing of a posthuman condition. It is the latter that most interests me in the following discussion. If it seems too abrupt to leap immediately into the many positions of the different tendencies found under its rubric, the effort is also bracing and has the advantage of preparing us for the radical claims on value that attend its general theory. I am thinking, for example, of the tendency to posit randomness or irresolvable uncertainty when analyzing any nonlinear or complex system, as though the latter automatically entailed the former; and of the tendency to posit autopoiesis in human and natural systems—claiming not only that organisms make themselves by recycling their own outputs as inputs, but that they respond to their environment in ways determined by their internal self-organization and are therefore powerless to recognize anything outside their internal points of reference. I am thinking as well of the redefinition of "communication" so that it no longer means the intentional exchange of information but rather the biomechanical exchange of chemical or electronic signals; of the proposal that when human systems become so large that they cannot be controlled by planning, they then supersede the human entirely, leaving it essentially behind or irrelevant to its structures—"human fabrications no human has made"(in Bruno Latour's dramatic words); and of the redefinition of the term "environment" to mean a hybrid of the natural and human worlds, not only without priority but without distinction. I am thinking, finally, of the postulate that "life" may be defined as "information" and that these information signals are immaterial—that messages that allow systems to function depend on no material substrate for their transmission (what Katherine Hayles aptly calls "disembodiment"). Specific examples of posthumanist theory at the moment include object-oriented criticism, cognitive hermeneutics, machine cultures, surface reading, thing theory, deep ecology, systems theory, some variants of animal studies, autopoiesis, and the theory of hybrid natural/human environments, but there are many others.

Posthumanism is generally thought to respond to an objective crisis in the concept "human," but it may be more accurate to say that it is a defection from the humanities. It maneuvers within a business climate and a media culture that assumes the supremacy of the natural sciences, above all the managerial wing of the applied sciences. To that extent, it gives a contemporary voice to a doctrine found in the seventeenth century—or what Jonathan Israel rightly calls (albeit for the wrong reasons) the "radical" Enlightenment as distinct from the more merely liberal and derivative era of the eighteenth-century philosophes, that is to say, the scientific Enlightenment rather than the political one focused on the Rights of Man.[46] Descartes considered the disciplines of history and philology (what we today call the humanities) arbitrary and largely pointless, and subsequently concludes that philosophy, in its combat with superstition, must divorce itself from metaphysics, merging its preoccupations with the logic of mathematics and a quantifiable, isolatable matter.

From the start, though, we can see that posthumanism is not a counter-Enlightenment philosophy, as it is usually assumed to be, but an homage to a particular Enlightenment constellation brought with some modifications into a vastly different modernity, technologically speaking. It sweeps through the academic humanities from a variety of quarters, leaving its mark on theory so that the humanities themselves, as theory's medium, come to stand in certain quarters for the demotion of the human, a rejection of the uniqueness, dignity, or priority of humans as a particular evolutionary form of natural life. Instead of being a rejection of the humanism of the Enlightenment, it is a devotion to one rather than another Enlightenment legacy. Its attractions to the achievements of science, together with its commentary on the implications for philosophy of the discoveries of science, are carried out, however, with no attention to the trenchant critiques of Cartesianism and its offshoots (above all Spinozism) in the seventeenth and eighteenth centuries themselves, forged from within the literary humanities (most definitively by Vico).

It would be easy to miss the philosophical oneness, with internal variations, of these different proposals even as their lessons revolve around a similar set of findings in the applied sciences, as well as (given their foundation) still earlier conjectures from specific philosophical positions in the seventeenth-century Enlightenment. What prompts this startling convergence, and where does it come from? Because these gestures are conducted explicitly at a foundational level, a constellation of unlike elements can be found to have a prior common ground. By circuitous paths, and by way of developing vocabularies and sensibilities often radically at odds with one another, we are witnessing a gathering of minds. Despite the fearsome technical knowledge that branded their various missions, they sought to carve out for themselves a political space—what Latour calls in regard to his own project a "Copernican counter-revolution."

In *We Have Never Been Modern* (1991), written on the heels of the fall of the Berlin Wall, Latour explicitly shapes his thesis to the form and scale of what he takes to be a welcome historical event. He concludes his argument with a blunt reflection in the book's closing pages on how the West "invented science, an activity totally distinct from conquest and trade, politics and morality."[47] In case we thought we had misheard his intent in relieving the West of its role in conquest and trade (one can only imagine Leonardo's design for cannons before the burghers of Venice), he declares that "exploitation" no longer exists and that "Eastern peoples"—who, he avers, unlike Westerners, *never* transformed nature, only commented on it—"can no longer be reduced to their proletarian avant-gardes."[48] The third world is no longer communist, in other words, and so, however happy an outcome from his point of view, we are, as the civilization of action and accomplishment, left with a cause for "anguish." For how will we in the West be able to absorb the peripheral masses clamoring to enter our modernity? He defines "modernity" as the "birth of 'nonhumanity'—things, or objects, or beasts—and the equally strange beginning of a crossed-out God, relegated to the sidelines."[49] Latour's surprisingly unguarded first-worldism, which frees him from an earlier historical dynamic of dissent and restlessness, is not an idiosyncracy within posthumanism but hovers over its very inception. There is nothing particularly Nietzschean about his language or modes of thought, and yet he confirms Nietzsche's prescience in naming the elements of the latter's "philosophy of the future," among other things, a first-world triumphalism: the death of God (Spirit) and the natural human object.

An example of this dynamic can be found in the intriguing return to early systems theory and the first-wave cybernetics of Norbert Wiener and the Macy conferences between 1946 and 1953 by some contemporary posthumanists. Kathryn Hayles and Cary Wolfe, for instance, have both seen these movements as foundational for their own departures.[50] The inaugural systems theorist, Ludwig von Bertalanffy, was an interwar Austrian biologist whose *General Theory of Systems* appeared in 1945 (a moment that, as we have seen in the discussions of Bataille, Lefebvre, and Kojève, was pivotal in the counterphilological post-Vichianism I have been tracing). He was drawn not to the "closed systems" of the laboratory but to "open systems," where predictability was vastly complicated not only by the multiple interactions of the systems' many parts but in which the interactions themselves were not static but dynamic, constantly changing themselves or being reconfigured by other stimuli. Reflecting philosophically on the experimental observation of biological systems, he wondered whether the biological models with which he was familiar might not fit every organizational system of whatever type. The idea was, as it had been for early nineteenth-century positivism, to explain all systems in all fields of science.

As for "cybernetics," the term comes from the Greek for "steersman," taking as the model for its inquiries the nineteenth-century practice of steering large ships by the use of rudders that compensated in response to "feedback" from their navigational systems. This idea of a self-correcting system that automatically makes adjustments according to environmental stimuli is its founding concept. Most directly and urgently, it wanted to apply the feedback concept to the daunting problem of improving the accuracy of anti-aircraft weapons. This involved designing mechanisms that could predict the future location of fast-moving, irregularly patterned objects. Hence, it was all about the search for a theory that would allow the same kind of confident control of objects in non-linear, complex systems as in the linear, managed world of discrete laboratory experiments. As Wiener makes clear in his classic study of 1948, *Cybernetics: Or Control and Communication in the Animal and the Machine,* "the deciding factor" for his research was "the war."[51] He and his colleagues were driven, he says, to perform a "function" in the context of a "national emergency." Essentially, what this demanded, from the early cyberneticists' point of view, was to give machines the self-correcting, problem-solving capabilities of advanced animals, most especially humans themselves. But by the same token, as he states explicitly, the "human must be mechanized to improve predictability."[52]

This common denominator is what Wiener famously calls—in a striking example of the parasitism of the sciences on the humanities—"communication," by which he means something very specific. Wiener establishes the analogy between the machine and the nervous system by way of the concept of "feedback" (kinesthesia, ataxia, etc.): oscillation as a result of overcorrection. The nervous system in combination with the muscles and the senses is, he argues—and here cybernetics begins to take on some of the same features as systems theory—a "circular" relationship. Control engineering = communications engineering, the management of three kinds of message—electrical, mechanical, and nervous. A "message" is defined as "a sequence of measurable events distributed in time."[53]

Let me pursue this idea of parasitism for a moment. As we read Wiener's remarkable book, its methods of argument become clearer. First, there are sudden deployments of analogy throughout the argument. He moves abruptly and without transition from the discussion of controlled microsystems to the human organism (often conflating these as well with the phrase "living organisms," as though the two were coterminous). The fusion he seeks is, to a degree, achieved verbally, or better, literarily, for, in his presentation at least, there is no experimental basis to witness an actualization of the assertion. He is primarily concerned with recalibrating our ways of thinking or seeing phenomena rather than inventing new hybrids. Second, he reduces the term "information" to any chemical or electrical transfer of energy that produces a response or is capable of being stored so long as it is low energy, since low energy characterizes the circuits of computers and information technologies generally, in contradistinction to the high-energy valve, cylinder, and motor machines of the industrial age. There is, in short, a reverse personification, which becomes very important for later posthumanism both methodologically and stylistically. This is crucial to his eventual move, in fact—also without transition—to the liberation of information itself from "the chemical and the electrical" so that it may become the purely signatory or semantic: a code without body (a body without organs).

Third, there is a clear aesthetic desire to achieve balance and symmetry between the control of information outputs and the resistance to predictive capacity within complex systems. In other words, unable to achieve the certainties upon which the exact sciences depend, given their objects' levels of complexity, cybernetics must philosophically posit certainty on the grounds of statistical probability—or, to put this less ceremoniously, a constantly receding referent. This operation necessitates the increasing abstraction of its terms and the reduction of the variables in play to make them manageable; it is a kind of gaming of complexity to bring back to the nonlinear an approximation of the linear's predictability.

It is a paradox, then, that Wiener would become a figurehead for posthumanism, although not at all that he would gravitate toward a presentation that, despite its mathematical armature in places, was importantly borrowing from the literary. In a connection whose significance has gone mostly unmarked, he was, after all, the son of the American philologist and polyglot Leo Wiener, who schooled Norbert at home using his own original methods, and who between 1917 and 1922 established himself as a heterodox critical voice and exploder of Western pretensions along lines that have been widely imitated in the work, for example, of Jan Carew, Martin Bernal, Ivan van Sertima, John Hope Franklin, and others. A Polish immigrant and leftist—one of the most prolific translators and editors of Tolstoy—he published two multivolume works in those years that together exceed two thousand pages and that effectively carry on the ethnic and national de-centering strategies inaugurated by Vico. The first, the four-volume *Contributions Towards a History of Arabico-Gothic Culture* (1917), set out to demonstrate the Arabic origins of Germanic languages and mythology in a configuration he called the "Gothic Renaissance"; the second, the three-volume *Africa and the Discovery of America* (1920–22), argued, according to extensive linguistic evidence, that African and native Caribbean cultures were in frequent contact in pre-Columbian times.[54]

The broad generational shift between interwar and postwar intellectual life symbolized by this radical change of focus from father to son reveals some of the alienation felt by eastern European intellectuals whose lively awareness of the politics of multilingual conflicts and contacts failed to register in the American melting pot. This dynamic flow from the poorer and more politically unstable European East toward the West is in many ways the story of twentieth-century literary theory. Many Soviet and eastern European scholars were, for this reason and others, poised to theorize the philological aspects of peripheral cultural emergence. They are the ones who largely brought that emphasis to the West in a sophisticated form unknown there. At the same time (in Prague linguistics, formalism, and structuralism), some critics within the same migration chose a different option, feeling the need to give to literary criticism the feel of the natural sciences.

At any rate, and for whatever reason, in (Norbert) Wiener's hands cybernetics achieves its intellectual leverage on the basis less of experimental verification than of philosophical position. The only example of an experiment in the book is an almost self-parodic account of his vivisection of a cat, with half of its brain removed, in order to witness its muscle twitchings when electricity was pumped into its body by a system of electrodes—an act that, from his account of it at least, accomplished nothing that could not have been predicted beforehand. The position in philosophy he embraced had, he implies, prepared the ground for his effort to make his own philosophy (that is, cybernetics) appear scientific in postwar American terms. He sought, in other words, to live up to a philosophy drawn above all from the Descartes/Spinoza/Leibniz axis of the seventeenth century that he used as his ideal and guide. The same is true of Bertalanffy in interwar Vienna. His inquiries into biology were deeply configured by his intense study in those years of the ontology, epistemology, and axiology all around him in that city. For Wiener, Leibniz in particular is the patron saint. In Leibniz there is a coming together, in Wiener's estimation, of "universal symbolism and calculus of reasoning."[55] Leibniz perfected the binary number system so central to the computer, invented a mechanical calculator, devised the infinitesimal calculus, and anticipated the dream of symbolic logic, a language shorn of all social connotations, found later in analytic philosophy—perhaps the twentieth century's best-known scientism of the humanities. He did this, moreover, while looking back to the Scholastic tradition and to Epicurus, where conclusions are produced by applying reason to first principles or prior definitions rather than to empirical evidence.

The posthumanist concessions to scientism, then, are paradoxical, for they draw their inspiration from the precise moment when the applied sciences themselves are beginning to find their way out of a narrowly focused technics, looking for ways to speak of the totality by taking their leads from philosophy, literature, and sociology. This would be another aspect of the convergence I have previously remarked upon. Wiener, for example, is eloquent in his interrogation of scientific methods as they had been conducted before him, but his critique is based on what was already second nature to the traditions of philosophy he ignores, which had already established the methodological necessity for interdisciplinarity and generalism against the prevailing doctrines of academic specialization. I am referring above all to Hegelian system philosophy—to the total interplay and mutual penetration in Hegel's project (and that of Marx later) of all the disciplines in a defiant, autodidactical generalism of the intellect—the heart of Vico's literary sociology and the definition of what he meant by philology. This was collectively reflected, among other things, in the team concept of the Institute for Social Research and critical theory prior to the Macy conferences. The early systems theory of Bertalanffy, for example, might be characterized as the discovery of the relevance to science of the discipline of sociology, now reduced to the compartmentalizing habits of science's categorical methodologies. It was an effort to take that methodology and insert it into a study of the supposedly unwavering certainties of a matter that one pretended to isolate from the social world in order to penetrate its secrets by simplifying its contexts and variables—above all, the variables embodied by an always inconvenient human will, resistance, argument, and whim.

The transition from cybernetics and systems theory to posthumanism is significant, I would argue, for reasons that ultimately have very little to do with matters of originality or the tracing of influences in the study of intellectual history. For apart from the way it illustrates Vico's predictive capacity in revealing the antidemocratic underpinnings of an uncritical scientism in the humanities, there is also—as with Bataille—a specific colonial setting that inflects the development. This is found, among other places, in the movement of anthropological antihumanism in Germany in the early decades of the century, discussed in Chapter 3, that is one of Bataille's direct forerunners. But posthumanism is also traceable, again, to the social upheavals of the interwar period, the residues left behind by the temporarily defeated ideologies of the European Right, later given articulation in the immediate postwar period by groups of scientists assembled for the war effort, operating still in a crisis mentality and composed now of recent European émigrés working in privately funded institutes and conferences in the United States of the Cold War. These included, for example, Bell Laboratories, which sought to apply the techniques of control first theorized under the pressures of world war to the functioning of the societies left behind. Bertalanffy worked throughout the interwar years untroubled in Nazi Austria. Heidegger's early mentor, Husserl, in his *Phenomenology and the Crisis of Philosophy* (1935), as we saw in an earlier chapter, anticipated Latour decades later by calling for Europe to do "endless battle" against those who would challenge (in his words) its "mission to humanity."

If the project of postmodernism now appears in retrospect to have been an effort to salvage something liberating from an abject defeat—that is, to embrace commodification as a form of transgression, concede the victory of corporate mass culture, and enter its logic freely by making it one's own in order to forge new subjectivities—so posthumanism might be seen as granting, with similar reluctance, legitimacy to alienation. It gives alienation a philosophical and scientific respectability: to disembody human skill and intelligence, to de-realize human will and effort, to unthink the human. The human subject alienated from his or her powers of cognition, divorced from the body, delivered from the uniqueness of the species, and deprived of will is the form of its sublime. And this is done as the recognition of necessity in the discovery of laws—a massively willed and historically determined effort to be done with will and history as human making. The politics of posthumanism is impossible to de-link from a postcritical attitude—what Latour programmatically outlines as a desired "End of Denunciation" or what Gianni Vattimo extols as "weak thought" or François Laruelle as "non-epistemology," "quantum thoughts," "fractal" thinking, and so on.[56] Iterations of the same idea are everywhere.

The viral object of posthumanist discourse, in the spirit of genealogy if not in direct contact with it, is not about counterpositions. It has no intention of refuting its opponents by pointing out their inadequacies. The more effective—more truly "natural" in the sense of precritical or even cellular—means of removing offensive thoughts is to explode thinking itself. And therefore the discourse (of Wolfe, of Laruelle, and even—in a different register—of Latour and Niklas Luhmann) acts as a virus feeding on communication and setting out to cripple its codes. It means to overburden readers with inadequate memory storage, constantly deflecting all reproach by the gaps it creates with missing files and intentionally (or recklessly) damaged programs. And this is its intention—expressed as the discounting of all expression and intentionality. To demonstrate the insufficiency of posthumanism's sources, the self-contradictions of its plans, or the chaotic leaps of its conceptualizations as they move from assertion to assertion would be to get lost in the maze of its system, which, quite unlike its own self-characterization as autopoietic, is much more like a blueprint for the virtualization of a doxological imperative: to deprive of choice that being which they contend has no choice.

As such, posthumanism rests ambiguously on the authority of contemporary cultures of control. The sources it draws on have, in the history of developing their ideas, been institutionally connected to the interests of government policy, the media, and the military. Cybernetics is a profoundly American project, despite its international corps of scientific collaborators or the fact that Wiener wrote its founding text in Mexico. At the dawn of the American Century when cybernetics was conceived (just after World War II), those conditions raise questions about the international dynamics of its conception of knowledge.

The everyday life of those living in U.S. and Western capitalist societies is not at all characterized by an exaggeration of human capacities. While it is true that market ideology relies on an acting subject who fashions and imagines—for there can be no entrepreneurship without it—the history of Western thought is marked throughout by the desire to cast the human within an indifferent nature as one of its expendable features, to blur its boundaries and repossess for the human being the image of his or her own bestiality and insignificance. The instauration of bourgeois modernity in the seventeenth-century Enlightenment begins with this articulation of a centerpiece of its later ideology: the objectification of human nature quite unlike the exaltation of the human in the Renaissance.

The demotion of the human in market ideology finds a home in the cyborg fascinations of early science fiction, expressing itself throughout popular culture in a cinema and television industry that displaces humans to other planets or machine worlds where their distinctness or superiority (from and to aliens and machines) is ambiguous, and to postapocalyptic scenarios where their pack instincts and supposedly antisocial cores can revealingly play themselves out. The central justification for the predatory lending that led to the recent banking collapse was that we cannot choose, that we are part of something larger, something structural, which directs us. Our humanity (in humanism's sense) is for these social evolutionists laughably obsolete.

Similarly, the calculations of the military regarding collateral fallout, or the expendability of village populations killed by drone aircraft, arguably derives from an ideology of the posthuman, as do the unfolding strategies only now becoming apparent in the biotechnology industries as they move beyond robotics and prostheses to human cloning, to an ever more refined form of eugenics, and to the commercially driven invention of entirely new forms of life. Admittedly, the claims for the posthuman can be viewed, at least in part, as critical and sorrowful responses to these developments, soberly drawing conclusions in order to forge new manifestos. But we are dealing with much more than a contradiction: it is the calling into being of an idea that seeks to shield itself in the act of calling.

We might even try to caption the twentieth-century Enlightenment and counter-Enlightenment in terms of an antipodal contrast found neatly at the halfway point of the century itself: the publication of Heidegger's "Letter on Humanism" in 1947 and the publication of the Universal Declaration of Human Rights in 1948, which was itself based on the Mexican revolutionary constitution of 1917 and largely written by delegates from Egypt, Chile, India, and other former colonies.[57] The contrast suggests the centrality of the struggle over the definition of the human being in the anticolonial arena. This is not to extol the comparative discourses of human rights that have too often become an instrument for justifying imperial intervention abroad on the bayonet point of NATO Atlanticism, but rather movements that conserve the human as a political project all by itself, defining him or her as a global and above all a civic subject.

To enshrine the posthuman, by contrast, is to take humanity away from the slave, the domestic servant, the illegal immigrant, the Chavista, the Tibetan Maoist. To condemn the arrogance of humanism is to exempt from inclusion all men and women so long as their struggles against injustice can be shunted onto machines or other species, leaving unchecked and unaddressed the injustice to the invisible within our own species who just now, in the last century, have started to come into focus. Just as the politics of imperial expansion has always depended on scientific technical superiority, so this diversion from a critique of imperialism is carried out in name of a curious kind of revolt: a revolt based on a dwelling in being.

The Zimmerwald manifesto (1915), the revolutionary constitution of Mexico (1917), the "April Theses" of the Russian Revolution (1917), the program of the short-lived Soviet Republic of Bavaria (1919), the Universal Declaration of Human Rights (1948), the Arusha Declaration in Tanzania (1967)—each outlines a view of the human as an international subject defined by the right to conscience, labor, livelihood, political activity, and cultural expression. These extraordinary statements of social rights may not have been brought to realization in the form of policies by the movements that imagined them, but then again, our own twenty-first century has not realized them either and is losing the ability to imagine them. They surpassed every conception of rights that had been conceived in earlier revolutions.[58] It is the philosophical foundation of these movements, together with the possibilities they intimate for the future, that should be explored further. We need now to look at the political milieu of their formation, as well as the literary and cultural universe they built in the early decades of the anticolonial century when the implications of Vico's philological politics found a new and more powerful articulation.

APPENDIX
Preview of Borrowed Light, Volume II

The second volume of *Borrowed Light* traces Vico's legacies in the twentieth century. His literary science is developed by later generations and takes shape as "imperial form": a response to empire centered on the vulgate, philological readings of the social, internationalist cultural value, and a critique of scientism and the posthuman.

The opening movement of the book attempts to understand on its own terms the estranged logic of interwar communism, aesthetically and hermeneutically. It treats the interwar period as one defined by its offering for the first time a truly global challenge to the imperial system in the wake of the Mexican and Russian revolutions. Philosophy and aesthetics themselves change radically in a milieu where dissidence is suddenly wed to the resources of state power and to vast international organizations. A "civic hermeneutics" is proposed.

The feel of the era is pursued in close readings of neglected works of anti-imperialist literature and film by figures such as Larissa Reissner, Ilya Ehrenburg, V. Pudovkin, and Carl Einstein. A theory is presented that key anticolonial concepts were developed by canonical Marxist thinkers—among them, "temporal discontinuity" (Ernst Bloch), the literary "age of imperialism" (Georg Lukács), the labor of the "fragment" (Walter Benjamin), "vulgarity" (Antonio Gramsci), and the "primitive" (Rosa Luxemburg).

It is argued that Marxism and philology belong together and that the era's central figures, moreover, consciously understood this to be the case. Marxism's importance to peripheral aesthetics is traced by way of three developments: (1) the socialist "republic of letters"—a worldly network of vernacular forms that continues to reflect the actual writing from the global periphery; (2) "Moscow philology": the neglected role of communist intellectuals in preserving, editing, and giving form to the endangered manuscripts of global dissidents; and (3) the persistent critique, and even mockery, of literary modernism and the avant-gardes, both as a style and a social outlook, across the global spectrum of Left anticolonial thought—a critique that spans from César Vallejo's parodies of surrealism to Bakhtin's introduction to *Rabelais and His World*. What arises is a literature opposed to *irony* itself—the inheritance of Vico's and Hegel's little-known philosophical assault on irony.

The last section of the book explores how Marxist literary and cultural criticism has always been one with the aesthetic outlooks of the global periphery. Marxist literary theory is not captured adequately by the familiar concepts of reflection theory, base and superstructure, agitprop, or ideology critique—it never has been. Rather, such criticism requires a new set of categories drawn, as they always have been, from anticolonial terrain: montage, unevenness, vulgarity, sacrifice, and polemic.

NOTES

INTRODUCTION

1. Antonio Gramsci, *Quaderni del carcere*, ed. Valentino Gerratana, vol. 2 (Turin: Einaudi, 1977), Q11 §25, 1430 (my translation).

2. Abbé Guillaume-Thomas-François Raynal, "Extract VIII (Chapters 24 and 26): Corruption and Decadence of the Portuguese in the Indies," in *A History of the Two Indies (A Translated Selection of Writings from Raynal's "Histoire philosophique et politique des établissements des Européens dans les Deux Indes")*, ed. Peter Jimack (Aldershot, UK: Ashgate, 2006), 12–14.

3. Alain Badiou, *The Communist Hypothesis*, trans. David Macey and Steve Corcoran (New York: Verso, 2010); Robert Kurz, *Schwarzbuch Kapitalismus: Ein Abgesang auf die Marktwirtschaft* (Cologne: Eichborn Verlag, 2009); The Invisible Committee, *The Coming Insurrection* (Los Angeles: Semiotext(e); Cambridge, MA: MIT Press, 2009); Sylvère Lotringer, ed., *Autonomia: Post-Political Politics* (Los Angeles: Semiotext(e), 2007).

4. "Places of Mind, Occupied Lands: Edward Said and Philology," in *Edward Said: A Critical Reader*, ed. Michael Sprinker (Oxford: Blackwell, 1992), 74–95.

5. Michael Ondaatje, *Anil's Ghost* (New York: Vintage, 2000), 83.

6. Ibid., 105.

7. For example, Robert Irwin, *For Lust of Knowing: The Orientalists and Their Enemies* (London: Allen Lane, 2006); Werner Hamacher, "95 Theses on Philology," *PMLA* 125:4 (October 2010): 994–1001; Hans Ulrich Gumbrecht, *The Powers of Philology: Dynamics of Literary Scholarship* (Urbana: U of Illinois P, 2003), 1; Sheldon Pollock, "Future Philology?: The Fate of a Soft Science in a Hard World," *Critical Inquiry* 35:4 (Summer 2009): 931–61; Jerome McGann, "Philology in a New Key," *Critical Inquiry* 39:2 (Winter 2013): 327–46.

8. Vico, *NS*, 6 (my emphasis).

9. See the excellent analysis of Vico's poetic politics in Andrea Battistini, *Principi di "Scienza Nuova" di Giambattista Vico* (Turin: Einaudi, 1992), where the open-ended structure of his narrative is stressed, as well as its anthropological and encyclopedic qualities.

10. Erich Auerbach, "Einleitung," in Giambattista Vico, *Die Neue Wissenschaft: Über die gemeinschaftliche Natur der Völker*, Nach der Ausgabe von 1744, trans. and intro. Erich Auerbach (Munich: Allgemeine Verlagsanstalt, 1924), 23 (my translation).

11. Ibid., 12 (my emphasis).

12. Johann Gottfried Herder, *Philosophical Writings*, ed. Michael N. Forster (Cambridge: Cambridge UP, 2002), 50.

13. Antonio Gramsci, *Prison Notebooks*, vol. 2, ed. and trans. Joseph A. Buttigieg (New York: Columbia UP, 1996), Notebook 4, §1, 137.

14. Gramsci, *Quaderni del carcere*, vol. 2, Q11, §25, 1429 (my translation).

15. Walter Benjamin, *The Arcades Project*, trans. Howard Eiland and Kevin McLaughlin, ed. Rolf Tiedemann (Cambridge, MA: Harvard UP, 1999), 476 [N11, 6].

16. Sebastiano Timpanaro, *On Materialism*, trans. Lawrence Garner (London: New Left Books, 1975), 159.

CHAPTER 1

1. Marcel Grilli, "The Nationality of Philosophy and Bertrando Spaventa," *Journal of the History of Ideas* 2 (1941): 361, 368.

2. Benedetto Croce, La filosofia de Giambattista Vico (1911; Bari: G. Laterza & Figli, 1922), translated as *The Philosophy of Giambattista Vico*, trans. R. G. Collingwood (London: Howard Latimer, 1913); Croce and Fausto Nicolini, *Bibliografia vichiana*, 2 vols. (Naples: R. Ricciardi, 1947–48).

3. Jules Michelet, *Mémoires de Vico écrits par lui-même. Suivis de quelques opuscules, lettres, etc. Précédées d'une introduction sur sa vie et ses ouvrages* (Brussels: Société Belge de Librairie, 1837). Michelet remarks, "Vico est encore si peu connu en-deçà des Alpes" (1). Michelet's forty-three-page biographical introduction, although highly appreciative, sticks closely to received wisdom and gives evidence of nothing like the research of Croce at the turn of the century.

4. Georges Sorel, *Étude sur Vico et autres textes*, ed. Anne-Sophie Menasseyre (1896; Paris: H. Champion, 2007); Paul Lafargue, *Le déterminisme économique de Karl Marx: Recherches sur l'origine et l'évolution des idées du justice, du bien, de l'âme and de Dieu* (1911; Paris: L'Harmattan, 1997).

5. Erich Auerbach, "Einleitung," in Giambattista Vico, *Die Neue Wissenschaft: Über die gemeinschaftliche Natur der Völker*, Nach der Ausgabe von 1744, trans. and intro. Erich Auerbach (Munich: Allgemeine Verlagsanstalt, 1924), 17 (my translation). Herder traveled to Naples in 1789, two years after Goethe, and mentions Vico by name in his "Letters in Furtherance of Humanity" (1797). In *The Idea of History* (1946; Oxford: Oxford UP, 1993), R. G. Collingwood identifies F. A. Wolf as knowing Vico too.

6. One meaning of *gens* is a technical one from Roman law, where it "denotes a degree of relationship for purposes of inheritance" (Max Harold Fisch, introduction to *NS*, xxi). But the adjective derived from it (*gentile*), since it refers to those humans who have no special pact with God and therefore had to make their own history, means "not Jewish."

7. Max Harold Fisch, introduction to *AGV*, 59.

8. Jonathan Israel's *Radical Enlightenment: Philosophy and the Making of Modernity 1650–1750* (New York: Oxford UP, 2001), for example, places Spinoza at the very center of the founding of modernity (not even Leibniz is given similar space), relegating Vico to a small entry where he is cast, quite inaccurately, as a reformulator of Spinozan motifs.

9. Fisch, introduction to *AGV*, 43.

10. For example, while he was still growing up, these would have included such people as "Giacomo Lubrano, a Jesuit of infinite erudition" and "Monsignor Geronimo Rocca, Bishop of Ischia and a distinguished jurist," whose nephews he tutored (*AGV,* 118).

11. Sorel, *Étude sur Vico,* 57.

12. Ibid., 69. By the same token, his reading of Vico's relevance to Marxism is very different from mine, and in my view, he fundamentally misunderstands key aspects of Vico's intentions. Sorel, in fact, leans on what he takes to be the idealist demerits of *The New Science* in order to settle accounts with Jean Jaurès while denouncing the "poetic character" of Vico's sociological conceptions, in that way depriving Vico of what makes his theories unique.

13. Raymond Williams, *Marxism and Literature* (New York: Oxford UP, 1977), 17.

14. Ibid.

15. In current anthropology, the reigning position seems to invert Vico's antidiffusion thesis. Recent genetic research strongly suggests that human beings have a uniquely African origin, a finding that challenges views popular as recently as the 1980s based on a multiregional model of human origins proposed by Franz Weidenreich in the 1930s. The African origins model arguably supports Vico's theory, however, since he emphasizes culture rather than physical characteristics; a single biological origin is its necessary precondition.

16. See James Joyce, *Finnegan's Wake* (1939; New York: Penguin, 1976), 599: "sullemn fulminance, sollemn nuptialism, sallemn sepulture and providential divining."

17. For the rejection of all law qua law, see Giorgio Agamben's *The Time That Remains: A Commentary on the Letter to the Romans,* trans. Patricia Dailey (Stanford, CA: Stanford UP, 2005); and *Potentialities: Collected Essays in Philosophy,* trans. Daniel Heller-Roazen (Stanford, CA: Stanford UP, 1999); see also Jacques Derrida, *The Beast and the Sovereign,* trans. Geoffrey Bennington (Chicago: U of Chicago P, 2009); and his "Force de loi: Le 'fondement mystique de l'autorité,'" *Cardozo Law Review* 11 (1989/90): 920–1046.

18. Excellent critiques of the diffusion thesis and the "European miracle" can be found in James Blaut, *The Colonizer's Model of the World: Geographic Diffusionism and Eurocentric History* (New York: Guilford Press, 1993) (esp. chap. 1); and Jack Goody, *The Theft of History* (Cambridge: Cambridge UP, 2006).

19. Contrast this emphasis, however, with Herder's otherwise Vichian account of the origins of language in "Fragments on Recent German Literature," where he contrasts the "bourgeois world" with the "shepherd's knowledge" of Hebrews and Arabs, who spoke "many-sidedly" through images rather than narrowly like our "city-dwelling Muses." *Philosophical Writings,* trans. and ed. Michael N. Forster (Cambridge: Cambridge UP, 2002), 33–34.

20. The term "savagery" has struck many critics in animal studies as inherently invidious. But several figures in the Vichian tradition inaugurate a democratic pantheism—a humanism intent on seeing the world from the point of view of animals themselves. This is the emphasis one finds in Herder, for instance ("Treatise on the Origin of Language," *Philosophical Writings,* esp. 74–96), as well as in Michelet's extraordinary books written from the point of view of other species or as an attorney on their

behalf, subordinating the centrality of the human in the order of nature—for example, his *L'insecte: Étude par M. Berthelot* (Paris: C. Lévy, 1903); and *L'oiseau: Étude par Françoise Coppée* (Paris: Calmann-Lévy, 1905).

21. Herder does not erase meaningful distinctions between animals and humans—his whole effort, in fact, is to find a meaningful difference. But he assigns souls to animals, argues that they possess language, and chastises theories that overstate on normative grounds the nonanimal characteristics of human beings.

22. Karl Marx and Frederick Engels, *Manifesto of the Communist Party*, in *Collected Works*, vol. 6, *Marx and Engels: 1845–1848* (New York: International Publishers, 1976), 488.

23. Karl Marx and Friederich Engels, *The German Ideology*, Parts I & II, ed. R. Pascal (New York: International Publishers, 1947), 43–4.

24. Marx sticks very closely to Vico's schema of the *famuli*: "The division of labour . . . [which] is based on the natural division of labour in the family and the separation of society into individual families opposed to one another, simultaneously implies the *distribution*, and indeed the *unequal* distribution, both quantitative and qualitative, of labour and its products, hence property." Marx and Engels, *German Ideology*, 46.

25. Max Horkheimer, "Beginnings of the Bourgeois Philosophy of History," in *Between Philosophy and Social Science: Selected Early Writings*, trans. G. Frederick Hunter, Matthew S. Kramer, and John Torpey (Cambridge, MA: MIT Press, 1993), 380–85, esp. 383.

26. J. G. A. Pocock, *Barbarism and Religion*, vol. 1, *The Enlightenments of Edward Gibbon, 1737–1764* (Cambridge: Cambridge UP, 1999), 172. For his part, John Robertson ("Gibbon and Giannone," in *Edward Gibbon: Bicentenary Essays*, with the assistance of John Burrow and John Pocock, ed. David Womersley [Oxford: Voltaire Foundation, 1997], 3–20) argues that Gibbon's history was directly inspired by Giannone's *Civil History of Naples*.

27. His pursuit of law can be said, in fact, to look forward to utopian socialist and communist notions of government: "the thought of meditating an ideal eternal law that should be observed in a universal city after the idea or design of providence, upon which idea have since been founded all the commonwealths of all times and all nations" (*AGV*, 122).

28. J. G. A. Pocock, *Barbarism and Religion*, vol. 2, *Narratives of Civil Government* (Cambridge: Cambridge UP, 1999), 60. Pocock points out how common these connections were in Naples, where philology was a privileged area of study: "Those there were, indeed, who became obsessed with philology, either in order to imitate the ancients or to anatomise their style when it was no longer imitable."

29. "There must be a mental language common to all nations, which uniformly grasps the substance of things feasible in human social life and expresses it with as many diverse modifications as these same things may have diverse aspects" (*NS*, 67).

30. In the same spirit, Hegel speaks in *The Philosophy of History* of "providentially determined processes" and the "plan of Providence," appealing not to religion but to actions whose similarity in difference suggests a larger human pattern (*PH*, 13).

31. He believes, somehow—or pretends to believe—that the Chinese and the Egyptians were unskilled at painting, pottery, and casting, that their work was "crude" (*NS*, 51).

32. Could this be at work, for instance, when he declares that "the extension of empires," since they expand on the logic of cities as asylums for the vulnerable, "comes by the practice of justice, strength and magnanimity, which are the most luminous virtues of princes and states" (*NS*, 12)? It would be easier to take this apparently colonialist position at face value if he were not so unflattering elsewhere to "princes and states."

33. Auerbach, "Einleitung," 23.

34. Giuseppe Mazzotta, *The New Map of the World: The Poetic Philosophy of Giambattista Vico* (Princeton, NJ: Princeton UP, 1999), 223.

35. In *Vico and the Transformation of Rhetoric in Early Modern Europe* (Cambridge: Cambridge UP, 2010), David L. Marshall cleverly argues that Vico "employs antilogy to remind us of the ironic structure of history itself where providence produces public goods out of private vices, or rather general interests out of particular ones" (61), but this seems out of step with his earnestness, for there is nothing arch about Vico.

36. One type of irony, as Mazzotta goes on to point out, is the Socratic kind, of which Vico approves since it does not depend on radical doubt but is a form of self-reflexiveness (*New Map of the World*, 224).

37. See Robertson, "Gibbon and Giannone," 10: "Anxious to legitimate his regime, the new viceroy, the Marchese di Villena, commissioned Vico to expose the history of the conspiracy: but while Vico was happy enough to inveigh against the feudal nobility responsible, his account of the scope of French ambition—to render what had been the greatest monarchy in the world virtually a 'colony' of the House of Bourbon—was quite unacceptable, and the history too had to be suppressed."

38. Croce and Nicolini, *Bibliografia vichiana*, quoted in translator's introduction to *SAC*, 11.

39. Robertson, "Gibbon and Giannone," 9.

40. J. G. A. Pocock, *Politics, Language and Time: Essays on Political Thought and History* (New York: Atheneum, 1971), 24. In a Herderian mode, Pocock goes on to say that "only after we have understood what means [an author] had of saying anything can we understand what he meant to say, what he succeeded in saying, what he was taken to have said, or what effects his utterance had in modifying or transforming the existing paradigm structures" (25).

41. See, for example, Charles Taylor, *A Secular Age* (Cambridge, MA: Belknap Press of Harvard UP, 2007); Talal Asad, *Formations of the Secular: Christianity, Islam, Modernity* (Stanford, CA: Stanford UP, 2003); Iain Chambers, "The 'Unseen Order': Religion, Secularism and Hegemony," in *The Postcolonial Gramsci* (New York: Routledge, 2012), 85. For a counterview, see Edward Said, "Conclusion: Religious Criticism," in *The World, The Text, and the Critic* (Cambridge, MA: Harvard UP, 1983), 290–94. Said, discussing Vico, writes of being depressed by "a dramatic increase in the number of appeals to the extrahuman, the vague abstraction, the divine, the esoteric and the secret" (291). He has in mind primarily deconstruction, the so-called Yale School, and Gadamerian hermeneutics by way of Frank Kermode.

42. Domenico Losurdo, *Heidegger and the Ideology of War* (1991; Amherst, NY: Humanity Books, 2001), 71.

43. Pocock expresses a similar idea in *Barbarism and Religion*, 1:63: "Scepticism, and the forms of authority which it attacked, alike rested, in that clerical culture, on erudition and the interpretation of texts; but there was a point at which skepticism became more than doubt—a way of life and even a way of, or substituting for, religion itself."

44. That false position was a theory of materialism that precluded social obligation: "By reading Lucretius he learned that Epicurus ... denied any generic difference of substance between mind and body and so for want of a sound metaphysic remained of limited mind.... He built on his mechanical physics a metaphysics entirely sensualistic just like that of John Locke, and a hedonistic morality suitable for men who are to live in solitude, as indeed he enjoined upon all his disciples" (*AGV*, 126).

45. This is precisely the line of attack adopted by Hegel in "On the Scientific Ways of Treating Natural Law, on Its Place in Practical Philosophy, and Its Relation to the Positive Sciences of Right" (1802–3), in *HPW*, 102.

46. Karl Marx, *Difference between the Democritean and Epicurean Philosophy of Nature*, in Marx and Engels, *Collected Works*, vol. 1, *Karl Marx: 1835–1843* (Moscow: Progress Publishers, 1975), 41, 45.

47. John Bellamy Foster, *Marx's Ecology: Materialism and Nature* (New York: Monthly Review Press, 2000).

48. Patrick Chamoiseau, Jean Bernabé, and Raphaël Confiant, *Éloge de la creolité* (Paris: Gallimard, 1993), 33–34.

49. J. G. A. Pocock, *Political Thought and History: Essays on Theory and Method* (Cambridge: Cambridge UP, 2009), 185.

50. Vico, quoted in editors' introduction to *UR*, li.

51. Andrea Battistini, *Principi di "Scienza Nuova" di Giambattista Vico* (Turin: Einaudi, 1992). Battistini analyzes the political dimensions of poetic reading, stressing the open-ended structure of Vico's essentially anthropological narrative.

52. Étienne Balibar inaccurately calls the book a "democratic manifesto" in *Spinoza and Politics*, trans. Peter Snowdon (1985; New York: Verso, 1998), 25.

53. Isaac Deutscher, *The Non-Jewish Jew and Other Essays* (London: Oxford UP, 1968), 27.

54. It should be noted that Deutscher says no more here than Spinoza himself in the *Theologico-Political Treatise* (46), where he finds the distinctive achievement of the Hebrews to be a worldly rather than a providential one: "The Hebrew nation was not chosen by God in respect to its wisdom nor its tranquility of mind, but in respect to its social organization ... their successful conduct of matters relating to government."

55. Antonio Negri explores it at some length, however, in *The Savage Anomaly: The Power of Spinoza's Metaphysics and Politics*, trans. Michael Hardt (1981; Minneapolis: U of Minnesota P, 1991), even invoking philology in one of the book's subtitles. His reading takes Spinoza to be arguing on behalf of revelation in accordance with the import Negri gives to Spinoza's phrase "lumen naturale" (natural light). In a Heideggerian mode, he finds "an excavation of reality that reveals the ontologically pregnant collec-

tive force of this human conquest, a conquest that renews being" (101). Spinoza is saying something very different, however: that biblical words find their meaning according to the light shed on them by material correspondents in nature. The entire movement of Spinoza's book positions itself against the imputed revelations enjoyed by prophets. Negri is uninterested in Spinoza's theory of reading, remarking that Spinoza's method is subsumed by his practice of ontological revelation. He avers that Spinoza is applauding the "imagination," whereas in fact he is attempting to curtail its uncritical deployment. Balibar's discussion of the book's implicit politics in *Spinoza and Politics* (1–49) is more balanced, exploring the implications of Spinoza's treatment of the Hebrew state as a political model, and yet he ignores entirely its most prominent feature: its hermeneutical theory.

56. He treats this at length in "On Miracles," in *TPT*, 80–91.

57. Ibid., 98.

58. As though anticipating *The New Science* even in particulars, he derives from this technique the observation that "we cannot wonder that very strong and tall men, though impious robbers and whoremongers, are in Genesis called sons of God" (*TPT*, 21)—exactly Vico's point about "heroes." They both view abstract reasoning and imaginative power as being at odds (although they value each differently).

59. One is "rightfully dependent" on another if under the other's authority, but is independent only insofar as "he is able to repel all violence and avenge to his heart's content all damages done to him" (*PT*, 295).

60. See also *TPT*, 28: "Prophetic knowledge is inferior to natural knowledge, which needs no sign, and in itself implies certitude."

61. See also ibid., 64: "A matter is understood when it is perceived simply by the mind without words or symbols." For Vico—and this is the point Herder stresses in his *Treatise on the Origin of Language*—thinking is impossible outside of language.

62. Pocock, *Politics, Language and Time*, 176.

63. "... existentia Entis absolute infiniti seu perfecti, hoc est Dei." Spinoza, "De Deo" (scholium of Prop. XI), in *EGD*, 7.

64. This certainly is Hegel's conclusion about Spinoza in his *Lectures on the History of Philosophy*, vol. 3, trans. E. S. Haldane and Frances H. Simpson (Lincoln, NE: U of Nebraska P: 1995), 269–80.

65. For Spinoza, a false idea is distinguished from a true one on the basis of its agreement with its object—its correspondence to an external world with independent properties. He is to that degree a materialist. And yet, as he stresses, the human mind cannot distinguish between the two, since both equally correspond to an "extrinsic denomination."

66. This is especially evident in Gilles Deleuze's *Expressionism in Philosophy: Spinoza*, trans. Martin Joughin (New York: Zone Books; Cambridge, MA: MIT Press, 1990), with its portrait of society as a flattened, consistent terrain without contradiction—a pure productivity.

67. He had in mind, for example, Louis Althusser, *Écrits philosophiques et politiques*, vol. 1 (1945–53; Paris: Stock/IMEC, 1994), translated by G. M. Goshgarian as *The Spectre*

of Hegel: Early Writings (London: Verso, 1997), 36–169; Pierre Macherey, *Hegel ou Spinoza* (Paris: Maspero–La Découverte, 1979); Gilles Deleuze, *Spinoza et le problème de l'expression* (Paris: Éditions de Minuit, 1969); Alexandre Matheron, *Individu et communauté chez Spinoza* (Paris: Éditions de Minuit, 1969); Antonio Negri, *The Savage Anomaly*; Étienne Balibar, *Spinoza and Politics.*

68. Perry Anderson, *Considerations on Western Marxism* (London: Verso, 1979), 65.

69. For an excellent summary of points in defense of philological reading as against the improvisations of theory's thought experiments and programmatic utilities, see Marcus E. Green, "On the Postcolonial Image of Gramsci," *Postcolonial Studies* 16, no. 1 (2013): 90–101.

70. His support of myth in *Reflections on Violence*, however, infamously inspired Mussolini, although myth in Vico is not the ground of a political strategy but a code of primitive reason that, once broken, allows us to read the past on its own terms rather than ours.

71. Warren Montag, *Bodies, Masses, Power: Spinoza and His Contemporaries* (London: Verso, 1999), 87.

72. Pierre Macherey, *In a Materialist Way*, ed. Warren Montag, trans. Ted Stolze (London: Verso, 1998), 125.

73. Ibid. (emphasis in original).

74. Louis Althusser, *Essays in Self-Criticism*, trans. Grahame Lock (1974; London: New Left Books, 1976), 132.

75. Herder, *Philosophical Writings*, esp. 3–177, 247–360.

76. Slavoj Žižek, *The Parallax View* (Boston: MIT Press, 2006), 391–92.

77. Walter Benjamin, *The Arcades Project*, trans. Howard Eiland and Kevin McLaughlin (Cambridge, MA: Harvard UP, 1999), 485.

78. Macherey, *In a Materialist Way*, 25. In *Dialectic of Enlightenment* (New York: Continuum, 1995), 203, Adorno and Horkheimer indict those who consider "fruitfulness" the major criterion for theory (it was, one notes, a common gesture even in the 1940s).

79. Paolo Virno, *A Grammar of the Multitude*, trans. Isabella Bertoletti, James Cascaito, and Andrea Casson (New York: Semiotext(e), 2004), 42–43.

80. Vico, for example, in *The New Science*, compares women to the feeble-minded (*NS*, 153) and commends the show of force in taking a wife (*NS*, 173). As for Spinoza, in *A Political Treatise* he is compelled to "exclude women from government" on the grounds of their weakness as compared to men and by virtue of the fact that they are not "equally distinguished by force of character and ability, in which human power and therefore human right chiefly consist" (*PT*, 387).

81. Antonio Negri, *Insurgencies: Constituent Power and the Modern State*, trans. Maurizia Boscagli (Minneapolis: U of Minnesota P, 1999), 24, 25.

82. Spinoza, *TPT*, 74. Not only in these words but in the long section that follows them as well, Spinoza reveals himself to be an advocate of laws that keep people "in bounds" by reasonable means, in the hope of a greater good, so that they are not placed in "subjection to equals." He does not on principle oppose a governmental power in "the hands of the few" provided it meets these standards.

83. "The right of the supreme authorities is nothing else than simple natural right, limited, indeed, by the power, not of every individual, but of the multitude, which is guided, as it were, by one mind" (*PT*, 301).

84. Althusser, *Essays in Self-Criticism*, 136.

85. Montag, *Bodies, Masses, Power*, xvi.

86. Said would appear to agree. He speaks of Vico's "frighteningly godless" vision, a "human vision" of "an excruciatingly gentile mind"—in other words, a mind "which has been denied the fully integrated revelation accorded the Hebrews[, creating instead] a neutral, amoral, and beautiful *mundus* of the mind that is—as he [Vico] is always ready to remind us—only an imagistic economy for the real thing" ("Vico: Autodidact and Humanist," *Centennial Review* 11, no. 3 [Summer 1967]: 341, 351). See also his reference to Vico's "vivid account . . . of human 'gentile' existence" in "Vico on the Discipline of Bodies and Texts," in *Reflections on Exile* (Cambridge, MA: Harvard UP, 2000), 84; and *Beginnings: Intention and Method* (Baltimore, MD: Johns Hopkins UP, 1975), 349–50.

87. Antonio Negri, *Subversive Spinoza* (Manchester, UK: Manchester UP, 2004), 51.

88. V. N. Volosinov, *Marxism and the Philosophy of Language*, trans. Ladislav Matejka and I. R. Titunik (Cambridge, MA: Harvard UP, 1986), 23.

89. Martin Bernal, *Black Athena: The Afroasiatic Roots of Classical Civilization* (New Brunswick, NJ: Rutgers UP, 1987), 23–24, 170; see also *NS*, 38–39.

90. Said, *The World, The Text, and the Critic*, 25.

91. Ibid., 337.

92. See, for example, the work of Maryam Jameela, Anouar Abdel-Malek, A. L. Tibawi, and others who set the stage for Said's book, providing leads that he took up in his own original way.

93. Among the Palestinian communists were Emile Habiby, Emil Touma, and Tawfiq Zayyad. This general point about predecessors is made in Said's own reassessment, "*Orientalism* Reconsidered," in *Reflections on Exile* (1985; Cambridge, MA: Harvard UP, 2000), 198–215, although without mentioning all of them. A similar observation is found in Robert Irwin's history of philology, *For Lust of Knowing: The Orientalists and Their Enemies* (London: Allen Lane, 2006), a book published after Said's death that portrays him as an incompetent scholar marred by overstatement and omission. See Timothy Brennan, "Settling Scores: The Orientalists Strike Back," *Race & Class* 48, no. 3 (January 2007): 94–100, for a discussion of the problems with this claim. For an account of the reception of Said's work and the debates surrounding it among Levantine Marxists, see Fadi A. Bardawil, "When All This Revolution Melts into Air: The Disenchantment of Levantine Marxist Intellectuals" (PhD diss., Columbia University, 2011).

94. Between 1979 and 1983, Said twice offered a seminar devoted to Lukács's "Reification and the Consciousness of the Proletariat" and Gramsci's "Certain Aspects of the Southern Question." In the same period, he offered two separate seminars on critical theory and the Frankfurt School.

95. Harry Levin, "Thematics and Criticism," in *Grounds for Comparison* (Cambridge, MA: Harvard UP, 1972), 92.

96. Edward Said, "Introduction to the Fiftieth Anniversary Edition," in Erich Auerbach, *Mimesis: The Representation of Reality in Western Literature*, trans. Willard R. Trask (Princeton, NJ: Princeton UP, 2003), xii.

97. Erich Auerbach, *Dante: Poet of the Secular World*, trans. Ralph Manheim (1929; Chicago: U of Chicago P, 1969), 110–11.

98. Marx and Engels, *Collected Works*, vol. 41, *Marx and Engels: 1860–64, Letters January 1860–September 1864* (Moscow: Progress Publishers, 1985), 355.

99. Karl Marx, *Grundrisse: Foundations of the Critique of Political Economy*, trans. Martin Nicolaus (New York: Penguin, 1993), 110.

100. Georg Lukács, "Reification and the Consciousness of the Proletariat," in *History and Class Consciousness* (Cambridge, MA: MIT Press, 1971), 145.

101. Ibid., 143.

102. Hannah Arendt, *The Portable Hannah Arendt*, ed. Peter Baehr (Harmondsworth, UK: Penguin, 2000), 169.

103. E. P. Thompson, *The Poverty of Theory and Other Essays* (New York: Monthly Review Press, 1978), 115.

104. Volosinov, *Marxism and the Philosophy of Language*, 71.

105. Ibid., 74–76.

106. Georg Lukács, "The Ideology of Modernism," in *The Lukács Reader*, ed. Arpad Kadarkay (Oxford: Blackwell, 1995).

107. Said, *The World, the Text, and the Critic*, 234.

CHAPTER 2

1. "A citation from Marx on the mutability of nature (in [Karl] Korsch, *Karl Marx*, Vol. 3, p. 9)," quoted in Walter Benjamin, *The Arcades Project*, trans. Howard Eiland and Kevin McLaughlin (after Rolf Tiedemann) (Cambridge, MA: Harvard UP, 1999), 484.

2. "Hegel ist immer an der Zeit." Ernst Bloch, "Postscript," in *Subjekt-Objekt: Erläuterungen zu Hegel* (Berlin: Aufbau Verlag, 1951).

3. Giambattista Vico, *Des J. B. Vico kleine Schriften*, vol. 1, ed. and trans. K. H. Müller (Neubrandenburg, 1854). The connection is explored as well in Benedetto Croce, *La filosofia di G. B. Vico* (Bari, Italy: Laterza, 1911); and Croce, *What Is Living and What Is Dead of the Philosophy of Hegel*, trans. Douglas Ainalie (London: Macmillan, 1915).

4. In this, too, he follows Vico: "By uniformity of ideas the orientals, Egyptians, Greeks and Latins, each in ignorance of the others, afterwards raised the gods to the planets" (*NS*, 4).

5. Compare, for example, the incorporative gesture of Vico in *The New Science* (*NS*, 139) with Hegel's almost identical move in *The Science of Logic* (*SL*, 511).

6. See Karl Löwith, *Meaning in History: The Theological Implications of the Philosophy of History* (Chicago: U of Chicago P, 1949); and Eckhard Kessler, "Vico's Attempt towards a Humanistic Foundation of Science," in *Vico: Past and Present*, ed. Giorgio Tagliacozzo (Atlantic Highlands, NJ: Humanities Press, 1981), 73–88. The Löwith book is cited in Sandra Rudnick Luft, *Vico's Uncanny Humanism: Reading "The New Science" between Modern and Postmodern* (Ithaca, NY: Cornell UP, 2003). Hegel sounds most

like Vico, perhaps, in his sustained dismantling of the pretensions of mathematics for science (*PhS*, 23–27).

7. Compare also his statement on secular providence in *PR*, 372.

8. G. W. F. Hegel, letter to Schelling, 16 April 1795, quoted in Georg Lukács, *The Young Hegel: Studies in the Relations between Dialectics and Economics* (1938; London: Merlin Press, 1975), 11.

9. In the work of Charles Taylor, Talal Asad, and Saba Mahmood, among others, and of several figures within subaltern studies—Dipesh Chakrabarty, for example.

10. The critique of secularity along contemporary lines can be found in an identical form in the work of a number of interwar thinkers on the political Right. Drawing on them, Raymond Aron gave the position a distinctive voice in 1944 in his exposure of secular thought as nothing more than another "religion." See Stefanos Geroulanos, *An Atheism That Is Not Humanist Emerges in French Thought* (Stanford, CA: Stanford UP, 2010), 6.

11. See *PhS*, 260–61, where the entire argument of the *Philosophy of Right* is expressed in a condensed form.

12. Stuart Barnett, introduction to *Hegel after Derrida*, ed. Stuart Barnett (London: Routledge, 1998), 25. As Jon Stewart puts it in *The Hegel Myths and Legends*, ed. Jon Stewart (Evanston, IL: Northwestern UP, 1996): "The tradition that is inaugurated after Hegel is most accurately understood not as a new beginning or a radical break with the past but rather as something continuous with what preceded it" (307).

13. The case was made thoroughly by Lukács in 1938 in *The Young Hegel* but has been added to since. See the Hegel scholarship cited in this chapter by Losurdo, Buck-Morss, and Anderson in this respect; see also Terry Pinkard, *Hegel: A Biography* (Cambridge: Cambridge UP, 2000), 53, 58.

14. Howard P. Kainz, in *An Introduction to Hegel: The Stages of Modern Philosophy* (Athens: Ohio UP, 1996), paraphrases Hegel's position on Kant in this respect: "[For Kant] outside us there are things-in-themselves devoid of space and time, while inside us there is a space that is not a space for anything, and a time which is not a time for any particular thing. What Kant fails to realize is that the universality of space and time does not prevent them from being *external* universals" (60).

15. Adorno captures this movement in "Skoteinos, or How to Read Hegel": "Hegel's publications are more like films of thought than texts" (*Three Studies on Hegel*, trans. Shierry Weber Nicholsen [1963; Cambridge, MA: MIT Press, 1994], 121).

16. Fredric Jameson, *Valences of the Dialectic* (London: Verso, 2009), 3.

17. See, for example, Keya Ganguly, *Cinema, Emergence, and the Films of Satyajit Ray* (Berkeley: U of California P, 2010), and *States of Exception: Everyday Life and Postcolonial Identity* (Minneapolis: U of Minnesota P, 2001); John K. Noyes, "Hegel and the Fate of Negativity after Empire," in *Postcolonialism Today: Theoretical Challenges and Pragmatic Issues*, Virtual Symposium of the Open Semiotics Resource Center (June 2003), http://www.semioticon.com/virtuals/postcolonialism_2/Noyes%20Hegel.htm; Loren Kruger, *Post-Imperial Brecht: Politics and Performance, East and South* (Cambridge: Cambridge UP, 2007); Crystal Bartolovich, "Figuring the (In)Visible in an Imperial *Weltstadt*: The Case of Benjamin's Moor," *Cultural Critique* 52 (Fall 2002), 167–208; Antonio Vasquez-

Arroyo, "Universal History Disavowed: On Critical Theory and Postcolonialism," *Postcolonial Studies* 11, no. 4 (December 2008), 450–73; and Domenico Losurdo, *Hegel and the Freedom of Moderns*, trans. Marella and Jon Morris (Durham, NC: Duke UP, 2004). The present book was completed before the appearance of Slavoj Žižek's *Less than Nothing: Hegel and the Shadow of Dialectical Materialism* (New York: Verso, 2012).

18. The revival of Hegel in analytic philosophical circles has been both sudden and wide-ranging. See John McDowell, *Having the World in View: Essays on Kant, Hegel, and Sellars* (Cambridge, MA: Harvard UP, 2009); Robert Brandom, *Reason in Philosophy: Animating Ideas* (Cambridge, MA: Belknap Press of Harvard UP, 2009); Raymond Geuss, *The Idea of a Critical Theory: Habermas and the Frankfurt School* (Cambridge: Cambridge UP, 1981); and Roy Bhaskar, *Dialectic: The Pulse of Freedom* (London: Verso, 1993).

19. Judith Butler, "Final Reflections on 'Overcoming' Hegel," in *Subjects of Desire: Hegelian Reflections in Twentieth-Century France* (New York: Columbia UP, 1987); Louis Althusser, *Essays in Self-Criticism*, trans. Grahame Lock (1974; Atlantic Highlands, NJ: Humanities Press; London: New Left Books, 1976), 134; Gilles Deleuze, *Negotiations, 1972–1990*, trans. Martin Joughin (1990; New York: Columbia UP, 1995), 6.

20. Lloyd Spencer and Andrzej Krauze, *Introducing Hegel* (New York: Totem Books, 1996), 157. They contend that Hegel was never very popular outside Berlin and that Hegelianism remained a "minority perspective" in a Germany dominated by neo-Kantianism and romanticism. This statement is partly valid, although only in a highly qualified sense, and is truer of the mid- to late nineteenth century than the twentieth, which is presumably the "our century" they are referring to. They fail to mention the role of Hegelianism in the positivism that emerged from Hegel's follower Ludwig Feuerbach, the meteoric rise of social democracy in the political arena, or the effects of Hegelian Marxism on the labor movement, on twentieth-century aesthetics, on *Kulturkritik*, and on the disciplines of anthropology and sociology, which Left Hegelianism wove out of Vichian and Herderian threads. Only by restricting Hegel to a school of academic philosophy can it be said that Hegelianism dissipated, and even then, only until the appearance of neo-Hegelians such as Georg Lasson, Hermann Nohl in the interwar period, and of course, Georg Lukács. After that, Hegelianism of various sorts can be said to have dominated philosophical thinking in the century, in however inverted a form—which was often the case, as the Barnett epigraph above suggests.

21. Edward Said, *Culture and Imperialism* (New York: Alfred A. Knopf, 1993), 110.

22. Ibid., 47.

23. Edward Said, *Orientalism* (New York: Vintage, 1979), 118.

24. Losurdo, *Hegel and the Freedom of Moderns*, 31.

25. Ellen Meiksins Wood, *Empire of Capital* (New York: Verso, 2003); Ulrich Beck, *What Is Globalization?*, trans. Patrick Camiller (Cambridge: Polity, 2000); Antonio Negri and Michael Hardt, *Empire* (Cambridge, MA: Harvard UP, 2000).

26. Hegel's analyses of the German constitution (1798–1802) and of the English Reform Bill (1831), although seminal to an understanding of his politics, are conjunctural. See *HPW*.

27. Think, for example, of the many references to Attic Greece in Martin Heidegger's essays on the world picture, the work of art, and "dwelling" in the earth, as well as in Hannah Arendt's political philosophy; the references to Roman law in the political theory of Giorgio Agamben; or the uses of Polybius in Negri. In the second case, I am alluding to the arguments of Louis Althusser and Gilles Deleuze that Spinoza was not simply an Enlightenment rationalist but a radical materialist and a revolutionary—views that I analyzed in the previous chapter.

28. It seems apparent to me, as to Said, that Fanon's thinking was based in a positive sense on Hegel's ideas, terms, and modes of expression. Others who take this view include Cedric Robinson (1993), Benita Parry (1994), Ato Sekyi-Oti (1996), Nigel Gibson (1999), Neil Lazarus (1999), and E. San Juan (1999). Since the mid-1980s, though, there have been attempts to deny this, seeing him rather in a Lacanian or post-identitarian frame. Some examples are Homi Bhabha (1986, 1994), Robert Young (1990), Stuart Hall (1996), Diana Fuss (1995), Kobena Mercer (1996), Françoise Vergès (1996), and Rey Chow (1998).

29. This point is made well by Vasant Kaiwar in "Postcolonialism, Eurocentrism, and the Question of Universalism: Subaltern Studies and Postcolonialism in India and USA," in *World Orders Revisited*, ed. Ulf Engel and Matthias Middell (Leipzig: Leipziger Universitätsverlag, 2010), 46, 17–50. For recent examples of work exploring reversals in the use of the term "Eurocentric," see Daniel Vukovich, "China in Theory: The Orientalist Production of Knowledge in the Global Economy," *Cultural Critique* 76 (Fall 2010), 148–72; Jamil Khader, "Zizek's Infidelity: Lenin, the National Question, and the Postcolonial Legacy of Revolutionary Internationalism," in *Žižek Now: Current Perspectives in Žižek Studies*, ed. Jamil Khader and Molly Anne Rothenberg (Cambridge: Polity, 2012); Sumit Sarkar, "The Decline of the Subaltern in *Subaltern Studies*," in *Mapping Subaltern Studies and the Postcolonial*, ed. Vinayak Chaturvedi (London: Verso, 2000), 300–323.

30. For example, George Anastaplo, *But Not Philosophy: Seven Introductions to Non-Western Thought* (Lanham, MD: Lexington Books, 2002); Emmanuel Chukwudi Eze, ed., *African Philosophy: An Anthology* (Cambridge, MA: Blackwell, 1998); Pieter Coetzee and A. P. J. Roux, eds., *The African Philosophy Reader* (London: Routledge, 1998); Tsenay Serequeberhan, ed., *African Philosophy: The Essential Readings* (New York: Paragon House, 1991).

31. Alfred Métraux, *Voodoo in Haiti*, trans. Hugo Charteris (New York: Oxford University Press, 1959); Lydia Cabrera, *El monte: Igbo, finda, ewe orisha, vititi nfinda: Notas sobre las religiones, la magia, las supersticiones y el folklore de los negros criollos y el pueblo de Cuba* (Miami: Ediciones Universal, 2006); Fernando Ortiz, *La africanía de la música folklórica de Cuba* (Havana: Editora Universitaria, 1965); Joan Dayan, *Haiti, History, and the Gods* (Berkeley: U of California P, 1995); Timothy Brennan, *Secular Devotion: Afro-Latin Music and Imperial Jazz* (New York: Verso, 2008).

32. See, for example, Bill Ashcroft, Gareth Griffiths, and Helen Tiffin, eds., *The Empire Writes Back: Theory and Practice in Post-Colonial Literatures* (London: Routledge, 1989): "[Postcolonial studies] first emerged not in metropolitan critical theory texts but in the cultural discourse of formerly colonized peoples" (196). Similar arguments can be

found under the rubric of "decoloniality": Walter Mignolo, "Mariátegui and Gramsci in 'Latin' America: Between Revolution and Decoloniality," in *The Postcolonial Gramsci* (New York: Routledge, 2012), 191–220. Here decoloniality (or "nativism") is said to be utterly untouched by an undifferentiated entity called "Western thought."

33. Jean-Luc Nancy, *Hegel: The Restlessness of the Negative*, trans. Jason Smith and Steven Miller (Minneapolis: U of Minnesota P, 2002), 3.

34. Hegel's reservations about Spinoza—a philosopher who is mentioned repeatedly in his work—revolve in part around the latter's one-sided assault on religion. By this line of attack, according to Hegel, Spinoza represents "negative pure insight," which is characterized as "a distinguishing of differences which are no longer differences." Making the Notion itself into an *object*, it thereby arrests movement by making of "*pure* thought" a "*pure Thing*" (*PhS*, 350). It is to this position that faith, now deprived of religion, sinks back after the illusions of religion are revealed. What Hegel is rejecting most of all is the tendency in early Enlightenment thought (especially Spinoza) of rendering the good always in terms of utility. He calls this philosophical stance, somewhat derisively, "pure insight," where the thought no longer "has any life within it" (*PhS*, 353). This destruction of the pictorial imagination has clear Vichian resonances and reminds one, negatively, of Vico's nonverbal, pictorial original words.

35. See Marx's concise way of putting the matter: although it could be mystified, still Hegel's dialectic "in its rational form is a scandal and an abomination to the bourgeoisie and its doctrinaire spokesmen, because it includes in its positive understanding of what exists a simultaneous recognition of its negation, its inevitable destruction . . . and because it does not let itself be impressed by anything, being in its very essence critical and revolutionary" (Karl Marx, *Capital*, vol. 1, trans. Ben Fowkes [New York: Penguin Books, 1990], 103).

36. Losurdo, *Hegel and the Freedom of Moderns*, 26.

37. Forster's radicalism was not unrelated to his colonial worldliness. He became famous at the age of twenty-four as the author of an account of Captain Cook's second voyage (1772–75).

38. Losurdo is particularly incisive when contrasting Hegel's radicalism to the vaunted freethinking of Enlightenment liberalism. Montesquieu, John Locke, Madame de Staël, Benjamin Constant, and others are quoted to great effect, denouncing the "rabble" and demonstrating their contempt for the democracy they nominally embraced—just the opposite of Hegel's populist emphases and tone as well as his sympathy for revolution. For Montesquieu, "freedom" meant the "freedom of the barons" (115); Taine similarly "will later condemn Rousseau's 'grudge (*rancune*) typical of the poor,' and Nietzsche, who declares he attended Taine's 'school,' will denounce Rousseau as the 'grudging man' (*Ranküne-Mensch*)" (183). Losurdo develops these ideas in *Liberalism: A Counter-History*, trans. Gregory Elliott (London: Verso, 2011).

39. Antonio Gramsci, *Pre-Prison writings*, trans. Virginia Cox, ed. Richard Bellamy (Cambridge: Cambridge UP, 1994), 50.

40. Lukács, *The Young Hegel*, 25.

41. Gillian Rose, *Hegel contra Sociology* (1981; Verso, 2009), 26–35, 226–27.

42. His rejection of the rationale for slavery occurs in several parts of the *Philosophy of Right*. Only by allowing these parts to shed light on one another within his *system* can one intrepret his implied meaning: "In the ethical realm, a human being has rights in so far as he has duties, and duties in so far as he has rights.... The slave can have no duties; only the free human being has these. If all rights were on one side and all duties on the other, the whole would disintegrate, for their identity is the only basis we have to hold on to here" (197).

43. For example, Robert Brenner, "The Origins of Capitalist Development: A Critique of Neo-Smithian Marxism," *New Left Review* 104 (July/August 1977), 25–93; and T. Aston and C. Philpin, eds., *The Brenner Debate: Agrarian Class Structure and Economic Development in Pre-Industrial Europe* (Cambridge: Cambridge UP, 1985).

44. Carl Siger, *Essai sur la colonisation* (Paris: Société du Mercure de France, 1907), 173.

45. Hegel, "The German Constitution," in *HPW*, 98.

46. What Lukács, in a Vichian reference, calls Hegel's "first faint glimmerings of an understanding of gentile society" (*The Young Hegel*, 48).

47. Ibid., 1–89.

48. Gayatri Chakravorty Spivak, *A Critique of Postcolonial Reason* (Cambridge, MA: Harvard UP, 1999), 78.

49. Martin Heidegger, *Hegel's Phenomenology of Spirit*, trans. Parvis Emad and Kenneth Maly (1930–31; Bloomington: Indiana UP, 1988), 13.

50. In *Glas*, Derrida misrepresents the role of the family in Hegel by missing this source and following a more expected Freudian line of interpretation. He fails to mark the Vichian character of Hegel's presentation, taking it instead as a mark of Christian heteronormativity that begs for disruption according to what Derrida describes as his intention to "violently intervene ... in the Hegelian systematics" (Jacques Derrida, *Glas*, trans. John P. Leavey, Jr., and Richard Rand [1974; Lincoln: U of Nebraska P, 1986], 4–45).

51. Lukács, *The Young Hegel*, 95–96.

52. For a large and varied, if not full, accounting of the typical charges against Hegel, see Jon Stewart, *The Hegel Myths and Legends*. These myths include the idea that Hegel believed all reality was reasonable (that is, defensible, acceptable); that he was a Prussian apologist and totalitarian theorist who glorified war; that he believed history had reached its highest possible stage in Germany; that he denied the law of contradiction; that he was interested only in the internal mental life of subjects; that his idea of absolute Spirit was crypto-theological; and that he relied on a pat formula based on the triad "thesis-antithesis-synthesis."

53. To get a clearer sense of the complexities of this interpretive difficulty, see the translator's preface to *PR*, xxxvi; and Georg Lasson's "Note on the Composition of the Text" in *LPH*, 4–11. One, then, must disagree with Jean Hyppolite in *Logic and Existence* when he writes that "Hegel is the author of the *Phenomenology* just as much as he is the author of the *Science of Logic*, the author of the *Philosophy of History* just as much as he is the author of the conclusion of the *Encyclopaedia*" (Jean Hyppolite, "Logic and Existence," in *Hegel and Contemporary Continental Philosophy*, ed. Dennis King Keenan [Albany: SUNY Press, 2004], 175). This is untrue if we consider that the other three

works were published in his lifetime and so do not include students' notes presented as his own words.

54. Susan Buck-Morss, *Hegel, Haiti and Universal History* (Pittsburgh: U of Pittsburgh P, 2009), 56–57.

55. C. L. R. James, *Notes on Dialectics: Hegel, Marx, Lenin* (1948; London: Allison and Busby, 1980). The revolutionary communist international (Third International), wrote James, was an embodiment "'in principle' of socialism, of the Universal." But those who mean to let the matter rest there "completely failed to study p. 244 of [Hegel's] *Logic*." If they had, they would "recognize that these, concrete as they were, were yet abstract Universals in the sense that Hegel has so carefully explained. They were only a form. They were not totality. And precisely because they were abstract Universality, they could become fearfully fixed and ferociously finite" (124). *Notes on Dialectics* does not explicitly explore the dynamic of colonialism, as do, for example, his essay "Lenin and the Problem" and other of his essays from the 1960s. It was written principally as a way to think himself out of Trotskyism without leaving socialism, to show that Trotsky was insufficiently Hegelian.

56. Said, *Culture and Imperialism*, 244–45.

57. A point made explicitly in Robert J. C. Young, *Colonial Desire: Hybridity in Theory, Culture, and Race* (New York: Routledge, 1995), 179.

58. Walter Mignolo, "(Post)Occidentalism, (Post)Coloniality, and (Post)Subaltern Rationality," in *The Pre-Occupation of Postcolonial Studies*, ed. Fawzia Afzal-Khan and Kalpana Seshadri (Durham, NC: Duke University Press, 2000), 89–90.

59. Bill Ashcroft, Gareth Griffiths, and Helen Tiffin, eds., *The Post-Colonial Studies Reader* (London: Routledge, 1995), 102.

60. Robert Young, *White Mythologies: Writing, History, and the West* (London: Routledge, 1990), 2.

61. Tsenay Serequeberhan, *Contested Memory: The Icons of the Occidental Tradition* (Trenton, NJ: Africa World Press, 2007), 93, 65, 64.

62. But there are other scholarly objections to raise about Serequeberhan's project. He enlists Herbert Marcuse in support of his argument that "Hegel reproduces, on the level of thought, the imperious relations that Europe imposes on the non-European world" (ibid., 65). Actually, in *Reason and Revolution* Marcuse quotes Hegel to opposite effect, summarizing Hegel's views in this way: "The old privileges of the estates have about as much basis in modern society as have 'sacrificial murder, slavery, feudal despotism, and countless other infamies'" (Herbert Marcuse, *Reason and Revolution: Hegel and the Rise of Social Theory*, 2nd ed. with suppl. chap. [London: Routledge & Kegan Paul, 1955], 176).

63. Serequeberhan, *Contested Memory*, 67.

64. See *PR*, 81, 83, where Hegel repeats the master/slave dialectic in other terms to make the point that slavery undermines the concept of ownership itself: "My *inner* idea [*Vorstellung*] and will that something should be *mine* is not enough to constitute property, which is the *existence* [*Dasein*] of personality; on the contrary, this requires that I should *take possession* of it. The *existence* which my willing thereby attains includes its ability to be recognized by others.—That a thing of which I can take possession should

be *ownerless* is . . . a self-evident negative condition. . . . Thus, there is nothing there which could be taken possession of by someone else."

65. Jameson, *Valences of the Dialectic*, 46–47.

66. This conflict and its condemnation, often attributed to Marx's radicalization of Hegel, is already present in Hegel himself: "The abstraction of production makes work increasingly *mechanical*, so that the human being is eventually able to step aside and let a *machine* take his place" (*PR*, 233).

67. Martin Heidegger, *Being and Time*, trans. John Macquarrie and Edward Robinson (New York: Harper, 1962), introduction, sec. 2.6.

68. Serequeberhan, *Contested Memory*, 93.

69. Robert Bernasconi, "Hegel at the Court of the Ashanti," in *Hegel after Derrida* (London: Routledge, 2002), 41–63.

70. Duncan Forbes, introduction to *LPH*, 5–9.

71. "The Thersites of Homer who abuses the kings is a standing figure for all times. . . . But our satisfaction at the fate of Thersitism also, may have its sinister side" (*PH*, 32).

72. In addition to James's *Notes on Dialectics*, see, for example, Babacar Camara's *Reason in History: Hegel and Social Changes in Africa* (Lanham, MD: Lexington Books, 2011).

73. Ronald Chilcote, "The Political Thought of Amilcar Cabral," *Journal of Modern African Studies* 6, no. 3 (1968): 373–88; Julius Nyerere, *The Arusha Declaration* (Dar es Salaam: Publicity Section, Tanganyika African National Union, 1967); Kirk A. Hawkins, *Venezuela's Chavismo and Populism in Comparative Perspective* (New York: Cambridge UP, 2010).

74. Bipan Chandra, *Modern India: A History Textbook for Class XII* (New Delhi: National Council of Educational Research and Training, 1990), 173–74.

75. Indira Gandhi, "Shaping the Future: Address to Andhra Pradesh Legislators, Hyderabad, July 26, 1972," in *The Years of Endeavour: Selected Speeches of Indira Gandhi, August 1969–August 1972* (New Delhi: Publications Division, Ministry of Information and Broadcasting, 1975), 234.

76. Walter Rodney, *How Europe Underdeveloped Africa* (Washington, DC: Howard UP, 1982), 21, 14. The problem is explored sensitively throughout the work of W. E. B. Du Bois as well, who directs his attention to the problem of overcoming underdeveloped capacities in the underfed, undereducated, and overworked rather than disputing the viability of the concept of backwardness. See, for example, *Darkwater: Voices from within the Veil* (New York: Harcourt, Brace, 1920), 59–60, 67–68, 98; and *The Negro* (New York: Henry Holt, 1915), 160–82.

77. Rodney, *How Europe Underdeveloped Africa*, 291; Mulk Raj Anand, *Is There a Contemporary Indian Civilisation?* (Bombay: Asia Publishing House, 1963), 105–6, 115–16; Rodney, "A Treasure Chest and a Rubbish Dump," in *Letters on India* (London: George Routledge & Sons, 1942), 72–78; "Speech by the President of Brazil, Luiz Inácio Lula da Silva, at the Plenary Meeting of the 61st UN General Assembly—New York," September 19, 2006, transcript online at http://www.brazil.org.uk/press/speeches_files/20060919.html.

78. Harry Harootunian, *History's Disquiet: Modernity, Cultural Practice, and the Question of Everyday Life* (New York: Columbia UP, 2000), 62–63.

79. Henri Lefebvre, "Logos, Logic, Dialectic," in *Critique of Everyday Life*, trans. John Moore (London: Verso, 2002), 2:252.

80. Amanda Anderson, *The Way We Argue Now: A Study in the Cultures of Theory* (Princeton, NJ: Princeton UP, 2006).

81. Raymond Geuss, *Outside Ethics* (Princeton, NJ: Princeton UP, 2005), 51.

82. This is a strategy that permeates much of the thinking of non-Hegelian Marxism. See, for example, Diana Coole, *Negativity and Politics: Dionysus and Dialectics from Kant to Poststructuralism* (London: Routledge, 2000).

83. The effort to link Marxist social and economic theory with Hegel's *Science of Logic* is one of the principal legacies of the Frankfurt School. Hans-Georg Backhaus is one of the most provocative thinkers of this sort, together with Helmut Reichelt, Alfred Schmidt, and Hans-Jürgen Krahl.

84. In *The Hegel Variations: On the "Phenomenology of Spirit"* (New York: Verso, 2010), Fredric Jameson goes so far as to say that "the *Phenomenology* is a profoundly structuralist work *avant la lettre*" (48).

85. A position that Jameson borrows from Paul de Man, "The Resistance to Theory," in *The Resistance to Theory* (Minneapolis: U of Minnesota P, 1986), 3–20.

86. Jameson, *Valences of the Dialectic*, 4; all subsequent references to *Valences* (V) will be cited parenthetically in the text. A similar idea is repeated in his *Hegel Variations*, where he associates "opposition" as such with merely commonsensical or naïvely empiricist thinking (Hegel's *Verstand*): in lieu of resolving a contradiction positively, "it is preferable to grasp each moment as an interminable play of oppositions without any stable resting places" (50). I am going to suggest that, first, this is not Hegel's position, and second, that it accommodates positions with which dialectics is in conflict.

87. Theodor Adorno, *Critical Models: Interventions and Catchwords*, trans. Henry W. Pickford (New York: Columbia UP, 1998), 5–36.

88. Martin Heidegger, "What Is Metaphysics?," in *Basic Writings*, ed. David Farrell Krell (1927–64; San Francisco: HarperSanFrancisco, 1993), 93–110.

89. The outlook is almost environmental today. See, for example, Jacques Rancière's recent writing on the aesthetic dimension of politics, where he employs the word "dissensus" but rushes to say that he does not mean conflict: "It is [rather] a perturbation of the normal relation between sense and sense" (Jacques Rancière, "The Aesthetic Dimension: Aesthetics, Politics, Knowledge," *Critical Inquiry* 36, no. 1 [2009]: 3). See also his *Dissensus: On Politics and Aesthetics*, trans. Steven Corcoran (London: Continuum, 2010), 29: "What is specific to politics is the existence of a subject defined by its participation in contraries," which is what Rancière wishes to overcome.

90. A similar point is made by Slavoj Žižek in *The Sublime Object of Ideology* (New York: Verso, 1989), 154–55; see also Timothy Brennan, "Running and Dodging: The Rhetoric of Doubleness in Contemporary Theory," *NLH* 41, no. 2 (Spring 2010): 277–300.

91. For Hegel's withering critique of utility in philosophy, see *PhS*, 353–55.

92. Karl Marx, from "Remarks on the New Instructions to the Prussian Censors" (1842), reprinted in *Marx and Engels on Literature and Art: A Selection of Writings*, ed. Lee Baxandall and Stefan Morawski (St. Louis: Telos Press, 1973), 59.

93. Johann Gottfried von Herder, *Philosophical Writings*, ed. Michael N. Forster (Cambridge: Cambridge UP, 2002), 76.

94. Robert Pippin, "Hegel's Metaphysics and the Problem of Contradiction," in Stewart, *The Hegel Myths and Legends*, 239–52.

95. Friedrich Nietzsche, *The Genealogy of Morals: A Polemic*, in *WFN*, 13:2–3.

96. Despite these affinities, Nietzsche was nonetheless quite critical of Spinoza in *The Joyful Wisdom*, denying that there is anything divine in humanity's interior (*WFN* 10:258) and considering Spinoza's philosophy too entangled with the natural sciences (*WFN* 10:290): "[W]hat *remains* of Spinoza, *amor intellectualis dei*, is rattling and nothing more!" (*WFN* 10:337).

97. Friedrich Nietzsche, "On the Genealogy of Morals," in *BW*, 452.

98. Karl Marx, "Preface to the First Edition" (1867), in *Capital*, 1:91.

99. In this regard, see Marx's inaccurate formulation in the "Postface to the Second Edition" (1873) of *Capital*, where he states that his dialectical method is "exactly the opposite" of Hegel's, for whom the process of thinking "is the creator of the real world," whereas for him "the ideal is nothing but the material world reflected in the mind of man" (102). It may seem odd of me to quote Heidegger against Marx, but the former was right to observe that after Hegel's death, Hegelian philosophy had not at all collapsed. The same cannot be said of his next observation, which argues that Hegel's "contemporaries and successors have not ever yet stood up so that they can be measured against his [Hegel's] greatness," a comment that seems churlishly aimed at Marx. Heidegger was not wrong to say, however, that "people managed to 'stand up' to him only by staging a mutiny" (Heidegger, *Hegel's Phenomenology of Spirit*, 40).

100. Karl Marx, preface to *A Contribution to the Critique of Political Economy*, in *Collected Works*, vol. 29, *Karl Marx: 1857–61* (New York: International Publishers, 1987), 262.

101. Ibid.

102. Karl Marx, "Letters from the *Deutsch-Französische Jahrbücher*," in *Collected Works*, vol. 3, *Marx and Engels: 1843–44* (New York: International Publishers, 1975), 143.

103. Georg Lukács, *Karl Marx und Friedrich Engels als Literaturhistoriker* (Berlin: Aufbau-Verlag, 1947), quoted in Losurdo, *Hegel and the Freedom of Moderns*, 287. Similarly, see Lenin's "Backward Europe and Advanced Asia," in *Collected Works*, vol. 19, *March–December 1913*, ed. Robert Daglish, trans. George Hanna (Moscow: Foreign Language Publishing House, 1963), 99–100.

104. Roberto Schwarz, *Misplaced Ideas: Essays on Brazilian Culture*, ed. John Gledson (London: Verso, 1992).

105. Some of the classic work establishing these points can be found in K. M. Panikkar, *Asia and Western Dominance: A Survey of the Vasco da Gama Epoch of Asian History, 1498–1945* (London: G. Allen & Unwin, 1959); M. N. Roy, *The Communist International* (Bombay: Radical Democratic Party Publication, 1943); and Stuart Schram and Hélène Carrère D'Encausse, eds. and trans., *Le marxisme et l'Asie, 1853–1964* (Paris: Armand Colin, 1965). See also Anthony Brewer, ed., *Marxist Theories of Imperialism: A Critical Survey* (London: Routledge, 1980).

106. Karl Marx, introduction to *Contribution to the Critique of Hegel's "Philosophy*

of Right," in *Collected Works*, vol. 3, *Marx and Engels: 1843–44* (New York: International Publishers, 1975), 176. All subsequent references to *Contribution to the Critique of Hegel's "Philosophy of Right"* (*CHPR*) will be cited parenthetically in the text.

107. Mikhail Lifshitz, *The Philosophy of Art of Karl Marx*, trans. Ralph B. Winn (1933; London: Pluto Press, 1973), 34.

108. Karl Marx and Frederick Engels, *Manifesto of the Communist Party*, in *Collected Works*, vol. 6, *Marx and Engels: 1845–48* (New York: International Publishers, 1976), 485.

109. For attempts to construct a Kantian Marx, see the work of Lucio Colletti, *Marxism and Hegel*, trans. Lawrence Garner (London: New Left Books, 1973); Kojin Karatani, *Transcritique: On Kant and Marx*, trans. Sabu Kohso (Cambridge, MA: MIT Press, 2005); and Jürgen Habermas, *Critique and Power: Recasting the Foucault/Habermas Debate*, ed. Michael Kelly (Cambridge, MA: MIT Press, 1995), 149–56.

110. Likewise, Losurdo's study of Hegel was written to counter the influence of Karl-Heinz Ilting, who in the 1970s discovered new Hegel materials thought lost and took the opportunity of revising the reconsideration of Hegel launched by Lukács.

111. Shadia Drury, *Alexandre Kojève: The Roots of Postmodern Politics* (New York: St. Martin's Press, 1994).

112. Alexandre Kojève, *Introduction to the Reading of Hegel: Lectures on the "Phenomenology of Spirit,"* trans. James H. Nichols, Jr. (Ithaca, NY: Cornell University Press, 1969). For characteristic positions in theory based on Kojève's reading of Hegel, see Keenan, *Hegel and Contemporary Continental Philosophy*.

113. Kojève, *Introduction to the Reading of Hegel*, 247.

114. Ibid., 160–61n.

115. Ibid., 239.

116. Jameson, *The Hegel Variations*, 35. He declares that in the *Phenomenology*, Hegel uses language "in what it is not anachronistic to call a deconstructive way" (35).

CHAPTER 3

Note on Translation The definitive edition of Nietzsche's complete works in German is the *Kritische Gesamtausgabe* (*KGW*) edited by Giorgio Colli and Mazzino Montinari, which began appearing (in German) in 1967. It is complemented by a shorter student edition of the same work known as the *Kritische Studienausgabe* (*KSA*). Although there is a definitive English edition based on *KSA* now in preparation (five volumes have appeared), my practice has been to use the earlier *Complete Works of Friedrich Nietzsche* (*WFN*, ed. Oscar Levy, 1909–13) rather than the varied publications by different translators of individual works widely available today in paperback editions. Although arguably not as scholarly as the newer editions based on *KSA* (which are, in any case, incomplete), *WFN* better captures the Nietzsche that English-speaking readers knew in the early twentieth century and continued to read until the 1960s. The variants in the translations between this and current editions, moreover, are insignificant apart from a few archaisms. In every case, I have compared Nietzsche's words against the German in *KGW* for accuracy.

For the individual works of Nietzsche that correspond to the citations, see the following: vol. 1: *Birth of Tragedy*; vol. 2: "The Greek State" (1–18) and "Homer's Contest"

(49–62), in *Early Greek Philosophy and Other Essays*; vol. 3: "On the Future of Our Educational Institutions" (15–144) and "Homer and Classical Philology" (145–70); vol. 4: "David Strauss, the Confessor and the Writer," in *Thoughts Out of Season*, bk. 1 (3–97); vol. 5: *Thoughts Out of Season*, bk. 2; vol. 6: *Human, All-Too-Human I*; vol. 7: *Human, All-Too-Human II*; vol. 8: "We Philologists" (109–90); vol. 9: *Dawn of Day*; vol. 10: *The Joyful Wisdom ("La Gaya Scienza")*; vol. 11: *Thus Spake Zarathustra*; vol. 12: *Beyond Good and Evil*; vol. 13: *The Genealogy of Morals: A Polemic*; vol. 14: *The Will to Power*, bks. 1 and 2; vol. 15: *The Will to Power*, bks. 3 and 4; vol. 16: *Twilight of the Idols* (1–124) and *The Antichrist* (125–236); vol. 17: *Ecce Homo* and poetry.

1. Raymond Geuss, *Outside Ethics* (Princeton, NJ: Princeton UP, 2005), 53.

2. One recent study, however, does deal with his years as a philologist: James I. Porter's *Nietzsche and the Philology of the Future* (Stanford, CA: Stanford UP, 2000). In this excellent book, Porter is, however, not interested in the colonial question and follows convention by seeing Nietzsche as a writer whose intentions can never be verified.

3. The standard English edition of Nietzsche's complete works translates this title as *Thoughts Out of Season*. I leave it as *Untimely Meditations* here because it is under that name that most contemporary readers will recognize it.

4. I am underscoring the fact that early Nietzsche is frequently driven to counterpose the "real" evidence of the record to conventional fantasies of an "ideal" he seeks to correct. See "We Philologists," in *WFN*, 8:122–23.

5. Distinctions between the two can also be more subtle. If we discount Vichian irony, Vico writes at times as though he had prepared Nietzsche's playbook. Those who deserve to rule cannot be "fainthearted" (*NS*, 422); "Men consist of these two parts, one of which is noble and should therefore command, and the other of which is base and should serve" (*NS*, 13); and he even identifies "nobler nature[s]" with specific peoples: the Egyptians, Greeks, and Latins, all of whom had "a presumed natural heroism" (*NS*, 13). The word "presumed," however, matters a great deal in this context, as becomes even clearer when he remarks that the aristocratic commonwealths "held themselves to have" a superior nature to that of the plebs (*NS*, 20). Natural heroism may be "presumed," but he does not share the presumption.

6. "The truly scientific people, the literary peoples, were the Egyptians, and not the Greeks"; "That which is really Greek is much less the result of natural aptitude than of adapted institutions, and also of an acquired language" (*WFN*, 8:167, 163).

7. See, for example, Giorgio Agamben's use of the term *Ausnahme* in *Homo Sacer: Sovereign Power and Bare Life*, trans. Daniel Heller-Roazen (Stanford, CA: Stanford UP, 1998). By taking the word apart, prefix and root, he makes it mean a "taking of the outside," whereas it simply means exception, just as the English word *suspend* does not mean in most contexts "to dangle over one's head" but "to delay an event." At the beginning of *The Coming Community*, similarly, he treats the word *quodlibet* (whatever) as though it meant (in his words) "that particular or special thing one desires," whereas in Latin it means "whatever one happens arbitrarily to pick." In Latin, choosing (*libet*) does not signify desire, with all its post-Freudian connotations, only whim.

8. There is some apparent counterevidence. If marriage as a civic institution is

praised by Vico because it allows humans for the first time to know who was born to whom, the story he tells of its rise is double-edged. The clan mentalities that arose brought social oppression and interethnic conflict. If the first families left the forests and built protective enclosures, they also assumed the role of priests, sacrificing the impious, who were defined as those who arrived later: "The first *hostiae* . . . [were] the first victims of the gentile religions. . . . [T]hey were called *hostes* because such impious men were rightly held to be enemies of the whole human race" (*NS*, 191, 194). These words could be taken to say that commoners were inherently inferior, except that, as I have already argued, Vico is ventriloquizing a position with which he disagrees.

9. For a characteristic view of Nietzsche on orality, see *WEN*, 19.

10. "[Philology] is composed of . . . natural science in so far as it strives to fathom the deepest instinct of man, that of speech" (*WFN*, 3:146).

11. This Zoroaster (Zarathustra) later makes an entrance in *The New Science* in words that may bear on Nietzsche's aristocratic sympathies: "The first monarchy was founded there, that of the Assyrians over the Chaldean people, from whom came the first wise men of the world, their prince being Zoroaster" (*NS*, 88–89).

12. In this effort, St. Paul targeted opponents of superstition such as medicine and philology, an "arch-Jewish" thing to do, argues Nietzsche, waging war on the good scholars and doctors of the Alexandrine schools.

13. Leela Gandhi, *Postcolonial Theory: A Critical Introduction* (New York: Columbia UP, 1998), 37–38.

14. Edward Said, *The World, the Text, and the Critic* (Cambridge, MA: Harvard UP, 1983), 133–34, 178; Said, *Culture and Imperialism* (New York: Alfred A. Knopf, 1993), 268–69.

15. Gandhi, *Postcolonial Theory*, 38. For an opposing view, see Sanjay Subrahmanyam, "One for the Money, Two for the Show: On Postcolonial Studies and South Asian History," *L'Homme* 187–88 (2008): 3–4, 93–104.

16. Bill Ashcroft, *On Postcolonial Futures: Transformations of Colonial Culture* (London: Continuum, 2001), 29.

17. Quoted in Joachim Köhler, *Zarathustra's Secret: The Interior Life of Friedrich Nietzsche*, trans. Ronald Taylor (New Haven, CT: Yale UP, 2002), xv.

18. In *States of Injury: Power and Freedom in Late Modernity* (Princeton, NJ: Princeton UP, 1995), however, Wendy Brown follows this lead in a different direction, arguing that Nietzsche is a thinker who might bring the identitarian focus back to a more agonistic and active political orientation: "His thought is useful in understanding the source and consequences of a contemporary tendency to moralize in the place of political argument, and to understand the codification of injury and powerlessness—the marked turn away from freedom's pursuit—that this kind of moralizing politics entails" (27). This is the precise opposite of the more textually supported view that Nietzsche ridicules all political argument: Pierre-André Taguieff, "The Traditionalist Paradigm—Horror of Modernity and Antiliberalism: Nietzsche in Reactionary Rhetoric," in *Why We Are Not Nietzscheans*, ed. Luc Ferry and Alain Renaut (Chicago: U of Chicago P, 1997), 158–224.

19. Jacques Derrida, *Margins of Philosophy*, ed. and trans. Alan Bass (Chicago: U of Chicago P, 1982).

20. Michel Foucault, *The Order of Things: An Archaeology of the Human Sciences* (London: Tavistock, 1970), 286. According to Said, "in Foucault, Nietzsche's legacy operat[ed] at a deep level." Edward Said, *Reflections on Exile* (Cambridge, MA: Harvard UP, 2002), 192.

21. Clearly not all postcolonial scholars see themselves as Nietzscheans, but the conformity of the reception is clear enough. A partial list would include, for example, Kalpana Seshadri-Crooks, *Desiring Whiteness: A Lacanian Analysis of Race* (London: Routledge, 2000), 57; Graham Huggan, *Interdisciplinary Measures: Literature and the Future of Postcolonial Studies* (Liverpool, UK: Liverpool UP, 2008), 28; Bill Ashcroft, *Caliban's Voice: The Transformation of English in Post-Colonial Literatures* (London: Routledge, 2009); Robert Young, *Postcolonialism: An Historical Introduction* (Oxford: Blackwell, 2001), 410; Simon Gikandi, *Writing in Limbo: Modernism and Caribbean Literature* (Ithaca, NY: Cornell UP, 1992), 126; Bill Ashcroft, Gareth Griffiths, and Helen Tiffin, eds., *The Empire Writes Back* (London: Routledge, 1989), 164.

22. Although some have managed to. See Geoff Waite, *Nietzsche's Corps/e: Aesthetics, Politics, Prophecy, or, The Spectacular Technoculture of Everyday Life* (Durham, NC: Duke UP, 1996); Steven E. Aschheim, *The Nietzsche Legacy in Germany 1890–1990* (Berkeley: U of California P, 1992); and, more recently, Malcolm Bull, *Anti-Nietzsche* (New York: Verso, 2011).

23. Jan Rehmann, *Postmoderner Links-Nietzscheanismus* (Berlin: Argument Verlag, 2004); Domenico Losurdo, *Nietzsche, Il ribelle aristocratico* (Turin: Bollati Boringhieri, 2002); David Brolin, *Friedrich Nietzsche: Liv, Filosofi, Politik* (Stockholm: Häften, 2010). Rehmann's significant accomplishment is to show primarily how Deleuze, Foucault, and others selectively created a Left Nietzsche. He does not focus on the prehistory of this postwar project, as I would like to do, nor on colonialism. None of these three formidable studies contends, however, with the more unsettling fact of Nietzsche's popularity among traditional Marxist philosophers such as Henri Lefebvre—hardly a postmodernist—or, in a very different context, the analytic philosopher Raymond Geuss.

24. Aimé Césaire, *Discourse on Colonialism* (New York: Monthly Review Press, 1972), 33.

25. Alejo Carpentier, *The Lost Steps*, trans. Harriet de Onis, intro. Timothy Brennan (Minneapolis: U of Minnesota P, 2001), 72.

26. Alejo Carpentier, *The Chase*, trans. Alfred MacAdam, intro. Timothy Brennan (Minneapolis: U of Minnesota P, 2001), 109.

27. A position they call "feudal socialism": Karl Marx and Friedrich Engels, *Manifesto of the Communist Party*, in *The Marx-Engels Reader*, ed. Robert C. Tucker, 2nd ed. (New York: W. W. Norton, 1978), 476. There were other premonitions as well: "the brutal display of vigour in the Middle Ages, which Reactionists so much admire" (476); and in *Capital*, in the section on primitive accumulation: "Its origin is supposed to be explained when it is told as an anecdote of the past. In times long gone by there were two sorts of people; one, the diligent, intelligent, and above all, frugal elite; the other, lazy rascals, spending their substance, and more, in riotous living" (431).

28. Walter Benjamin, "Capitalism as Religion," in *Walter Benjamin: Selected Writings*, vol. 1, *1913–1926*, ed. Marcus Bullock and Michael W. Jennings (Cambridge, MA: Belknap Press of Harvard UP, 1996), 289.

29. Max Horkheimer and Theodor W. Adorno, *Dialectic of Enlightenment*, trans. Edmund Jephcott (Palo Alto, CA: Stanford UP, 2002), 77. They may have had in mind passages such as the following: "Who can attain to anything great if he does not feel in himself the force and will *to inflict* great pain? . . . that belongs to greatness" (*WFN*, 10:250).

30. Horkheimer and Adorno, *Dialectic of Enlightenment*, 76.

31. Ibid., 79. Horkheimer and Adorno, of course, recognize Nietzsche's attempt to subvert dominant political culture, and they also describe his project as a "protest against civilization." They go so far as to thank him for betraying the "consoling affirmation" that accompanies official power as well as the hypocritical utopia of grand philosophies (93). But the realization of Nietzsche's doctrines, they add, "both refutes them and reveals their truth." Against the current assumptions of mainstream thinking in political and postcolonial theory, their view of Nietzsche's link to Nazism is unyielding: German fascism brought Nietzsche's philosophy "to its absurd conclusion" (79), in part because his contempt for reality served the movement's fantasies of dominance, neglecting the positive side of the Enlightenment dialectic. That positive side for them is the ability of reason to *critique* its object, and by doing so, to say no to it.

32. Geoff Waite, "Heidegger, Schmitt, Strauss: The Hidden Monologue, or, Conserving Esotericism to Justify the High Hand of Violence," in "Radical Conservative Thought in Transition: Martin Heidegger, Ernst Jünger, Carl Schmitt 1940–1960," ed. Peter Uwe Hohendahl, special issue, *Cultural Critique* 69 (Spring 2008), 113–44.

33. Wilhelm Carl Becker, *Der Nietzschekultus: Ein Kapitel aus der Geschichte der Verirrungen des menschlichen Geistes* (Leipzig: Verlag von Richard Lipinski, 1908).

34. Alfred Bäumler, *Nietzsche der Philosophe und Politiker* (Leipzig: Reclam, 1931); cited in David Quigley, *Carl Einstein: A Defense of the Real* (Vienna: Akademie der bildenden Künste, 2006), 183.

35. No one has explored the ups and downs of Nietzsche criticism more impressively than Geoff Waite in his Althusserian study, *Nietzsche's Corps/e*—by far the most informed and creative take on Nietzsche's writings and influence in English. But his brilliant capture of Nietzschean illocutionary effects (mastered fully in his own prose) gives everything away to the Nietzschean position of unreadability (see esp. 27–28)— "it is necessary to be 'after' hermeneutics"—rendering a philological reading not only irrelevant but indeed a simplistic error doomed to miss its mark." Although he seems mortified by the conclusion, Waite considers Nietzsche the master puppeteer who conquered everyone and who now is literally everything (TV, technoculture, *us*). By internalizing him, he abandons the project of exposing him to his own meaning.

36. Alexander Nehamas, introduction to Nietzsche, *WEN*, ix.

37. Martin Heidegger, *Nietzsche*, 4 vols., trans. David Farrell Krell (1961; San Francisco: Harper & Row, 1979–82); Jacques Derrida, *Spurs: Nietzsche's Styles*, trans. Barbara Harlow (Chicago: U of Chicago P, 1979).

38. Pierre Bourdieu, *The Political Ontology of Martin Heidegger*, trans. Peter Collier (Stanford, CA: Stanford UP, 1991); Waite, "Heidegger, Schmitt, Strauss," 113–44, esp. 122.

39. Nietzsche's appeal to an elect is often couched, metaphorically, in the imagery of world conquest, as in *The Gay Science* (*The Joyful Wisdom*): "Many brave pioneers are now needed . . . men silent, solitary and resolute, who know how to be content and persistent in invisible activity" (*WFN*, 10:219).

40. Waite, *Nietzsche's Corps/e*, 154.

41. Thomas Mann, *Nietzsche's Philosophy in the Light of Contemporary Events* (Washington, DC: Library of Congress, 1947), 29.

42. "Das viele Lesen der Philologen: Daher die Armuth an originellen Gedanken" (*NGW*, 2:30; my translation).

43. A summary description of what Nietzsche admires about the ancients can be found in *WFN*, 16:225.

44. The translation is from *The Portable Nietzsche*, trans. Walter Kaufmann (New York: Penguin, 1968), 44. Kaufmann's exerpt from this work is substantially shorter than the original.

45. Walter Benjamin, *The Arcades Project*, trans. Howard Eiland and Kevin McLaughlin (Cambridge, MA: Harvard UP, 1999), 117.

46. "Odysseus, the typical Hellene of the Old Art" (*WFN*, 1:87).

47. Homer, *The Odyssey*, trans. Robert Fitzgerald (Garden City, NY: Doubleday, 1961), 9:158. All subsequent references to the *Odyssey* (*O*) will be cited parenthetically in the text.

48. Nietzsche praises piracy in *The Antichrist*, *WFN*, 16:227.

49. James I. Porter, "Nietzsche, Homer, and the Classical Tradition," in *Nietzsche and Antiquity: His Reaction and Response to the Classical Tradition*, ed. Paul Bishop (Rochester, NY: Camden House, 2004), 9.

50. Porter, *Nietzsche and the Philology of the Future*, 8.

51. Although the form of the entries is often very similar, Nietzsche uses different terms interchangeably when referring to them: "maxim" in *Human, All-Too-Human*; "aphorism" in *On the Genealogy of Morals, Human, All-Too-Human*, and *The Antichrist*; and "epigram" in *The Antichrist*.

52. Benjamin, *Arcades Project*, 117.

53. Massimo Cacciari, *Geofilosofia dell'Europa* (Milan: Adelphi, 1994), 8. The epigraph is in German in Cacciari's original (my translation).

54. Robert C. Holub, "Nietzsche's Colonialist Imagination: Nueva Germania, Good Europeanism, and Great Politics," in *The Imperialist Imagination: German Colonialism and its Legacy*, ed. Sara Friedrichsmeyer, Sara Lennox, and Susanne Zantop (Ann Arbor: U of Michigan P, 1998), 33–50.

55. Peter Bergmann, *Nietzsche, "The Last Antipolitical German"* (Bloomington: Indiana UP), 1987.

56. Nietzsche addresses socialism consistently, especially in the unpublished work: "In a socialistic society, life denies itself"; their affairs are "childish" and "lamblike"; and their movement will never "signify anything more than an attack of illness"; "I am op-

posed to ... socialism, because it dreams ingenuously of 'goodness, truth, beauty, and equal rights' [and to] parliamentary government and the power of the press, because these are the means by which cattle become masters" (*WFN*, 14:102–3; 15:206).

57. *Große Politik* (great, or high, politics) is a term that Nietzsche summons to mock Bismarck, who used the phrase to describe his patriotic project of German colonial expansion. Nietzsche, in a jest, echoes the term to refer to his different strategy of creating a new society of "philosophers of the future" (*WFN*, 9:186).

58. Andrew Zimmerman, *Anthropology and Antihumanism in Imperial Germany* (Chicago: U of Chicago P, 2001), 3.

59. Ibid., 241.

60. Ibid., 7, 246.

61. Bergmann, *Nietzsche, "The Last Antipolitical German,"* 53.

62. Ibid.

63. Ibid., 52–53.

64. Frederick Engels, *Herr Eugen Dühring's Revolution in Science* [*Anti-Dühring*], trans. Emile Burns (New York: International Publishers, 1966), 126–27. The reference is to both men's self-flattery, since they thought of themselves as "the only real philosophers of today and of the 'foreseeable future,'" who possess "a final and ultimate truth" (34).

65. Bergmann, *Nietzsche, "The Last Antipolitical German,"* 119.

66. Ibid., 121.

67. Arendt finds society undesirable as such. Similar to Nietzsche, she argues that moderns have misread the Greeks, who wished to keep the private and public realms radically separate from one another. The tragedy of modernity for Arendt is that concerns and interests once associated only with the private realm of the *oikos*, or "home" (such as satisfying the physical needs of existence), had been brought into the public realm as virtues under the banner of productivity, labor, and the circulation of goods. Arendt in effect dismantles the modern conception of "labor" as it was received from political economy and sets out to contravene Hegel's influential efforts in the *Philosophy of Right* (in the spirit of Vico) to bring social productive labor into the purview of philosophy.

68. Domenico Losurdo, *Hegel and the Freedom of Moderns*, trans. Marella and Jon Morris (Durham, NC: Duke UP, 2004), 147–48.

69. See, for example, *Ecce Homo* (*WFN*, 17:10): "Dialectic a symptom of decadence. ... All the morbid disturbances of the intellect, even that semi-stupor which accompanies fever ... etc."

70. Reinhart Kosellek, *Futures Past: On the Semantics of Historical Time*, trans. and intro. Keith Tribe (1979; New York: Columbia UP, 2004), 189.

71. In some respects (not all) a social Darwinist, Nietzsche thought that Darwin was wrong on key points; the weak, not the strong, have triumphed (*WFN*, 14: 158–59). The weak have more intellect, whereas the strong neither need nor want it; let the intellect fall away and still "the *Empire* will remain" (*WFN*, 16:72). His rejection is immersed in many of the conventional ideas of his time regarding the Darwinian themes of heredity, the weak, and genetic destiny. His disagreement ultimately is summarized in this way: "Man as a species is *not* progressing" (*WFN*, 14:157).

72. See also Waite's persuasive argument in "Heidegger, Schmitt, Strauss."
73. Georg Lukács, "Friedrich Nietzsche," in *The Lukács Reader*, ed. Arpad Kadarkay (Oxford: Blackwell, 1995), 250.
74. "*By which means does a virtue attain to power?*—With precisely the same means as a political party: slander, suspicion, the undermining of opposing virtues that happen to be already in power, the changing of their names, systematic persecution and scorn; in short, *by means of acts of general 'immorality'*" (*WFN*, 14:252).
75. See also Bergmann, *Nietzsche, "The Last Antipolitical German,"* 87.
76. In literary criticism, "signifying on" is a practice performed by trickster figures (especially in African American culture). A dominant image or term is seized upon in order to deflate its status, mock its goals, or redirect its meanings. The idea is to share a joke with an audience of like thinkers who do not have the social capital to directly contest an entrenched value system.
77. Nietzsche meant by cosmopolitan Europe—that is, by what he calls "good Europeans" as opposed to "patriots" (nationalists)—irony, attention to crossbreeding, the discipline of the will, and the wearing of masks. This amounts, he says, to thinking in a "super-European" way. See *WFN*, 14:106–8.
78. Slavoj Žižek, *Interrogating the Real* (New York: Continuum, 2005), 12.
79. His view of Germans, although complex, is not really ambiguous. His hope was to "kindle the flame of enthusiasm ... for that which is truly German ... [for the] reformation and purification of the German spirit" (*WFN*, 3:67–68).
80. See *Human, All-Too-Human*, *WFN*, 6:346–47, where he sees a positive outcome in the "destruction of nationalities." This will involve "perpetual crossings" and the "mixed race, that of the European man." This mixing, he argues, will produce "*good Europeans*," with the German as their natural "hereditary ... interpreters and intermediaries."
81. Bergmann, *Nietzsche, "The Last Antipolitical German,"* 123, 122.
82. Sara Friedrichsmeyer, Sara Lennox, and Susanne Zantop, introduction to *The Imperialist Imagination: German Colonialism and Its Legacy* (Ann Arbor: U of Michigan P, 1998), 10.
83. For more on this, see Bradley D. Naranch, "Inventing the *Auslandsdeutsche*: Emigration, Colonial Fantasy, and German National Identity, 1848–71," in *Germany's Colonial Pasts*, ed. Eric Ames, Marcia Klotz, and Lora Wildenthal (Lincoln: U of Nebraska P, 2005), 21–40.
84. "It might still be possible for the Germans to make an honourable name ultimately out of their old name of reproach, by becoming the first *non-Christian* nation of Europe" (*The Joyful Wisdom*, *WFN*, 10:181).
85. "Nueva Germania," *ABC Color*, March 29, 2009. According to this unsigned article, the project eventually failed, in part because the male colonists found it difficult to resist the amorous approaches of the local women, who were moved to reach out to the German settlers given the paucity of men in the area (the male population had been severely depleted in the war of 1870). "With his project in shambles, Förster relocated to San Bernardino where, disillusioned, he poisoned himself with strychnine and morphine, killing himself."

86. Holub, "Nietzsche's Colonialist Imagination," 36–37.

87. Michael Hardt and Antonio Negri, in *Empire* (Cambridge, MA: Harvard UP, 2000), give a similar misreading. They celebrate what they call Nietzsche's embrace of a "new nomad horde, a new race of barbarians, [that] will arise to invade or evacuate Empire." They then quote Nietzsche directly: "'Problem: where are the *barbarians* of the twentieth century? Obviously they will come into view and consolidate themselves only after tremendous socialist crises." As noted above, cultural "barbarism" is—in this context at least—what Nietzsche considered to be the downfall of the worker in his or her militant mode (the Communards are his nightmare vision); it does not have a positive connotation, at least not here. He is saying that the workers can nevertheless redeem themselves on behalf of Europe by participating in a wave of emigration to colonize distant climes.

88. Sylvère Lotringer and Christian Marazzi quote only part of this passage, excluding the lines where he talks about Chinese "ants," in *Italy: Autonomia: Post-Political Politics* (Los Angeles: Semiotext(e), 2007), 8.

89. Holub, "Nietzsche's Colonialist Imagination," 41.

90. Ibid., 42.

91. Ibid., 43, 47.

92. Antonio Gramsci, *Pre-Prison Writings*, ed. Richard Bellamy (Cambridge: Cambridge UP, 1994), 77.

93. See Peter Uwe Hohendahl, ed., "Radical Conservative Thought in Transition," special issue, *Cultural Critique* 69 (Spring 2008), which examines the postwar careers of writers of the Right who sought to retain, while refashioning, their discredited interwar views.

94. In his own edition and translation of *On the Genealogy of Morals* (*BW*, 437–599), Walter Kaufmann argues that "the 'blond beast' is not a racial concept and does not refer to the 'Nordic race'" (*BW*, 477). Only a few pages earlier, though, Nietzsche has declared that Germans must submit to "blood-poisoning" in order to fulfill their "world-historic mission." He has spent long passages (*BW*, 466–70) associating the Greek terms for ugly, ill-born, and vile with the slippage (in Latin) between "bad" (*malus*) and "dark" (*melas*), declaring that the "common man [is] the dark-colored, above all as the black-haired man . . . as the pre-Aryan occupant of the soil of Italy who was distinguished most obviously from the blond, that is Aryan, conqueror race by his color." Nietzsche's point may not be racist in the sense of Arthur de Gobineau, since for him the earlier suppressed races were gradually recovering the upper hand (and because blending, rather than racial purity, was his key to creating the master race). But it is absurd to say the "blond beast" is not a racial concept.

95. Irina Gutkin, *The Cultural Origins of the Socialist Realist Aesthetic* (Evanston, IL: Northwestern UP, 1999), 33.

96. Oswald Spengler, *Jahre der Entscheidung: Deutschland und die weltgeschichtliche Entwicklung* (Munich: C. H. Beck, 1933), 147.

97. Lothrop Stoddard, *The Rising Tide of Color* (New York: Charles Scribner's Sons, 1926), 120, 196, 232.

98. Lothrop Stoddard, *The Revolt against Civilization: The Menace of the Under-Man* (London: Chapman & Hall, 1923), 125-6, 132, 214.

99. Georges Sorel, *Reflections on Violence*, ed. Jeremy Jennings (Cambridge: Cambridge UP, 1999), 230–38. Nietzsche is cited often in this edition, but not by Sorel as much as by his contemporary editor.

100. Henri Massis, *Defense of the West* (1927; New York: Harcourt, Brace, 1928), 247–48. All subsequent references to *Defense of the West* (*DW*) will be cited parenthetically in the text.

101. René Guénon, *East and West*, trans. William Massey (London: Luzac, 1941), 42, 46–48.

102. Edmund Husserl, *Phenomenology and the Crisis of Philosophy*, trans. Quentin Lauer (New York: HarperCollins, 1965).

103. For example, *Beyond Good and Evil* (*WFN*, 12:224): in aristocratic culture there were "more *complete* men (which at every point also implies the same as 'more complete beasts') . . . men with a still natural nature, barbarians in every terrible sense of the word."

104. *WEN*, 161.

105. Michel Foucault, "Nietzsche, Genealogy, History," in *Language, Counter-Memory, Practice*, ed. Donald F. Bouchard (New York: Cornell UP, 1977), 140. All subsequent references to "Nietzsche, Genealogy, History" (*NGH*) will be cited parenthetically in the text.

106. The claim that Nietzsche resists origins has circulated widely. It is found again, for example, in Gilles Deleuze's *Nietzsche and Philosophy*, trans. Hugh Tomlinson (New York: Columbia UP, 1983), 2, positing the "indifferent origin for values" in genealogy.

107. Friedrich Nietzsche, *Zur Genealogie der Moral*, KGW, 6.2:260, 261, 263: "Über die Herkunft unserer moralischen Vorurtheile"; "gegen Umgebung, Beispiel, Alter, Herkunft auftrat"; "Herkunfts-Hypothesen."

108. The influence of Foucault's essay is widespread. See, for instance, Robert Guay, "The Philosophical Function of Genealogy," in *A Companion to Nietzsche* (Oxford: Blackwell, 2006), 353–55. Guay also sees genealogy as a method that shows "the ruptures, lacunae, arbitrariness, and randomness of all of our sense-making" and that considers the origin of a thing to be at odds with its utility, examining the logic of practices rather than the past causes that led to present effects.

109. Raymond Geuss, "Nietzsche and Genealogy," *European Journal of Philosophy* 2, no. 3 (1994): 276.

110. For it is not that there is no evidence for Geuss's position. See, for example, *The Dawn of Day*, (*WFN*, 9:51): "The salvation of mankind [once] depended upon *insight into the origin of things*—whereas now . . . the more we examine into origins, the less do they concern our interests."

111. "In dem eine längere Reihe spezifischer und bisher vereinzelter Erscheinungen zusammengeschaut und als verschiedene Wirkungen *einer* Ursache an verschiednem Material erkannt wird" (Friedrich Nietzsche, "Über die Methode der philologischen Quellenkritik," *NGW*, 1:430).

112. It is relevant that Herder, after Vico, argued that a lack of interest in sources,

or the view that sources are illusory, produces the monological option, not the other way round: "Whence have so many confusions arisen as from the fact that one took the later condition of a thing, a language, an art for its first condition, and forgot the origin? Whence so many errors as from the fact that *a single* condition [that is, the immediate condition of its present appearance] in which one considered everything inevitably yielded nothing but *single-sided* observations, divided and incomplete judgments?" (Johann Gottfried Herder, "Fragments on Recent German Literature," in *Philosophical Writings*, trans. and ed. Michael N. Forster (Cambridge: Cambridge, UP, 2002), 53).

113. "Was sagt dein Gewissen?—Du sollst der werden, der du bist" (And what does your conscience say? "You should be the one you are"). Friedrich Nietzsche, *Die fröhliche Wissenschaft*, KGW, 2:197, an adaptation of Goethe's famous line for Mephistopheles: "Du bist am Ende—was du bist" (*Faust*, trans. Walter Kaufmann [New York: Anchor, 1963], 190).

114. Sebastiano Timpanaro, *The Genesis of Lachmann's Method*, ed. and trans. Glenn W. Most (1981; Chicago: U of Chicago P, 2005), 10.

115. L. D. Reynolds and N. G. Wilson, *Scribes and Scholars: A Guide to the Transmission of Greek and Latin Literature* (Oxford: Clarendon Press, 1991), 209.

116. Timpanaro, *The Genesis of Lachmann's Method*, 120; Reynolds and Wilson, *Scribes and Scholars*, 210.

117. Timpanaro, *The Genesis of Lachmann's Method*, 119.

118. Ibid., 128.

119. He refers to this secret as one that brought him along the road of questioning morality and ethics, calling it a "personal scruple." See the full treatment of this passage in Joachim Köhler's study on the philosopher's young adulthood and sexuality, *Zarathustra's Secret*.

120. For an example of a particularly bitter exchange carried out with a studied insouciance of this sort, see the very genealogical encounter between Derrida and Agamben in Jacques Derrida, *The Beast and the Sovereign*, trans. Geoffrey Bennington (Chicago: U of Chicago P, 2009); Giorgio Agamben, *The Time That Remains: A Commentary on the Letter to the Romans*, trans. Patricia Dailey (Stanford, CA: Stanford UP, 2005); and Agamben, *Potentialities: Collected Essays in Philosophy*, trans. Daniel Heller-Roazen (Stanford, CA: Stanford University Press, 1999).

CHAPTER 4

1. Georges Bataille, *The Accursed Share: An Essay on General Economy*, vols. 2 and 3, trans. Robert Hurley (New York: Zone Books, 1993), 373. All subsequent references to *The Accursed Share*, vols. 2 and 3 (*AS*) will be cited parenthetically in the text. The first volume was published as Georges Bataille, *La part maudite: Essai d'économie générale (La consumation)* (Paris: Éditions de Minuit, 1949).

2. Geoff Waite, for example, in his near-encyclopedic study of Nietzsche's influence, does not dwell on *The Accursed Share*, nor is he especially interested in the anticolonial angle. I follow him completely, though, when he observes that all postwar Nietzsche-

ans "have hardly managed to get beyond" the problematic of his [Bataille's] principal binary challenge: Nietzsche or communism?" (*Nietzsche's Corps/e* [Durham, NC: Duke UP, 1996], 97).

3. *Bibliothèque de l'école des chartes* 83 (1922): 235–44.

4. Georges Bataille, *Choix de lettres*, ed. Michel Surya (Paris: Gallimard, 1997), letter of March 14, 1918, 15 (my translation).

5. For "transformism," see Antonio Gramsci, *Selections from the Prison Notebooks*, ed. and trans. Quintin Hoare and Geoffrey Nowell Smith (New York: International Publishers, 1971), 58–59. Gramsci describes it as a process in which "Left and Right parties tended to merge in terms of program" and "new formations arose to assert the autonomy of the subaltern groups, but within the old framework."

6. Didier Eribon, *Michel Foucault* (Cambridge, MA: Harvard UP, 1991): 52, 137.

7. This is not unlike what Said alludes to in *Culture and Imperialism* (New York: Alfred A. Knopf, 1993), when writing about André Gide's *L'immoraliste*—a narrative that, in Said's view, "entitled the European authorial subject to hold on to an overseas territory, derive benefits from it, depend on it, but ultimately refuse it autonomy or independence" (193).

8. Friedrich Nietzsche, *Twilight of the Idols*, WFN, 16:62; *Contra Wagner*, WFN, 8:77.

9. Charles Baudelaire, *The Parisian Prowler: Le spleen de Paris: petits poèmes en prose*, ed. Edward K. Kaplan (Athens: U of Georgia P, 1989), 21–22.

10. Charles Baudelaire, *Intimate Journals*, trans. Christopher Isherwood (London: Blackamore Press, 1930), 69.

11. Nietzsche, *Twilight of the Idols*, WFN, 16:104.

12. "Être un homme utile m'a paru toujours quelque chose de bien hideux" and "Le goût du néant" (Charles Baudelaire, *Oeuvres complètes*, ed. with notes by Y.-G. Le Dantec [Paris: Gallimard, 1968], 1:679, 76).

13. Georges Bataille, *The Accursed Share: An Essay on General Economy*, vol. 1, trans. Robert Hurley (New York: Zone Books, 1991), 76–77. Hereafter referred to as "*AS1*."

14. " . . . aus der allgemeinen thierischen Ökonomie"; Johann Gottfried Herder, *Abhandlung über den Ursprung der Sprache*, ed. Wolfgang Frühwald (Munich: Carl Hanser, 1978), 26. For English, see Johann Gottfried Herder, "Treatise on the Origins of Language," in *Philosophical Writings*, ed. Michael N. Forster (Cambridge: Cambridge UP, 2002), 82; in the same volume, compare "How Philosophy Can Become More Universal," 22.

15. Thorstein Veblen, *The Theory of the Leisure Class* (1899; Boston: Houghton Mifflin, 1971), chap. 4.

16. Henri Lefebvre, *Frédéric Nietzsche* (1939; Paris: Éditions Syllepse, 2003). The elementary study was written as an intellectual biographical primer, and so lacks the analysis found in Lefebvre's major statements. Its enthusiasms are clear, however. Lefebvre compares Nietzsche's oeuvre to a "vast fugue" of themes difficult to grasp in their "total movement" and enlists him in the company of Stendhal, Heine, Goethe, and Hegel as one of the authors of the "great works of the Napoleonic cycle" (86, 87).

17. Alexandre Kojève, *Introduction to the Reading of Hegel*, trans. James H. Hichols, Jr., ed. Allan Bloom (1947; Ithaca, NY: Cornell UP, 1969), 241.

18. Kevin Anderson, *Lenin, Hegel, and Western Marxism: A Critical Study* (Urbana: U of Illinois P, 1995). Anderson points out that some scholars have found these notebooks to be crucial to the formation of early Soviet policies on national minorities and the national question, explored in volume 2 of the present work. See also Kevin Anderson, *Marx at the Margins: On Nationalism, Ethnicity, and Non-Western Societies* (Chicago: U of Chicago P, 2010).

19. Anderson, *Lenin, Hegel, and Western Marxism*, 187.

20. One notorious instance is Bataille's reading of the photographs of a gruesome public execution in China in 1905—the death by "one hundred pieces"—in *The Tears of Eros* (1961; San Francisco: City Lights Books, 2001), where he writes of his obsession with the images, his feeling of ecstasy in their presence, and that he imagined Sade wanting to see them in "relative solitude, without which the ecstatic and voluptuous effect is inconceivable" (206).

21. Henri Lefebvre, *Critique of Everyday Life*, trans. John Moore (1947; London: Verso, 1991), 1:108, 122.

22. Henri Lefebvre, *Critique de la vie quotidienne II: Fondements d'une sociologie de la quotidienneté* (Paris: L'Arche, 1961).

23. Lefebvre, *Critique of Everyday Life*, 1:120–22.

24. For an illuminating discussion of "reactionary modernism" in the interwar years (Jünger, Schmitt, Jaspers, and others), see Domenico Losurdo, *Heidegger and the Ideology of War: Community, Death and the West* (1991; Amherst, NY: Humanity Books, 2001), 101. As for the "discordances," even though Heidegger shared Nietzsche's desire to aestheticize philosophy, to idolize (if not idealize) ancient Greece, and to adapt a rhetoric of secrecy and disguise, Nietzsche considered ontology (Heidegger's area of innovation) a dead letter in German philosophy. See, for example, Friedrich Nietzsche, *Thoughts Out of Season*, *WFN*, 5:8, 75, 77; and *The Joyful Wisdom*, *WFN*, 10:111.

25. "Cela pouvait seduire, mais ne renseignait pas. . . . Nul ne peut dire sans être comique qu'il s'apprête à quelque intervention renversante: il doit renverser, voilà tout"; Bataille, *La part maudite*, 12 For English, see *AS1*, 9–10.

26. With a different focus and arguments, Georg Lukács also explores theories of revolt that obviate reform in *A Defense of History and Class Consciousness: Tailism and the Dialectic*, trans. Esther Leslie (1923; New York: Verso, 2002).

27. Michael Trebitsch, preface to Lefebvre, *Critique of Everyday Life*, 1:xvii.

28. For example, in the failure to appreciate the significance of the passages on Hegel in Simone de Beauvoir's *The Second Sex*, which appeared in 1949—the same year as volume 1 of *The Accursed Share*. In these passages she traces the idea of social construction to Hegel's writing on the absolute Other and uses his paradigm of the master/slave relationship from the *Phenemenology* to organize her book's understanding of gender relations.

29. Maurice Merleau-Ponty, preface to *Phenomenology of Perception*, trans. Donald A. Landes (1945; New York: Routledge, 2012).

30. Alain Badiou, *Conditions*, trans. Steven Corcoran (New York: Continuum, 2008), 4.

31. Christoph Demmerling, "Heidegger-Marxismus (Herbert Marcuse und an-

dere). Von der Ontologie zur Gesellschaftstheorie, in *Heidegger-Handbuch: Leben, Werk, Wirkung*, ed. Dieter Thomä (Stuttgart: Verlag J. B. Metzler, 2003), 575–78.

32. Lucien Goldmann, *Lukács and Heidegger: Toward a New Philosophy*, trans. William Q. Boelhower (London: Routledge & Kegan Paul, 1977), 36–38.

33. Martin Heidegger, *Basic Writings* (San Francisco: HarperSanFrancisco, 1993), 99.

34. The *Kriegsideologie* is explored at length in Losurdo, *Heidegger and the Ideology of War*, 36–87.

35. See, for example, Iain Chambers, "The 'Unseen Order': Religion, Secularism and Hegemony," in *The Postcolonial Gramsci*, ed. Neelam Srivastava and Baidik Bhattacharya (New York: Routledge, 2012).

36. Nietzsche, *The Joyful Wisdom*, WFN, 10:213; *Human, All-Too-Human*, WFN, 6:621.

37. Gilles Deleuze, "Letter to a Harsh Critic," in *Negotiations* (1990; New York: Columbia UP, 1995), 6.

38. Anderson relates this anecdote in *Lenin, Hegel, and Western Marxism*, 237.

39. Jane Bennett, "Systems and Things: A Response to Graham Harman and Timothy Morton," *new literary history* 43, no. 2 (Spring 2012): 230.

40. Ibid., 225.

41. Stephen Best and Sharon Marcus, "Surface Reading: An Introduction," *Representations* 108, no. 1 (Fall 2009): 9.

42. Ibid., 10.

43. Ibid., 17.

44. The position that meaning forecloses possibilities is taken, for example, by Gayatri Chakravorty Spivak in *Death of a Discipline* (New York: Columbia UP, 2003); for the rejection of hermeneutic meaning in neophilological circles, see Hans Ulrich Gumbrecht's Heideggerian homage in *The Powers of Philology: Dynamics of Textual Scholarship* (Urbana: U of Illinois P, 2003), 32, 62–63.

45. Jacques Rancière, *The Flesh of Words: The Politics of Writing*, trans. Charlotte Mandell (Stanford, CA: Stanford UP, 2004), 4, 13.

46. Jonathan Israel, *The Radical Enlightenment: Philosophy and the Making of Modernity 1650–1750* (Oxford: Oxford UP, 2002).

47. Bruno Latour, *We Have Never Been Modern*, trans. Catherine Porter (1991; New York: Harvester Wheatsheaf, 1993), 97.

48. Ibid., 77.

49. Ibid., 13.

50. N. Katherine Hayles, *How We Became Posthuman: Virtual Bodies in Cybernetics, Literature and Informatics* (Chicago: U of Chicago P, 1999), xiv, 6–20; Cary Wolfe, *What Is Posthumanism?* (Minneapolis: U of Minnesota P, 2010), xviii–xix.

51. Norbert Wiener, *Cybernetics; or, Control and Communication in the Animal and the Machine* (1948; Cambridge, MA: MIT Press, 1965), 3.

52. Ibid., 6.

53. Ibid., 8.

54. Eric Owens, "The Authenticity of Jargon: Leo Wiener and the Comparative Method," unpublished essay, Duke University, 2011.

55. Wiener, *Cybernetics*, 12.

56. Latour, *Why We Have Never Been Modern*, 145; Gianni Vattimo, "Dialectics, Difference, Weak Thought," in *Weak Thought*, ed. Gianni Vattimo and Pier Aldo Rovatti, trans. Peter Carravetta (Albany: SUNY Press, 2013), 39–53; François Laruelle, *Philosophies of Difference: A Critical Introduction to Non-Philosophy* (London: Continuum, 2010).

57. Susan Eileen Waltz, "Universalizing Human Rights: The Role of Small States in the Construction of the Universal Declaration of Human Rights," *Human Rights Quarterly* 23, no. 1 (February 2001), 44–72.

58. Among the social rights they proposed, which advanced the scope of rights as they are found in the era of Samuel Adams, Tom Paine, and Mary Wollstonecraft, or any other era for that matter, are the socialization of industry, reorganization of the banks, the legal and financial equality of women, equal treatment of all races and creeds, the prohibition of monopolies, the prohibition of exemption from taxation, the right to a "just return" on one's labor, economic justice by means of state regulation, free job training, guaranteed social security, and an end to imperialism.

INDEX

(the) Absolute, 76, 91, 107–8
Abu-Lughod, Ibrahim, 65
Abu-Lughod, Janet, 87
Academia degli Investiganti, 35, 38
actualization, 76, 85
Adorno, Theodor W., 122, 174, 260n31
aesthetic: autonomy, 4; of continuity and rupture 12; peripheral vs. modernist, 42, 69, 109, 139; 180, 199, 221–22; working-class form, 205
affect, 6, 22, 51–52, 108, 194, 220
African influence, 11, 14, 86, 100, 103–5, 139, 142, 162, 175, 206, 210
Agamben, Giorgio, 136–37, 199, 211, 257n7, 266n120
Ahmad, Eqbal, 65
alienation, 76, 101, 126, 207; as homelessness, 216; see labor
Althusser, Louis, 19–20, 52–57, 60–67, 82, 86, 92, 113, 131, 218, 221
Amin, Samir, 80,
anarchism, 162–4, 168, 170, 209–10
Anderson, Kevin, 98, 268n18
Anderson, Perry, 52
anthropology, 7; as antihumanism, 141, 153, 162, 188, 199–214; heroic origins of the state, 95, 97; as a literary soci-ology, 28–29, 42, 138, 200. *See also* posthumanism
anticolonial intellectuals, 14–15, 208; libera-tion movements, 60, 99, 200; literature, 5; thought, 2–4, 13;
anticritique, 193
antihumanism, 1, 6, 45, 61, 63, 161–62, 182, 207. *See also* posthumanism
Apollinian, 152–53, 170, 177
Aragon, Louis, 62
Arendt, Hannah, 67, 136–37, 164, 199, 208, 216, 262n67
Aricó, José, 80
Arusha declaration, 234
Aryan, 151, 174, 176, 182–83, 193
Aschheim, Steven, 174
Ascoli, Graziadio Isaia, 68
Ashanti, 103, 105
Attila, 31
Auerbach, Erich, 7, 9, 18–19, 32, 63, 66
autopoiesis, 224–25

backwardness, 24, 34, 48, 80, 134, 150; in anticolonial thought, 105–7, 253n76
Bacon, Francis, 9, 20, 23, 43
Badiou, Alain, 216
Bakhtin, Mikhail, 43, 69, 75

Bakunin, Mikhail, 163
barbarism, 135–6, 140, 155, 175, 177, 183–84, 210, 264n87
Barnett, Stuart, 80
Bartoli, Matteo, 68
Bataille, Georges, 15, 197–215; against Marxism, 212; in colonialist thought, 210–11; impersonation of Nietzsche, 198–203; vs. Lefebvre, 208–9; literary anthropology, 211–12; in philology, 198; subversion as conformism, 211–13; *The Accursed Share*, 15, 197–215
Battistini, Andrea, 237n9
Baudelaire, Charles, 39, 202, 205
Baudrillard, Jean, 208
Bauer, Bruno, 99
Bäumler, Alfred, 144
Bayle, Pierre, 45
Bebel, August, 163–65
Becker, Wilhelm Carl, 144
Beckerath, Herbert von, 178
Beethoven, Ludwig von, 171
Bell, Daniel, 216
Benjamin, Walter: against Nietzsche, 143, 154, 159, 179; for philology, 10–11; and Vichian Marxism, 57, 62, 73, 174;
Bennett, Jane, 221
Bentham, Jeremy, 37, 91
Bergmann, Peter, 161–62
Bernabé, Jean, 40
Bernal, Martin, 11, 64, 136, 229
Bernasconi, Robert, 103–5
Bertalanffy, Ludwig von, 227, 231
Berth, Édouard, 179
Bhaskar, Roy, 82
Bible, 3, 21, 30, 33–34, 46–47, 134, 153, 155, 158, 182, 193
Biedermann, Karl, 163
Bismarck, Otto von, 134, 160, 164, 171, 176, 184
Blackmur, Richard, 66
Blavatsky, Madame, 180
Bloch, Ernst, 36, 62, 75, 98, 121
blond brute, 175–76, 264n94
(the) body, 141, 185–86, 193, 211; as anti-intellect, 213, 221
Bolshevism, 177, 181
borrowed light, 2, 15, 215–18

Bossuet, Jacques-Bénigne, 29, 120
Bourdieu, Pierre, 3, 145
Brathwaite, Edward Kamau, 40
Brecht, Bertolt, 75, 83, 98
Brolin, David, 259n23
Brown, Dan, 37
Brown, Wendy, 258n18
Buck-Morss, Susan, 81, 98
buddhism, 87, 140, 180, 182
byt (everyday life), 205–6; Alltäglichkeit, 215

Cacciari, Massimo, 160
Caillois, Roger, 210
Camões, Luís de, 154
Carafa, Antonio, 35
Caravita, Nicola, 38
Carew, Jan, 229
Catullus, 41
Cecrops, 34
Césaire, Aimé, 98, 142
Chamoiseau, Patrick, 40
Chavista, 234
China, 2, 31, 129, 161, 173, 176, 181, 206
Christianity, 25, 29–30, 34–36, 62; and Afroasiatic influence on Europe, 11; Hegel's critique of, 79, 87, 96; Nietzsche's critique of, 139–40, 153, 167, 176
Churchill, Winston, 212
Cicero, 38
civic, 4, 24, 76–77, 84, 97, 116, 152; in etymology, 137; hermeneutics, 4, 139, 206
civil society, 102
class, 14, 67, 81, 90, 165; as colonial conquest, 26–29; in Nietzsche, 140, 161–74; war, 14, 21, 25–28, 101, 138
classics, 4, 15, 134, 154–59, 156; departments, 8; classical philology, 9, 134
Cold War, 129
Coleridge, Samuel Taylor, 17
Collège de sociologie, 206, 210
colonialism, 3, 13, 25; in Germany, 15, 133–34
communism, 15, 54, 65–66, 99, 125, 129; and anticolonial movements, 197, 200–201, 208, 215, 226

comparative literature, 4, 82
conatus, 48, 212

Condillac, Étienne Bonnot de, 120
Confiant, Raphaël, 40
Confucius, 153
constituent power, 59, 91
content of form, 4, 41, 44, 68, 116, 147, 157–59, 194–95, 217
continuity (historical), 11–14, 20, 65, 80
contradiction, 111, 122
Copernican, 11, 80, 226
corporeal, 4
corsi (and *ricorsi*), 17, 20, 24, 76, 80, 138
cosa ("institutions"), 23–24
cosmopolitanism, 150, 160, 171, 199, 218
counterphilology, 15, 97, 134, 144, 147–51, 157, 174, 185, 189, 200, 213, 218, 221–23, 227. *See also* philology; reading, theories of
Critical Theory (and empire), 81, 223
Croce, Benedetto, 8, 17, 32, 53, 63, 73
Cubism, 206
Cunard, Nancy, 99
Curtius, Ernst Robert, 66
Cuvier, Georges, 11
cybernetics, 7, 226–30; aesthetics of, 228; as an American movement, 232; reliance on humanities, 229–30
Cyclops, 26, 32, 154–55, 159

Damasio, Antonio, 57
Darwin, Charles, 11, 151–52, 167, 262n71
deconstruction, 86, 107–8, 113
Deleuze, Gilles, 57, 82, 109, 113, 219–21
Della Volpe, Galvano, 222
Demmerling, Christoph, 216
Democritus, 38, 144
demotic, 4, 44, 64, 135
dependency, 3
Derrida, Jacques, 3, 107, 109, 111, 114–16, 141, 145, 181, 211, 252n50, 266n120
Descartes, René, 22–23, 35, 38, 44, 75, 107, 120, 225, 230
Deutscher, Isaac, 46, 242n54
dialectics, 14–15, 53, 63, 85, 100, 108–18, 213, 250n35, 252n55, 255n99; Kojèvian, 129–30
dialogical, 111
diffusion thesis (of human origins), 239n15
Diogenes Laertius, 145, 157
Dionysian, 134, 139, 142, 152–53, 170, 177, 182

dissimulation (lying), 138, 144, 150–54, 157, 201–2; in Bataille, 213; in Nietzsche, 171, 183, 187–88, 194–95
distant reading, 222
Dostoevsky, Fyodor, 177, 182, 202
du Bois, W. E. B., 253n76
Dühring, Eugen, 163, 168

(the) East, 4, 10, 14, 33, 81, 86, 139, 176, 179–80, 226
Eastern (peripheral) Europe, 2, 4
Eco, Umberto, 37
École des chartes, 198
ecological crisis, 6
economics, 199, 202–4; "general economy," 203, 207, 219
Egypt, 12, 33–34, 38, 64, 103, 151, 154, 233
Einstein, Albert, 37
Eleatics, 104
English studies, 8
Enlightenment, 24, 36, 39, 42, 51, 79, 84, 87–88, 119, 141, 168, 225
Epicureans (Epicurus), 35, 37–38, 45, 114–15, 139, 242n4
epigram, 145–47, 157–59
ethical life (*Sittlichkeit*), 84, 94–96
Ethiopian, 103–4
etymology, 80, 155, 257n7; difference between Vico and Nietzsche on, 135–38; in Nietzsche, 167–68, 175, 185–88, 194
eugenics, 184
Euripides, 152
Eurocentrism, 3, 12, 100, 249n29
Europe, decentering of, 13, 20, 24–25, 30, 82, 103, 139, 160, 175, 210, 249n29
"European miracle," critique of, 239n18
Eusebius, 20

family (in society), 79, 93, 97, 190, 251n50, 258n8
Fanon, Frantz, 82, 84–85, 98, 249n28
Feuerbach, Ludwig, 57, 92, 99, 163
Fichte, Johann Gottlieb, 74
Forbes, Duncan, 103
Forster, Georg, 88
Förster, Bernhard, 173
Foster, John Bellamy, 39

Foucault, Michel, 114, 120, 141, 202; and genealogy, 185–87
Francis, St. 60
Franco-Prussian War, 169
Frankfurt School, 11, 82, 112, 208, 254n83
Franklin, John Hope, 229
Frederick the Great, 121
free will (human choice), 9, 50, 58, 76, 89, 266n113
French Communist Party, 208
French Revolution, 60, 74, 84, 93
Freud, Sigmund, 42, 120, 141, 206, 221
Frobenius, Leo, 162
Fukuyama, Francis, 82

Gadamer, Hans Georg, 83
Galileo, 35, 120
(the) "game," 211, 213
Gandhi, Indira, 105
Gandhi, Mohandas, 86, 181
Gassendi, Pierre, 35–36
Geheimschrift (secret writing), 145, 202, 220, 266n119
genealogy: as family lineage, 79, 97, 190, 218; as a mode of argument, 15, 134, 147, 184–95, 198, 207, 209, 216–18, 266n120
generalism, 9, 19–20, 101, 122, 206
gentile, 21, 26, 30, 39, 43, 64
Gersdorff, Carl von, 169
Geuss, Raymond, 109, 133, 159, 187–88
Giannone, Pietro, 29, 31
Gilles de Rais, 198
Gibbon, Edward, 29
Goethe, Johann Wolfgang von, 17, 45, 148, 166, 172
Gothic invasions, 31
Gramsci, Antonio: on country and city, 126; contra Nietzsche, 174–75; for philology, 1, 7–8, 68, 222; his theory of reading, 10, 108; on transformism, 201, 267n5; and Vichian Marxism, 32, 53, 89, 98, 136, 208, 220
Great Imperialist War (World War I), 99
Greece, 140; as *not* the origin of Europe, 12, 14, 24, 33–34, 75, 136; as origin of Europe, 176; 249n27
Green, Marcus, 244n69

Greenblatt, Stephen, 36–39
Grilli, Marcel, 17
große Politik, 161, 174
Grotius, Hugo, 26
Guénon, Réné, 180
Guterman, Norbert, 204
Gutkin, Irina, 177

Habermas, Jürgen, 216
Halévy, Daniel, 179
Hamann, Johann Georg, 17, 78
Harootunian, Harry, 87, 106
Hauptstücke, 159
Hayles, Katherine, 225, 227
Hazlitt, William, 195
Hegel, Georg Wilhelm Friedrich, 51, 250n38, 251n42, 251n52; in anticolonial thought, 65–66, 81–88, 91, 95–96, 98, 181, 201, 204; on the civic, 4, 12, 28, 74–81, 84–86, 89–97; critique of Spinoza, 250n34; on philology, 74, 130–31; theory's reliance on, 55, 57, 95, 213–6, 218, 220, 247n14, 248n20; as a Vichian, 1, 4–5, 7, 12, 14, 18, 25–26, 32, 36, 62–63, 73–80, 147, 206; *Philosophy of Right*, 4, 14–15, 74–81, 84–86, 89–97, 100–103, 114, 118, 252n64; *Phenomenology of Spirit*, 87–88, 102, 108–23; *Lectures on the Philosophy of History*, 103–8
Hegel revival, 81, 119
Heidegger, Martin, 3, 69, 97, 102–3, 115, 122, 136–37, 145, 175, 181, 199; and the posthuman, 233; reliance on Hegel, 215–16
Heraclitus, 134
Herder, Johann Gottfried, 45; and Hegel, 72, 78, 88, 130–31; on human vs. animal life, 239n20; on nomadic style, 239n19; as Vichian, 9, 17–18, 24, 42–43, 56, 63, 120, 200, 203, 238n5, 266n112; and world literature, 82
hermeneutic, 4, 21, 37, 56, 60–61, 63–64, 83, 168, 221, 269n44
Hermes Trismegistos, 64
Hinduism, 75, 86, 180
historical continuity (and rupture), 1, 3, 218
historical recurrence, 80, 134–35, 138, 159
Hobbes, Thomas, 26, 37, 48, 59–60, 130, 200
Hoffmeister, Johannes, 128

Holy Book, 5, 46, 139
Holy Roman Empire, 35
Homer, 31, 104, 135, 148, 152–56, 174, 179, 193, 210
Hook, Sidney, 112
Hugues de Tabarie, 198
(the) human, 1, 26, 29, 34, 36–39, 50, 103, 129, 200, 206, 209, 221; according to Hegel, 131; according to Nietzsche, 143; as actor, 7, 38, 49, 53, 62, 70, 131, 190, 192, 222–23; as non-animal, 214
humanism, 1, 7, 29, 61, 69, 107, 141, 162, 221
humanities, 1, 6, 9, 15, 20, 36–37, 79, 84; and the sciences, 6, 14, 22, 91, 148, 225
human rights, 233, 270n58
Hume, David, 37, 107, 200
Husserl, Edmund, 87, 180, 231

Ibn Khaldun, 42
immanence, 49, 53–54, 59
imperialism, 3, 7, 13, 54, 95, 156, 199; British, 171–72; U.S., 6
indecisionism, and post-critical thought, 6, 83, 114–18
independence movements, 15
India, 38, 75, 140, 181, 233
indigenous (native), 12, 86, 105
intellectual history, 1, 3
intellectuals, 27, 127; of the periphery, 2
international, 3–5, 26, 105
interwar era (and anticolonial thought), 1–2, 4, 12, 15, 18, 36, 51, 130, 139, 146, 174–84; Marxism, 200, 215–17; reception of Nietzsche, 197–98
irony, 32–34, 118, 120–21, 178, 189, 195, 213, 223; compared with antilogy, 241nn35–36
Islam, 31, 35, 42, 66, 81, 86, 107, 140, 200
Israel, Jonathan, 225; on Vico, 238n8

Jacobi, Friedrich Heinrich, 38, 108
Jahn, Otto, 191
James, C. L. R., 98, 100, 112, 252n55
Jameson, Fredric, 14, 81, 87, 102, 109, 111–15, 119, 130, 254n86
Japan, 175–76
Jaspers, Karl, 199
Jefferson, Thomas, 37

Jeremiah, 160
Jesus, 168, 199–200
Jewish, 167, 174, 210
Judaism, 30, 43, 46, 153; and Nietzsche, 168, 176, 188
Jünger, Ernst, 175, 199

Kant, Immanuel, 3, 18, 74–75, 81, 107, 114, 128
Kaufmann, Walter, 141, 264n96
Kojève, Alexandre, 15, 128–31, 204, 227
Kollontai, Alexandra, 4
Korsch, Karl, 57
Krauss, Karl, 11
Kupka, František, 175

labor: in class civilization, 27, 73; in Hegel's economics, 84, 94, 101, 126, 204–5, 214–15; labor movement, 164, 167; theory's antipathy towards, 67, 199, 201, 208, 262n67; as Vichian self-making, 5, 76;
Labriola, Antonio, 4, 53
Lacan, Jacques, 3
Lachmann, Karl, 191
Lafargue, Paul, 18, 53
Lamaism, 200
language, material, 14; Saussurean, 11; "secret," 27
Laruelle, François, 232
de Las Casas, Bartolomé, 5
Lassalle, Ferdinand, 53, 66, 163
Lasson, Georg, 128
Latin, 20, 35, 49–51, 54, 137, 157
Latour, Bruno, 224, 226, 232
law, 48, 77; civil, 5; natural, 5, 50, 91–92; as *Recht*, 90, 160
Lefebvre, Henri, 108, 126, 227, 267n16; vs. Bataille, 208–9; and Vichian literary sociology, 205–6, 208
Left (and Right), 2, 161, 164, 174–75, 201, 213
Left Hegelian thought, 9, 20, 28, 66, 70, 84, 99, 208
Leibniz, Gottfried Wilhelm von, 23, 43, 230
Leiris, Michel, 210
Lenin, V. I., 4, 6, 99–100, 178, 181, 204, 220
Levin, Harry, 66
Lévinas, Emmanuel, 3
liberalism, 88–89, 95–96, 116, 206, 250n38

Liebknecht, Wilhelm, 162, 165
Locke, John, 91
Lorians, 8
Losurdo, Domenico, 83, 88, 146, 250n38, 268n24
Luhmann, Niklas, 232
Lukács, Georg, 53, 67, 70, 98, 122, 125, 128, 174, 215–16, 247n13, 268n26; on Homeric idyll, 156
Lucretius (Titus Lucretius Carus), 23, 37–38, 191
Luther, Martin, 121, 184
Luxemburg, Rosa, 6, 99, 195

Macherey, Pierre, 49, 53, 58, 218
machine culture, 7
Mahabharata, 154
Mandela, Nelson, 195
Mann, Thomas, 141
Manu, 153
Marcuse, Herbert, 98, 112, 252n62
Mariátegui, José Carlos, 53
market (capitalism), 5, 55, 60, 62, 77, 94, 101, 124, 126, 233
Marshall Plan, 200
Marx, Karl, 3, 4, 6, 45, 89, 143; and anticolonial thought, 15, 73, 84–5, 99, 199–200, 210; as critic of Epicurus, 37–39; as critic of Hegel, 15, 124–29; on Greek art, 156; polemic, 119; theory's deference towards, 207–8, 216, 221; as Vichian, 20, 26–28, 35, 42, 52, 66–67, 78, 80, 240n24
Marxism, 11, 53, 162–63, 209; and anticolonial thought, 124, 201; and the civic sense, 12; international Marxism, 4–5; and interwar moment, 12; and philology, 7–8, 10, 20, 55, 63–70; theory of "crisis," 11
Massis, Henri, 178–82
materialism, 11, 14, 37–8, 42–3, 49, 51, 57, 78, 92–93; Spinoza's, 243n65
Mayakovsky, Vladimir, 41
Mazzotta, Giuseppe, 32
mediation, 92, 108, 116
Menelik, 175
Merezhkovsky, Dmitry, 177
Merleau-Ponty, Maurice, 216
metaphysics, 11, 23, 40, 48

Mexico, 2, 234
Michelet, Jules, 18, 35, 238n3; on the animal, 239–40, 239n20
Mill, John Stuart, 164
Mills, C. Wright, 75
Mithras, 139
modernism (aesthetic and literary), 4, 8, 10, 12, 39, 69–70, 116, 130, 177; and colonialist thought, 206, 268n24; and economic theory, 202
modernity, 12–13, 69, 74–75, 87, 101, 105, 127, 160, 164, 178, 187, 226
monarchy, 211; constitutional, 47, 58, 60, 94
Montag, Warren, 54, 61
Montesquieu, 17
Müller, K. H., 73
multitude, 47, 55, 58–61, 93
Muret, Maurice, 178, 182

Naples (in Vico's time), 22, 29, 35–38
Napoleon, 88, 160
nationalism, 171–72, 174, 176
NATO, 234
natural (objective) history, 6–7
natural law, 26
negation, 109, 121, 206–8, 213–14
Negri, Antonio, 49, 54, 57–58, 60, 62, 242n55, 264n89
Nehamas, Alexander, 145
Neoplatonism, 11–12, 64
neo-Spinozism, 14, 52–63; as Nietzschean movement, 5, 52, 199, 211; a revitalization of Marxism, 5, 52–53;
New Criticism, 86
The New Science, 4, 9, 20, 31; summarized, 21–23
Newton, Isaac, 20, 23, 43
Nicolini, Fausto, 17
Niebuhr, Barthold Georg, 184
Nietzsche, Elisabeth, 142
Nietzsche, Friedrich, 45, 51, 57, 87, 123; as anti-Vico, 5–6, 133–39, 148; on class, 140, 187; as capitalist, 155, 159, 179, 201; in colonialist thought, 139–47, 160–62, 173–74, 259n23, 260n31, 261n39; as foil to Hegel, 135, 159, 164–66, 168–69; on Germany and Germans, 155, 160, 168–70; as philologist,

5, 9, 15, 133–39, 203, 257n2; in postcolonial studies, 141–44, 181; on race, 152, 161–62, 170–71, 175, 182–84, 186, 258n18, 262n71; relationship to Spinoza, 5, 124, 255n96; on slavery, 167, 171–72; on socialism (as a colonial barbarism), 159, 161–65, 176–78, 182–84, 259n27, 261n56, 264n89; his theory of reading, 186–95, 220–21; views of anticolonial intellectuals, 142–43; and women, 165
Nizan, Paul, 75
Nohl, Herman, 128
nomadism, 24, 26, 29, 140, 150, 155, 202
Novalis, 108
Nubian, 103
Nueva Germania, 173, 263n85

object-oriented criticism, 221, 225
Odysseus, 28, 154–55
Ondaatje, Michael, 8
ontology, 222; political, 50, 81; and race, 12, 81
opposition (antagonism), 108–9, 112–113, 218, 254n86; as negation, 121
orality, 29, 40; deconstruction's opposition to, 107–8, 130–31; in etymology, 137–38
oriental, 88, 134, 163
orientalist, 104, 128, 180
origins (historical), 11, 48, 69–70, 134, 135–36, 168, 185–87, 218, 265n106, 266n112; *Herrkunft* vs. *Ursprung*, 185–86
Osten, Franz, 180
(the) other, 76, 81, 87, 89, 97, 153; epistemological, 109, 114
Overton, Richard, 49

Panikkar, K. M., 80
Paraguay, 161, 173
Paris Commune, 165, 170
Pater, Walter, 37
Paul, St. 139, 162, 198
(the) people (popular), 10, 29, 40–41, 59, 62, 93, 135, 165, 170–71
periphery (global), 106, 133, 161, 181, 201, 217; influence on Europe, 128
periphery (of Europe), 63–64, 73, 80, 85, 125–26

Persia, 38, 140
phenomenology, 51, 75, 129, 214; in colonialist thought, 217
philology, 7–10; and anticolonial thought, 7, 65, 67–68; and colonialist thought, 134, 165; generalism, 10, 19, 64; "living philology," 1, 63; and Marxism, 7, 10, 20, 55; philological method, 4, 9, 123, 149, 223, 240n28, 244n69, 266n112; as philosophy, 9–10, 148; as a social science and politics, 9, 29. *See also* reading, theories of; counterphilology
Phoenician, 12, 28, 151, 154
Pippin, Robert, 122
piracy (and empire), 25
Planck, Max, 37
Plato, 64, 92, 108, 134, 153, 155
"play," 208, 211; and genealogy, 218
Plekhanov, Georgi, 57
polemic, 14–15, 43–45, 89, 109, 119–24
Pocock, J. G. A., 36, 42, 49, 240n28
Poe, Edgar Allen, 202
Porter, James I., 257n2
positivism, 8, 23, 57, 91, 162, 192, 222
postcolonial theory, 2–4, 6, 36, 75, 85–86, 115, 128, 200–201; attraction to Nietzsche, 15, 140–42, 175, 181; critical tendencies within, 98; hostility to Hegel, 98–108; non-Western or postcolonial literatures, 4, 40
postcritical thought, and indecisionism, 6, 254n89, 260n5 *See also* reading, theories of
posthumanism, 6–7, 19, 107, 116, 131, 161, 222–23; as fear of colonial independence, 197–99, 206, 218; as an imperial ideology, 224, 226–34. *See also* anthropology; antihumanism
potlatch, 200, 203–4
pragmatism, 86
Prague linguistic circles (and Copenhagen), 11
presentism, 3, 20, 36, 60–61
(the) primitive, 202, 206, 210
primitive accumulation, 99
productive reading, 14, 53, 55, 62, 83, 218–19
property, 77, 101–2

278 INDEX

providence, 29, 60, 62, 78, 104
Psammeticus, 34
Pufendorf, Samuel, 26, 200
Pyrrhonism, 37

Rai, Himansu, 180
Raleigh, Walter, 5
Rancière, Jacques, 222, 254n89
Raynal, Guillaume Thomas François, 5
reading, theories of, 5, 9–10, 22, 39–44, 46–48, 55–56, 64, 103, 139, 144, 266n112; adjacency, 65, 119, 187; "against the grain," 56, 218; biological, 138; Derridean, 115–116; distant reading, 222; early Nietzsche's, 150–1, 220; genealogical, 15, 200; Gramscian, 10, 108; indeterminacy and undecidability 145–47, 153, 178, 184, 192, 202, 220–2, 254n89, 260n35, 265n108, 269n44; Kojèvian, 129–30; "play," 208, 211; "productive" reading, 14, 53, 55, 62, 83, 218; surface reading, 220–23; "symptomatic" reading, 56, 218, 220–23. *See also* counterphilology; philology; postcritical thought
realism, 32, 41–2, 108–9
Rehmann, Jan, 259n23
reification, 215
reportage, 75
revolution, 6, 234; as performance, 211, 268n26; as tradition, 12
rhetoric, 32, 41–42, 46, 48, 51, 109, 118, 120–21, 134–35, 184, 214, 219. See also dissimulation (lying)
Right (and Left), 2, 161, 164, 174; philosophical Right, 199
Ritschl, Friedrich Wilhelm, 191–92
Robertson, John, 35
Roman Empire, 31, 35, 96, 136, 153
Romanticism, 10, 24
Rose, Gillian, 91
Rousseau, Jean-Jacques, 17, 91, 178
rupture (historical), 1, 11–14, 65, 70, 80, 218, 265n108
Russia, 177–78, 181, 205; Orient of Europe, 181
Russian Revolution, 165; of 1905, 177, 234
Russo-Japanese War, 177, 179

Sade, Marquis de, 199–200, 212
Saladin, 198
Sallust, 134, 157
Sanskrit, 9
Said, Edward, 7–8, 19, 24, 63–66, 82, 87, 100, 136; and Marxism, 7–8, 65–66, 69, 245nn93–94; on Nietzsche, 141; and philology, 9
Saussure, Ferdinand de, 11, 68
Schäffle, Albert, 164
Schelling, Friedrich Wilhelm Joseph, 79, 91
Schiller, Friedrich, 148
Schlegel, Karl Wilhelm Friedrich, 108, 121, 223
Schleiermacher, Friedrich, 168
Schmitt, Carl, 50, 144, 175
Schopenhauer, Arthur, 87, 140, 165
Schwarz, Roberto, 126
science, and the humanities, 6, 15, 19, 37–38, 91, 224
scientism, 6, 14, 42, 63–64, 224; reliance on humanist methods, 230–31; and the seventeenth-century Enlightenment, 6, 224
Second International, 57
secular, 3, 30, 36, 56, 61–62, 79, 247n10; *irdische* (worldly), 66
Serequeberhan, Tsenay, 100–103, 252n62
Sertima, Ivan van, 229
Siculus, Diodorus, 20
signifying on Hegel (mimicry and mockery), 15, 116, 171, 193, 207–15, 208–9, 218; term explained, 262n78
Simmel, Georg, 206
Skeptics, 119–21
slavery, 14, 54–55, 84, 94, 99, 124, 137–38, 156, 164, 167, 202, 208, 251n42, 252n64
Smith, Adam, 200
socialism, 15, 23, 29, 60, 125, 143, 161–64, 168, 170; as anticolonial, 176–78, 182–84, 202; socialist wonder, 206
socialist realism, 39
Socrates, 152
Solovyov, Vladimir, 177
Sophocles, 41, 145
Sorel, Georges, 18, 23–24, 53, 56, 63, 174, 179, 244n70; on Vico's idealism, 239n12
sovereignty, 47, 58–59, 61, 100, 105, 127, 199, 201, 207, 209–11

Soviet Union, 15, 129, 197, 200–201, 206, 229
Spengler, Oswald, 178
Spinoza, Benedict de, 28, 35, 78, 87, 90, 123, 128, 130, 143, 230; affinities to mercantile thought, 14, 54, 58–62; and Hegel, 90–92, 94–95, 108; his hermeneutics, 5, 14, 45–9; and Nietzsche, 5, 218; political impact summarized, 45–47, 51–52; and posthumanism, 15, 45; on race, 107; and science, 158; "Spinoza," 52–62, 218; his style without affect, 19–20; and Vico, 21, 36, 43, 47–48, 61, 63, 67; and women, 244n80; *Ethics*, 48–51; *Theologico-Political Treatise*, 14, 45–50, 243n58, 243n60, 243n61; 244n82
Spirit, 91, 102, 104
Spitzer, Leo, 7, 9, 66
(the) state, 5, 14, 26, 48, 54, 77–78, 84, 89–97, 125, 164, 170
Stirner, Max, 99
Stoddard, Lothrup, 178
Stoics, 38, 119–20
Strauss, David Friedrich, 134, 168–69
Strauss, Leo, 57
subaltern studies, 86, 217
(the) subject, 10, 39, 53, 58, 61, 67, 76, 91, 97, 119, 207, 223
Sufism, 180
surface reading, 220
Surrealism, 205
system character of philosophy, 14–15, 43, 51, 63, 76, 89–90, 101, 112, 122–23
systems theory, 98, 225–27

Tacitus, Publius Cornelius, 9, 33
Tagore, Rabindranath, 86, 179
Taine, Hippolyte, 165
Taoism, 180
Tasso, Torquato, 154
teleology (historical vs. rhetorical), 58, 63, 91, 100, 116, 122, 213
Terence, 32
"theory," 1–2, 7, 36, 43, 45, 56, 83, 109, 112, 114, 119–22, 136, 161, 199, 201, 209, 218; vs. intellectual history, 1, 80; as Marxism's borrowed light, 4, 202–15
Thersites, 104
third world, 205, 210, 226

Thompson, E. P., 67
Thorez, Maurice, 99
Timpanaro, Sebastiano, 11, 192, 222
totality, 9, 13, 36, 69, 110, 117, 204, 214–15, 217
transformism, 267n5
transgression, 204, 208, 212–13
Tretyakov, Sergei, 41
Trotsky, Leon, 53, 100, 126
Truman, Harry, 212
turn to language, 20, 63, 86
Tzara, Tristan, 62

uneven development, 3, 99, 125
(the) universal, 12, 26, 31, 36, 43, 100, 131, 161, 181, 202
Ur-Eine, 136
utility, 88, 144, 157, 187, 190; 197–98, 203–4, 220; of disutility, 202, 207, 213

Vallejo, Camila, 195
Valletta, Giuseppe, 38
Varro, Marcus Terentius, 20, 64
Vattimo, Gianni, 232
Veblen, Thorstein, 203
Vedantic philosophy (and dialectics), 86, 88, 103, 153
Vergil, 41
vernacular, 3, 20, 64, 108, 137
Vichian tradition, 11, 13, 37, 44, 53, 62–63, 73, 113, 122, 130, 143, 156, 206, 224
Vico, Giambattista, 3, 94–95, 120, 122, 135, 139, 147, 158, 200, 224; anticolonial ideas, 19–28, 241n37; and class conflict, 19, 21, 25–28, 73, 203–4; as critic of science, 20, 22–23, 37–38, 63, 76, 225; critique of the Cartesian Left, 22, 38, 41; critique of Spinoza, 6, 225; his definition of philology, 9; influence on anticolonial intellectuals, 1–5, 14, 19, 63, 241n41, 245n86; influence on Marxism, 11, 14, 17–18, 20, 23–24, 28, 53, 63–70, 204, 240n27; inventor of sociologically informed culture, 9, 24, 42, 205–6, 208; origins of language and poetic speech, 3, 22, 29–31, 39–43, 73; politics of literature, 29–31, 41, 64, 136; relationship to Hegel, 1, 4–5, 7, 14; theory of history, 4, 20; theory of reading, 22, 39–44, 64; and

women, 244n80; and world literature, 18, 20
Vinci, Leonardo da, 226
Vivekananda, Swami, 105
Volosinov, Valentin, 53, 63, 67
vulgarity, 75
vulgate, 4, 40, 74, 108, 191

Wagner, Richard, 163
Waite, Geoff, 145, 260n35, 267n2
war of positions, 3
Weber, Max, 200
West, Cornel, 86
West, 136, 226; Western, conceptual form, 4
White, Hayden, 24
Wiener, Leo, 229

Wiener, Norbert, 226–30
Williams, Eric, 99
Williams, Raymond, 24, 126, 205
Winckelmann, Johann, 136
Wolfe, Cary, 227, 232
Wordsworth, William, 40, 53
world literature, 3, 20, 124, 172

Xenophon, 31

Young Hegelians, 78

Zinoviev, Grigory, 181
Zionism, 86
Zimmerwald manifeso, 234
Žižek, Slavoj, 57, 81, 112

The authorized representative in the EU for product safety and compliance is:
Mare Nostrum Group
B.V Doelen 72
4831 GR Breda
The Netherlands

www.ingramcontent.com/pod-product-compliance
Lightning Source LLC
Chambersburg PA
CBHW030526230426
43665CB00010B/782